DEVON AND CORNWALL RECORD SOCIETY

New Series

Volume 61

A LORD LIEUTENANT IN WARTIME

The Experiences of the Fourth Earl Fortescue during the First World War

Edited by RICHARD BATTEN

DEVON AND CORNWALL RECORD SOCIETY

THE BOYDELL PRESS

© Devon and Cornwall Record Society and Richard Batten 2018

All Rights Reserved. Except as permitted under current legislation
no part of this work may be photocopied, stored in a retrieval system,
published, performed in public, adapted, broadcast,
transmitted, recorded or reproduced in any form or by any means,
without the prior permission of the copyright owner

The right of Richard Batten to be identified as
the author of this work has been asserted in accordance with
sections 77 and 78 of the Copyright, Designs and Patents Act 1988

First published 2018

A publication of the
Devon and Cornwall Record Society
published by The Boydell Press
an imprint of Boydell & Brewer Ltd
PO Box 9, Woodbridge, Suffolk IP12 3DF, UK
and of Boydell & Brewer Inc.
668 Mt Hope Avenue, Rochester, NY 14620–2731, USA
website: www.boydellandbrewer.com

ISBN 978 0 90185 361 5

Series information is printed at the back of this volume

A CIP catalogue record for this book is available
from the British Library

The publisher has no responsibility for the continued existence or accuracy
of URLs for external or third-party internet websites referred to in this book,
and does not guarantee that any content on such websites is,
or will remain, accurate or appropriate

This publication is printed on acid-free paper

Printed and bound in Great Britain by TJ International Ltd, Padstow, Cornwall

CONTENTS

FIGURES

PREFACE

The First World War was an important period in the life of the fourth Earl Fortescue, who as the Lord Lieutenant of Devon played a significant role in the county's war effort. From the vantage point of Lord Lieutenant, Fortescue was an unparalleled observer of the county during the war years and compiled a large archive of materials relating to his wartime activities. This book reveals how Fortescue referred to his memories from the war and consulted with his diaries and his private papers to help him construct a retrospective account of his experiences as the county's Lord Lieutenant from 1914 to 1918. By presenting a selection of records from the Fortescue of Castle Hill archive, these documents reveal the priorities, trials and tribulations of a member of the county's local elite during the Great War. In addition, the retrospective account and Earl Fortescue's diaries provide a personal chronicle of his experiences of the First World War as well as those of other members of the Fortescue family including Lady Fortescue and their sons, Viscount Ebrington and Denzil Fortescue. As a result, these documents impart a nuanced, insightful and illuminating portrait of the fourth Earl Fortescue and the Fortescue family from 1914 to 1918. This is a unique volume that considers the First World War on a local level primarily through the perspective and records of the Lord Lieutenant of a county.

ACKNOWLEDGEMENTS

In the course of the journey to complete this book, I would like to express my appreciation to the following people who have helped to make the journey both an intellectually stimulating and rewarding one. First, I would like to thank Professor Andrew Thorpe, who approached me to produce a volume related to my doctoral research for the Devon and Cornwall Record Society. I am especially grateful for his support through the book's development and the great confidence that he placed in both me and the project. I would like to thank Lady Arran for granting her permission as the great-granddaughter of the 4th Earl Fortescue for the documents from the Fortescue at Castle Hill archive to be featured in this volume. The documents in this volume are reproduced with the kind permission of Devon Archives and Local Studies Service. I would like to thank Dr Todd Gray MBE for his efforts to help ensure that the book could be ready to be published in time for 2018. Moreover, I greatly appreciate his assistance in gaining the permission from Devon County Council to use the portrait of the fourth Earl Fortescue for this book.

I would like to express my thanks to the Devon and Cornwall Record Society for this opportunity to produce a volume related to Devon during the First World War. Indeed, this book follows from the research that I completed for my doctoral thesis; I would like to thank my former supervisors Dr Tim Rees and Professor Richard Toye for their valuable input and sustained support. My doctoral research also benefited from the insightful feedback of Professor Andrew Thorpe, Dr Pierre Purseigle and Dr Catriona Pennell.

Finally, I would like to acknowledge the support of my brother Simon, my sister Anna and my uncle Robin Loosmore, and dedicate this book to my mother Valerie and father Anthony for their ceaseless encouragement and boundless faith in me through the highs and lows of the great journey to complete the work.

ABBREVIATIONS

ACC	Army Canteen Council
ADC	Aide-de-Corps
ADMS	Assistant Director Medical Services
AG	Adjutant General
ASC	Army Service Corps
BRCS	British Red Cross Society
CB	Companion of the Order of Bath
CBE	Commander of the British Empire
CC	County Council
CFO	County Fire Office
CH	Castle Hill
CMC	Canteen & Mess Cooperative or the Canteen & Mess Society
CO	Commanding Officer
COS	Charity Organisation Society
DCLI	Duke of Cornwall Light Infantry
DCM	Distinguished Conduct Medal
DDMS	Deputy Director Medical Services
DG	Dragoon Guards
DHC	Devon Heritage Centre
DL	Deputy Lieutenant
DPF	Devon Patriotic Fund
DSO	Distinguished Service Order
FA	Field Artillery
FP	Food Production
GBE	Grand Cross of the British Empire
GOC	General Officer Commanding
GPO	General Post Office
GWR	Great Western Railway
HC	Holy Communion
HM	His Majesty's
HO	Heavy Ordinance
HP	Horse Power
HQ	Head Quarters
HRH	His/Her Royal Highness
JP	Justice of the Peace
KCB	Knight Commander of Bath (Military Award)
KCVO	Knight Commander of the Victorian Order
KRRC	Kings Royal Rifle Corps
L & SWR	London and South Western Railway
MB	Bachelor of Medicine
MBE	Member of the British Empire
MD	Doctor of Medicine

MFH	Master of Foxhounds
MG	Machine Gun
MGC	Machine Gun Corps
MP	Member of Parliament
MRCS	Member of the Royal College of Surgeons
MT	Mechanical Transport
NCO	Non-Commissioned Officer
NZ	New Zealand
OBE	Officer of the British Empire
OC	Officer Commanding
OR	Ordinary Regulars
PC	Police Constable
PO	Post Office
QMG	Quartermaster-General
RAMC	Royal Army Medical Corps
RE	Royal Engineers
RFA	Royal Field Artillery
RGA	Royal Garrison Artillery
RMC	Royal Medical Corps
RNDH	Royal North Devon Hussars
RRC	Royal Red Cross
RSM	Regimental Sergeant Major
SJ	Standing Joint
SSFA	Soldiers, Sailors Families Association
SSHS	Soldiers, Sailors Help Society
TF	Territorial Force
TFA	Territorial Force Association
TNA	The National Archives
USA	United States of America
VA	Voluntary Aid
VAD	Voluntary Aid Detachment
WO	War Office

INTRODUCTION

This book is a study of the British Home Front of the First World War on a local level from the perspective of the Lord Lieutenant of Devonshire: the fourth Earl Fortescue. As a Lord Lieutenant during the Great War, Hugh Fortescue was a pre-eminent figure in Devon's local elite, to whom his involvement with the war effort in the county was significant. This volume considers the wartime experiences of a county's Lord Lieutenant through a presentation of records from Fortescue's private papers. It contains the original typescript that Fortescue wrote in 1924 as a retrospective account of his experiences during the conflict as well as the diaries that he kept from 1914 to 1918. Alongside the original typescript and his wartime diaries, this book also presents a selection of documents related to the Great War from the *Fortescue at Castle Hill* archive. This selection is organised into four sections: mobilising the county for war; recruitment; charities and voluntary aid; and food production and agriculture. By presenting these documents from Lord Fortescue, this book raises awareness of his involvement with the war effort in the county and the momentous challenges that he faced as the Lord Lieutenant of Devon during the First World War.

Hugh Fortescue, the Fourth Earl Fortescue (1854–1932)

Hugh Fortescue was born in London on 16 April 1854.[1] He was the eldest son of the third Earl Fortescue, Hugh Fortescue, and Georgina Augusta Charlotte Caroline Dawson-Damer. The Fortescues were lauded as a highly distinguished Devonshire family, and their home was the country seat of Castle Hill near Filleigh in north Devon.[2] The family were also well-established landowners with extensive estates in the West Country, Lincolnshire and Waterford in Ireland.[3] As the third Earl Fortescue's eldest son, he was appointed with the courtesy title of Viscount Ebrington to indicate that he was the earl's heir apparent before his eventual succession from Viscount Ebrington to Earl Fortescue. After his education at the public school of Harrow, Ebrington attended Trinity College at the University of Cambridge, where he attained a first-class degree in Law.[4] Upon finishing his BA in 1876, he continued his studies at Trinity College to

---

[1] *The Western Times*, 4 November 1932, p. 10; 'Ebrington, Hugh, Viscount (EBRN872H)', Cambridge Alumni Database, University of Cambridge, http://venn.lib. cam.ac.uk/cgi-bin/search-2016.pl?sur=&suro=w&fir=&firo=c&cit=&cito=c&c=all&z= all&tex=EBRN872H&sye=&eye=&col=all&maxcount=50 (accessed 20 November 2017).

[2] *The North Devon Journal*, 3 November 1932, p. 3; Gerald Gliddon, *The Aristocracy and the Great War* (Norwich: Gliddon Books, 2002), p. 84.

[3] David Parker, *Edwardian Devon, 1900–1914: Before the Lights Went Out* (Stroud: The History Press, 2016), p. 79; Anthony Michael Dawson, 'Politics in Devon and Cornwall, 1900–1931', PhD thesis, London School of Economics, 1991, pp. 36–37.

[4] Robert Henry Mair, ed., *Debrett's House of Commons and the Judicial Bench* (London: Dean & Son, 1886), p. 45.

complete an MA in 1879. Ebrington also participated with the University's
Pitt Club, a Conservative dining club in honour of the former prime minister
William Pitt.[5] From an early age, Ebrington developed an interest in stag
hunting.[6] His enthusiasm for the sport meant that he became proficient in the
field of hunting red deer and achieved a measure of celebrity within hunting
circles.[7] He became the Master of the Devon and Somerset Stag Hounds from
1881 to 1887.[8] Ebrington was also a prominent Freemason: he was chosen as the
Grand Master of the Freemasons in Devon from 1879 to 1896.[9]

Like his father and grandfather, Ebrington decided to pursue a career in
politics. Upon the death of William Nathaniel Massey, one of the two Liberal
MPs for the mid-Devon constituency of Tiverton, there was a by-election
in November 1881. As Viscount Ebrington, he was selected as the Liberal
party's candidate; he won the seat with a majority of 252 votes.[10] From
1881 to 1885, he was one of the two Liberal MPs for Tiverton alongside Sir
John Heathcoat-Amory, the first Baronet Heathcoat-Amory.[11] However, the
political representation for Tiverton was reduced to one member due to the
Redistribution of Seats Act of 1885. Accordingly, Ebrington moved from
Tiverton to become the Liberal party candidate for the west Devon constituency
of Tavistock in the general election of November 1885. He was elected as the
Liberal MP for Tavistock with a majority of 2,218 votes.[12] However, after
his election victory, Ebrington's future as a Liberal MP was short-lived. As a
result of William Gladstone's proposals to introduce Home Rule for Ireland,
Ebrington moved from the Liberals to the breakaway Liberal Unionist party
since he opposed the prospect of Irish Home Rule.[13] Indeed, Ebrington was
a member of the moderate faction of Liberal MPs who opposed Home Rule
which was formed by George Goshen, first Viscount Goshen, and thus was
separate from the Marquess of Hartington's Whigs.[14] It was during the early
months of 1886 that this grouping, which included Viscount Lymington and Sir
John Lubbock, began to make contact with 'those who might be able to organise
an alternative Liberal campaign at [a] grass-roots level'.[15] An example of this
reconnaissance to ascertain the position of various members of Parliament was

[5]   Walter Morley Fletcher, *The University Pitt Club: 1835–1935* (Cambridge: Cambridge
University Press, 1935), p. 83.
[6]   *The Times*, 8 November 1932, p. 16.
[7]   *Baily's Monthly Magazine or Sports and Pastimes*, Vol. 43, 301, pp. 389–390; Viscount
Ebrington, 'Stag Hunting', in A. E. T. Watson, ed., *Fur and Feather Series: The Red
Deer* (London: Longmans, Green, and Co., 1896), pp. 197–284; *The Daily Telegraph*,
31 October 1932, p. 6.
[8]   Fred Goss, *Memories of a Stag Harbourer* (London: H. F. & G. Witherby, 1931),
p. 211.
[9]   *The Western Morning News and Daily Gazette*, 31 October 1932, p. 6.
[10] F. W. S. Craig, ed., *British Parliamentary Results: 1832–1885* (London: The Macmillan
Press, 1977), p. 309.
[11] *Ibid.*
[12] F. W. S. Craig, ed., *British Parliamentary Results: 1885–1918* (London: The Macmillan
Press, 1974), p. 259.
[13] *The Western Morning News and Daily Gazette*, 31 October 1932, p. 3.
[14] Ian Cawood, *The Liberal Unionist Party* (London: I. B. Tauris, 2012), p. 19
[15] *Ibid.*

evident in a letter that Ebrington wrote to Hartington on 1 March 1886.[16] In his letter, Fortescue revealed to Hartington that, based on a survey of 159 election addresses that were delivered by Liberal MPs in England, Wales and Scotland, there were thirteen members of Parliament, including Hartington himself, who 'declared their opposition to a separate parliament for Ireland'.[17]

By the summer of 1886, the splinter group of discontented Liberal MPs had permanently split from the Liberal party and had established the Liberal Unionist party as a distinct alternative political movement. In the general election of July 1886, otherwise known as the Home Rule Election, Ebrington stood as the Liberal Unionist candidate for Tiverton, and he won the seat with a majority of 1,195 votes.[18] From 1886, the Liberal Unionists were well supported in parts of both Devon and Cornwall, to the extent that both counties were regarded as the main bastion for the party outside of Birmingham.[19] Henry Pelling suggests that the reason why the Liberal Unionists were popular in areas of Devon was that it indicated a 'persistence of [a] body of opinion which, while radical on domestic questions, was conservative on Imperial matters'.[20] From 1886 to 1892, Ebrington was the Liberal Unionist MP for Tavistock. However, he decided to retire as a constituency MP with the announcement of the election of 1892.[21] According to The Times, the reason why he had decided to retire from politics was due to ill health, which 'after a time compelled him to give up the House of Commons'.[22] Although he was no longer an MP, Ebrington retained a strong interest in British politics. This was evident when he made speeches in north Devon in 1910 that defended the House of Lords against the attacks that it had received after the Lords had blocked Lloyd George's People's budget.[23] Additionally, Ebrington also continued to support the Liberal Unionists at their party conferences into the twentieth century.[24]

At the same time that he was busy campaigning for the 1886 general election, Ebrington married his cousin Emily Ormsby-Gore on 15 July 1886, and she was appointed Lady Fortescue.[25] She was the daughter of the Anglo-Irish peer and the second Baron Harlech, William Ormsby-Gore.[26] Emily and Hugh's marriage bore three children: Hugh, Geoffrey and Denzil. While both Hugh and Denzil survived through to adulthood, Geoffrey died in 1900. Upon the death of his father in 1905, Hugh Fortescue became the fourth Earl Fortescue

[16] Ibid.
[17] Ibid.; T. A. Jenkins, Gladstone, Whiggery and the Liberal Party, 1874–1886 (Oxford: Clarendon Press, 1988), p. 288.
[18] Craig, ed., British Parliamentary Results: 1885–1918, p. 259.
[19] Cawood, The Liberal Unionist Party, p. 171.
[20] Henry Pelling, Social Geography of British Elections, 1885–1910 (London: Macmillan, 1967), p. 173.
[21] The Western Times, 4 November 1932, p. 10.
[22] The Times, 8 November 1932, p. 16.
[23] The North Devon Journal, 1 December 1910, p. 3.
[24] The Daily Telegraph, 22 March 1904, p. 10.
[25] Burke's Peerage and Baronetage, 1914 (London: Harrison & Sons, 1914), p. 808.
[26] Who's Who, 1914 (London: Adam & Charles Black, 1914), p. 732.

and inherited his father's peerage in the House of Lords.[27] As a result, the fourth Earl Fortescue's eldest son and heir apparent, Hugh William Fortescue, was bestowed with the courtesy title of Viscount Ebrington in 1905. David Parker has described the fourth Earl Fortescue as a 'typical late Victorian paternal aristocrat'.[28] This was due to the fact that the fourth Earl 'epitomised the traditional role of wealthy estate owners as social leaders, patrons of morally sound institutions, leading supporters of charities and local guardians of law and order'.[29] Indeed, Earl Fortescue was a diligent member of Devon's landed gentry and held a number of civic appointments in the county. Fortescue held the position of Justice of the Peace for Devon and he was also the chairman of the Devon Quarter Sessions.[30] In 1908, Fortescue held the office of High Steward for Devon as well as the post of Deputy Lieutenant.[31] Fortescue's services to the State were recognised in 1911 when he was invested with the honour of Knight Commander of Bath (KCB).[32] Alongside his civic engagements, Fortescue also had a number of business interests. From 1906 to 1923, he was the director of the insurance company the County Fire Office.[33] Fortescue was also part of a consortium that submitted an unsuccessful application to construct a railway line from Filleigh to the north Devon seaside village of Lynton.[34]

Upon the decision of King Edward VII, Fortescue was appointed the office of Lord Lieutenant of Devonshire on 28 March 1904 when Charles Henry Rolle Hepburn-Stuart-Forbes-Trefusis, the twentieth Baron Clinton, retired from the Lord Lieutenancy due to his declining health.[35] The post of Lord Lieutenant was chosen by the monarch and was appointed to a male figure from well-established county families and aristocratic landowners.[36] In fact, Miles Jebb reveals that this was still mainly the case by 1906 as the 'aristocratic tenor of the Lieutenancies remained dominant'.[37] The Lord Lieutenant acted as the representative of the monarch in each county across the United Kingdom. Accordingly, as the Lord Lieutenant of Devon from 1904 to 1928, Fortescue was the representative of King Edward VII and later King George V in the county. Simultaneously, he was also Aide-de-Camp to both King Edward VII and King George V.[38] The appointment of Lord Lieutenant was a great honour for the fourth Earl Fortescue. Both the first and second Earl Fortescue

[27] *Whitaker's Peerage, Baronetage, Knightage and Companionage for the Year 1909* (London, 1909), p. 338.
[28] David Parker, *Exeter: Remembering 1914–18* (Stroud: The History Press, 2014), p. 32.
[29] Parker, *Edwardian Devon, 1900–1914*, p. 79.
[30] *The North Devon Journal*, 3 November 1932, p. 3.
[31] Mair, ed., *Debrett's House of Commons and the Judicial Bench*, p. 45; *Burke's Peerage and Baronetage*, 1914, p. 808.
[32] *The Western Times*, 4 November 1932, p. 10.
[33] Aubrey Noakes, *The County Fire Office, 1807–1957: A Commemorative History* (London: H. F. & G. Witherby Ltd, 1957), p. 179.
[34] Trevor Jarvis, *The Rise of the Devon Seaside Resorts, 1750–1900* (Exeter: University of Exeter Press, 1993), p. 133.
[35] *The Devon and Exeter Gazette*, 29 March 1904, p. 10.
[36] Miles Jebb, *The Lord Lieutenant and his Deputies* (Chichester: Phillimore, 2007), pp. 87–96.
[37] *Ibid.*, p. 94.
[38] *The Times*, 31 October 1932, p. 8.

had also held the office of Lord Lieutenant of Devonshire. The first Earl Fortescue, in particular, had played a prominent role in the county during the Napoleonic wars.[39] The Lord Lieutenancy also carried with it the role of '*Custos Rotulorum*' (Keeper of the rolls) for which he kept the records of judicial trials for his respective county.[40] The office of Lord Lieutenant was a historic post: its 'origins lay in preceding systems of local government and military control'.[41] Previously, the Lord Lieutenant held the jurisdiction over local militias for the purposes of national defence. However, this changed with the Regulation of the Forces Act of 1871 which completely removed the military jurisdiction of the County Lieutenants over the local militia and this jurisdiction was 'revested in the Crown'.[42] Yet, there were some County Lieutenants who still had a minor involvement with local volunteer units.

During the Edwardian era, the county Yeomanry regiments became an important feature on a local level as well as a 'rallying-point for the local gentry and their supporting countrymen'.[43] Although the Lord Lieutenants did not possess any official links with these regiments, several of the County Lieutenants 'presided over them as Honorary Colonel'.[44] Indeed, Lord Fortescue was an Honorary Colonel in the North Devon Yeomanry cavalry from 1889 to 1903.[45] However, the involvement of the Lord Lieutenant with local volunteer military units was subject to reform by the Secretary of State for War, Richard Haldane.[46] The Territorial and Reserve Forces Bill of 1907 established a territorial force in specific counties as a voluntary reserve military unit. These territorials were administered through the creation of County Associations and the president of these associations was to be 'the Lord-Lieutenant though his position was anomalous'.[47] As the Lord Lieutenant of Devon, it fell to Fortescue to carry out Haldane's army reforms for the establishment of a territorial force in the county in 1907.[48] Fortescue had raised concerns about the Bill in the House of Lords as he wanted clarity on the role of the Lord Lieutenant within these County Associations.[49] However, Fortescue held a strong interest in Haldane's Territorial Force scheme.[50] In fact, Fortescue was one of two Lord Lieutenants to who Haldane had 'referred all [the] more formidable problems of his Territorial scheme for solution and to whom he acknowledged special obligations'.[51]

---

[39] John Fortescue, *The County Lieutenancies and the Army, 1803–1814* (London: Macmillan and Co. Ltd, 1909), pp. 36–37, 77, 92, 99, 100.

[40] 'The Office of Lord Lieutenant', in W. M. Ormrod, ed., *The Lord Lieutenant and High Sheriffs of Yorkshire, 1066–2000* (Barnsley: Wharncliffe Books, 2000), p. 3.

[41] Jebb, *The Lord Lieutenant and his Deputies*, p. 1.

[42] *Ibid.*, p. 101.

[43] *Ibid.*, p. 102.

[44] *Ibid.*

[45] 'Denzil Fortescue b. 1893 Recollections 1974', http://fortescue.org/site/wp-content/uploads/2012/11/DGFRecollections2.pdf (accessed 12 December 2017), p. 2.

[46] Jebb, *The Lord Lieutenant and his Deputies*, p. 102.

[47] *Ibid.*, p. 103.

[48] *The Times*, 31 October 1932, p. 8.

[49] Jebb, *The Lord Lieutenant and his Deputies*, p. 104.

[50] *The Times*, 8 November 1932, p. 16.

[51] *Ibid.*

After the bill received royal assent in 1907, the Lord Lieutenant was conferred with the chairmanship of the County Associations of the Territorial Force in their respective county. Accordingly, Fortescue became the Chairman of the Territorial Force Association in Devon. It is clear that the Lord Lieutenant was a key figure on a local level in early twentieth-century Britain.

As the Lord Lieutenant of Devonshire, Earl Fortescue was an industrious figure in the county due to his involvement in the public activities and civic entities of Devon's civil society.[52] Earl Fortescue was an original member and alderman of Devon County Council. In fact, he was chairman of the county council from 1904 to 1916.[53] As the county council's chairman, Fortescue held a privileged position and was able to preside over the affairs of local government in the county.[54] Indeed, local government entities presented opportunities for notable figures within the aristocracy to extend their influence and prestige within Edwardian society.[55] It was only when Lord Fortescue shouldered the three roles of Lord Lieutenant of Devonshire, chairman of Devon County Council and chairman of the county's Territorial Association that he 'found [the] full scope for his powers'.[56] As a result of these combined undertakings, Fortescue was both an eminent and well-connected figure in Devon and he 'shared indefatigably also in the social activities of the county'.[57] Thus, Lord Fortescue possessed a considerable influence upon the socio-economic fabric of the county on the eve of the First World War.[58]

Earl Fortescue and the First World War

The assassination of Archduke Franz Ferdinand by Serbian terrorists on 28 June 1914 produced a crisis which enveloped the nations of Europe and ultimately became a global conflict.[59] In Great Britain, the European crisis overshadowed the British population's domestic concerns and fears of a civil war in Ireland.[60] After the British Government's demand for the withdrawal of the German army from Belgium had expired on 4 August 1914 at 11 pm, Britain declared war on Germany.[61] In Devon, the county's population in rural and urban areas observed the transition of the county from peacetime to wartime. On 4 August, Lord

---

[52] 'The Family of Fortescue', in R. Pearse Chope, ed., *The London Devonian Year Book 1910* (London: The London Devonian Association, 1910), p. 36.
[53] Jeffrey Stanyer, *A History of Devon County Council, 1889–1989* (Exeter: Devon Books, 1989), p. 93.
[54] *Ibid.*
[55] David Cannadine, *The Decline & Fall of the British Aristocracy* (London: Picador, 1992), pp. 139–181.
[56] *The Times*, 8 November 1932, p. 16.
[57] *The Times*, 31 October 1932, p. 8.
[58] *The Western Morning News and Daily Gazette*, 31 October 1932, p. 3.
[59] Hew Strachan, *The First World War, Volume I: To Arms* (Oxford: Oxford University Press, 2001), p. 1114.
[60] Catriona Pennell, *A Kingdom United: Popular Responses to the Outbreak of the First World War in Britain and Ireland* (Oxford: Oxford University Press, 2012), pp. 24–25; *The North Devon Journal*, 6 August 1914, p. 5.
[61] David Stevenson, 1914–1918: *The History of the First World War* (London: Penguin, 2004), p. 32.

Fortescue witnessed the mobilisation of the third Battalion of the Devonshire Regiment as they travelled from Woodbury Common to embark by rail from Exeter St David's railway station to Plymouth. After witnessing how the citizens of Exeter reacted to the news of the outbreak of war and the sight of the battalion marching through the city's streets, Fortescue commented that the 'attitude & behaviours of [the] men & [the] people [were] quite satisfactory'.[62]

After the outbreak of war, worries over German spies and enemy sabotage escalated significantly when individuals were accused of crimes such as 'reconnoitring likely invasion areas or sabotaging telephone lines' and 'signalling from the coast to enemy ships'.[63] For Lord Fortescue, the most pressing concern was the protection of vulnerable points in Devon. In his view, the railway line from Exeter to Plymouth was of vital importance to the British war effort since it was used to transport troops and material to one of the most important ports in the United Kingdom. Accordingly, Fortescue went to great lengths to find individuals such as special constables and in one instance a rector with his party of boy scouts to protect and patrol particular places, including viaducts and tunnels along the Exeter to Plymouth railway line.[64] Nonetheless, in response to Fortescue's efforts the military stated that 'they cared little if the railways into Plymouth were interfered with as they had got all the troops they wanted into the fortress and could supply them by sea'.[65] Notwithstanding Fortescue's concerns to safeguard the vulnerable points in Devon, it was clear that the military had prepared for the possible sabotage of the railway line from Exeter to Plymouth. Yet, Fortescue's efforts reveal that he considered the protection of susceptible locations in the county from subversive enemy action to be a vital priority. Similarly, precautions were coordinated by the Lord Lieutenant of Sussex, the Duke of Norfolk, who was concerned about vulnerable areas in Sussex.[66]

In the transition from peacetime to wartime, there was a great flourishing of charities in Devon because fundraising and charitable relief were important activities among individuals and communities in the county.[67] This was evident with the mobilisation of the women of Devon into charitable efforts related to the war effort. Earl Fortescue revealed that the queen's appeal for the women of England to knit socks and belts for servicemen in the armed forces proved to be very successful in the county during the beginning of the war. In his view, the appeal was a 'wise move for though many socks were [so] badly made that they were useless except to put over the breech action of the rifles as [a] mud

---

[62] DHC: 1262M/0/FD/46, Personal diary of the 3rd Lord Ebrington, 1914–1916, 4 August 1914.

[63] David French, 'Spy Fever in Britain, 1900–1915', *The Historical Journal*, Vol. 12, 2 (June 1978), p. 365.

[64] DHC: 1262M/0/FH/42, Typescript of work of Lord Fortescue during 1st World War, post 1919, 1924, pp. 7–11.

[65] *Ibid.*, p. 11.

[66] Keith Grieves, 'Introduction', in K. Grieves, ed., *Sussex in the First World War* (Lewes: Sussex Record Office, 2004), pp. xvi–xvii.

[67] R. Richardson, *Through War to Peace, 1914–1918: Being a Short Account of the Part Played by Tavistock and Neighbourhood in the Great War* (Tavistock: Jolliffe & Son, 1919), p. 82–95; Gerard Wasley, *Devon in the Great War, 1914–1918* (Tiverton: Devon Books, 2000), pp. 70–71.

guard it gave occupation to numberless restless women: 5000 pairs of socks and 1500 body belts were sent to Lady Fortescue in six weeks'.[68] Another philanthropic success in Devon was the reception of the Belgian refugees. In Exeter, the efforts of the Mayoress of Exeter, who was supported by Lady Fortescue, led to the establishment of the Exeter Committee for Relief of War Refugees on 25 September 1914.[69] Within a fortnight of the committee's creation, the fundraising efforts for the Belgian refugees across Devon had produced £450 with 'offers of many homes'.[70] Miss Clara Andrew became the honorary secretary for the organisation and was sent to London.[71] Upon her return, Andrew arrived with '150 refugees who were promptly placed with benevolent people and by the end of October the numbers had risen to 800 [refugees]'.[72] This meant that Exeter was the first provincial centre to receive and house Belgian refugees.[73] By February 1915, the number of refugees in the county had risen to 3,000. However, it had become clear at this time that the large number of charities created for the reception of Belgian refugees across Devon and Cornwall had meant that 'the movement had outgrown their unconnected and somewhat haphazard methods'.[74] This led Fortescue to attempt to arrange a greater co-ordination between 'all the many committees' related to Belgian refugees in both counties and for them all to be merged into a larger refugees committee to cover both Devon and Cornwall.[75]

On 15 March 1915, the Devon and Cornwall War Refugees Committee was formed with the intention to secure housing and offer hospitality to Belgian and other war refugees in both counties.[76] Lord Fortescue and Lord Mount Edgcumbe, the Lord Lieutenant of Cornwall, were appointed as Joint Presidents of the Committee since it covered Devon and Cornwall.[77] However, the Exeter Committee stood out for a year before it was amalgamated into the Devon and Cornwall War Refugees Committee in February 1916.[78] Behind the scenes, this spirit of co-operation among the local elite towards the Belgian refugees was undermined by upper-class tribalism.[79] According to Fortescue, there was 'a

---

[68] DHC: 1262M/0/FH/42, Typescript of work of Lord Fortescue during 1st World War, p. 17.
[69] Ibid., p. 26; DHC: 1262M/0/O/LD/139/1, Pamphlet on the history of the Devon & Cornwall War Refugees Committee, c. 1915, p. 1.
[70] DHC: 1262M/0/FH/42, Typescript of work of Lord Fortescue during 1st World War, p. 26.
[71] Ibid.
[72] Ibid.
[73] DHC: 1262M/0/O/LD/139/1, Pamphlet on the history of the Devon & Cornwall war refugees committee, c. 1915, p. 1.
[74] DHC: 1262M/0/FH/42, Typescript of work of Lord Fortescue during 1st World War, p. 26.
[75] Ibid.
[76] TNA: CHAR 4/4, WAR CHARITIES ACT 1916: List of Registers, Cheshire (Maple)-Devon (Exeter), Devon and Cornwall War Refugees Committee, 1916, p. 745.
[77] DHC: 1262M/0/FH/42, Typescript of work of Lord Fortescue during 1st World War, p. 26.
[78] Ibid.
[79] Peter Cahalan, Belgian Refugee Relief in England during the Great War (London: Garland Publishing Inc., 1982), p. 505.

considerable amount of personal jealousy and personal self-importance with not least among the Andrew's family'.[80] In fact, Clara Andrew's brother and sister were key figures of the original city committee.[81] Similarly, there were significant disagreements between Lord Fortescue and the Mayor of Exeter, James Owen during 1915 which were rooted in the issue of the organisation's jurisdiction and finances.[82] The reception and charitable efforts of the Belgian refugees did result in great difficulties for Fortescue. Indeed, most of Fortescue's time was 'spent pacifying ruffled feelings and ensuring effective appointments were made'.[83] He noted in the typescript that among all who were connected with the office, there was a sense of great relief when the office finally closed in around January 1920.[84] Fortescue concluded that the Belgian refugees were 'not a very nice lot; they were exacting and tiresome, and a proportion were criminal and amoral'.[85] Nevertheless, the Devon and Cornwall War Refugees Committee did achieve great success as the Committee received and accommodated 8,000 refugees during the war.[86]

After 4 August 1914, voluntary recruitment efforts to answer Lord Kitchener's call to arms began in earnest across the British Isles.[87] In Devon, the county's landowning, social and economic elite intended to transform Devon into a county at arms. They envisaged themselves as holding a central role in the county's preparations for war and hoped that, through their involvement in recruitment efforts, Devon would excel at recruitment for the armed forces. Like the Lord Lieutenant of Sussex, Fortescue as Lord Lieutenant was the '*defacto* principal recruiting officer' in Devon and he was instrumental in the promotion of recruitment efforts across the county.[88] For the first few weeks of August, Fortescue claimed that recruiting was as brisk in Devon 'as it was everywhere else'.[89] However, there was some trouble in that 'men came in much faster than either accommodation or bedding or clothing or arms could be provided, and neither examining doctors nor the clerical staff could keep pace with the demands on their time'.[90] Across the United Kingdom, it was reported that

---

[80] DHC: 1262M/0/FH/42, Typescript of work of Lord Fortescue during 1st World War, p. 26.

[81] *Ibid.*

[82] DHC: 1262M/0/O/LD/117/10, Letter to Earl Fortescue from Clara Andrew, Belgian Refugees' and Relief Committees, 11 March 1915; DHC: 1262M/0/O/LD/117/36, Letter to Earl Fortescue from James Owen, Mayor of Exeter, 29 May 1915, item, p. 1.

[83] David Parker, *The People of Devon in the First World War* (Stroud: The History Press, 2013), p. 103.

[84] DHC: 1262M/0/FH/42, Typescript of work of Lord Fortescue during 1st World War, p. 27.

[85] *Ibid.*

[86] *Ibid.*

[87] John Morton Osborne, *The Voluntary Recruiting Movement in Britain, 1914–1916* (New York: Garland Publishing, 1982).

[88] Keith Grieves, "'Lowther's Lambs": Rural Paternalism and Voluntary Recruitment in the First World War', *Rural History*, Vol. 4, 1 (1993), p. 57.

[89] DHC: 1262M/0/O/LD/153/5, Speech (incomplete), 1 December 1914, p. 1.

[90] *Ibid.*

many recruiting offices had become bottlenecks of recruitment after they had
been swamped by floods of volunteers.[91]

Yet, despite the high hopes of Devon's elite for the county to excel in volun-
teering and set a fine patriotic example for other counties in England, the reality
of recruitment efforts did not reach their high expectations. An example of this
was in late August 1914 when Lord Fortescue voiced his scepticism about the
loyalty of the men from the north Devon town of Bideford.[92] Similarly, Stanley
Jackson, a resident of Oakleigh in Torrington, had regretfully to admit to Lord
Fortescue in October 1914 that despite gaining 147 recruits for the regular army
and the territorials after nine weeks recruiting, there were 'still hundreds of
men in this district that will not do their duty'.[93] The recruiting statistics which
chronicled recruitment figures in the South West up to 10 October 1914 revealed
that the number of recruits that Devon had raised compared 'unfavourably with
many other counties'.[94] The perception of a strong naval tradition in Devon had
led some to propose that the county's menfolk had joined the navy instead of
the army. In their view, this would then explain why Devon had low recruitment
figures for the army.[95] However, Fortescue disputed this explanation and said
that it was only an excuse for 'not having done better in general recruiting'.[96]

In the rural areas of Devon, recruitment efforts had encountered hesitation
and indifference from the county's farmers.[97] Some farmers had argued that
their patriotic duty was not to enlist but rather produce food for the nation.[98]
However, Fortescue was frustrated with what he believed were excuses from
Devon's farmers against military service and contended that farmers in the
county were more concerned about their own businesses than the war effort.[99]
Fortescue warned that the consequences would be extremely severe if Devon's
agriculturalists did not undertake their duty.[100] Likewise, the Lord Lieutenant of
Kent, Lord Harris, also struggled with how to convey the importance of the war
to the farmers of Kent.[101] Based on the low recruitment figures and the sceptical
responses from some of Devon's menfolk, Fortescue declared that in the matter

[91] Peter Simkins, *Kitchener's Army: The Raising of the New Armies, 1914–1916* (Barnsley:
Pen & Sword Military, 2007), pp. 72–73.
[92] DHC: 1262M/L129, Lord Lieutenant's Papers, 31 August 1914 as cited in Pennell,
A Kingdom United, p. 150.
[93] DHC: 1262M/L129, Lord Lieutenant's Papers, 18 October 1914 as cited in Pennell,
A Kingdom United, p. 150.
[94] 'Devonshire and the War', in R. Pearse Chope, ed., *Devonian Year Book 1915* (London:
The London Devonian Association, 1915), p. 40.
[95] *The North Devon Journal*, 10 December 1914, p. 2; Stuart Dalley, 'The Response in
Cornwall to the Outbreak of the First World War', *Cornish Studies*, Vol. 11 (2003), pp.
102–103.
[96] *The North Devon Journal*, 10 December 1914, p. 2.
[97] *The Western Times*, 19 November 1914, p. 2; *The Devon and Exeter Gazette*,
11 December 1914, p. 12.
[98] *The Western Morning News*, 3 December 1914, p. 6; *The Devon and Exeter Gazette*,
11 December 1914, p. 13.
[99] DHC: 1262M/0/O/LD/153/5, Speech (incomplete), 1 December 1914, pp. 3, 5.
[100] *Ibid.*, p. 3.
[101] *Kentish Gazette and Canterbury Press*, 5 September 1914, as cited in Mark Connelly,
Steady the Buffs! A Regiment, a Region, and the Great War (Oxford: Oxford University
Press, 2006), p. 10.

of recruiting 'Devon had nothing to be proud of'.[102] In fact, the county had one
of the lowest recruitment returns for the army across the United Kingdom and
authorities on both a 'local and [a] national level were concerned about Devon's
recruitment returns'.[103] Nonetheless, Fortescue hoped that recruitment efforts
across the county in 1915 would 'be pushed more diligently, for more men are
badly wanted'.[104] Like the local elite of Sussex, Devon's notable figures changed
their recruiting techniques so that by April 1915 the 'language and imagery
of recruitment had shifted significantly from the controlling presumptions of
August 1914'.[105] Through new dedication and collaboration, it was hoped that
recruitment efforts in Devon could be reinvigorated with new strategies and
more convincing appeals to enlist.

A new strategy that was employed to revive the fortunes of recruitment
efforts in Devon were the route marches.[106] A route march, otherwise known
as a recruitment march, would involve units from the Devonshire Regiment
travelling along a specific route through towns, villages and hamlets with
recruiting sergeants and local notables. These marches were intended to raise
'public awareness and advertised well in advance to enable the population to
come out and see the local battalion'.[107] It was expected that the presence of
local troops, along with appeals from local notable figures, would help to win
over the hearts and minds of Devon men who were reluctant to volunteer.
The county's elite subscribed private money to help finance the route marches
and the 'military authorities readily co-operated' with local notable figures
to organise them.[108] Under the management of the clerk to the Lieutenancy,
Mr H. Ford, the recruitment marches began in earnest across the county in the
spring of 1915.[109] The first route march in Devon took place from 12 to 15 January
1915. A small party of the third Battalion of the Devonshire Regiment left
from Exeter bound for the town of South Molton. From South Molton,
the regiment and local recruiting authorities visited all the hamlets and other
habitations en route to the village of Witheridge.[110] Fortescue revealed that
the first route march achieved a certain amount of success and that the
soldiers had received a very cordial reception among the local populations.[111]
On 15 January 1915, Fortescue noted that the route march had gained around
48 to 60 recruits.[112]

[102] *The Western Times*, 24 November 1914, p. 5.
[103] Pennell, *A Kingdom United*, p. 150.
[104] 'Devonshire and the War', p. 41.
[105] Grieves, 'Introduction', p. 2.
[106] DHC: 1262M/0/FH/42, Typescript of work of Lord Fortescue during 1st World War,
p. 32.
[107] Derek Rutherford Young, 'Voluntary Recruitment in Scotland, 1914–1916', PhD
thesis, University of Glasgow, 2001, p. 170.
[108] DHC: 1262M/0/FH/42, Typescript of work of Lord Fortescue during 1st World War,
p. 32.
[109] *Ibid*.
[110] *The Western Times*, 12 January 1915, p. 3.
[111] DHC: 1262M/0/FH/42, Typescript of work of Lord Fortescue during 1st World War,
p. 32.
[112] DHC: 1262M/0/FD/46, Personal diary of the 3rd Lord Ebrington, 1914–1916,
5 January 1915.

Despite the intention of the recruitment marches as a form of outreach to change and shape public understanding of the war across the county, many of the marches exposed the depth of apathy and indifference present among some of Devon's menfolk towards military service.[113] Fortescue claimed that there were parishes in the county which seemed to be 'divided from the first-named by some mysterious indefinable line of demarcation, showed only ignorance, apathy and utter want of appreciation of their responsibilities to their county'.[114] It was clear that there were distinct limits to the self-mobilisation of Devon's menfolk. This was apparent during a recruitment march on 3 June 1915. After the Devonshire Regiment had passed through the north Devon villages of Chittlehampton, Swimbridge and Landkey, Fortescue noted in his diary that the march had produced 'lots of food &c, but no men'.[115] Many of the route marches in Devon prompted the local residents to support the troops in a humanitarian way with generous hospitality. Instead of encouraging their menfolk to enlist, the villages of Devon provided 'endless food [to the troops], but few recruits presented themselves' on the recruiting marches.[116] Similarly, the recruitment marches in the 'other parts [of the county] though reinforced by bandsmen and chara bancs effected little'.[117] Although there were some successes, the route marches generally achieved mixed success across the county.[118] Nevertheless, Devon's notable figures persevered in their attempts to increase Devon's recruitment returns. There were also reports in the local press of Devonians who heckled, criticised and accosted notable figures and recruiting sergeants in 1915.[119] On 23 October 1915, Fortescue revealed that for the first six months of the year the number of recruits in the county 'averaged 500 a month for the Regular Forces, and a similar number of the Territorials'.[120] Indeed, recruitment numbers in Devon had rebounded by June 1915.[121] However, this was only a fleeting improvement. Fortescue revealed that since the beginning of July the numbers for Devon had shown a 'grave falling off, only 400 men had been obtained for the Regulars and 300 for the Territorials'.[122] While recruitment figures from certain districts of Devon had risen in 1915, there were still many instances where this intensified campaign of voluntary recruitment had failed to change the attitudes of Devon's menfolk towards military service.[123]

[113] *The Devon and Exeter Gazette*, 5 March 1915, p. 3.

[114] *Ibid.*

[115] DHC: 1262M/0/FD/46, Personal diary of the 3rd Lord Ebrington, 1914-1916, 3 June 1915.

[116] DHC: 1262M/0/FH/42, Typescript of work of Lord Fortescue during 1st World War, p. 32.

[117] *Ibid.*

[118] *The Western Times*, 2 March 1915, p. 3; *The Devon and Exeter Gazette*, 19 June 1915, p. 4; *The Devon and Exeter Gazette*, 3 September 1915, p. 2.

[119] Bonnie J. White, 'Volunteerism and Early Recruitment Efforts in Devonshire, August 1914–December 1915', *The Historical Journal*, Vol. 52, 3 (2009), pp. 641–666.

[120] *The Devon and Exeter Gazette*, 23 October 1915, p. 4.

[121] White, 'Volunteerism and Early Recruitment Efforts in Devonshire, August 1914–December 1915', p. 661.

[122] *Ibid.*

[123] *Ibid.*, pp. 641–666; *The Western Times*, 20 February 1915, p. 4; *The Devon and Exeter Gazette*, 3 September 1915, p. 2.

Two groups that Fortescue believed were to blame for low recruitment figures in the county were the Nonconformists and Devon's farmers.[124] In the case of the county's farmers, local newspapers reported that during the route marches both farmers and their sons were either conspicuous by their absence or had responded with indifference towards appeals to enlist.[125] In Cornwall, the marked absence of farmers' sons at recruiting events had provided other classes with an excuse not to volunteer.[126] This was also the case in Devon.[127] It was proposed that a special battalion, modelled upon the successful Pals or class battalions, should be created to convince farmers and their sons to enlist.[128] In 1915, there were 4,532 farmers' sons still working on Devon's farms.[129] In an attempt to reverse the perception of farmers as shirkers from military service, Fortescue submitted a proposal to raise a Farmers Battalion. Major Champion, the Recruiting Officer for Gloucestershire, as well as other military figures and the War Office had all expressed confidence in the project.[130] However, the plan to create this unit was entirely dependent on the condition that the army could establish and maintain good relations with the National Farmers Union. Champion was certain that if this could be achieved the scheme to raise a Farmers' Union Battalion was 'well worth proceeding with'.[131] Nonetheless, despite the positive correspondence that Fortescue received about the Farmers Battalion, the project was ultimately abandoned.[132] Fortescue confessed that he did not think that it was a 'very hopeful undertaking as the margin of farmer's sons available for an Infantry Battalion with its second line was not large after providing for the Yeomanry and its second line'.[133] In addition, the War Office had refused the conditions of his proposal which was in his view just as well because 'all the good men available of farmer class were wanted as officers in the next three years'.[134] Although the project was unsuccessful, the Farmers Battalion was still an important project for Lord Fortescue.[135]

---

[124] DHC: 1262M/0/O/LD/153/25, Recruitment of Non-conformists, 13 May 1915, p. 2.

[125] *The Western Morning News*, 16 February 1915, p. 7; *The Western Express and Torrington Chronicle*, 20 February 1915, p. 4; *The Devon and Exeter Gazette*, 3 September 1915, p. 2.

[126] DHC: 1262M/0/O/LD/114/5, Extract from Report on Recruiting work in CORNWALL by Major Pike, 7 July 1915, p. 1.

[127] DHC: 1262M/0/O/LD/114/4, Letter to Fortescue from Pitcairn-Campbell, 12 July 1915.

[128] DHC: 1262M/0/FH/42, Typescript of work of Lord Fortescue during 1st World War, p. 32.

[129] DHC: 1262M/L140, Labour Officer's Report, 17 April 1918, as cited in Bonnie White, 'Feeding the War Effort: Agricultural Experiences in First World War Devon, 1914–1917', *Agricultural History Review*, Vol. 58, part I (2010), p. 102.

[130] DHC: 1262M/0/O/LD/114/4, Letter to Fortescue from Pitcairn-Campbell, 12 July 1915, p. 1.

[131] DHC: 1262M/0/O/LD/114/10, Letter from Major S. S. Champion about recruitment for farmers' battalions, 21 July 1915, p. 2.

[132] DHC: 1262M/0/O/LD/114/29, Telegram from General Campbell to Lord Fortescue, 4 September 1915.

[133] DHC: 1262M/0/FH/42, Typescript of work of Lord Fortescue during 1st World War, p. 32.

[134] *Ibid.*

[135] *Ibid.*

Yet, in light of the frustrations with the county's low recruitment returns, it was understandable why contemporaries in Devon discussed the prospect of a scheme of compulsory military service.[136] Many politicians and army recruiters had also come to similar conclusions that the existing system of voluntary recruitment was inadequate.[137] On 10 February 1916, this system was replaced with the introduction of conscription in England, Wales and Scotland with the Military Service Act.[138]

From the autumn of 1915, Lord Fortescue became involved in the efforts to increase food production in the county. According to Fortescue, these undertakings remained 'constant and exacting till the end of the war'.[139] In September 1915, Lord Selborne, the President of the Board of Agriculture, issued a circular to call upon farmers to increase their arable land. To accompany this directive, county councils across the United Kingdom were directed to form county-based War Agricultural Committees.[140] As a result, Devon County Council formed the Devon War Agricultural Committee and William Tremlett, the chairman of the Devon Farmer's Union, was appointed as the committee's chairman.[141] These War Agriculture Committees were to 'organise the supply of labour (especially female), to consider how food production could best be maintained or increased, and to report on shortages in the supply of fertiliser, feed, machinery or other supplies'.[142] However, without statutory powers or additional staff to oversee the work, the efforts of the Devon War Agricultural Committee to encourage greater organisation of food production in the county were ineffective during 1916.[143] Yet, by December 1916, the situation in respect to food supplies had worsened. The poor harvest of 1916, along with the campaign of unrestricted submarine warfare across the Atlantic which restarted in February 1917 had taken a heavy toll upon food imports.[144] During 1917 and 1918, the food shortages and high food prices in Britain heightened 'working-class resentment and disenchantment with the war effort, especially when this hardship was coupled with an awareness of social contrasts'.[145] In Devon, by

---

[136] *Devon and Exeter Gazette*, 15 October 1915, p. 10.

[137] Osborne, *The Voluntary Recruiting Movement in Britain, 1914–1916*, pp. 130–133.

[138] James McDermott, 'The Work of the Military Service Tribunals in Northamptonshire, 1916–1918', PhD thesis, University of Northampton, 2009, p. 19.

[139] DHC: 1262M/0/FH/42, Typescript of work of Lord Fortescue during 1st World War, p. 40.

[140] *Ibid.*

[141] TNA: MAF 80/4998, Devon War Agricultural Committee, War Agricultural Committee minutes, 15 October 1915, p. 1.

[142] P. E. Dewey, *British Agriculture in the First World War* (Routledge: London, 1989), pp. 26–27.

[143] Julia Neville, 'Devon County Council and First World War Food Production Policy: A Challenge to Landlordism and Squirearchy?', *The Devon Historian*, Vol. 86 (2017), p. 67.

[144] Peter Dewey, 'Food Production and Policy in the United Kingdom, 1914–1918: The Alexander Prize Essay', *Transactions of the Royal Historical Society*, Vol. 30 (1980), pp. 71–73; Avner Offer, *The First World War: An Agrarian Interpretation* (Oxford: Clarendon Press, 1989), p. 366.

[145] George Robb, *British Culture and the First World War* (Basingstoke: Palgrave Macmillan, 2002), p. 82.

1917 there was also an 'acute shortage of basic foods'.[146] As a response to this crisis in British food supplies, Roland Prothero, the President of the Board of Agriculture, developed a government programme that was accompanied by a set 'quota of land [that was] to be broken up and tiled to corn or potatoes in every county'.[147]

Through an amendment in the Defence of the Realm Act, the Board of Agriculture gained additional powers to intervene into domestic food production and these powers were delegated to the county War Agricultural Committees in England and Wales.[148] Prothero also intended to make the county War Agricultural Committees more efficient with the 'creation of Executive Committees of four to seven members'.[149] Through this greater co-ordination and authority, the county War Agricultural Committees were able to fulfil their potential and they became the 'backbone of the food production campaigns of 1917 and 1918'.[150] The Devon War Agricultural Executive Committee organised the county into four divisions 'based on those already adopted by the County Council for the administration of the Small Holdings Act'.[151] These four divisions were presided over by notable figures from the county: the Western Division was chaired by Sir Henry Lopes, the Southern Division would be administered under the chairmanship of William Coulton and the Eastern Division was under the jurisdiction of Sir Ian Heathcoat-Amory. Fortescue was appointed as Chairman of the Northern Division and Mr G. Smyth-Richards, his estate agent, acted as surveyor and correspondent. The division covered around 414,000 acres and the areas of the Barnstaple, Bideford, South Molton and Torrington Poor Law Unions.[152] Consequently, the chairmen of these four divisions formed the Devon War Agricultural Executive Committee and Fortescue was the Executive Committee's chairman.[153]

Although the calls to increase the quantity of corn grown in Devon did encounter some resistance in 1917, these appeals did achieve success by 1918.[154] This was evident with a large increase of 34,815 acres of corn harvested in the county in 1918 compared to that obtained in 1917.[155] This was due to the

---

[146] Bonnie J. White, 'War and the Home Front: Devon in the First World War', PhD thesis, McMaster University, 2008, p. 94.

[147] DHC: 1262M/0/FH/42, Typescript of work of Lord Fortescue during 1st World War, p. 41.

[148] L. Margaret Barnett, *British Food Policy during the First World War* (Boston, MA: George Allen & Unwin, 1985), p. 198.

[149] *Ibid.*, p. 198.

[150] *Ibid.*, p. 64.

[151] DHC: 1262M/0/FH/42, Typescript of work of Lord Fortescue during 1st World War, p. 42.

[152] *Ibid.*

[153] *Ibid.*, p. 42; Parker, *People of Devon in the First World War*, p. 224.

[154] Parliamentary Debates, House of Commons, Fifth Series, Vol. 90, 8 February 1917, Column 154.

[155] House of Commons Parliamentary Papers Online, '[Cd. 9006, 9089, 9163] Agricultural Statistics for Great Britain, with Summaries for the United Kingdom, 1917', http://parlipapers.chadwyck.co.uk (accessed 21 January 2009); House of Commons Parliamentary Papers Online, '[Cmd. 13, 298, 375] Agricultural Statistics for Great Britain, with Summaries for the United Kingdom, 1918', http://parlipapers.chadwyck.co.uk (accessed 21 January 2009).

Corn Production Act of 1917 which had guaranteed prices for domestically produced wheat and oats.[156] As the 'new food production policy got into its stride', there was also an increase of 6,396 acres of potatoes grown in Devon in 1918 compared to what was recorded in 1917.[157] The attempts to increase food production in Devon were also evident with the introduction of the tractor. However, according to Fortescue, the new tractor ploughs were not well received by Devon's farmers because 'no one really knew how to build them and they had to learn how to manage them when built'.[158] He concluded that the tractors 'cost much money and were a doubtful success' to agriculturalists in the county.[159] Hence, Devon's farmers remained unconvinced by this novel piece of machinery, the benefits of which appeared to be outweighed by the negatives.

By the spring of 1918, Lord Fortescue and members of Devon County Council were concerned that if any more men were removed from agriculture, fishing and forestry it would hamper their production in the county. They were concerned about the mood in Devon in that there seemed to be a 'fair degree of contradiction between the needs of the armed forces and the needs of the county'.[160] Fortescue was adamant that the National Service Department would understand his concerns 'once the dizziness of war has past'.[161] Indeed, he revealed that there 'were endless struggles about men' of which the 'War Office very properly claimed all able bodied men for the Army'.[162] However, after the failure to defend against the Spring Offensive on the Western front in the spring of 1918, the demand for additional manpower became especially acute.[163] As a result, the Devon War Agricultural Executive Committee was assigned the task known as the 'Clean-Cut' to obtain additional men for the army from the county's agricultural sector. The quota of men that Devon had to provide was 1,000 farmers of which 250 had to be supplied from the county's Northern Division.[164] Fortescue suggested that the 'Clean-Cut' was an arduous and cruel undertaking for those who had to review the list of the 2,500 men employed on Devon's farms.[165] In fact, he admitted that it was the worst task set to the Devon War Agricultural Executive Committee to which 'the whole of the Committee

[156] Dewey, *British Agriculture in the First World War*, p. 93.

[157] Peter Dewey, 'Nutrition and Living Standards in Wartime Britain', in J. Winter and R. Wall, eds, *The Upheaval of War: Family, Work and Welfare in Europe, 1914–1918* (Cambridge: Cambridge University Press, 2005), p. 204; House of Commons Parliamentary Papers Online, '[Cd. 9006, 9089, 9163] Agricultural Statistics for Great Britain, with Summaries for the United Kingdom, 1917', http://parlipapers.chadwyck.co.uk (accessed 21 January 2009), House of Commons Parliamentary Papers Online, '[Cmd. 13, 298, 375] Agricultural Statistics for Great Britain, with Summaries for the United Kingdom, 1918', http://parlipapers.chadwyck.co.uk (accessed 21 January 2009).

[158] DHC: 1262M/0/FH/42, Typescript of work of Lord Fortescue during 1st World War, p. 45.

[159] *Ibid.*

[160] DHC: 1262M/151, Letter to Hughes-Buller from Lord Fortescue, March 1918, as cited in White, 'War and the Home Front', p. 240.

[161] *Ibid.*

[162] DHC: 1262M/0/FH/42, Typescript of work of Lord Fortescue during 1st World War, p. 44.

[163] *Ibid.*, p. 47.

[164] *Ibid.*

[165] *Ibid.*

was thankful when the job was done – fortunately within six months the defeat of the Germans put a different complexion on the situation'.[166] On 11 November 1918, the First World War ended with the signing of the Armistice.

After the war, Earl Fortescue continued to undertake his public duties as Lord Lieutenant and maintained his commitments to organisations that were part of Devon's civil society.[167] However, on 16 October 1922 both Earl and Lady Fortescue were involved in an accident when they were driving a small carriage which overturned after the horse had become restless.[168] Although Fortescue emerged from the accident with minor injuries, Lady Fortescue suffered serious injuries as she was 'thrown violently upon her head'.[169] While she did regain consciousness and continued courageously to fulfil her civic commitments, Lady Fortescue never recovered fully from the effects of the accident.[170] As a result, it could be argued that her declining health since the accident, as well as Earl Fortescue's age, may have contributed to his decision to retire as Lord Lieutenant of Devon.[171] In July 1928, after he had held the post of Lord Lieutenant for 24 years, Fortescue relayed his decision to retire from the Lord Lieutenancy to King George V. Accordingly, the king appointed notable politician Francis Bingham Mildmay, the first Baron Mildmay, as the new Lord Lieutenant of Devon.[172] Upon review of Earl Fortescue's term as the Lord Lieutenant of Devon, *The North Devon Journal* proclaimed that he had set a high standard for the Lord Lieutenancy to which fourth Earl had 'discharged the many duties associated with that office with tact, diligence, and conscientiousness'.[173]

One year after Earl Fortescue had retired from the Lord Lieutenancy, his wife Emily Lady Fortescue died on 12 July 1929 after a long illness.[174] It was suggested in Lady Fortescue's obituary in *The Times* that her later life was one of 'continued battle against intense bodily suffering, to which she succumbed at last through sheer exhaustion'.[175] Although Earl Fortescue had withdrawn from his responsibilities as Lord Lieutenant and other affairs in the county, he kept himself busy. Indeed, he was still an active figure as he was 'constantly in the saddle perambulating the estate, hunting regularly, and riding among the foremost with the staghounds'.[176] In April 1929, Earl Fortescue finished compiling a history of his family and the Castle Hill estate which was privately published by W. H. Smith. Into his later years, Earl Fortescue continued to be a passionate advocate for stag hunting and wild deer hunting on Exmoor

---

[166] *Ibid.*, p. 48.
[167] *The Devon and Exeter Gazette*, 17 June 1920, p. 1; *The Western Times*, 15 July 1920, p.2; *The Times*, 7 March 1921, p. 13; *The North Devon Journal*, 2 June 1921, p. 6.
[168] *The Times*, 17 October 1922, p. 9.
[169] *The Times*, 13 July 1929, p. 16.
[170] *The Western Times*, 19 July 1929, p. 10.
[171] 'Denzil Fortescue b.1893 Recollections 1974', pp. 3–4.
[172] *The Devon and Exeter Gazette*, 7 July 1928, p. 8.
[173] *The North Devon Journal*, 12 July 1928, p. 5.
[174] *The Times*, 13 July 1929, p. 16.
[175] *Ibid.*
[176] *The Times*, 8 November 1932, p. 16.

against anti-stag hunting demonstrations.[177] However, in late October 1932, Earl Fortescue was taken ill and he underwent an operation at Castle Hill by London surgeon Sir Percy Sargent.[178] While the operation was a success and he appeared to make good progress in his recovery, the fourth Earl Fortescue died on 29 October 1932 from heart failure in his 79th year.[179] As a result, the fourth Earl's eldest son, Hugh William Fortescue, who was the Viscount Ebrington from 1905 to 1932, became the fifth Earl Fortescue.

According to his brother, Denzil Fortescue, the fifth Earl Fortescue followed very much in their father's footsteps in respect to both 'County and Duchy work'.[180] This was also evident when the fifth Earl held the office of the Lord Lieutenant of Devon from 1936 to 1958 to which he was both 'very active and assiduous'.[181] It could be argued that the fifth Earl upheld the noble tradition of his male forebears who were previously Lord Lieutenant and, in particular, he was inspired by his father's example of dutiful public service as the Lord Lieutenant of Devon from 1904 to 1928. During his tenure as the Lord Lieutenant of Devon, the fifth Earl was also ably assisted in his duties by his wife, Margaret Countess Fortescue.[182] After Hugh William Fortescue became the fifth Earl Fortescue in October 1932, his only son, (Hugh) Peter Fortescue, was appointed with the courtesy title of Viscount Ebrington. However, Viscount Ebrington did not inherit his father's peerage as he was killed in action at El Alamein on 17 July 1942 while serving with the Royal Scots Greys.[183] Consequently, the fifth Earl Fortescue's brother, Denzil Fortescue, was the next in line to inherit the peerage and he became the sixth Earl Fortescue upon his brother's death in 1958.

The Typescript, Diaries and Supplementary Materials
as Primary Sources

In the postwar period, Fortescue decided to write an account of his wartime experiences and work as the Lord Lieutenant of Devon during the Great War. The result of his endeavours was the 'typescript of work' that Fortescue typed up in 1924. It delivers a great number of insightful observations about Fortescue's participation with aspects of the war effort in the county that include agriculture, recruitment efforts and the Belgian refugees. The typescript reveals the great responsibilities that Fortescue had to shoulder during the First World War as the Lord Lieutenant of Devon, alongside his commitments to both Devon County Council and the county's Territorial Force Association. This is evident when Fortescue recalled that the First World War to him was

---

[177] *The Devon and Exeter Gazette*, 4 April 1930, p. 11; *The Western Times*, 14 August 1931, p. 9; *The Western Times*, 12 August 1932, p. 16.

[178] *The North Devon Journal*, 3 November 1932, p. 3.

[179] *Ibid.*; *The Times*, 31 October 1932, p. 8.

[180] 'Denzil Fortescue b. 1893 Recollections 1974', p. 43.

[181] *Ibid.*

[182] 'Lady Margaret Fortescue summary1', Exmoor Oral History Archive, 2001, http://www1.somerset.gov.uk/archives/Exmoor/fortescuesummary1.htm (accessed 20 March 2018).

[183] *The North Devon Journal-Herald*, 17 June 1943, p. 4.

mainly a 'confused mass of perpetual correspondence, committee meetings and anxiety'.[184] For Earl Fortescue, the Great War was a 'trying period [to which] not only recruiting but the agricultural organisation of the county occupied much of his attention'.[185] It is clear that the combination of three important posts in one person had 'naturally made the correspondence and work of that person heavy'.[186] According to his son Denzil Fortescue, Earl Fortescue was a diligent man who worked 'himself as hard as he could; still more so as Lord Lieutenant'.[187] The time-consuming and challenging nature of all of Fortescue's wartime responsibilities proved to be very strenuous for just one man's shoulders and hardworking sensibilities. This strain took a heavy toll upon him and in March 1916, Fortescue decided to retire as the Chairman of Devon County Council upon the advice of his doctor.[188] In his letter of resignation to the council, he stressed that 'the Government finds something fresh every week for the Chairman of the County Council or the Lord Lieutenant or the Chairman of the Territorial Force Association (or all three of them) to do'.[189] These unrelenting and increasing responsibilities could also explain why Fortescue recalled the conflict as a 'confused mass'.[190] It was claimed that the strain of the conflict had 'very nearly broke him down'.[191] Yet, while these three positions in wartime were a heavy burden for one individual, Fortescue acknowledged that in hindsight it 'prevented over-lapping and saved a lot of trouble'.[192]

The primary reason why Fortescue had decided to construct the typescript was as a result of his investigation of the papers and letters from the first Earl Fortescue in connection with his efforts as Lord Lieutenant to prepare for an invasion by Napoleon in 1803. After this survey of the first Earl's surviving papers, he had found 'a good deal that was of interest'.[193] It was through this consultation with his forebear's private papers that it had occurred to the fourth Earl that a record of his own wartime experiences from 1914 to 1918 'may similarly interest my descendants'.[194] The typescript was a gift to his descendants that presented a narrative of the 'sort of work that fell to my lot in the Great War'.[195] To Fortescue, this account was especially significant if the head of the family had the honour to be appointed Lord Lieutenant of the county. As mentioned previously, the appointment of Lord Lieutenant of

---

[184] DHC: 1262M/0/FH/42, Typescript of work of Lord Fortescue during 1st World War, p. 1.
[185] *The Western Morning News and Daily Gazette*, 31 October 1932, p. 6.
[186] DHC: 1262M/0/FH/42, Typescript of work of Lord Fortescue during 1st World War, p. 2.
[187] 'Denzil Fortescue b. 1893 Recollections 1974', p. 2; *The North Devon Journal*, 3 November 1932, p. 4.
[188] *The North Devon Journal*, 23 March 1916, p. 7.
[189] *Ibid.*
[190] DHC: 1262M/0/FH/42, Typescript of work of Lord Fortescue during 1st World War, p. 1.
[191] *The Times*, 8 November 1932, p. 16.
[192] DHC: 1262M/0/FH/42, Typescript of work of Lord Fortescue during 1st World War, p. 2.
[193] *Ibid.*, p. 1.
[194] *Ibid.*
[195] *Ibid.*

Devon was viewed as both a high distinction and a noble tradition bestowed upon the Fortescue family. This declaration is a noteworthy point to underscore due to the fact that Fortescue described the typescript as a 'memorandum'. By reading the typescript as a memorandum, it can be viewed as an account not intended for general publication but rather a written communication that was envisioned to be read by a selective and privileged audience.[196] Indeed, the typescript contains confidential and sensitive information that explains the work that fell within Fortescue's remit as the Lord Lieutenant of a county during the First World War. As a result, the content of the typescript is more of a personal reflection of the war years because it contains many candid and revealing opinions, insights and judgements. The typescript is, therefore, Lord Fortescue's commentary upon a number of wartime subjects, specific events and key individuals related to the war effort in the county. To construct the typescript, Fortescue revealed that he had consulted with a number of primary sources that he had at his disposal. These included the diaries that he had kept during the war as well as his private papers from the war years. By consulting with these combined sources, Fortescue explained that he could 'reconstruct a good deal' of his experiences as the Lord Lieutenant of Devon during the Great War.[197] Through the process of reconstruction that Fortescue employed in the typescript, he claimed that he was able, with greater confidence, to add clarity to his account of the conflict.

The diaries that Lord Fortescue kept from 1914 to 1918 are an extensive chronicle of his day-to-day activities and routines during the war years. These diaries are an important resource that Fortescue consulted to fashion the content of the typescript and it is possible to trace the individual diary entries that he referred to. An example of this in the typescript is when Fortescue described how the citizens of Exeter adapted to the new culture of wartime in August 1914. He revealed that apart from 'some middle-class members of the community who had begun to lay in stores of food: the public generally were helpful and calm'.[198] It is clear that Fortescue had directly referred to an entry from his diary dated 9 August 1914 because this section of the typescript mirrors the sentiments noted in his diary. On 9 August 1914, both he and Countess Fortescue went to Exeter to attend a service at Exeter Cathedral. Fortescue observed in his diary that in the city, 'Everyone is helpful & calm. No one has behaved ill but a few middle class who have got in stores of food.'[199] It is also interesting to point out that included in the folder that contains the typescript there are several sheets in Fortescue's handwriting. These sheets are organised for each year of the war and list important dates with corresponding events from Fortescue's wartime diaries. Similarly, it is evident that Fortescue used these entries as a guide to refer to various topics related to the war years and

---

[196] Kristina Spohr Readman, 'Memoranda', in M. Dobson and B. Ziemann, eds, *Reading Primary Sources: The Interpretation of Texts from Nineteenth- and Twentieth-Century History* (Abingdon: Routledge, 2009), pp. 123–125.

[197] DHC: 1262M/0/FH/42, Typescript of work of Lord Fortescue during 1st World War, p. 1.

[198] *Ibid.*, p. 12.

[199] DHC: 1262M/0/FD/46, Personal diary of the 3rd Lord Ebrington, 1914–1916, 9 August 1914.

there are ticks marked next to several entries. Through a cross-examination of these marked entries from his diaries alongside the typescript, it is possible to ascertain the individual diary entries that Fortescue had selected to help him during his research. An example of this is the section of the typescript which reveals the efforts that were made by Fortescue and others to raise a Farmers Battalion in Devon. For the sheet dedicated to 1915, Fortescue has ticked two dates, 29 July and 24 August 1915 respectively. Both of these diary entries reveal that Fortescue went to great lengths to try to establish this Farmers Battalion.[200] Similarly, there are letters between him and the military authorities that relate to the Farmers Battalion contained within the *Fortescue at Castle Hill* archive. Evidently, Fortescue also referred to these materials to construct this segment of the typescript.

As a retrospective account of the war years, it is important to be aware of the merits and drawbacks of the process of reconstruction that Fortescue employed to fashion his reminiscences of the conflict. In the typescript, Fortescue recalled that the First World War was mainly as a 'confused mass of perpetual correspondence, committee meetings and anxiety' but he does not clarify what this anxiety was. [201] The next time that the word anxiety was used in the typescript was when he referred to the number of red deer.[202] According to Fortescue, the dense population of these animals on Exmoor had produced a crisis.[203] He reveals that various figures, including Fred Goss, the Stag Harbourer for the Devon and Somerset Stag Hounds, had proposed and employed various solutions in the hope to decrease the size of the deer population and ultimately reduce the amount of compensation that was granted to farmers for damage caused by the roaming deer.[204] The typescript is primarily framed around Fortescue's personal recollections of the war years. In composing it, he benefited greatly from using his diaries and private papers to support or fill in the gaps in his memories of the period. It was through this process that Fortescue constructed a narrative of his wartime experiences. This means that the typescript could be assessed as an exercise in the use of memory. In the document, this is evident when Fortescue employed phrases that place a great emphasis upon the limitations of his memories. These include: 'as far as I recollect', 'if memory serves me correct' and 'if I remember right'.[205] These phrases also establish an important point in that they underscore the heavily reliance that he has placed upon his memories of the war years. Fortescue acknowledged this in that while he wrote the typescript six years after the Armistice of 1918, he stated: 'I cannot pretend my memory of the period is very clear.'[206] It is important to point out that

---

[200] DHC: 1262M/0/FD/46, Personal diary of the 3rd Lord Ebrington, 1914–1916, 29 July 1915; DHC: 1262M/0/FD/46, Personal diary of the 3rd Lord Ebrington, 1914–1916, 24 August 1915.

[201] DHC: 1262M/0/FH/42, Typescript of work of Lord Fortescue during 1st World War, p. 1.

[202] *Ibid.*, p. 29.

[203] *Ibid.*

[204] *Ibid.*, pp. 29–31.

[205] *Ibid.*, pp. 3, 4, 28.

[206] *Ibid.*, p. 1.

Fortescue was 'a little over 60' when war was declared in August 1914.[207] This could possibly help to explain why Fortescue's memories of the war were not as clear when compared to memories from earlier in his life. However, Fortescue stressed that despite his age he was still 'pretty tough and active'.[208] Upon evaluation of Fortescue's diaries, he was quite an active individual indeed. From 1914 to 1918, he managed to find time for his hunting pursuits, overseeing the Castle Hill estate, his obligations to activities related to the war effort in Devon as well as regular trips to London to fulfil his duties in the House of Lords. As a result, the entries contained in the fourth Earl Fortescue's diaries reflect the active and varied life that he led during the First World War.

Alongside his diaries, Fortescue also referred to documents from the war contained within his private papers. He stated that he had organised these materials which were 'filed in one of the cabinets under various headings'.[209] Fortescue does state in the typescript that fuller information on the 'subjects of these notes will be found in the newspaper cuttings &c. that I have filed, and in the papers I kept about the war'.[210] Based on this, Fortescue provided his descendants with the opportunity that if they wanted to know more about his wartime experiences after they had read the typescript they could consult the papers that he kept from the war. It is also clear that Fortescue did refer to newspaper cuttings that he had kept which related to his involvement with the war effort. Nevertheless, apart from this statement, Fortescue does not explicitly state which individual documents from his private papers that he referred to in order to construct the typescript. The sheer volume and variety of documents present in the *Fortescue at Castle Hill* archive reflects the scale of Fortescue's involvement in the war effort. As a result of this extensive repository of materials, Fortescue possessed a wide range of primary sources that he could consult with for the typescript. This uncertainty presents an issue in how to ascertain which specific documents Fortescue had used to help him to reconstruct his memories of the conflict. Yet, through a process of cross-examination of the typescript alongside a survey of the materials in the *Fortescue at Castle Hill* archive, it is possible to propose individual documents that Fortescue probably consulted to fashion his account. For instance, in the section of the typescript that addresses the 'Clean Cut' in June 1918, it is highly likely that Fortescue consulted with the document titled 'Notes as to the Clean Cut in Devonshire. June 1918'. In these notes, Fortescue documented the difficulties that were involved with the 'Clean Cut' as well as the anxiety felt by those involved in this process.[211] Thus, while Fortescue reconstructed a good deal of his wartime experiences, it must be said that through this process of recollection the typescript is a noteworthy albeit incomplete account.

It is also important to point out the strengths and limitations of the typescript itself. As a primary source, the typescript concentrates on subjects that relate to Fortescue's involvement in the war effort. This is particularly evident with

[207] *Ibid.*

[208] *Ibid.*

[209] *Ibid.*

[210] *Ibid.*, p. 48.

[211] DHC: 1262M/0/O/LD/155/45, Typed notes, entitled – as to the Clean Cut in Devonshire and additional hand written notes, June 1918.

how Fortescue only briefly touches upon the Volunteer Training Corps in the typescript. He describes the corps as a military unit that somewhat resembled an amateur home defence force to which units were raised 'among men who were too old or really too busy for more active service'.[212] Hence, the typescript contains only a small amount of information about the activities of the corps in Devon; Fortescue explains that in his view there was not 'much scope for them in Devonshire' and they were an unnecessary and wasteful distraction for the war effort in the county.[213]

It is clear that Fortescue had composed the typescript as an assembled draft version from his working notes. This is evident in the fact that Fortescue did not finish the typescript. Although he stated his intention to close 'these memoranda with', there is no information after this declaration.[214] Yet, in 1927, Fortescue added this conclusion when he revisited the original typescript and refashioned it into a chapter of *A Chronicle of Castle Hill, 1459–1919*. This was a book that Fortescue wrote and compiled as both a history of the Castle Hill estate and a testament of the lives and achievements of his notable forebears. In 1929, it was privately printed by W. H. Smith. Upon review of the version of the typescript that was printed in the book, it is identical to the original albeit with minor alterations as well as the inclusion of bonus material and primary sources. He included additional information that expanded upon a number of subjects that were touched upon in the typescript which include the Devonshire Patriotic Fund and the billeting of soldiers in Devon.[215] To close the memorandum, Fortescue included two letters that he had found amusing about the Separation Allowance, the entries from his diary for the last three days of the war (9, 10 and 11 November 1918) and three letters from Lady Fortescue.[216] Parker has suggested that this privately printed manuscript is a 'particularly illuminating source'.[217] However, this description can also be applied to the original typescript because it is an insightful and important primary source in its own right. As a draft version of his reminiscences of the war years, the typescript contains additions, amendments and deletions that provide an impression of Fortescue's thought processes when he reviewed the document. This is evident with the short statement on page four of the typescript to which Fortescue inserted the comment: 'the G. O. C. at Plymouth was a useless person'.[218] This opinion about the General Officer Commanding at Plymouth was later added in pen by Fortescue in the space between two paragraphs. Yet, in the printed version he decided to omit this comment. Nevertheless, this observation provides a valuable insight from Fortescue and it reveals his workings when he reviewed the content of the typescript. In this volume, the original

---

[212] DHC: 1262M/0/FH/42, Typescript of work of Lord Fortescue during 1st World War, p. 36.
[213] *Ibid.*
[214] *Ibid.*, p. 48.
[215] Hugh Fortescue, *A Chronicle of Castle Hill: 1454–1919* (London: W. H. Smith & Son, 1929), pp. 152–153, 159–160.
[216] Ibid., pp. 177–182.
[217] Parker, *The People of Devon in the First World War*, p. 11.
[218] DHC: 1262M/0/FH/42, Typescript of work of Lord Fortescue during 1st World War, p. 4.

typescript is presented in full with the corrections, additions and amendments that Fortescue added in pen and pencil. There are also footnotes which provide explanations of the major differences between the original typescript and the printed version.

It is also vital to shed a critical light upon Fortescue's wartime diaries. In the typescript, Fortescue described the diary that he kept during the war as a 'diary of a sort'.[219] This is an apt description because Fortescue's diaries are not what could be described as a conventional diary that contains regular statements with detailed self-reflection and self-observation.[220] The content of the diary entries are not consistent where upon an individual would comprehensively chronicle the events of the day. Rather, the length and nature of Fortescue's diary entries vary significantly. He confessed that repeatedly his diary entries were 'very brief indeed, sometimes no more than "work as usual"'.[221] There are many entries that reflect this as they simply state Fortescue's routines and activities during a particular day. This is evident when he records his activities on the Castle Hill estate such as his involvement with haymaking and shooting. There are also a number of brief diary entries that relate to the war effort in Devon. He noted in his diary that he attended recruiting meetings and route marches across the county but he rarely provides further descriptions about these events.[222] This is also the case in the diary entries where Fortescue stated that he was present at the National War Aims Committee events in Barnstaple.[223] These very brief entries reinforce how active Fortescue was during the war years and in several entries he revealed that he was exhausted after long and eventful days.

Simultaneously, Lord Fortescue's diaries also contain occasional longer entries. These are especially revealing about Fortescue's priorities as to what he considered was significant to record in greater detail. In the typescript, Fortescue explained why the diaries occasionally contained longer entries about the events of a particular day. This was especially the case if he had met and 'talked with anyone who had inside knowledge of what was going on'.[224] There are a number of entries that reflect this because they reveal Lord and Lady Fortescue's involvement in upper-class social circles. He recorded the conversations, some of which he documented verbatim, that they had experienced with notable contemporary figures on subjects related to the war. He chronicles the discussions that he and Lady Fortescue had with prominent members of both Houses of Parliament, other peers, foreign envoys and other notable figures of

---

[219] *Ibid.*, p. 1.

[220] Christa Hammerle, 'Diaries', trans. by Andrew Evans, in M. Dobson and B. Ziemann, eds, *Reading Primary Sources: The Interpretation of Texts from Nineteenth- and Twentieth-Century History* (Abingdon: Routledge, 2009), pp. 141–155.

[221] DHC: 1262M/0/FH/42, Typescript of work of Lord Fortescue during 1st World War, p. 1.

[222] DHC: 1262M/0/FD/46, Personal diary of the 3rd Lord Ebrington, 1914–1916, 20 August 1914; DHC: 1262M/0/FD/46, Personal diary of the 3rd Lord Ebrington, 1914–1916, 18 May 1915.

[223] DHC: 1262M/0/FD/47, Personal diary of the 3rd Lord Ebrington, 1916–1918, 26 October 1917; DHC: 1262M/0/FD/47, Personal diary of the 3rd Lord Ebrington, 1916–1918, 19 December 1917.

[224] DHC: 1262M/0/FH/42, Typescript of work of Lord Fortescue during 1st World War, p. 1.

the British aristocracy. One example of this was on 15 December 1915, which Fortescue labelled as a meeting of 'dissatisfied peers'. In his diary, Fortescue recorded who attended the meeting and the contributions that were made by individual peers, including Lords Milner and Morley who objected to how the Asquith coalition government was waging the war.[225] There are occasional longer entries that contain Lord Fortescue's thoughts upon what was discussed in these conversations. This is evident for his diary entry for 18 April 1918. While staying in London, Fortescue met the veteran British diplomat, Sir Arthur Nicholson. During dinner, both men spoke about the war's progress, where Nicholson held 'strongly that the Kaiser did not want war with us a bit & was rather let in for it by Austria'.[226] Fortescue confided in his diary in a satirical tone that after three and half years of war he believed that the 'feeling seems to be that we are past the crisis'.[227]

It must also be said that the diaries of the fourth Earl Fortescue present a valuable perspective upon the personal lives of both Earl Fortescue and other members of the Fortescue family during the Great War. This is due to the fact that he recorded important events that happened to himself and his family from 1914 to 1918. These include his son Denzil being involved with the mobilisation of C (Cavalry) Squadron of the Royal North Devon Yeomanry in August 1914, Lady Fortescue's frequent trips to Windsor due to the fact that she was a Lady in Waiting to Queen Mary, and the wedding of Viscount Ebrington to Margaret 'Daisy' Beaumont, the daughter of the first Viscount Allendale, on 8 February 1917.[228] Likewise, Earl Fortescue touched upon the wartime experiences of Lady Fortescue and their sons Ebrington and Denzil in the typescript.[229] Accordingly, both documents impart a portrait of the Fortescue family during the First World War. Upon review of the diaries that the fourth Earl Fortescue kept throughout the war years, it is clear that the diary entries present a great amount of variety. This is a reflection of Earl Fortescue's industrious work ethic as well as his own diverse interests and engagements. These various observations cover a wide range of subjects that document Fortescue's many commitments during the war as the Lord Lieutenant of Devon, a peer of the realm and a member of the county's landed gentry. At the same time, he combines this catalogue of entries related to his wartime experiences with personal insights about other members of the Fortescue family. Thus, the diaries of the fourth Earl Fortescue are a significant primary source because they are a rich and multifaceted document of the war years.

[225] DHC: 1262M/0/FD/46, Personal diary of the 3rd Lord Ebrington, 1914–1916, 15 December 1915.
[226] DHC: 1262M/0/FD/47, Personal diary of the 3rd Lord Ebrington, 1916–1918, 18 April 1918.
[227] *Ibid.*
[228] DHC: 1262M/0/FD/46, Personal diary of the 3rd Lord Ebrington, 1914–1916, 5 August 1914; DHC: 1262M/0/FD/46, Personal diary of the 3rd Lord Ebrington, 1914–1916, 29 April 1915; DHC: 1262M/0/FD/46, Personal diary of the 3rd Lord Ebrington, 1914–1916, 3 September 1915; 'Denzil Fortescue b. 1893 Recollections 1974', pp. 4, 21; DHC: 1262M/0/FD/47, Personal diary of the 3rd Lord Ebrington, 1916–1918, 8 February 1917.
[229] DHC: 1262M/0/FH/42, Typescript of work of Lord Fortescue during 1st World War, pp. 14–15, 37.

It could be argued that the documents that Fortescue had kept from the war in his private papers provide a valuable indication of his priorities as to what he wished to keep for posterity. This is particularly evident with the cuttings from local newspapers that Fortescue had decided to keep, especially in the case of two articles by Sydney Harper that were published in the *North Devon Journal* on 13 and 20 August 1914 respectively. In the two articles, Harper compared recruitment efforts in Devon in 1914 with the recruitment drive that occurred in the county in 1794. While Harper makes a comparison between the first and fourth Earl Fortescue, the two articles are mainly a history of the barracks at Barnstaple from 1794 to 1807.[230] Although these articles provide a small amount of information about the fourth Earl as such, the fact that Fortescue kept these two articles is significant. These articles reveal that contemporary figures sought to promote historical parallels with what was happening in 1914 as a means to inform and reassure readers who were uncertain and worried about what the war would bring. It can also be observed that these articles probably helped to establish or further confirm to Fortescue the noteworthy connection between his wartime experiences as Lord Lieutenant and those of his great-grandfather. The primary sources presented in this volume also include letters and other correspondence to various officials, statistics for the acreage ploughed in the county, and officially published booklets containing histories of various organisations and committees. Therefore, this collection of documents act as a representative sample of Fortescue's private papers that reveals much about Devon from 1914 to 1918.

Historiography and the Significance of the Lord Lieutenant
on the British Home Front of the Great War

The historiography of the Home Fronts of the First World War has expanded significantly since the 1960s.[231] An important shift in this historiography is the consideration of how the belligerent nations mobilised for war. John Horne has defined mobilisation during the First World War as the 'engagement of the different belligerent nations in their war efforts both imaginatively, through collective representations and the belief and value systems giving rise to these, and organizationally, through the state and civil society'.[232] The mobilisation of the belligerent nations for war was ultimately a 'political and cultural process'.[233] To consider mobilisation as a process or a 'totalizing logic' rather than an achieved result, is that it not only 'encourages analysis of its form and evolution but also of its constraints and limitations'.[234] Britain, France and Germany appear to 'share a common pattern of national mobilization in which the first two years of the war were strongly characterized by persuasion rather

[230] DHC: 1262M/0/O/LD/136/3, Newspaper cutting of an article comparing recruitment in Devonshire for the First World War with that of a recruitment drive in 1794, c. 1914.
[231] Jay Winter and Antoine Prost, *The Great War in History: Debates and Controversies, 1914 to the Present* (Cambridge: Cambridge University Press, 2007), pp. 156–159.
[232] John Horne, 'Introduction: Mobilizing for "Total War", 1914–1918' in J. Horne, ed., *State, Society and Mobilization in Europe during the First World War* (Cambridge: Cambridge University Press, 1997), p. 3.
[233] *Ibid.*, p. 1.
[234] *Ibid.*, p. 5.

than coercion, and by a high degree of "self-mobilization" in civil society'.[235] However, the meaning of wartime mobilisation shifted during the war from its 'original military definition to encompass the contribution of civil society, whose resources were also expected to directly support the armed forces in the field'.[236] In 1917, there was a distinct shift from self-mobilisation to remobilisation. This second mobilisation or remobilisation entailed the recognition of sacrifices which were previously deemed unacceptable to guarantee the prospect of victory. In Britain and France, during 1917 and 1918 the state became 'involved in a broad-fronted campaign to sustain civilian morale for outright military victory'.[237]

The mobilisation efforts and work of civilians in the belligerent nations during the war constituted 'a front (albeit a secondary one) that supported or complemented the [military] front'.[238] The secondary front that emerged has become defined as the Home Front. Socio-cultural histories of the Home Fronts of the belligerent nations have taken into consideration a number of different aspects of the civilian experience and reflected on the nature of wartime mobilisation. These include the means by which the belligerent nations attempted to mobilise popular support for the war effort, and how various groups of civilians (e.g. farmers, fishermen, women and children) engaged with the war effort.[239] Through comparative analysis with the Home Fronts of the belligerent nations, the wartime experiences on the British Home Front have been positioned within a wider international context.[240] Yet, studies of the Home Front during the Great War have, usually, concentrated their analytical focus on the administrative framework of the nation-state.[241] In response to this, Jay Winter has advocated that the best method to move beyond this and 'penetrate behind

[235] *Ibid.*

[236] Pierre Purseigle, 'Violence and Solidarity. Urban Experiences of the First World War', 27 September 2012, http://www.pierrepurseigle.info/violence-and-solidarity-urban-experiences-of-the-first-world-war (accessed 20 February 2013).

[237] John Horne, 'Remobilizing for "Total war": France and Britain, 1917–1918', in J. Horne, ed., *State, Society and Mobilization in Europe during the First World War* (Cambridge: Cambridge University Press, 1997), p. 198.

[238] Maureen Healy, *Vienna and the Fall of the Habsburg Empire: Total War and Everyday Life in World War I* (Cambridge: Cambridge University Press, 2004), p. 5.

[239] Bernard Waites, *A Class Society at War: England, 1914–18* (Leamington Spa: Berg Publishers, 1987); Susan R. Grayzel, *Women's Identities at War: Gender, Motherhood, and Politics in Britain and France during the First World War* (Chapel Hill, NC: The University of North Carolina Press, 1999); Nicoletta F. Gullace, *"The Blood of Our Sons": Men, Women and the Renegotiation of British Citizenship during the Great War* (New York: Palgrave Macmillan, 2002); David Bilton, *The Home Front in the Great War: Aspects of the Conflict, 1914–1918* (Barnsley: Leo Cooper, 2003), pp. 195–201; Adrian Gregory, *The Last Great War: British Society and the First World War* (Cambridge: Cambridge University Press, 2008); Rosie Kennedy, *The Children's War: Britain, 1914–1918* (Basingstoke: Palgrave Macmillan, 2014).

[240] Jay Winter, 'Recent Trends in the Historiography of Britain and the First World War: Cultural History, Comparative History, Public History', in H. Berghoff and R. von Friedeburg, eds, *Change and Inertia: Britain under the Impact of the Great War* (Bodenheim: Philo, 1998), pp. 94–97; Tammy M. Proctor, *Civilians in a World at War, 1914–1918* (New York: New York University Press, 2010).

[241] John Williams, *The Home Fronts: Britain, France and Germany, 1914–1918* (London: Constable, 1972).

the illusory veil of a unitary "national experience" is to describe the character of community life in wartime'.[242] As a result, studies of the Home Front have shifted their analytical focus away from the administrative framework of the nation-state to examine the wartime experiences of civilians in specific localities such as cities, towns, villages and hamlets. Accordingly, micro-histories of individual localities represent a 'new' cultural history of the Great War in that these studies are informed from below with a greater 'emphasis on the effects of war on local communities in their distinctive settings'.[243] This has also led to an initiative to look beyond and below the nations with a cross-examination of specific localities across the belligerent nations.

In his comparative examination of two small towns, Béziers in France and Northampton in Britain, Pierre Purseigle suggests that the 'local elite was the critical group'.[244] The reason for this is that the local elite reflected and shaped the mediation of the war experience on a local level.[245] As a result, the local elite were important intermediaries and campaigners for the war effort on the Home Front. In Purseigle's view, the local elite acted as the 'transmitters of national bodies or organisations that rallied to the war effort'.[246] The vision of the war which was transmitted and mediated by the local elite to their respective communities 'fell into line with the national mobilization whose "totalizing logic" enlisted the cultural, moral, and ideological commitment of each nation to fight an uncivilised enemy to its total destruction, lest its victory should lead to the end of one's culture, identity and way of life'.[247] The complex cultures of war with their distinct depictions of sacrifice, patriotism and duty provided a means for individuals, communities and societies across the belligerent nations to understand and participate in the war. The discourses and iconography of 'war cultures' that are evident in the materials produced by 'civic authorities, newspapers and voluntary organizations show how local elites used the main symbols of local identity to stress that victory would belong to the urban community as well as to the nation'.[248] The employment of national representations and the connection to this wider war culture were evident in the reactions of the local elites of Northampton and Béziers to the fate of Belgium.[249] However, despite the growth of the state in both Britain and France during the war, local civil society were not stripped of their mediating role.[250] Purseigle

[242] Jay Winter, 'Paris, London, Berlin 1914–1919: Capital Cities at War', in J. Winter and J-L. Robert, eds, *Capital Cities at War: Paris, London, Berlin, 1914–1919* (Cambridge: Cambridge University Press, 1999), p. 3.

[243] Keith Grieves, 'The Quiet of the Country and the Restless Excitement of the Towns: Rural Perspectives on the Home Front, 1914–1918', in M. Tebbutt, ed., *Rural and Urban Encounters in the Nineteenth and Twentieth Centuries: Regional Perspectives* (Manchester: Conference of Regional and Local Historians, 2004), p. 80.

[244] Pierre Purseigle, 'Beyond and Below the Nations: Towards a Comparative History of Local Communities at War', in J. Macleod and P. Purseigle, eds, *Uncovered Fields: Perspectives in First World War Studies* (Leiden: Brill, 2004), p. 96.

[245] *Ibid.*, pp. 96–99.

[246] *Ibid.*, p. 98.

[247] *Ibid.*

[248] Purseigle, 'Violence and Solidarity'.

[249] Purseigle, 'Beyond and Below the Nations', p. 99.

[250] *Ibid.*, p. 120.

advocates that the experiences of the local elite should be studied because an inquiry of this critical group allows the 'historian to deal comprehensively with both the local commitment to the national mobilization and the mental imagery which allowed the transcendence of the war experience'.[251]

During the war, the status of the local elite as self-appointed figures of civil society gave them another avenue to exert their influence upon wartime society. This was evident with the participation of Ireland's peers in various activities to support the war effort because it was a natural 'extension of their traditional role as landlords and patrons of charitable societies'.[252] This was also the case in Devon. Both Lord and Lady Fortescue respectively had existing roles in areas such as welfare and education in the county.[253] Although the Fortescues occupied new roles and responsibilities on various wartime committees in the county, it could be argued that these undertakings also acted as a natural extension of their traditional role in local civil society.[254] It must also be said that, alongside her involvement in the county's civic society, Lady Fortescue ably supported her husband in his duties as the Lord Lieutenant of Devon both before and during the First World War.[255] In Devon, the county's local elite were intermediaries of the war effort on a local level to which they shaped and mediated the war experience. Devon's local elite were agents who broadcasted, reflected upon and policed the nature of sacrifice and the social morality of wartime in the county.[256]

Yet, it is important to recognise the limitations of wartime mobilisation and the efficacy of the local elite on a local level. The discourses of national mobilisation could also unintentionally create vocabularies of counter-mobilisation through the powerful agents of class and nation.[257] Winter notes that class consciousness was an important factor in the mobilisation process because industrial conflict during the war revealed that patriotism itself was a contested term.[258] Maureen Healy is sceptical about the success of mobilisation in Vienna as the attempts to mobilise the city's population caused 'communal disintegration'.[259] Purseigle advances that the 'war cultures' that were 'most forcefully articulated by the elites were neither uncritically endorsed by the masses, nor merely imposed from above through the state ideological apparatus'.[260] It must also be said that when 'common sense on the popular level diverged from state propaganda, the official

---

[251] *Ibid.*, p. 96.

[252] Peter Martin, '*Dulce et Decorum*: Irish Nobles and the Great War, 1914–19', in A. Gregory and S. Pašeta, eds, *Ireland and the Great War: 'A War to Unite Us All'?* (Manchester: Manchester University Press, 2002), p. 37.

[253] 'Denzil Fortescue b. 1893 Recollections 1974', pp. 2–5.

[254] *The Devon and Exeter Gazette*, 13 July 1929, p. 4.

[255] *The North Devon Journal*, 12 July 1928, p. 5.

[256] Richard Batten, 'Devon and the First World War', PhD thesis, University of Exeter, 2013.

[257] Horne, 'Introduction', p. 12.

[258] Winter, 'Paris, London, Berlin, 1914–1919', p. 17.

[259] Healy, *Vienna and the Fall of the Habsburg Empire*, p. 4.

[260] Pierre Purseigle, 'Introduction, Warfare and Belligerence: Approaches to the First World War', in P. Purseigle, ed., *Warfare and Belligerence: Perspectives in First World War Studies* (Leiden: Brill, 2005), p. 26.

message turned hollow or simply vanished'.[261] The contribution that the local
elite could make on a local level to disseminate this 'war culture' and promote
wartime initiatives was crucial for the war effort of the belligerent nations. This
was evident with the efficacy of the Tsarist war effort in rural areas of Russia.
Although Russia's gentry were expected to accept their wartime responsibilities
and organise public support for the Russian war effort, the reputation of these
notable figures had greatly diminished before the war to the extent that by 1914
they were 'something of a spent force'.[262] Peter Gatrell suggests that Russia's
landed elite were unreliable and could not 'underpin an effective propaganda
offensive in the countryside'.[263] The fact that Russia's rural elite were ineffective
intermediaries of the war experience undermined efforts to mobilise Russia's
rural populace for war.

It would be wrong to propose that Devon's local elite were constantly an
effective and cohesive group because to gain the participation of the people of
Devon in the war effort was dependent on the efforts of individual members
of civil society in the county.[264] The evidence from the *Fortescue at Castle Hill*
archive underscores that not all forms of wartime mobilisation were universally
accepted on a local level across the county. These documents also reinforce the
agency of the county's population during the First World War in that many
Devonians placed individual priorities above national ones. The county's elite
struggled to convince all of Devon's population that the Great War was every-
body's war and there were Devonians who were partially resistant to the logic of
modern industrial war.[265] The Lord Lieutenant was one of the most significant
members of the local elite as they exerted significant socio-political influence
in local civil society in counties across the United Kingdom. During the Great
War, the Lord Lieutenant played a pivotal role in promoting the war effort on
a local level. Through their involvement with the activities of committees and
organisations related to the war effort, Lord Lieutenants were able to extend
their influence as intermediaries of the war experience on a local level. They
disseminated and broadcast this war culture to their local communities through
addresses, speeches and statements.[266] Through their leadership on a local level,
the Lord Lieutenants could set a positive example for other figures in civil
society and local populations to follow.[267] Studies of the British Home Front
of the First World War have only occasionally included the figure of Lord

[261] J. M. Winter, 'Propaganda and the Mobilization of Consent', in H. Strachan, ed.,
The Oxford Illustrated History of the First World War (Oxford: Oxford University Press,
1998), p. 217.
[262] Peter Gatrell, *Russia's First World War: A Social and Economic History* (Harlow:
Pearson Education, 2005), p. 50.
[263] *Ibid.*, p. 56.
[264] *The Western Times*, 2 March 1915, p. 3.
[265] Plymouth and West Devon Record Office: Acc 1306/22, Diary of Edrica de la Pole,
1914, 1 September 1914, as cited in Pennell, *A Kingdom United*, p. 151; *The Western
Morning News and Daily Gazette*, 10 December 1914; *The Devon and Exeter Gazette*,
20 January 1916, p. 4.
[266] DHC: 1262M/0/O/LD/153/5, Speech (incomplete), 1 December 1914.
[267] William Collins, *Herefordshire and the Great War, with the City and County's Roll of
Honour* (Hereford: Jakeman & Carver, 1919), p. 41.

Lieutenant.[268] However, there are exceptions. In his research on Sussex in the Great War, Keith Grieves has considered the wartime role and activities of the Duke of Norfolk as the Lord Lieutenant of Sussex.[269] Similarly, works by David Parker and Bonnie White have explored the involvement of Lord Fortescue as the Lord Lieutenant of Devon with the county's war effort from 1914 to 1918.[270] There are also works that have considered the Lord Lieutenant in respect to their involvement in the commemoration of the conflict with war memorials.[271] However, the wartime experiences of the Lord Lieutenant can offer important contributions to the history of the British Home Front on a local level.

From the unique and towering vantage point of the Lord Lieutenant of Devonshire, Earl Fortescue was an unparalleled observer of the county from 1914 to 1918. He was one of the most dedicated and diligent campaigners of the war effort across Devon.[272] Fortescue was responsible for voluntary recruitment and agricultural organisation in the county with the chairmanship of the Devon Parliamentary Recruiting Committee and the Devon War Agricultural Executive Committee respectively.[273] Purseigle has advocated that the history of the local elite 'is an inquiry into the war experience through a cross-section of the local societies, an intermediary level of that experience'.[274] The typescript, diaries and other documents included in this volume reveal this intermediary level of the war experience between Devon's local elite and the county's population. Fortescue acted as a pivotal intermediary for the war experience on a local level in Devon but he was also a moderator between conflicted parties on the Home Front.[275]

The First World War was a crucial period in Lord Fortescue's life and this is reflected in how the printed version of the typescript functions as a chapter in *A Chronicle of Castle Hill*. With the exception of three chapters, the book is structured as a series of biographies on the previous Earl Fortescue. However, the chapter that should stand as the fourth Earl's memoirs is in fact a refashioned version of the typescript.[276] As he oversaw many aspects related to the war effort in Devon during the Great War, the fourth Earl Fortescue believed that he had followed in the footsteps of the first Earl Fortescue. The fact that Fortescue presented a revised version of the typescript reinforces that he wished what he had endured and accomplished during the Great War to be remembered as the defining period of his life. In fact, Fortescue's service to the state from 1914 to 1918 was recognised by Roland Prothero, who stated in a letter on 16

[268] Pennell, *A Kingdom United*, pp. 82, 105, 150, 155 ; Connelly, *Steady the Buffs!*, p. 10.
[269] Grieves, 'Lowther's Lambs', pp. 57–58; Grieves, 'Introduction', pp. xvi–xvii.
[270] Parker, *The People of Devon in the First World War*; White, 'War and the Home Front'.
[271] Todd Gray, *Lest Devon Forgets: Service, Sacrifice and the Creation of War Memorials* (Exeter: Mint Press, 2010), pp. 24, 77–78, 105–106; Alex King, *Memorials of the Great War in Britain: The Symbolism and Politics of Remembrance* (Oxford: Berg, 1998), pp. 43, 79–81.
[272] *The North Devon Journal*, 18 July 1929, p. 3.
[273] *The Western Times*, 4 November 1932, p. 10.
[274] Purseigle, 'Beyond and Below the Nations', p. 96.
[275] DHC: 1262M/0/FH/42, Typescript of work of Lord Fortescue during 1st World War, pp. 26–27, 37–39.
[276] Fortescue, *A Chronicle of Castle Hill*, pp. 144–182.

January 1919 that 'We owe you a heavy debt for all the help you have given us in Devonshire.'[277] Upon Earl Fortescue's death on 29 October 1932, the obituaries of him in the local and national press stressed the importance of his service to the state during the First World War. In their obituary of Fortescue, the *Western Times* declared that during the war he had 'maintained the noble traditions of the family in regard to service to the State by playing a practical part in the recruiting campaign conducted throughout the county in those tragic days'.[278] In their tribute to Lord Fortescue, a correspondent for *The Times* suggested that it fell to the fourth Earl Fortescue to 'guide Devon through the War of 1914–18 as his great-grandfather had guided her through that of 1793–1814'.[279] Similarly, another *Times* correspondent stressed his fortitude in that 'Devon owes him a debt of gratitude for the unsparing work of many years'.[280]

The typescript is an indispensable and personal survey of Devon as a Home Front during the First World War from one of the county's pre-eminent figures at the time. It is Fortescue's original recollection of his wartime experiences as the Lord Lieutenant of Devonshire. Fortescue's diaries reveal his day-to-day activities as a Lord Lieutenant, a peer of the realm and a member of the landed gentry during the Great War. The longer diary entries also provide an insider's viewpoint upon important events and reveal his participation, along with Lady Fortescue, in prominent social circles. The documents that accompany the typescript and the diaries also contain many fascinating observations into the county during the war years. Accordingly, all of the documents presented in this book are a significant historical record of the priorities, trials and tribulations of a prominent member of Devon's local elite from 1914 to 1918.

---

[277] DHC: 1262M/0/O/LD/112/35, Private Letter to Lord Fortescue from the Board of Agriculture and Fisheries, 16 Jan 1919, p. 1.
[278] *The Western Times*, 4 November 1932, p. 10.
[279] *The Times*, 8 November 1932, p. 16.
[280] *The Times*, 31 October 1932, p. 8.

TYPESCRIPT OF THE
WORK OF LORD FORTESCUE DURING
THE FIRST WORLD WAR (1924)

Devon Heritage Centre (DHC hereafter): 1262M/o/FH/42

TYPESCRIPT OF WORK OF LORD FORTESCUE DURING FIRST WORLD WAR, Post 1919

Having found a great deal that was of interest in the letters and papers received and sent by our great grandfather the first Earl Fortescue[1] when in 1803 invasion by Napoleon[2] was anticipated and much work in connection with the Defence of the Realm was imposed on him as on all other Lords Lieutenant, it has occurred to me that it may similarly interest my descendants especially if the head of the family has again the honour of being H. M. Lieutenant, to see the sort of work that fell to my lot in the Great War 1914 – 1918.

Though I am writing only in 1924 I cannot pretend that my memory of the period is very clear: I recall it mainly as a confused mass of perpetual correspondence, committee meetings and anxiety.

I kept a diary of a sort: occasionally there are long notes about the events of the day especially if I had met and talked with anyone who had inside knowledge of what was going on; but more often the entries are very brief indeed, sometimes no more than "work as usual".

However, between it and the papers I kept (which are filed in ~~the library~~ one of the cabinets[3] under various headings) I can reconstruct a good deal. My activities were varied as in addition to being Lord Lieutenant I was Chairman of the County Council[4] and also Chairman of the Territorial Force Association. As all government communications were with the holder of one of these offices this prevented over-lapping and saved a lot of trouble in that way, but the combination of three important posts in one person naturally made the correspondence and work of that person heavy.

It is just worth mentioning that the area of the County is 1,671,364 acres and the population (1911) 699,703. The Territorial Force of the County

[1] Hugh Fortescue (1753–1841). He was the first Earl Fortescue and the Member of Parliament for Beaumaris from 1784 to 1785. Fortescue was also the Lord Lieutenant of Devon from 1788 to 1839.

[2] Napoléon Bonaparte (1769–1821). He was a French army general and statesman who later became the emperor of the French from 1804 to 1814/1815.

[3] Originally, the typescript stated that these papers were filed in 'the library'. However, Fortescue crossed this out and replaced this with 'one of the cabinets' in pen. This was subject to further change in the printed version of the typescript in *A Chronicle of Castle Hill* where Fortescue added a footnote which stated that this cabinet was at present (1927) located 'under the clock in the hall'.

[4] Lord Fortescue was the Chairman of Devon County Council from 1904 to 1916.

comprised two regiments of Yeomanry, Cavalry, R.G.A, R.F.A., R.E., four infantry battalions a company of A.S.C. and two field Ambulances. Their establishment was 6596 O.R. and their strength in August 1914 was 5601 O.R. The Administrative County, i.e. that under the jurisdiction of the County Council was the whole geographical county less the city of Exeter and the borough of Plymouth. Exeter had a population of 57,925 and Plymouth newly formed out of the three independent urban authorities of Plymouth, Devonport and Stonehouse[5] had a population of nearly 200,000. The administration County thus had a population of 440,000 and the County Council consisted of one hundred members.

When war broke out I was a little over 60, but pretty tough and active. Communication by rail between North and South Devon was slow and inconvenient and there was no telephone at Castle Hill.[6]

On 28th. July 1914 we moved our hunting box on Exmoor, and hunted with the Devon and Somerset Staghounds on that day and on Saturday 1st. August. I had been in communication wit[h] the Secretary of the Territorial Force Association, Col[onel]. Smith Rewse,[7] who wrote me on 1st. August that there seemed no prospect of mobilisation and there was no need for me to come to Exeter.

On the evening of Sunday 2nd. the Master of the Staghounds, Mr. Greig,[8] afterwards killed at Gallipoli,[9] and Mr. Aston, a stockbroker who had a house at Exford for his wife's hunting, came over with the news that Germany had declared war on France and Russia, and added many rumours about the attitude and intentions of our Government.

Next morning I motored early to Exeter, taking a change of clothes on the chance of having to stay the night, but expecting to get home. There was as far as I recollect nothing very definite to be done, beyond consideration of contingencies. I went to Woodbury where the Territorial Infantry Brigade had been in camp since 25th. July and the found them awaiting orders, but with little idea beyond. In the evening however the order for mobilisation came, and 24 hours later they marched into Exeter and entrained for Plymouth where they were detailed for garrison duty in outlying forts. I have a note "Attitude and behaviour of men and people quite satisfactory".[10]

[5]   This refers to the amalgamation of the three towns of Devonport, Plymouth and Stonehouse into the greater city of Plymouth in 1914.
[6]   Castle Hill was the historic residence of the Fortescue family located near Filleigh in north Devon.
[7]   Colonel Henry Whistler Smith-Rewse (1850–1930). He had a distinguished military career in the British army and had fought in the Second Anglo-Afghan war from 1878 to 1880. Smith-Rewse was the Secretary of the Territorial Force Association in Devon from 1907 to 1922.
[8]   Major Morland John Greig (1865–1915). He was the Master of the Devon and Somerset Stag Hounds from 1911 to 1914 and a major in the Royal North Devon Yeomanry Territorial Force. Greig was killed at Gallipoli on 17 October 1915.
[9]   The Allied campaign at Gallipoli against Ottoman forces in the peninsula from February 1915 to January 1916 was intended to open up the Dardanelles to the Allied powers.
[10]   This note is taken directly from Lord Fortescue's diary. See Devon Heritage Centre: 1262M/0/FD46, Personal diary of the 3rd Lord Ebrington, 1914–1916, 4 August 1914.

This move to their mobilisation stations[11] was a trying experience for the battalion: they had done a fair day's work striking camp etc. before they left Woodbury; the march to Exeter (8 miles) in the cool of the evening was accomplished without difficulty, and they were given a light meal before entraining, but next morning after a short and uncomfortable night in the train they had to face the march to their various outlying forts, 8 to 10 miles away. No arrangements had been made for giving them breakfast before starting, the roads were dusty and the sun soon got hot. Men fell out by scores, especially in the 4th. Devons who lost if memory is correct, a lot of equipment.

This was not a creditable episode: eith[e]r the Brigadier a good officer enough, or the staff at Plymouth ought to have made sure that the men would be provided with some food before they left the station for the forts, and the Battalion C.O.'s. ~~should~~ shewed[12] a lamentable lack of initiative in not doing any thing [sic] to help their men over a trying journey, whether by sending on an advance party, or commandeering a few farm carts.

The G.O.C. at Plymouth was a useless person.[13]

Mobilisation of the rest of the Territorial Units proceeded rapidly, and they were all ready by or in advance of scheduled time. Fortunately the funds at the disposal of the County T.F. Association had enabled it to buy a lot of new equipment in 1913 and 1914, and at the request of the G.O.C. Wessex Division I had given a good deal of personal attention to the provision of mobilisation stores earlier in the year: all C.O's had realized what they had to get and had ascertained what local tradesmen could supply. Some of them, or their Adjutants, were extraordinarily helpless when the question was first brought to their notice. The R[oyal]. 1st. Devon Yeomanry and the 7th. Cyclists professed themselves unable to obtain flannelette (or an equivalent) for cleaning their rifles. The R[oyal]. North Devon Hussars and the R.F.A. had made difficulties about bags for farriers tools and picketing gear, and the latter corps with H.Q. in Exeter did not think they could get 36 whistles ! Nonsence [sic] of this sort however had been disposed of long before, and lists had been sent to the Military authorities of semi technical articles like wire cutters and operating lamps for camp hospitals which really were not procurable in the county.

It may be mentioned as incidental evidence that the British Government had no deep laid and secret schemes for declaring war on Germany that Major Mudge of the Wessex Divisional Staff wrote me on 15th. May that a letter I had sent to his General as to mobilization stores would strengthen his hands enormously. "He really seems at last to be getting the higher military authority to take an interest in the matter and I have not the least doubt will send on your letter as the one and only effort made by an association "to tackle the subject" : and that H.Q. Southern Command wrote on 6th. June 1914 asking for a report by 15th. December whether satisfactory arrangements had been made for

---

[11] The statement 'move to their mobilisation stations' was added later by Fortescue in pen.

[12] Fortescue had originally typed the word 'should'. However, he crossed this out in pen and replaced this with 'shewed'.

[13] This sentence was added by Fortescue in pen and it was not included in the printed version.

completing the kits of those Territorials who might join on mobilization with incomplete sets.

The War Office Memo. 476 of 13th. December 1913 on this subject was perfectly hopeless. A complete kit of soldiers[14] "necessaries" i.e. change of underclothing, brushes and the like[15] could not be procured under 30/-, but even if a man bought every article he was only to be entitled to 10/- and if a single article even a threepenny shaving brush was deficient the newly mobilised Terrier was to get nothing.

I took the responsibility of directing C.O's in May to disregard this. To pay the men at vocabulary rates for whatever kit they bought (if serviceable) and to buy the rest.

Enquiries made in South Molton – population 3600 – as to local resources showed that country towns could probably provide out of stock a pair of stout boots for 10/- or 12/- a flannel shirt at 4/- or 5/- at the rate of 10 % of its inhabitants, and that the three banks in the little town normally held between them about £11,000 in gold and silver and some £8,500 in Bank of England notes.

Although as noted already the mere mobilisation of the Territorial units presented few difficulties, questions soon began to arise about the protection of vulnerable points.

Both the railways to Plymouth ran through Exeter and Brig[ider]. Gen[eral]. Donald,[16] the G.O.C. Wessex Division was not at all happy about them. He had a guard at Cowley Bridge just outside Exeter, but there was nothing to prevent evil disposed persons tampering with the permanent way anywhere else.

The most dangerous place was the Meldon Viaduct about 3 miles on the Plymouth side of Okehampton. This was a light iron structure in a wild unfrequented spot which could easily be wrecked with a few pounds of gun cotton: there were also some short masonry viaducts near North Tawton about which he was uneasy.

Discussion showed that he had no means of providing protection so I offered to enrol special constables for the purpose if he so desired.

Accordingly I motored to Okehampton in the afternoon of Thursday 6th. August and sought the assistance of the Police Sergeant there. He undertook to collect some sturdy men in the course of an hour of so, and in due course reported he had got them waiting for me, I think, in the Town Hall.

I gathered that they were not all very good characters, and the man recommended for the charge of the party was a poacher, but after I had explained what the job was they were ready enough to undertake it and promised to play up, so they were sworn in as Special Constables. I had omitted to bring a copy of the regulation oath from Exeter and the Police Sergeant has not got one so I had to invent one on the spur of the moment and "by virtue of the powers vested in me" gave them authority to commandeer some shot guns and to use them if necessary.

[14]   The word 'soldiers' was later added by Fortescue in pen.
[15]   Fortescue later added the comment 'i.e. change of underclothing, brushes and the like' in pen.
[16]   Major-General Colin George Donald, CBE (1854–1939). He had served in the Second Anglo-Afghan War in 1879. During the Second Boer War of 1899 to 1902, Donald was in command of the second Battalion of the Royal Fusiliers. He was involved with the Wessex Territorial Division from 1911 to 1914 and fought in the Great War.

The whole thing was of course entirely irregular and to crown it I accepted the offer of the Rector to visit the party with his Boy Scouts from time to time to see that they were not neglecting their duties.

By this time it was nearly dark, but I was able to repeat the performance at North Tawton with less delay and returned thence late and very tired to Exeter for I had been on the move since 7.30 a.m. On the way we passed a motor van in distress in charge of two or three men of the Cyclist Battalion of our Territorials who were following their Unit 7th.[17] Devons to Falmouth. Before they could have got there the Battalion was ordered to Durham so the little party must have had plenty of travelling on their own before they reached their Head Quarters.

The next day Friday 7th. August we had a county meeting to initiate a Patriotic Fund.[18] The Assize Court was packed and there was no mistake about the loyalty or steadfast purpose of those present.[19]

At the request of the military authorities I asked people occupying land beside the railways especially those in the vicinity of tunnels etc. to keep an eye to them. Acting on this Lord Devon[20] and his gamekeepers spent the nest [sic] [next] two or three nights patrolling the G.W.R. line about Starcross and Dawlish. He was an indolent useless man and though he did some military duty at the depot at Exeter or Taunton[21] I fancy this was quite the hardest work he did in the War.

More serious arrangements were initiated by me on 10th. after conference with the staff of No. 8 District to put magistrates with organised bodies of police and special constables in charge of certain areas, but these has [sic] [had] to be cancelled next day on receipt of a letter from Southern Command saying that Government had decided not to guard vulnerable points except on certain special lines, and did not approve of paying civilian guards.

On the 12th. however Col[onel]. Western[22] the O.C. 8th. District (Devon Cornwall Dorset and Somerset, H.Q. Exeter) sent on a letter from Southern Command saying it was for the Lord Lieutenant to direct what measures should be taken by the civil authorities to protect railways against individual evil doers. While the following day 13th. brought from the Southern Command War Office letters impressing on that General the importance of cooperation with local authorities not only in preserving order but also in safeguarding railways.

[17] Originally this was transcribed as '2nd.' However, Fortescue altered this in pencil to state the 7th.

[18] This refers to the creation of the Devon Patriotic Fund. Originally, the DPF raised funds to help and assist those in distress in the county. As the war progressed, the DPF made financial contributions to the British Red Cross in the county and the VAD hospitals in Devon.

[19] This sentence was omitted from the printed version.

[20] Charles Pepys Courtenay (1870–1927). He was the fourteenth Earl of Devon and a major in the third Battalion of the Prince Albert's (Somerset Light Infantry). Courtenay was also an inspector for the Board of Agriculture from 1895 to 1904.

[21] Fortescue later added 'at Exeter or Taunton' in pen.

[22] Major-General Sir William George Balfour Western (1861–1936). He had served with the 1st Battalion of the Royal West Kent Regiment in the Nile Expedition from 1884 to 1885. During the Second Boer War, Western served with the 2nd Battalion of the Royal West Kent Regiment. He also fought in the First World War. In the printed version, Fortescue added a footnote about Colonel Western: 'He was made Major-General and K.C.B. for his services at the evacuation of Gallipoli.'

A retired R.E. Colonel was now set to work to report as to the points where the railways needed protection, and the number of men required; and a letter was drafted for issue by the Lord Lieutenant to Magistrates designated to take charge of sections of railway.

On 18th. August the letter received on 13th. was superceded [sic] and with it the local arrangements proposed and the G.O.C. Southern Command was directed to determine what guards were needed and to employ for the purpose Territorials or National Reserve men.

The Home Office simultaneously decided an increase of the Police Force.

After conference with the Chief Constable and the Chairman of the Standing Joint Committee I went to Salisbury on 21st. and saw the G.O.C. Southern Command who approved our proposals except that 20 men instead of 41 were detailed to the G.W.R. which was very solidly built and also regularly patrolled from end to end by their own permanent way men while the guards for the L. & S.W.R. were increased from 29 to 36, Meldon Viaduct and Tamerton bridge absorbing half the number.

The expert reported that tunnels could almost take care of themselves, considerable time and much high explosive being needed to block them effectively, while the military said that they cared little if the railways into Plymouth were interfered with as they had got all the troops they wanted into the fortress and could supply them by sea. Whether the Naval authorities took the same view about Dockyard requirements did not transpire.

Be that as it may I was troubled no more about vulnerable points, and their immunity while unprotected shows that either the German preparations were not so very thorough after all, or else that our arrangements for dealing with their spies and agents was exceedingly efficient.

I have put the whole of the incidents about vulnerable points together, but there was plenty going on otherwise between 6th. and 21st. August.

On 7th. August as already mentioned we had a County meeting at the Castle.[23] The Court the usual scene of such affairs was packed to its utmost capacity and everyone was keen and earnest.

Lord Coleridge,[24] a strong radical, struck rather a jarring note when urging that our quarrel was with the German government and not with the people, but he was no less insistent than others on giving the maximum of support to our own authorities. Lord Iddesleigh[25] made rather a good speech, and then relapsed for the rest of the war into his accustomed lethargy.

The Mayor of Exeter[26] played up, and threatened pains and penalties to some middle class members of the community who had begun to lay [sic] in stores of food: the public generally were helpful and calm. The soldiers, reservists,

---

[23] This refers to Rougemont Castle which is located in the city of Exeter. It is also known as Exeter Castle.

[24] Bernard Coleridge, Q.C. (1851–1927). He was the second Baron Coleridge and a prominent High Court Judge on the King's Bench Division from 1907 to 1923.

[25] Walter Stafford Northcote (1845–1927). He was the second Earl of Iddesleigh and served as a member of the Inland Revenue Board from 1877 to 1892.

[26] Sir James Owen (1869–1939). He was a prominent newspaperman in Devon and managing director of the Western Times Company Limited. Owen was also the Mayor of Exeter from 1914 to 1919.

recruits etc. of whom there were some hundreds in Exeter were very sober and well behaved.

5 Private houses with 324 beds were used as First Line Hospitals and 29 with 1159 beds as Second Line Hospitals. Convalescents & Officers on leave were taken in at others beside all rent free.[27]

There were many offers of houses for Hospitals and the appeal for a County Patriotic Fund met with most generous response and reached eventually more than £35,000,[28] and a small Committee whose sittings Lady Fortescue[29] and I usually attended sat at this time almost daily.

She had made a hurried visit to York to see our elder son[30] before he embarked with the [Scot's] Greys[31] for France and then joined me on 17th. August in a lodging in Exeter and worked hard in connection with the Red Cross, Linen League[32], Hospitals, D. P. F. &c. Devon Patriotic Fund etc.

As at first neither sailors nor Territorials' wives drawing drew[33] separation allowance and wives of soldiers not "on the married establishment" were not recognised the Fund had plenty of applications. Beside these there were many women who when their husbands disappeared over sea for an uncertain time had to be helped to make new arrangements.

Lord Portsmouth,[34] Prebendary Buckingham,[35] Miss Sanders, Mr. T. Snow[36] as Members and Mr. Joseph Gould[37] the local organiser of the Conservative Party, as Secretary, were conspicuous for their good service.

[27] These two sentences were inscribed in pen by Fortescue in the left-hand margin of the typescript. In the printed version, this short paragraph was included as a footnote.

[28] In the printed version, Fortescue listed this amount as £45,000.

[29] Emily Fortescue (1859–1929). She was known as Lady or Countess Fortescue and was a Lady-in-Waiting to Queen Mary. Emily was a key figure in both the Devonshire Branch of the British Red Cross and the Voluntary Aid Detachment in the county.

[30] Colonel Hugh William Fortescue (1888–1958). He was the fourth Earl Fortescue's eldest son who later became the fifth Earl Fortescue. Hugh served with the Royal Scots Greys in the First World War. He held the office of the Lord Lieutenant of Devon from 1936 to 1958 and served as the Conservative Chief Whip in the House of Lords from 1945 to 1957.

[31] This refers to the Royal Scots Greys which was a calvary regiment within the British army.

[32] This, presumably, refers to the Devon Linen League of which Countess Fortescue was its President.

[33] Fortescue had typed 'Drawing'. He crossed this out and replaced this with 'drew' which he added in pen.

[34] Newton Wallop (1856–1917). He was the sixth Earl of Portsmouth and served as the Liberal MP for Barnstaple from 1880 to 1885. Portsmouth moved to the Liberal Unionists and was the Liberal Unionist MP for North Devon from 1885 to 1891.

[35] Reverend Frederick Finney Buckingham (1855–1934). He was the Rector of Doddiscombsleigh from 1883 to 1925 and a chairman of the St Thomas Board of Guardians. Buckingham also served as the Prebendary of Exeter and was referred to as Prebendary Buckingham.

[36] Thomas Snow (1852–1927). He was involved with the bank Messrs. Milford and Snow, Exeter. The business was later merged with the National Provincial Bank in 1918 to which Snow became a local director. Snow was also the Mayor of Exeter from 1889 to 1890 and a Justice of the Peace (JP).

[37] Joseph Gould (1852–1922). He was a keen organiser and political agent for the Conservative and Unionist Party in Devon. Gould was also secretary to the Exeter and Plymouth Gazette company and a JP.

Most of the work if not all should by right have been done by the S.S.F.A. and S.S.H.S. but these organizations though existing on paper were not going concerns. One of the first things to be done was to scrap the Secretary of one of them Col[onel]. Croft a charming ex officer of the K.R.R.C. but he was very old and quite inefficient. The D.P.F. took over the working members of the S.S.F.A.[38] and soon had willing ~~workers~~ helpers[39] in every parish in the county except those in the Plymouth fortress area which the Plymouth people worked themselves.[40]

My usual routine in Exeter was to go to the office of the Territorial Association by 9.15 and to stay there less a luncheon interval till 5 ot [sic] [or] 6 going in and out for frequent Committee Meetings and conferences. In the evening whenever whenever [sic] possible we took a run in the motor car into the country. After dinner there was generally more work. Col[onel]. Western who commanded No. 8 district and his staff officer Major Godman lived in the same house as we did at Southernhay West, indeed when we came in they kindly gave up their sitting room to Lady Fortescue.

We became great friends and were able to work off a lot of business as to recruiting and other things with the minimum of correspondence or formality.

On 12th. August C Squadron of the North Devon Yeomanry the Regiment of our younger son Denzil[41] which had mobilized at South Molton were due to entrain in the evening for their war station at Winchester, so we motored there in the afternoon giving a lift to Portsmouth Arms to Mr. Davis[42] the County Director of the Voluntary Aid Organization.

He and I were both about dead beat and comparing notes found that he had never been so tired since famine duty in India,[43] nor I since the Home Rule Election in the Tavistock Division in the hot summer of 1886.[44]

We got to South Molton about an hour before the time appointed for Parade, and said good bye quietly to Denzil in his bedroom, his mother putting up a short prayer.

---

[38]   Originally, Fortescue had typed 'S.S.H.S.' However, he later drew a line through H.S. and added F.A. in pencil.

[39]   In the typescript, Fortescue had typed the word 'workers'. Later, he crossed this out and replaced it with 'helpers' which he added in pen.

[40]   In the printed version, Fortescue added a section of six paragraphs which provides more information on the VAD hospitals in Exeter, the Devon Patriotic Fund and his wife's journey to York to see their son, Hugh, before he headed off to France. This section also incorporates a letter from his wife from 8 August 1914 while she was in York.

[41]   Denzil George Fortescue, MC (1893–1977). The fourth Earl Fortescue's third-born son who later became the sixth Earl Fortescue. He pursued a military career and fought in both the First and Second World Wars. Denzil had served with the Royal North Devon Hussars, the Royal Devon Yeomanry and he became a Lieutenant-Colonel in the first Heavy Regiment of the Royal Artillery.

[42]   John Samuel Champion Davis (1859–1926). He was in the Indian Civil Service from 1880 to 1906. Davis was the County Director of the Devonshire Branch of the British Red Cross and a member of the Council of the British Red Cross.

[43]   This could either refer to the Indian famine of 1896 to 1897 or the famine of 1899 to 1900.

[44]   This refers to the general election of 1886 to which the fourth Earl Fortescue as Viscount Ebrington stood as the Liberal Unionist candidate for Tavistock.

Mercifully granted for his and Hugh's safe return, and then we joined the officers at a hurried and indifferent meal.

We knew them all well especially the O.C. squadron, Greig the Master of the Staghounds who was almost the first man in the regiment to be killed at Gallipoli in September 1915. There were all so uncomfortable at the George at South Molton that they had all been eating and sleeping by turns at Castle Hill.

The squadron paraded in the Square just before dark and Den's old hunter Magpie all but started bucking. We followed them to the station and how long they were entraining their 120-130 horses I do not know – the horses were green, the men were green and the railway men except Porter Hall specially imported from Dulverton by reason of his experience in boxing horses, were greener still. There was little light and no facilities. I sat down on the ground and tried to go to sleep against a wall. In the time they got the work done, the train steamed out and we went back for the night to the empty house at Castle Hill.

Next morning we went together to Barnstaple to see the Headquarters of the Yeomanry. Then to Exeter where I worked till past 5 and then went on to London. Next morning I had a long talk with the Manager of the Canteen & Mess Cooperative Society of which I was a Chairman as to the way in which many demands were to be met. Saw various people at the War Office and returned to Exeter in the afternoon.

Recruiting at first presented no difficulties. The trouble was that men came in much faster than either accommodation or bedding or clothing or arms could be provided, and neither examining doctors nor the clerical staff could keep pace with the demands on their time.

Good willing men were thus exposed to considerable hardship. It would have been far better to have sent them home as soon as their names had been registered to wait a few days till some arrangements has been made for them. This method was in fact adopted by Drummond,[45] afterwards Sir Hugh, when raising the second line of the North Devon Yeomanry rather later.

The military officers did their best, but they were worked to death, and it was some time before they got authority to procure even such necessaries as socks and blankets from other than regulation sources. In response to an appeal from Plymouth I took 500 shirts there on September 19th. which I got from the newly established Linen League but that would not have provided over ten per company if as many as that.[46]

The Queen[47] at this time made an appeal to the Women of England to knit socks and belts for the soldiers. This was a wise move for though many of the socks were so badly made that they were useless except to put over the breech action of the rifles to protect them from the mud as mud guards[48] it gave

---

[45] Brigadier-General Sir Hugh Henry John Drummond (1859–1924). He joined the Royal North Devon Hussars (Yeomanry) and fought in the Great War. Drummond was the Chairman of the Southern Railway Company and was a Director of the National Provincial and Union Bank of England. He was also a JP.

[46] At this point, Fortescue wrote in the left-hand margin in pen 'Insert here M.S. para from p. 17'.

[47] Queen Mary (1867–1953). She was queen of the United Kingdom from 1910 to 1936 and the wife of King George V.

[48] Originally, Fortescue had typed 'to protect them from the mud'. However, he later crossed this out and he substituted this with 'as mud guards' in pen.

occupation to numberless restless women: 5000 pairs of socks and 1500 body belts were sent to Lady Fortescue in six weeks.

The General at Plymouth, one Penton,[49] was a hopeless person, quite unfit for an emergency and his men were for some weeks very ill supplied even with blankets and a second shirt.

Much greater relief as far as Exeter was concerned was afforded by the Superintendent of the County Lunatic Asylum at Exminster, an Institution with 1000 inmates. As soon as I explained the position to him he was most helpful, both in lending blankets and helping with facilities for laundry and disinfection.[50]

The establishment of the County Territorial Units were 6596 O.R. and the strength on 1st. August 5601, a deficiency of about 1000, but they all very quickly recruited their full number: there was however much waste of effort through the Regulars, the Territorials, and the New Army, all recruiting against each other at the same time, and after the first crop of keen eager men had been absorbed the less keen began to join the Territorials instead of the others, because they had a safe and comfortable job in garrisons in the East, but by the time they had put in four to five years without leave in India, Mesopotamia, and Palestine they must have doubted whether the ~~troubles~~ Trenches[51] in France were not preferable.

The two New Army units the 8th. and 9th. Devons were very fine battalions and did good work especially on their first big day at Loos, where they took some German guns, but they were trained away from the County and though their captured guns were paraded round Exeter on 12th. November 1915 they never established much county connection. At the end of the War they ~~first~~ just[52] dropped out of the Army List unsung and except by the Battalion who had fought alongside them I am afraid hardly remembered.

The County Territorial Association had to maintain the clothing of its old units and clothe and equip the new ones[53] who more than doubled its numbers: as every other County Association had similar duties we were all bidding against each other and against the Government who were buying all the khaki leather etc. they could lay their hands on. The result was no small profit to contractors and the supply of some very poor stuff to the troops.

I know we bought at least one lot of very inferior boots but with the help of an Exeter cloth merchant and by arrangements made by Col[onel]. Smith Rewse, Secretary of the T.F. Association, with many local tailors for making up we made such progress than in a comparatively short period our issues were

---

[49] Major-General Arthur Pole Penton (1854–1920). He joined the Royal Artillery (RA) in 1873 and he commanded the RA in Malta from 1908 to 1912. Penton was involved in the South West Defences from 1912 to 1916.

[50] These two sentences are a paragraph that Fortescue added later in pencil with a note in the left-hand margin: 'to go at bottom of previous page'.

[51] Fortescue had originally typed the word 'troubles'. He later crossed this word out and replaced it with 'trenches' which he added in pen.

[52] Fortescue had originally typed the word 'first'. He later crossed this out and replaced it with the word 'just'.

[53] In the printed version, Fortescue altered this to state 'new ones of the second and third line'.

abreast of requirements, and by the time that the Government took over all supply our units were pretty well found.

By 28th. February 1915 the strength of the Territorial Force was 12,612 as against 5,601 on 1st. August 1914, over 5,900 being abroad (1000 gunners, 4000 Infantry, R.E., R.M.C. &c and the issue of clothing from 1st. August 1914 to 28th. Feb. 1915 were 10,497 caps, 14,470 jackets, 4671 pants, 11,091 trousers, 8007 great coats and 10,725 pairs of putties and leggings and we had a great deal more besides on order being made or actually in store. The cost of these articles was about :- Caps 2/6, Jackets 15/5, Pants 17/6, Trousers 10/1, Great Coats 30/-, Leggings 8/-, Putties [puttees][54] 2/6.

All this meant very heavy work for Col[onel]. Smith Rewse who poor man lost a one son, a gunner[55] in August or September 1914 and another,[56] his favourite, a year or two later.[57]

We were very lucky in having such a man for our Secretary. He was untiring, always courteous, and thoroughly efficient. I had the satisfaction later of recommending him successfully for the C.B. and of appointing him a Deputy Lieutenant[58] for the County, two honours that gave him much gratification.

The Territorials had only been enlisted for home service which at any rate was better than the limited engagement to service in their own county under which most of the Volunteers had enlisted in 1803: but it very soon became apparent that they were wanted overseas, so they were "invited" to volunteer. Most of them did, but the required proportion was not too readily obtainable in some units. Col[onel]. Acland[59] of the 1st. Devon Yeomanry, a very unpopular C.O. had to discharge his bandsmen and sundry others in order to get the requisite percentage,[60] and many patriotic men who had business ties were placed in a very difficult position. However the Wessex Division as a whole was selected to relieve an equal number of regular gunners and infantry in India and in response to a mysterious "urgent" telegram I betook myself on 28th. September to Salisbury and Perham Down where the King[61] & Queen were inspecting the troops prior to their departure.

In the morning His Majesty reviewed the Cavalry Brigade that was just going out with the 7th. Division and in the afternoon he went roung [sic] [round]

---

[54] Puttees were strips of cloth used by soldiers in the First World War to cover their lower legs.
[55] Major Henry Bingham Whistler Smith-Rewse (1876–1914). He joined the Royal Artillery in 1897 and was killed at the first battle of Ypres on 22 November 1914.
[56] Lieutenant Meyrick Bingham Whistler Smith-Rewse (1887–1915). He joined the eighth Battalion of the Canadian Infantry in 1914 and was killed in action at Festubert on 22 May 1915.
[57] Fortescue had added 'and another, his favourite, a year or two later' in pen.
[58] A Deputy Lieutenant (DL) is nominated by the Lord Lieutenant to a notable local figure who is required to assist the office of Lord Lieutenant. Whilst a DL is nominated by a county's Lord Lieutenant, it is still a crown appointment.
[59] Colonel Alfred Dyke Acland, CBE (1858–1937). He commanded the Royal 1st Devon Yeomanry from 1910 to 1914. He also served as a JP.
[60] In the printed version, Fortescue changed this to 'get the percentage of volunteers required to qualify a corps for foreign service'.
[61] King George V (1865–1936). He was the king of the United Kingdom from 1910 to 1936 and husband to Queen Mary.

the Territorials who were drawn up on two sides of a shallow valley ,[.] Each battalion in column of companies closed up. A number of men were in mufti or only partly in uniform and a number were short of rifles and belts.

The Brigadier, Pinney,[62] was much disappointed at not going out with them as the Battalions had made great progress since mobilisation and he felt they would do themselves and him credit. It was really lucky for him though that he did not go to India, for the Brigade was broken up as soon as it got there, while he was sent to France where he got first a brigade and then a division, coming out of the war Maj[or]. General and K.C.B.

I paid a good many visits to Territorial Troops in these early months to see into matters of clothing and equipment, to hear complaints and relieve them as far as I could and to buck up all hands generally.

The difficulties of the new units were very great. We had officers who knew something in command of each, some ex-Regulars and some who had been in the Territorials, but they had very few officers or N.C.O. to help them who had any military knowledge or training.

In one newly raised Battalion the best Adjutant the C.O. could find was a lad whose only qualification was that he had had some business training in his father's office. I think this battalion was the 2nd. of the 4th. and the Adjutant was young Reed, subsequently killed, whose father had a paper mill near Exeter. Their methods naturally were casual but their keenness and devotion were unbounded.

There were troops of some sort during the first few months all over the county, Ilfracombe, Barnstaple, Crediton, Exmouth, Topsham, Teignmouth, Dawlish, Newton Abbot, Torquay, Totnes, beside Plymouth and Exeter, and they had to be billeted in all sorts of places.

A R.F.A. Battery at Topsham had a lot of men in a disused shipbuilding place. They had a little bantam-cock as Mascot and pet who was ready to fight anybody.

The flow of Government money and the advantages of supplying troops brought applications from many quarters, all sorts of unsuitable places discovering that they had every facility for troops whether in buildings, ranges or training ground, but by degrees the second and third line units were withdrawn from the outlying quarters and concentrated with much advantage and economy at regular training camps.[63]

The activities of the Territorial Association may be gauged to some extent by a statement submitted to the members at the Quarterly Meeting in December 1914

Postages from April to November   1913 were   £27. 18.[s]   10[d]

     Do.   Do.   1914 were   £127. 7.[s]   7½[d]

the cheques dawn since the September meeting were 839 for £62,242.

---

[62] Major-General Sir Reginald (John) Pinney, KCB (1863–1943). He commanded the Devon and Cornwall Brigade from 1913 to 1914. During the First World War, Pinney fought in both France and Belgium. He was also the High Sheriff of Dorset in 1923.

[63] In the printed version, Fortescue expanded upon the experiences of billeting troops in Devon and provided statistics of the number of troops who were quartered in various towns across the county in January 1915.

By 30th. June 1916 there were second line formations for all units (except some medical ones) and third lines for most of them, the Establishment was 692 Officers and 18,485 O.R. and the Strength 740 Officers 17,786 O.R. Approximately 35,000 men passed through the ranks of the County T.F. Units during the War.

Three hundred and forty eight Officers and 5,840 men had been registered for the National Reserve (all with some previous service in Regulars or Auxiliary Forces) 6 companies of 117 men each had been formed and assigned to various duties: another was forming and the clerical staff[64] had risen from 7 to 22, at wages that ran from 9/- to 50/- a week.

Eight of the clerks including three women were employed on Separation Allowance duties.

Very early in the war the Government abolished the rule that limited separation allowance to the few women in the regular army who were married "on the strength" and extended it to all married women in the Navy, Army or Territorials and even to "unmarried wives".

The Territorial Association in each county had to deal with the Separation Allowance for their own Units. At the end of August when the first issue of separation allowance was completed we had 1443 [women] on our books, but by December the number had grown to 4250 with additions just then at the rate of 300 per week.

We were fortunate enough to find a first rate man to take charge of this department in Mr. F.W. Askham a retired War Office official who had been educated at West Buckland. Besides helping about clothing and finance he took entire charge of separation allowances and neither Col[onel]. Smith Rewse nor I ever had any more trouble with it.

By the time the troops were demobilised Mr. Askham had dealt with and "put into payment" 11,711 married cases, and 13,492 dependants and paid out in all £1,827,983.

In February 1917 when the work was about at its highest his staff consisted of 5 men (one a part timer) 10 female clerks and a girl. The cost per 1000 cases per week was £1. 19.[s] 5[d] and each clerk on an average dealt with 770 cases. Overtime was not worked and it was generally possible to allow one half holiday weekly.

A comical little incident happened in these early days. The War Office enquired if I knew of any suitable place for German prisoners. Dartmoor prison to which the French and American prisoners had been relegated a century before[65] seemed obvious, so I wired the Governor for information as to the numbers he had in the place and the spare accommodation, signing the wire "Fortescue, Lord Lieutenant". Hours passed without reply, but at last there came a telegram addressed to "Lieutenant Lord" declining to reveal anything to unauthorised persons.

After that I got on to his clerk by telephone and soon extracted the particulars required.

The Governor's apprehension of losing his job was justified, for though no prisoners of war were sent to Dartmoor the convicts later on were all removed

---

[64]   This refers to the clerical staff of the Territorial Force Association in Devon.

[65]   This refers to when French and American prisoners of war during the Napoleonic Wars and the War of 1812, respectively, were housed in Dartmoor Prison at Princetown.

to other gaols and their places filled up with conscientious objectors, who were employed on reclamation and similar work: I was told at Princetown that the men who seemed to have genuine religious scruples about war and the shedding of blood did as little work as might be whereas the political minded objectors, those whose objections were really based on cowardice or socialism did a fair days labour ![66]

Before the end of September 1914 the County began to deal with Belgian Refugees. The first meeting of the War Refugees Committee was held at Exeter on 25th. of that month under the Mayoress,[67] Lady Fortescue being among those present and supporting her. An appeal produced within a fortnight £450 and offers of many homes, and a Miss Andrew[68] sister of a solicitor in the City was sent to London. She was energetic and kind-hearted, though lacking ballast. She returned with 120 refugees who were promptly placed with benevolent people and by the end of October the numbers had risen to 800 and by February 1915 to 3000. We had some for a time in two vacant cottages at Stag's Head,[69] and were glad enough when they left.[70]

Up to that time i.e. Feb[ruary] 1915[71] the arrangements for them were made in rather hand to mouth fashion[72] by Miss Andrew and numerous local committees in our County and in Cornwall, but it was now found that the movement had outgrown their unconnected and somewhat haphazard methods, and I was asked to arrange for more methodical procedure and for co-ordination. It soon became evident that there was a considerable element of local jealousy and personal self-importance to be dealt with not least among the Andrews family, but with a little persuasion all the local committees – except Exeter which stood out for a year – were merged in a Devon & Cornwall War Refugees Committee with the two Lords Lieutenant – Lord Mount Edgcumbe[73] and myself – as Joint Presidents.

Lord Mount Edgcumbe was very old and in feeble health so he was only a figure head and the headquarters were established in Exeter, with Miss Bannatyne and Miss Harrison as Secretaries.

---

[66] In the printed version, Fortescue also added: 'The reclamations were of little permanent value.'

[67] Janie Kirk Gibson Owen (1866–1943). She was the wife of Sir James Owen and was the Mayoress of Exeter from 1914 to 1919. During the Great War, Janie played an important role in charitable efforts in the city and the Mayoress's Depot that provided refreshments for troops at Exeter St David's railway station. She was also a JP.

[68] Clara Andrew (1862–1939). She was the Honorary secretary of the Devon and Cornwall War Refugees Committee from 1914 to 1916. Andrew established the Children Adoption Association in 1918 which later became the National Children Adoption Association.

[69] This refers to the Stag's Head public house at Filleigh.

[70] This sentence was later added by Fortescue in pen.

[71] Fortescue added 'i.e. Feb 1915' in pen.

[72] In the printed version, 'made in rather hand to mouth fashion' was omitted.

[73] William Edgcumbe (1833–1917). He was the fourth Earl of Mount Edgcumbe and he was the Conservative MP for Plymouth from 1859 to 1861. Mount Edgcumbe held the office of the Lord Lieutenant of Cornwall from 1877 to 1917 and he was Aide-de-Corps to Queen Victoria from 1887 to 1897.

The former was the attractive daughter of an Irish gentleman[74] who had recently bought Haldon:[75] the latter many years older was the daughter of General Sir R. Harrison[76] a veteran of the Indian mutiny.

They did not look a well matched pair, but they pulled well together and gave time and trouble freely and ungrudgingly.

The correspondence averaged fifty letters a day and the disbursements at one time ran to £2000 a month. Eight thousand refugees were received and provided for first and last, the maximum number on charge at any one time being 6000: and this was all done without employing a single salaried official though the operations of the committee lasted four years and a half. Repatriation began in January 1919 and lasted nearly six months, and it was nearly a year after that before the last account was collected and paid and the office finally closed to the great relief of all connected with it, for the refugees were not a nice lot; they were exacting and tiresome, and a proportion were criminal and immoral.

The latter however were gradually drafted to a sort of segregation camp which the government established near London and that made things much easier both for the Committee and the local sub-committees who in about a score of places in Devon & Cornwall were arranging to board, lodge, doctor and often clothe their uncongenial guests, few of whom contributed by work or otherwise to their maintenance which cost if I remember right about 10/- a week per head all round.

Local contributions both in cash and kind were at first given on a generous scale. As these failed the Government gave an adequate allowance. The Committee dealt so carefully with their resources that they were able in 1920 to return a substantial sum to the Treasury. I can claim very little credit for all this, my part being confined to attendance at a limited number of committee meetings and to writing or seeing officials when difficulties arose.

It is worthy of notice that Prebendary Buckingham and the Priest at the head of the Roman Catholic community at Exeter worked side by side on the committee from its initiation with the utmost cordiality.

Among the miscellaneous questions with which I had to deal was that of the wild red deer hunted by the Devon & Somerset Staghounds over most of the country between Bratton on the West and Dunster on the East.

The master Mr. Greig was doing duty with the R.N.D.H. in the East Coast, the Secretary with his Regiment somewhere else, and the show was being run by a small sub-committee of which the working members were Mr. P.F. Hancock of Wiveliscombe and the late Secretary, Mr. Everard. Greig had taken many of his stablemen and hunt horses away with him in the ranks of his squadron on mobilisation, and though the hounds went out when they could without advertising for the purpose of keeping down the deer, the establishment on its

[74] James Fitzgerald Bannatyne (1836–1915). He was an Anglo-Irish notable figure who had country seats in Devon and Limerick in Ireland. Bannatyne held the post of DL and JP for the county of Limerick.

[75] Haldon House was a country seat that was located near Exeter.

[76] General Sir Richard Harrison (1837–1931). He was a British army engineer who had a prolific military career. Harrison had served in the Indian Rebellion of 1857 (otherwise known as the Indian Mutiny), the Second Opium War in 1859 to 1860 and the Anglo-Egyptian War of 1882.

reduced scale was quite incapable of killing in the season the number, over a hundred, by which it was indispensable that the herd should be reduced if they were not to become a nuisance.

For some years past the number of the deer had been a cause of anxiety. Various expedients had been tried – killing calves in July, wire cages into which it was tried to drive the deer, and snaring. None had achieved more than a limited success. The expediency of employing an official executioner to shoot a lot of deer had been discussed, but rejected on two grounds. First that through a good shot could easily kill 20 or 30 deer they would soon become shy, and he would have great difficulty in killing the next 20; and secondly because if one person was authorised to shoot he would rapidly have been reinforced by any number of unauthorised assistants, who would shoot indiscriminately, and wound as many as they killed.

The crisis brought on by the state of affairs above related made it necessary to do something and that pretty soon so I arranged with Mr. Hancock that he and I should make a tour of the country to see keepers and others in the districts most thickly populated with deer and decide what should be done.

Accordingly on 3rd. October [1914] I started in the car from Castle Hill for Dulverton Station, met Mr. Hancock there, saw Goos[77] [sic] the harbourer who lived near by [sic], Mr Everard at his house near Bridgetown, and went on by Cutcombe and Dunkery Gate over Dunkery to Holnicote and Porlock and back by Exford to Castle Hill.

Fred Goss[78] proved far the most practical and helpful of those we consulted. He was positive that the poor results obtained from snaring were due to faulty methods, and confident that if it was done scientifically and if the Hunt servants with a few couple of hounds were detailed to assist in driving the deer he could catch as many deer as might be thought necessary.

I must own I did not entirely share his confidence but it seemed the best course, and he was put in charge of the snaring arrangements.

Thanks to his tact and woodcraft the first no less than the second they proved quite a success.

In the course of the season 1914–15 the Devon and Somerset accounted for 164 deer, and Capt. Amory[79] who hunted instead of rejoining the Army accounted for 62 more North of the railway plus 26 South of it. More than 100 of them were snared.

In 1915–16 the Devon and Somerset killed 39 stags in 52 days (13 days spring hunting) and 27 hinds in 30 days hunting, and 95 hinds etc. were taking in 17 days snaring.

This reduction of the herd combined with the liberal portions of venison distributed gave great satisfaction to the farmers, who did little or nothing in

---

[77]   It is clear that Fortescue is referring to Fred Goss.

[78]   Fred Goss (1872–1937). He was a stag harbourer for the Devon and Somerset Stag Hounds for 28 years and he wrote about his experiences in *Memories of a Stag Harbourer: A Record of Twenty-Eight Years with the Devon and Somerset Stag Hounds, 1894–1921.* The book was published in 1931. Goss was also a member of Dulverton Rural Council.

[79]   Captain Ludovic Heathcoat-Amory (1881–1918). He was the son of Sir John Heathcoat-Amory. Ludovic served in the Royal 1st Devon Yeomanry and the Royal Artillery during the Great War and was killed on 25 August 1918.

the way of destroying deer on their own account, and most generously reduced their claims for deer damage to very ~~small~~ moderate[80] dimensions. The payments for 1914–15 being only £434 up to 4th. August 1914 and £187 more to 1st. April 1915, while those for 1915-16 were £304. The compensation paid in 1913–14 ~~having~~ had[81] been £1253.

Early in 1915 it was decided to try and increase the supply of recruits by means of Recruiting Marches. Some money was privately subscribed, the military authorities readily co-operated and under the energetic management of Mr. H. Ford[82] the Clerk to the Lieutenancy, a beginning was made. A small party of the Devons under an officer marching from Exeter to South Molton via Witheridge.

They proceeded by early stages and halted in every village and hamlet. In that desolate country they had a certain success but similar at[t]empts in other parts though reinforced by bandsmen and chara bancs[83] effected little. The troops were ~~wll~~ very cordially[84] received and the villages provided endless food, but few recruits presented themselves.

At this period class battalions were being raised.[85] Sportsmen, Footballers, and so forth, and I was asked to help raise a Farmers Battalion in the Western Counties.

I never thought it a very hopeful undertaking as the margin of farmers sons available for an Infantry Battalion with its second line was not large after providing for the Yeomanry and its second line. However I got Lord Valletort[86] then with the 3rd. Battalion D.C.L.I. in the Isle of Wight to say he would accept the command if it were offered him, and he and I agreed to undertake the job provided he was allowed to choose his own Adjutant and to nominate his company commanders: the latter to be sons of country gentlemen in the several counties of the area.

The War Office refused these conditions so nothing came of the proposal, which was just as well for all the good men available of farmer class were wanted as officers in the next three years.

One's other work was hindered and delayed in the earlier days by the illness of Mr. Bailey[87] the Clerk to the County Council. He was a very hardworking official who had raised himself from a humble position, but he had not the gift

[80] Originally, Fortescue had typed 'small dimensions'. He later crossed out 'small' and substituted this with the word 'moderate' in pen.

[81] Fortescue had originally typed 'having'. Later, he decided to erase this word and he replaced it with 'had'.

[82] Henry Ford (1867–1937). He was the Clerk to the Devon Lieutenancy and an Under-Sheriff of Devon. Ford was also a senior partner of the solicitor firm, Messrs. Ford, Harris, Ford, and Simey.

[83] Chara bancs were an early form of motor coach.

[84] Originally, Fortescue had typed 'Wll'. However, he later crossed this out and replaced it with 'very cordially' in pen.

[85] These were also known as Pals Battalions.

[86] Piers Edgcumbe (1865–1944). He was Lord/Viscount Valletort from 1865 to 1917 before he inherited his father's title. He was the fifth Earl of Mount Edgcumbe. Piers served in the Second Boer War and was second in command to the 3rd Battalion of the Duke of Cornwall's Light Infantry. He was a DL for Devon.

[87] Frank Bailey (1857–1919). He was the clerk to Devon County Council and a Clerk of the Peace for Devon.

of devolution, and trying to do everything himself he got softening of the brain
and had to be got rid of, pensioned, and replaced in 1915.

It was not very easy to do this without upsetting him and making him worse,
and there were technical difficulties about the pension everyone wished to give
him, which could only be circumvented by personal interviews at the Local
Government Board and persuading them to approve of our giving an excessive
salary to his successor on the understanding that that gentleman should be out
of his superfluity provide Mr. Bailey's pension.

The Canteen and Mess Society were another side show. This Society had been
founded by my brother Lionel[88] and some Guards Officers in 1896. Beginning in
a very small way it had done much to reduce the abuses of the existing canteen
system and to benefit the rank and file, and when war broke out it was running
and supplying about a third of the Canteens of the Army at home, Messrs.
Dickeson[89] having practically all the remainder except some stations in Ireland.

After Lionel was killed in action in 1900 in South Africa[90] I had become
Chairman of the Managing Committee so when mobilisation, new units and
the advent of the Canadian troops doubled and trebled all canteen requirements
there was a good deal to do, and incidentally nearly all the active members of
the committee had gone overseas with their units, and a great many of our
employees being old soldiers were recalled to the colours. Fortunately our
Manager, Mr. Benson,[91] an old Haileybury[92] boy, was a man of energy and
resource who was not afraid of responsibility.

Once or twice he came to Exeter and I used to go to London once a month or
so, and I believe the Society accomplished everything it was asked to undertake.

Before many months there was practical amalgamation with the Dickesons,
and though their Manager Mr. Prince[93] (afterwards Sir A) was the original figure
head of the Expeditionary Force Canteens, that organization which at the end
of the war was able to return £1,000,000 or more to the troops, was framed and
directed from the beginning by Mr. Benson, who spent much time in France in
official charge.[94]

Some time [sic] in 1916 or 1917 canteen supply became a branch practically of
the Q.M.G. Department under the title of Navy, Army and Air Force Institutes;

[88] Lionel H. Fortescue (1857–1900). He was the third-born son of the third Earl Fortescue
and he was killed in the Second Boer War.
[89] This refers to the company founded by Sir Richard Dickeson (1823–1900), who was a
prominent businessman and merchant.
[90] This refers to Second Boer War otherwise known as the South African War that took
place from 1899 to 1902.
[91] Sir Frank Benson, CBE (1878–1952). He was the general manager of the Canteen
and Mess Co-operative Society in 1912. Benson was involved with the organisation
of Expeditionary Force Canteens and was appointed General Manager. He became a
director of the Navy-Army Canteen Board.
[92] Haileybury is an independent boarding school in Hertfordshire.
[93] Sir Alexander William Prince (1870–1933). He became a managing director of Messrs.
R. Dickeson & Company in 1907 and was appointed chairman of directors in 1909. From
January 1917 to December 1918, Prince was the managing director of the Navy and Army
Canteen Board.
[94] Fortescue added in the printed version that while in France, Benson gained the rank
of colonel.

the buildings stock etc. of the C.M.C. were taken over by the Government and the Society was dissolved. Its voluntary liquidation presented unusual features as its assets were so much in excess of its liabilities that the liquidator had to go to the Court for directions. Ultimately the original shareholders none of whom had more than £200 in it, were paid off in full with 200% bonus, in all £37,381, and over £192,000 were returned to the Units which were trading members.

The turnover of the society had risen in 22 years from £5,500 per annum to £2,000,000.

In 1916 there began a movement for raising Volunteer Corps[95] for purely local purposes among men who were too old or really too busy for more active service.

I did not think there was much scope for them in Devonshire and that they would really occupy time and cost money that could be better used, so I did not trouble myself about them. Five weak battalions were raised, General Sir R[ichard]. Harrison, a Mutiny Veteran, being County Commandant, with Mr. G. H. Harris, the standing Sub-Sheriff of the County as County Adjutant.

There was a test mobilisation on 18th. November 1915 when a certain number turned out and took charge of certain railway stations, bridges etc. and I accompanied Col. Golightly,[96] D.S.O. on his inspection, and very cold it was. That was all I had to do with the Volunteers beyond attending an inspection of samples of all the battalions by Field Marshal Lord French[97] on Sunday 29th. April 1917.[98]

He let me travel back with him to London in his special. Miss Buller[99] delayed his departure by taking him off to inspect a hospital, so we were rushed up by the L.S.W.R. in a little over three hours – a sinful waste of coal and money.

Some busy person at Buckfastleigh wrote to me in a fuss about possible spying by the priests at Buckfast Abbey, some of whom were Austrians and Germans. I suggested that it would be a nice job for the local volunteers to keep them under observation. Needless to say I heard no more about it.

Mention of Miss Buller brings up her connection with the Medical Services in the war, and the squabbling in connection therewith which gave me a lot of trouble as both to my wife who was President of the Devon Branch of the Red Cross Society and me, as both sides[100] sought our help in composing their

---

[95] These were known as Volunteer Training Corps (VTC).

[96] Colonel Robert Edmund Golightly, CBE (1856–1935). He had served in Kandahar and Ghuzni and commanded the Imperial Yeomanry in South Africa. Golightly was an assistant director in the War Office from 1917 to 1918.

[97] Field Marshal John Denton Pinkstone French (1852–1925). He was the first Earl of Ypres and had a prolific military career in the British army. He was the Commander-in-Chief of the British Expeditionary Force in France from 1914 to 1915. After this, French was the Commander-in-Chief of the troops stationed in the United Kingdom from 1915 to 1918. He also held the office of the Lord Lieutenant of Ireland from 1918 to 1921.

[98] This inspection took place at Exeter.

[99] Dame (Audrey Charlotte) Georgiana Buller (1884–1953). She was heavily involved with the efforts of the British Red Cross in Devon during the First World War. In 1920, Georgina was recognised for her efforts by the Red Cross Society with the award of the Royal Red Star (first class).

[100] Fortescue later added in pen 'to my wife who was President of the Devon Branch of the Red Cross Society and me, as both'.

differences and one (Miss B)[101] at any rate consistently refrained from taking my advice.

In 1909 the Secretary of State[102] had urged the formation in every County of Voluntary Aid Detachments, or the extension of the organization of the St. John's Ambulance Association. The latter had no status in the County so the Territorial Association went in for the V.A.D. system and appointed Mr. J.S.C. Davis to be County Director. He was an ex Indian civilian methodical and business like, but a little slow and precise. He took up his task with energy raised by 1912 thirteen men's and twenty four women's detachments, wrote an exhaustive handbook which was freely borrowed by other counties and ran into a fourth edition in three years, arranged Field days for his detachments who flattered themselves that their duties would consist in nursing Devonshire Territorials within the County, and built up with very limited resources a comprehensive organization which included an Assistant County Director,[103] and nearly sixty local secretaries.

When the Army was mobilised the V.A.D. were warned and before the end of August the County Director has been required to prepare hospitals on a considerable scale for the sick and wounded of the [British] Expeditionary Force and made emergency arrangements accordingly.

I do not think any patients actually arrived before the beginning of September[104] at earliest, but the V.A.D. got a little practice among the Territorials and New Army Battalions, whose medical arrangements were as yet exceedingly sketchy, and 3 hospitals with 271 beds were definitely mobilised in Exeter during October 1914 and five more with 252 beds elsewhere.

With the establishment of Hospitals in Exeter trouble began. Miss Buller was Assistant County Director for the Exeter Division and as much subordinate to the County Director as any of his other assistants, but she had inherited capability and some obstinacy from her father, Sir Redvers Buller;[105] she was masterful and aspired to the role of Florence Nightingale,[106] and there was endless friction between her and Mr. Davis – sometime pin pricking, sometimes serious, and I got more than my share of confidences and complaints from both.

In the end Miss Buller got rather the best of it, for thanks to a friend in the War Office who had served under her father and had very grateful recollections

[101] This was added later by Fortescue in pen.
[102] Richard Haldane (1856–1928). He was the first Viscount Haldane and the Liberal MP for Haddingtonshire from 1885 to 1911. As the Minister for War from 1905 to 1912, Haldane supervised what became known as the 'Haldane reforms' of the British armed forces. He was also the Lord High Chancellor of Great Britain from 1912 to 1915 and also in 1924.
[103] Fortescue changed this in the printed version to state that this included 'several Assistant County Directors (mostly ladies)'.
[104] Fortescue later inscribed the words 'the beginning of' onto the typescript in pen.
[105] Sir Redvers Buller, VC (1839–1908). He was a celebrated general in the British army. Buller had served in China in 1860, Ashanti in 1878, the Anglo-Zulu War of 1878 to 1879 and the Mahdist War of 1884. He had also served in South Africa from 1899 to 1900 during the Second Boer War. He was also the Under-Secretary for Ireland in 1887.
[106] Florence Nightingale (1820–1910). She was noted for her nursing career and was lauded as a role model of the nursing profession. As a result, Nightingale was otherwise known by her nickname of the 'Lady with the lamp'.

of him, she was made the independent commandant of the Exeter group of hospitals with their 500 beds. Such commands were held everywhere else by fully qualified medical men with the rank of at least Major in the R.A.M.C. and some of her officer patients and subordinates got a bit restive at having to take orders from an unqualified woman.[107] However she was exceedingly efficient and made good, working her staff unsparingly and herself so remorselessly that in 1919 her health complet[e]ly broke down.

Mr ~~Drastic~~ Davis[108] meanwhile whose methods were less drastic organised first and last 34 hospitals with 3905 beds to which 45,007 patients were admitted. The personnel he commanded was 2735 and the funds he administered exceeded a quarter of a million (£115,000 subscriptions and donations and £146,504 War Office grants) and his expenses in administration, including all rents and s[a]laries were only .7 %.

Though a very dry and undemonstrative man he was beloved of his staff who would do anything for him.

He finished the war with £12,000 in hand with which he endowed the V.A.D. organization in the County and gave large and welcome gifts to hospitals and the like.

In the autumn of 1915 began the work about Food Production which remained constant and exacting till the end of the war. A Royal Commission on Food Supply has [sic] reported in 1905 that we were drawing four-fifths of our bread corn and nearly half of our meat from across the sea.

Though German raiders and submarines had interfered but little with our supplies ~~at the time~~ so far,[109] Lord Selborne[110] as President of the Board of Agriculture issued in September 1915 a circular appealing to farmers to increase their arable land and County Councils were directed to form War Agricultural Committees to deal with the difficulties as to labour etc. that was involved.

We formed the Committee accordingly and as Chairman of the County Council I took charge of it superseding the Chairman of the standing Committee which normally dealt with agricultural affairs.

He was a Mr. Tremlett[111] a yeoman near Crediton, highly respected [sic] a rather slovenly farmer and quite useless for emergency.

He did not like being shunted and gave a little trouble, but not much, and not very long after the loss of his son in action broke him down and he died.

[107] In the printed version, Fortescue changed this to: 'at having to take orders from a woman who was neither a doctor nor a field officer'.
[108] Fortescue had originally typed the word 'Drastic'. However, he crossed this out and substituted this with 'Davis' which he later added in pen.
[109] Originally, Fortescue had typed 'at the time'. However, he later crossed this out and replaced this with 'so far' in pen.
[110] William Palmer (1859–1942). He was the second Earl Selborne and was the Liberal MP for East Hampshire from 1885 to 1886. Selborne moved to the Liberal Unionists and was the Liberal Unionist MP for East Hampshire from 1886 to 1892. He was also the Liberal Unionist MP for West Edinburgh from 1892 to 1895. Selborne was the First Lord of the Admiralty from 1900 to 1905 and the President of the Board of Agriculture from May 1915 to July 1916.
[111] William Tremlett (1851–1920). He was a prominent Devon agriculturalist and one of the founders and a chairman of the Devon Farmers Union. Tremlett was also an Alderman of Devon County Council and served as the Chairman of the Devon War Agricultural Committee.

For some months after the issue of Lord Selborne's circular nothing special happened. The growing of potatoes was stimulated and agricultural workers were encouraged to register themselves in categories exempt from recruiting, whereby there was in some quarters discreditable shirking.

Towards the end of 1916 however the German submarines got so busy that the situation began to cause anxiety.[112]

The authorities aimed at holding at least thirteen weeks supply of bread corn but after the war it transpired that in April 1917 when the losses of shipping exceeded 500,000 tons the Government stock of wheat and flour was no more than enough to feed the nation for 39 days, and there were in fact only five weeks between that time and the Armistice when the prescribed standard of 13 weeks consumption was obtained.

There was therefore ample reason for emergency measures.

Mr. Prothero[113] afterwards Lord Ernie[114] who had succeeded Lord Selborne[115] at the Ministry of Agriculture began to develop the Government programme in December 1916 –

A fixed price of 60/- per quarter for wheat:

Ploughing up of grass land under compulsory orders from
    County Committees,[:]

An assurance that a farmer who got women works in addition
    to his scale allowance of male labour would not have
    his men taken away in consequence

This was shortly supplemented by a minimum agricultural wage and a quota of land to be broken up and tilled to corn or potatoes in [e]very county.

Following on this "Executive Food Production Committees" were formed in every county and under the Defence of the Realm Act[116] were given very large powers. The Organisation adopted in Devonshire was one of four divisions based on those already adopted by the County Council for the administration of the Small Holdings Act.

North. Barnstaple, Bideford, South Molton & Torrington Poor Law Unions about 414,000 acres in charge Lord Fortescue with Mr. G. Smyth-Richards[117] (his estate agent) as Surveyor & Correspondent.

South. Newton Abbot, Kingsbridge, Plympton & Totnes Unions about 335,000 acres in charge Mr. W. Coulton of Dean Prior, a Yeoman-Farmer, with Mr. May a local Surveyor & Auctioneer, as Surveyor & Correspondent.

East.   Axminster, Crediton, Honiton, St. Thomas & Tiverton Unions with

---

[112] The campaign of unrestricted submarine warfare was restarted in February 1917.

[113] Rowland Prothero (1851–1937). He was the first Baron Ernle and was the Conservative MP for the University of Oxford from 1914 to 1919. Prothero was the President of the Board of Agriculture from December 1916 to August 1919.

[114] This should read Lord Ernle.

[115] In fact, Prothero succeeded the post from David Lindsay who was the twenty-seventh Earl of Crawford (1871–1940). Crawford was the President of the Board of Agriculture from 11 July 1916 to 5 December 1916.

[116] The Defence of the Realm Act was revised several times during the Great War.

[117] This refers to George Cobley Smyth-Richards who was the steward of the Castle Hill estate from 1900 until his death in 1929.

Culmstock 493,000 acres in charge Sir Ian Amory[118] of Tiverton with Mr. Ellis a leading Land Agent in Exeter as Surveyor & Correspondent.

West.   Holsworthy (to include Broadwoodwidger) Okehampton & Tavistock Unions about 396,000 acres of which 50,000 on Dartmoor hardly count in charge Sir H. Lopes[119] of Roborough with Mr. Ward, Auctioneer &c of Brentor, as Surveyor etc.[120]

Sir H. Lopes from an early date associated with himself Mr. Rundle the Duke of Bedford's[121] Agent at Tavistock, who worked very well.

The four chairmen with Mr. Tremlett who in fact boycotted the Committee and hardly even attended[122] formed the War Agricultural Executive Committee for the County.

Mr. Woodcock who was in charge of the Exeter branch of the New Land Valuation Department of the Inland Revenue was lent [to] us as Clerk.

He was a radical East Country farmer who had been given his job by political friends, and did us excellent service. Mr. Horne[123] of the Board of Agriculture[,] Lord Portsmouth in charge of pigs & seed potatoes and a few others including a lady or two were added as work developed.

Mr. Coulton in the Southern Division had about the hardest job as a very large proportion of the land in it was high class grass, the breaking of which was hard to justify or enforce: and among his opponents was the Hon. Edgar Forester, a sort of Agent of Sir R. Harvey's[124] both of whom ought to have known better.

The original quota we were expected to bring into tillage was between 150,000 acres & 200,000 acres, a big addition to the 479,000 acres shown by the Agricultural Returns for 1916 as "arable", "Permanent Grass" being 731,500 acres and "rough pasture" nearly 175,000 acres more. Over 150,000 acres additional were in fact put to corn in the Spring of 1917 but it was difficult of accomplishment. Labour was short generally – ploughmen in particular were deficient. Horses were short and so were seed, ploughs, implements & manure,

---

[118] Sir Ian Heathcoat-Amory, CBE (1865–1931). He was the second Baronet Heathcoat-Amory and a managing partner of John Heathcoat & Co. that manufactured lace in Tiverton. From 1911, Ian was the Master and Huntsmen of the Tiverton fox-hounds. He was also a member of Tiverton Town Council and served as the Vice Chairman of Devon County Council. Ian also held the office of High Sheriff of Devon in 1924.

[119] Sir Henry Lopes (1859–1938). He was the first Baron Roborough and was the Conservative MP for Grantham from 1892 to 1900. Lopes was the chairman of Devon County Council from 1916 to 1937.

[120] Fortescue later added 'as Surveyor etc' in pen.

[121] Herbrand Arthur Russell (1858–1940). He was the eleventh Duke of Bedford and he held the office of the Lord Lieutenant of Middlesex from 1898 to 1926. Bedford served as the Chairman of Bedfordshire County Council from 1895 to 1928 and he was the President of the Imperial Cancer Research Fund from 1910 to 1936.

[122] Fortescue added 'hardly even attended' later in pen.

[123] Frederic Horne (1863–1927). He was an experienced agriculturalist and served as the Vice-Chairman of the Shropshire Chamber of Agriculture. Horne was the Small Holdings Commissioner in the Ministry of Agriculture and Fisheries.

[124] Sir Robert Harvey (1847–1930). He was a notable figure in both Devon and Cornwall. Harvey was a prominent businessman with business interests in South America. He was the High Sheriff of Devon from 1896 to 1897. Harvey also served as a DL and JP for Devon.

and the weather in harvest was so bad that hundreds of acres were quite or almost worthless.

Some German prisoners were supplied in 1918. At first the farmer look askance at them and the Military regulations were altogether too stringent but the men were soon found to be useful adaptable fellows and they became popular. They had to be returned to their barracks at a fixed hour and in charge of a responsible farmer; but a farmer Bishopsnympton way sent his gang back one evening, when all hands were busy harvesting with rain in prospect, in charge of his little daughter, who herded them back on her pony to their "barrack" in South Molton. This was not the only funny incident in connection with prisoners – one of the early Commandants at South Molton where there were 30 men or so, was a ranker officer of R.A. who took his interpreter (himself a prisoner I think) and the bar maid of the "George" a joy ride all round [sic] the district in a Government car: and all came back drunk.

There were endless struggles about men: the War Office very properly claimed all able bodied men for the army, offering in return men who were only fit for Home Service and releasing men in training on Agricultural Furlough at busy times.

The Ministry of Agriculture on their part protested that they could not relieve the Navy by producing more food if all the skilled workers in Agriculture of Military age were drafted to the Army: so both parties had to compromise on terms that were not unreasonable. Though even in the atmosphere of good will that prevailed as between us and the Recruiting Authorities in Devon there was some friction and a good many hard cases; in which the truthful & patriotic man was more likely to suffer than the plausible shirker. However the work got done somehow. The police sent a few ex-labourers back to the land and we had a school for ploughmen near Exeter and with a London policeman formerly a ploughboy as head instructor; which turned out a certain number of useful men. Mr. Patterson, a retired planter from the East took charge of this, and of all the men sent us from the Army & elsewhere and of the horses; being greatly assisted about the latter by Mr. Pape[125] M.F.H. a Yeoman of Silverton. Our horses were so well bought that we made a small profit on them after the War.

As on the 22nd Dec[ember]. 1917 we had 1698 soldiers on the land: 10 applications outstanding & 52 men (only five of them skilled) available to meet them; 67 men on farms from the ploughing school and 27 more at the School. We had 233 horses working on farms and 51 at the Depot.

Tractor ploughs were introduced to help in breaking up land. They gave us no end of trouble, cost much money and were a doubtful success. It was nobodys [sic] fault, they were absolute novelties and no one knew really how to build them and they had to learn how to manage them when built.

Delivery was very uncertain owing to submarine activity and slow at the best.

Not a few farmers called on the drivers to attempt unfair if not impossible tasks, just to see what the machines could do, and not a few drivers neglected and abused them shamefully. I have a note of the results obtained from 15

[125] From a reading of how the original typescript was typed up, there is a large space between Mr. and M.F.H., and Pape is added in pen. It is evident that Fortescue searched through his private papers to check the name of this individual.

tractors between early May & 21st September. Two 20 h.p. "Bulls" were returned to the Department[126] after three months effort in which one ploughed 14 acres and the other nothing. In the same period 4½ acres was the record of a Wyle. On the other hand a 16 h.p. Mogul worked continuously for 19 weeks & ploughed 13 acres a week for its first three weeks. A 16 h.p. Avery worked for 16 weeks on end; and two other Avery[s] for 14 weeks out of 16. But another was only effective for 10 weeks and part of two more out of 17, and 10 or 12 acres per week seemed to be as much as could be reckoned on. Yet when the tractors were sold after the war many if not most were bought by farmers.

In the Northern Division we were lucky enough to secure as Tractor Officer a man who by profession was a Tailor or something of that kind, and who was consequently refused by one of the other divisions; but he had a turn for mechanics and kept his Tractors and their drivers going with great success.

A feature of the Food Production Movements was the way in which householders utilised any scrap of ground for growing a few vegetables. These could not be measured up and included in any returns but they with the plots round every signal box on the railways amounted to a considerable aggregate and their produce was very welcome.

The Rationing of the Nation under Lord Rhondda's[127] direction was admirably done, and no one suffered for want of food, but a great many would have been glad of more. Even we who as self suppliers had many advantages in the way of rabbits & game ~~home made butter~~ and ~~the~~ "offal" ~~from home killed sheep~~ often left the table regretting there had not been more on it and unappreciative of the difference in calories between lentils (102 per oz.) and fresh fruit which had only 18.

Medical herbs were grown in the flower beds in front of Castle Hill and potatoes in those in front of Buckingham Palace[128] – the latter much to the King's annoyance were killed by the fumes of the perpetually passing motors.

The worst task set to the Agricultural Executive Committee was that known as the clean cut in 1918 ~~when in~~ consequent on the Spring disasters in France,[129] disasters that might have been avoided had not the Cabinet[130] kept 200,000 men at home against Naval advice to resist a possible German invasion.

To meet the emergency it was ordered that Agriculture should give up so many of the men who had been exempted for farm work.

Our Quota in Devon was 1000 of whom about a quarter had to be found by the Northern Division.

---

[126] Fortescue added 'returned to the Department' later in pen.

[127] David Alfred Thomas (1856–1918). He was the first Viscount Rhondda and the Liberal MP for Merthyr Burghs from 1888 to 1910. Rhondda was also the Liberal MP for Cardiff from January 1910 to December 1910. He was appointed in June 1917 as the Minister for Food Control in the Lloyd George Coalition government.

[128] This is the official residence of the king and queen of the United Kingdom located in London.

[129] This refers to the German Spring offensive of 1918 otherwise known as Kaiserschlacht (Kaiser's Battle), which was co-ordinated by General Erich Ludendorff. This was an attack by the German army from March to June 1918. While it did break through the Allied lines on the Western Front, the offensive did not produce a decisive victory for the German army.

[130] This refers to the War Cabinet of the Lloyd George Coalition government.

It was cruel work going through the lists of the men employed on every one of our farms – 2500 more or less. The other members of the Committee were nearly all farmers but they played up well – partly I think because I had quite by accident insisted early in the proceedings that the son of one of them should join up: and he on the principle of the Fox who had lost his tail was thereafter all for drastic measures with other people.

We got our numbers; but if a man of middle age was working a 100 acre farm with a grown up son and a big boy we had to enlist the son, leaving him to get what additional labour he was bound to have by employing women or prisoners or more likely by working himself and the rest of his family a bit harder.

The whole of the Committee was thankful when the job was done – fortunately within six months the defeat of the Germans put a different complexion on the situation.

Fuller information on the subjects of these notes will be found in the newspaper cuttings &c. that I have filed and in the papers I have kept about the War.

I may close these memoranda with[131]

[131] Fortescue did not add the materials with which he wished to close the original version of the typescript. However, these materials were incorporated into the printed version. These include two separation allowance letters that Fortescue found amusing, the entries from his diary for the last three days of the war and three letters from Lady Fortescue.

THE PERSONAL DIARY OF THE
3RD LORD EBRINGTON (EARL FORTESCUE)
1914–1918

The diary entries reproduced below are taken from DHC: 1262M/0/FD/46 (Personal Diary of the 3rd Lord Ebrington 1914–1916), DHC: 1262M/0/FD/47 (Personal Diary of the 3rd Lord Ebrington 1916–1918), and DHC: 1262M/0/FD/48 (Personal Diary of the 3rd Lord Ebrington 1918–1921). Those from 1 August 1914 to 22 July 1916 are taken from DHC: 1262M/0/FD/46; those from 23 July 1916 to 30 September 1918 are taken from DHC: 1262M/0/FD/47; and those from 1 October 1918 to 28 November 1918 are taken from DHC: 1262M/0/FD/48. The entries are displayed consecutively here for clarity.

1914

1 Aug S Exmoor	Stag H[oun]ds at Culbone Stables. Found a good stag in Yanworthy clear & killed in the plantations. No sport. Very wet pm. The European prospect gets steadily worse.
2 Aug Sunday	Church am. Sacrament. Mr Aston & Greig, came over in ev[ening] with the news of Germany's declaring war on both France and Russia[.]
3 Aug M	Motored to Exeter early & was at various jobs all day.
4 Aug T	Mobilisation ordered in evening. I met all the 3 Batt[alion] at S[t] Davids[1] as they came in from Woodbury[2] to entrain for Plymouth in ev[ening]. [T]he attitude of men & people quite satisfactory.
5 Aug W C Hill	Got home in Mr Bampfylde'[s] car at 4. Denny[3] very busy about mobilising C[avalry] Sq[uadron].[,] & showing himself very capable.
6 Aug Th	Back to Exeter by 8 train to Okehampton v[ia] N[orth] Tawton at 4 to arrange for guarding railway. [B]ack at 11.30.
7 Aug F	Work all day. County meeting. Went well. Just saw P.[4]

---

[1]   This refers to Exeter St David's railway station.
[2]   This refers to the army training camp at Woodbury Common.
[3]   This is presumably Denzil Fortescue.
[4]   This is presumably Emily Fortescue as the fourth Earl Fortescue affectionately nicknamed her 'Pussy'.

8 Aug S	Work all day. Interesting interview with new GOC Southern Command Campbell. Saw the 3rd Devons off 900 strong. Very different to what they were in Honiton.
9 Aug Sunday	Went to the Cathedral5 pm[.] Work the rest of the day. Everybody is helpful & calm. No one has behaved ill but a few middle class who have got in stores of food. The soldiers very sober & well behaved.
10 Aug M Exeter	The Military have at last made up their minds to leave the protection of the railways to the County. Saw P for five min[utes] passing through for York. Much over wrought poor dear.
11 Aug T	Another hard day. Saw the gunners & the 1st FA nearly ready, & saw the 1st Yeo[manry] off.
12 Aug W	Got away at 4 to Portsmouth Arms with Mr Davis & P who had come in for the day. Then to S[outh] Molton to see Den[zil] & C[avalry] Squadron off. A long dragging business. [G]ot home to Castle Hill by 11 – about beat.
13 Aug Th	To Barnstaple with P to see [o]ff th[e] RNDH. [T]hen to Exeter. Work till 5.15 but not a very hard day & to London by 5.27[.]
14 Aug F	Saw Benson from 8.45 – 10[,] then to War Office where saw Sir C. Harris6 & Range Officer. Back to Exeter by the 12. An easy afternoon there & I feel much fitter. The news from Belgium mostly good.
15 Aug S	Got home in the ev[ening] after rather a strenuous day.
16 Aug Sunday C H	Fine after yesterday's rain. Church twice. Had a rare sleep.
17 Aug M	Motored to Exeter together by 10.45 & went into lodgings there.
18 Aug T	Hot. P went to Torquay & Paignton pm. We have today received 4th or 5th edition of orders as to vulnerable points.
19 Aug W	Had a most enjoyable motor run from 5.45 to 8 to Great Fulford. The house dates from 15th Cent[ury]. Some excellent carving in a well proportioned [sic] hall & much good furniture & china.
20 Aug Th	Hot & Stuffy. Meeting at the guildhall7 for recruiting in ev[ening]. Went off well: but as it turned out of 13 who offered only 2 passed the entry[.]

---

5   This refers to Exeter Cathedral.
6   Sir Charles Harris (1864–1943). He was a civil servant and joined the War Office as a clerk in 1887. During his time at the War Office, he became Principal Clerk in 1900, Assistant Financial Secretary in 1908, and Joint Secretary of the War Office in 1920.
7   This is presumably the Guildhall at Exeter.

21 Aug F Exeter	Went to Salisbury pm to see G.O.C. about Railway Protection. Late home.
22 Aug S	Motored back to Castle Hill in ev[ening].
23 Aug Sunday	Fine. Church twice. Walked to Higher Beer pm.
24 Aug M	Back to Exeter by 10.30. Usual succession of Com[mi]^{tees} &c.
25 Aug T	Work till 3. [T]hen to London. H[ouse] of Lords up long before I got there at 7. Dined with Clive[8] who had seen Burn[9] M.P. fresh from France. Having dined with French[10] on Mon[day]. Our men fought very well & did not lose much till they retired, which they only did in conformity with the French.
26 Aug W.	Went to SSFA. War Office. CFO[11] & Economic. [T]hen back by the 4.15 to Exeter. Heavy rain in morning.
27 Aug Thu	Motored to Haldon & back by Starcross in ev[ening]; after having motored down the 13 ladies & 4 persons who represent the Exeter SSFA.
28 Aug F	Motored to Broadclyst & back by Whimple.
29 Aug S	Went to Castle Hill in ev[ening].
30 Aug Sunday	Church twice. Greig came over about recruiting & Hounds.
31 Aug M	Back to Exeter. Hot[.]
1 Sept T	Work as usual. Motored in ev[ening].
2 " W	D^{itto}[.]
3 Sept Th	Distress Com[mi]^{tee} pm. Motored to Indio[12] for dinner.

---

[8]   Percy Robert Herbert (1892–1916). He was Viscount Clive and joined the army in 1914. He served with both the Scots Guards and the Welsh Guards. In October 1916, Clive died of his wounds.

[9]   Sir Charles Rosdew Forbes-Leith (1859–1930). He was originally known as Charles Burn before he changed his name by deed poll in 1925 to Charles Forbes-Leith. Charles was the first Baron of Forbes-Leith of Fyvie and had a lengthy career in the British army to which he had served in the Second Boer War and the First World War. He was the Conservative MP for Torquay from December 1910 to 1923.

[10]   This is presumably Field Marshall John French.

[11]   This refers to the County Fire Office in Piccadilly Circus of which the fourth Earl Fortescue was a director.

[12]   This refers to Indio House near Bovey Tracey.

| 4 Sept F | Got away at 6.30 to <u>Castle Hill</u>. |

5 Sept
S
Motored with S[myth] R[ichards] to Exmoor & had a good ride to Brendon.[13]

6 Sept
<u>Sunday</u>
Church twice. Took it easy else. Hot[.]

7 Sept
M
Left before 8 <u>for Exeter.</u>
The usual grind there.

8 Sept
T
<u>To London</u> by the 12. Saw Bethune[14] at the W.O. & Sir C. Harris. Kitchener[15] has not saved the Dept[artment]. from some appalling muddles. The foolish decision to have a linked Batt[alion] at home for every T.F. Batt[alion] that goes abroad was adopted by him on Eshers[16] advice against that of Bethune.

9 Sept
W
Saw Tudor Craig[17] at 10. [T]hen to Sandilands. [T]hen to Basto [sic] to see A. Barrow. [T]hen to War Office then Education Office. [T]hen to meet Davis at Waterloo.[18] [T]hen the Education Office again. [T]hen to the Economic & caught the 3.30 to <u>Exeter</u>. An awful hustle.

10 Sept
Th
A heavy day. Den[zil] came in ev[ening].

11 Sept
F
To Barnstaple in ev[ening] for a meeting. <u>To Castle Hill</u> after. Very tired.

12 Sept
S
Shot two hours with Den[zil] on Bradbury in steady rain, but we had a nice morning & got 6 hares, 1 pig[eon], 1 rab[bit]. I shot well.

13 Sept
<u>Sunday</u>
Church twice. Did very little else. Good news.

14 Sept
M
To Exeter by early train. Much rain last night.

[13] Brendon is a village on Exmoor.
[14] Sir Edward Cecil Bethune, KCB (1855–1930). He had a lengthy career in the British army and had served in the Anglo-Afghan War and the Second Boer War. Bethune commanded the West Lancashire Territorial Division from 1909 to 1912. He was the Director-General of the Territorial Force from 1912 to 1917.
[15] Horatio Herbert Kitchener (1850–1916). He was the first Earl Kitchener of Khartoum and a field marshall in the British army. Kitchener was the British agent and Consul-General in Egypt from 1911 to 1914 and the Secretary of State for War from 1914 to 1916.
[16] Reginald Baliol Brett, GCB (1852–1930). He was the second Viscount Esher and he was the Liberal MP for Penryn and Falmouth from 1880 to 1885. In 1904, he was Chairman of the War Office Reconstitution Committee, and based on the committee's findings the "Esher report" was produced. From 1909 to 1913, he was the Chairman of the Territorial Force Association for the county of London.
[17] This is presumably Sir Algernon Tudor-Craig (1873–1943). He was a major in the British army. Tudor-Craig was the Secretary, Inc. of the Soldiers' and Sailors' Help Society from 1903 to 1921 and the Veterans Relief Fund from 1908 to 1921.
[18] This refers to London Waterloo railway station.

15 Sept T	Motored to Killerton[19] in ev[ening]. Den[zil] left.

16 Sept W	Motored to Haldon[20] in ev[ening].

17 Sept Th	Motored to Pynes[21] in ev[ening] and walked back. Chilly.

18 Sept F	Got back <u>to Castle Hill by</u> 8.

19 Sept S	Had to go to Plymouth about shirts &c for the men. Saw the General & Bastard & went to <u>Saltram</u>[22] to stay. Rifle Pits in ther[e]in drive [sic] & entanglements outside.

20 Sept Sunday <u>Saltram</u>	Walked to Plymouth am[,] & went on to lunch with Gen[eral] Penton who jumps short. Went with him after to the Coast defence batteries, the Hospital where there were 4 or 5 Scots Greys & Efford fort. Much of interest. Lovely day.

21 Sept M	Back <u>to Exeter</u> by early train. Bright but chilly.

22 – 24 [Sept] Usual thing[s].

25 Sept F	<u>Motored home</u> in ev[ening]. Inspecting the men in temporary barracks at Crediton en route [sic]. 2 letters from Hugh.

26 Sept S	Shot for about 3 hours with Buttle on Park & Crossbury. Lovely day but could not kill clean.

27 Sept Sunday	Church am. Motored back to <u>Exeter</u> pm. Lovely day.

28 Sept M <u>Exeter</u>	[B]y the 7.15 to Salisbury. Motored to Tidworth. Saw Gen[eral] Donald. Then to Perham Down. Saw Pinney & went with him to the Kings inspection of the Life Guards &c. Very well housed. [T]hen lunch with Pinney[.] [T]hen Kings inspection of D[evon] & C[ornwall] Brigade before they go to India. Back to Tidworth & then to West Down camp to see the Gunners. Back to Salisbury to catch the 5.8 [sic] & returned to Exeter. Tired.

29 Sept T	Motored to the Markers in ev[ening].

---

[19] This refers to Killerton House which is located in Killerton near Exeter.
[20] This is probably Haldon House which was located in the Haldon Hills near Exeter.
[21] This is Pynes House which is located in Upton Pyne near Exeter.
[22] This refers to Saltram House which is located near Plymouth.

30 Sept W	Motored to Knightshayes[23] for dinner.
1 Oct Th	Office work light, so motored over Woodbury & took S[mith]. Rewse between 2.15 & 4.15.
2 Oct F	Got home by 7[.]
3 Oct S C Hill	Motored to Dulverton Station & thence with T. Hannock to Wheddon x [Cross] Porlock Exford & home. [S]eeing keepers &c. A pleasant run in fine weather. Polly Stucley came.
4 Oct Sunday	Church twice[.]
5 Oct M	To Exeter by early train.
6 Oct T	To London by the 10.15. Did Com[mi]^{tee} at Economic & caught the 2.15 to Colchester. [O]n to Tendring to stay with the Yeo[manry].
7 Oct W	Out early to look at saddles & clothing both the worn for wear. Then to Brigade Field Day[,] the troops look & work very well. Back to London by the 1.12. Economic. CMC.[,] & dined with Sue[.]
8 Oct Th	Back to Exeter[.]
9 Oct [F]	Sent some of the wounded out in the car[.]
10 Oct S	Early morning & left after lunch for Castle Hill. Cloudy & less warm.
11 Oct Sunday	Church twice. Colder. Walk to Leary pm.
12 Oct M	To Barnstaple early about Yeomanry. [T]hen by 12.39 to Exeter[.]
13 Oct T	Motored pm to Heavitree, Topsham & Exmouth to see the RFA batteries[.] [S]ome of whose methods are very casual.
14 Oct W	Rainy.
15 Oct [Th]	[No entry]

---

[23] This refers to Knightshayes Court located on the outskirts of Tiverton, the country seat of the Heathcoat-Amory's.

16 Oct F	P went to London for the christening of Billy Gore's[24] baby.[25] I went to Killerton to see Acland[26] about deer killing & then to C. Hill arriving 7.30.
17 Oct S	Lovely day. Rode with S[myth] R[ichards] to Bushton[27] Middle Hill[28] & N[orth] Aller[.]
18 Oct Sunday	Church twice. Fine & pleasant. Good news from the fleet.
19 Oct M	Back to Exeter by 10.30. Every one cheerful over present prospects.
20 Oct T	Both the VAD Hospitals here are now nearly full. Went over the Middle School one in ev[ening].
21 Oct W	To London by the 10.15. CFO Com[mi]^tee & Economic.
22 Oct Th	Back to Exeter after Econ. Com[mi]^tee by the 11. Rainy.
23 Oct F	Back to Castle Hill[.]
24 Oct S	Shot a little am with O Chichester about Stoodleigh &c. Lovely day.
25 Oct Sunday	Church twice. Wet.
26 Oct M	Back to Exeter by 10.30. Weather pleasant again.
27 Oct T	About my easiest day since 5 Aug[ust].
28 Oct [W]	Went to Cathedral service at 1. Very few there.
29 Oct Th	Motored in ev[ening] to Newton Abbot & Teignmouth & see the 5th Reserve Batt[alion] & the 1st Dev[on] Yeo[manry] R[egiment].

[24] William Ormsby-Gore (1885–1964). He was the fourth Baron Harlech and the Lord Lieutenant of Merionethshire from 1938 to 1957. He was the Conservative MP for Denbigh Boroughs from January 1910 to 1918 and the MP for Stafford from 1918 to 1938. In March 1917, Harlech was appointed as the Parliamentary Private Secretary to Lord Milner. From 1917 to 1918, he was an Assistant Secretary to the Lloyd George War Cabinet.
[25] This was William Ormsby-Gore's first child, Mary Hermoine Ormsby-Gore (1914–2006), who was born on 7 September 1914.
[26] This must be presumably Sir Charles Thomas Dyke Acland (1842–1919). He was the twelfth Baron Acland of Columb Major. He was the Liberal MP for East Cornwall from 1882 to 1885 and the MP for North East Cornwall from 1885 to 1892. He served as the Chairman of the Technical Education Committee of Devon County Council from 1890 to 1910. Acland was also the Sheriff of Devon from 1903 to 1904.
[27] This is presumably Bushton Wood.
[28] This is Middle Hill Farm.

30 Oct	Went to Exmouth in ev[ening] to see the 4th Reserve Batt[alion]. I have now
F	got fairly complete information about the venereal disease[s] among the
	troops in the County which results as follows.

Exeter.	About 4000 men.	5 cases.
Newton Abbot.	581 (5th Batt[alion])	Nil
Exmouth	670 (4th Batt[alion])	Nil.
Teignmouth	189 (1st Yeo[manry])	Nil.
Plymouth	27 000.	138 cases
of wh[ich]. 14 were Canadians.		

31 Oct	Left at 12 & got to <u>Castle Hill</u> by 2. The Herberts[29] came to luncheon. He
S	said the feeling about being let down by the French was very strong among
	the Troops who had to retreat from Mons.[30] Rode to W[est]. Buckland p.m.

1 Nov	Church twice. Sacrament am.
Sunday	Walked to Fullabrook[31] pm. Wet am.
C Hill	

| 2 Nov | To Exmoor with S[myth] R[ichards] & had a very wet ride to Larkbarrow |
| M | and Badgworthy. Fine pm. |

| 3 Nov | <u>To London</u> by the 9.10 with P. |
| T | |

| 4 Nov | Started for Aldershot by the 8.50 but was only at Surbiton when we ought |
| W | to have arrived so gave it up. CFO & Econ & CMC. |

| 5 Nov | Com[mi]tee at Econ. |
| Th | [T]hen War Office to <u>Exeter</u> by the 3.30. |

| 6 Nov | A long day's work. Rainy. |
| F | |

| 7 Nov | <u>Got home</u> by the 4.30. Fine[.] |
| S | |

| 8 Nov | Church twice. Walk pm. Raw am but warmer after. |
| Sunday | |

9 Nov	<u>To Exeter.</u> Astor[32] came to see me about defence of the Coast ports as to
M	which even on the E[ast] coast they are only now taking steps ~~relative for~~
	denying the conveniences of quays cranes & power plants to invaders.

[29] This is presumably George Charles Herbert (1862–1952). He was the fourth Earl of Powis and the Lord Lieutenant of Shropshire from 1896 to 1951. He was an Alderman of Shropshire County Council and President of the Shropshire Territorial Force Association; Violet Herbert (1865–1929). She was the Countess of Powis and the Baroness Darcy de Knayth.

[30] This refers to Battle of Mons on 23 August 1914 and the retreat from Mons of the British Expeditionary Force in August and September 1914.

[31] This could refer to Fullabrook farm near Umberleigh.

[32] Waldorf Astor (1879–1952). He was the second Viscount Astor and the Conservative MP for Plymouth from December 1910 to 1918. He was the MP for Plymouth Sutton from 1918 to 1919. He was the Inspector of Quartermaster General Services from October 1914 to January 1917. From December 1916, Astor was the Parliamentary Private Secretary to the Prime Minister, David Lloyd George, and he was appointed as the Parliamentary Secretary to the Ministry of Food in 1918.

10 Nov
T

Capt[ain] Godman. Staff officer told me that a P2000 Marshall had had to be sent round to collect Canadian Officers who were breaking their leave. There were 40 at Plymouth. There is very little discipline in the force.

11 Nov
W

All this corroborated by Benson who came down to see me about CMC affairs. The camps at Codford & on the plain[33] are horribly uncomfortable & the Canadians have looted the canteens & even stolen money freely. L[or]d K[itchener]. will take no action on the recommendations of the Rotherham Com[mit]tee[34] & there is a deadlock. Went down to meet a Hospital train. No stretcher came. The casualties are fewer now & less severe. Back to Castle Hill by the 4.30[.]

12 Nov
Th

Walked with Buttle am & rode pm. Clinton Drummond & Lesks came.

13 Nov
F

Den[zil] arrived by 9.36. Shot White Hill. Gale of wind & rain till 1.30. Got 116 ph[easants]. 4 wood[cocks]. A good day spoilt by weather.

14 Nov
S

Shot Higher Beer & Smalldons bottom. Weather fine & Buttle showed his birds well but the shooting was poor & we only brought in about 120. Den[zil] & I went up to London by the mail[35] after to meet Hugh.

15 Nov
Sunday

Church am & we all lunched with the S[t]. Aldwyns. Hugh had a touch of ptomaine poisoning a week ago but seems little the worse now. He does not pretend to be one of those who enjoy the war.

Nov 16
M
London

About with the boys am: CMC later. Den[zil] left in ev[ening]. for his Reg[imen]t[.]

17 Nov
T

Com[mi]tee at Econ. H[ouse] of Lords pm where Curzon[36] spoke very well on L[or]d Roberts,[37] insinuating "I told you so" about Nat[ional] Service without putting it offensively. He emphasized also the religious side of L[or]d R[oberts]. Hugh went to Clacton.

18 Nov
W

To Aldershot by 8.55 to see the 8th Devons. A fine batt[alion] but not all completely clothed, many having civilian great coats; some no rifles & manky leather or no equipment.
Economic after & then letters.

---

[33] This refers to Salisbury Plain.

[34] This refers to Rotherham Committee which was chaired by the first Baron Rotherham, William Holland, (1849–1927). See John Fortescue, *A Short Account of Canteens in the British Army* (Cambridge: Cambridge University Press, 1928), p. 48.

[35] This refers to the mail train.

[36] George Curzon (1859–1925). He was the first Marquess Curzon of Kedleston and the Conservative MP for Southport from 1886 to 1898. He was the Governor General of India from 1899 to 1905 and the Representative peer for Ireland from 1908 to 1925. Curzon was the Lord Privy Seal from 1915 to 1916 and the President of the Air Board in 1916. He was the Lord President of the Council from 1916 to 1919.

[37] Frederick Sleigh Roberts, VC (1832–1914). He was the first Earl Roberts and a veteran general in the British army in the late nineteenth century. He was the Commander-in-Chief in India from 1885 to 1893 and the Commander-in-Chief in Ireland from 1895 to 1900. Roberts was Commander-in-Chief of the Forces from 1900 to 1904 and was appointed the Colonel-in-Chief of the Empire ('Overseas') troops in 1914.

19 Nov Th	BCWS: Com[mi]^tee at Econ. & an hour with Ford about recruiting before lunch. After that with Hugh: & tried to get saddles for Yeomanry then <u>to Exeter by</u> 5.50.
~~Nov 20~~	Travelled down with Curzon who told me the French were not very comfortable allies as they were unpunctual in concerted movements which accounted at any rate in part for the very heavy losses of the 7th Div[ision]. We had a bad defeat in E[ast] Africa due apparently to gross mismanagement, & the Russian defeat this week was likely to delay their advance for weeks. Wet.
20 Nov F	Work of sorts till 5.30: then to <u>Castle Hill</u> with P. She had seen Hugh off to the front again at 8.30 this morning. Fine but cold.
21 Nov S	About the place with S[myth]. R[ichards]. [C]old[.]
22 Nov <u>Sunday</u>	Church twice. Cold with fresh E[ast] wind. Clinton[38] came to luncheon. The L&SWR were warned to have 660 trains ready with steam up last Mon[day], Tues[day] & Wed[nesday]. A German raid was fully expected, & all of the T.F. down here that had rifles. Not over many – were ready to move at three hours notice.
23 Nov M	To Exeter for meeting to stir up recruiting. It went off well. Less cold in ev[ening].
24 Nov T	Shot with Dick & Buttle over S[outh] Aller &c. [G]ot 16 ph[easants] & 9 rab[bits]. No one very accurate.
25 Nov W	To Exeter for S. J.[39] Com[mi]^tee &c : warmer.
26 Nov Th	Shot Cawses Barton[40] which took barely 3½ hours. Long walk Spa Wood & Heddon Bottom. With a mixed team. Mr. Francis, C[harles]. Slader, Buttle, Dick & self. I shot poorly all the morning though I got 3 woodc[ocks] but did better toward the end. [B]ut no one was in good form. We got 151 ph[easants] 6 woodc[ocks] 16 H[ares] 4 rab[bits]. Fine till 3. [T]hen wet. Pick up next day was 15 ph[easants] 1 H[are].
27 Nov F <u>C Hill</u>	To Exeter with P by the 8.39 for C.C. Finances + Patriotic[41] meeting.
28 Nov S	Rode with S[myth] R[ichards] am. Miss Andrew[42] came.

---

[38] Charles Hepburn-Stuart-Forbes-Trefusis (1863–1957). He was the twenty-first Baron Clinton and a lieutenant-colonel in the North Devon Yeomanry (Hussars). He was the Joint Parliamentary Secretary for the Board of Agriculture in 1918 and Chairman of the Forestry Commissioners from 1927 to 1932.

[39] This refers to the Standing Joint Committee of the Devon Constabulary.

[40] This presumably refers to Cawsey's Barton which is located close to the Castle Hill estate..

[41] This refers to the Devon Patriotic Fund.

[42] This refers to Miss Clara Andrew.

29 Nov Sunday	Church a.m. [D]id very little.
30 Nov M	26 wounded men were to have come to dinner at 12 but it was too rough & wet. Walked with P pm.
1 Dec T	To Exeter by the 10.30 then ~~with~~ in Ford's car to Tiverton for recruiting meeting & motored home with P. The Bomicks [*sic*] came.
2 Dec W	To London for Economic & CMC dined with /: [*sic*] [St] Aldwyn.
3 Dec Th	Com[mi]^{tee} at Economic. Then to Exeter for work & on home.
4 Dec F	Very wet & stormy. To Tavistock for recruiting meeting & back to Exeter.
5 Dec S	Work am. Meeting at S[outh] Brent pm. Back late to Castle Hill.
6 Dec Sunday	Church twice.
7 Dec M	To Exeter. Recruiting Meeting &c. Hugh came back.
8 Dec T	Recruiting meeting at Eggsford. Den[zil] came with a broken collar bone. Shot the ponds & Spa Wood with Hugh a.m. [R]ather a sporting morning.
9 Dec W	To Exeter & Newton Abbot[.]
10 Dec Th	Shot Long Walk Temple & Bray with the boys, Dick & Buttle. Den[zil] did pretty well with one hand, & we got 180. Fine day. Hugh gazetted Capt[ain]. [T]oday & went back at 8.30 to the front.
11 Dec F	Exeter again – A long day, & no luncheon.
12 Dec S	To Barnstaple by 7.30 to see the 6th Batt[alion] leave for India.
13 Dec Sunday	Church twice. Wet[.]
14 Dec M	To Exeter by the 10.30 for T.F. work[.]
15 Dec T	Christine went. Shot Tilery & Lower Beer with Den[zil]. 26 ph[easants] 1 w[oodcock] 1 pig[eon] 5 rab[bits]. Neither of us very deadly. Showers.

16 Dec W	<u>To Exeter</u> for TF. [G]ave away prizes at Crediton School pm.
17 Dec Th	County Council. DPF after not <u>home</u> till 7. Very tired.
18 Dec F	Shot E[ast] Buckland Covers with Den[zil] & C Slader 28 ph[easants] 3 rab[bits] 1 pig[eon]. Lovely day after heavy rain.
19 Dec S	Had a wet ride with Smyth Richards to E[ast] Buckland.
20 Dec Sunday	Church twice.
21 Dec M	A long day in Exeter. Sue came.
22 Dec T	Shot White Hill with Den[zil] & C. Slader. [G]ot 73 ph[easants]. Shot fairly till the last half hour when missed everything. Frost.
23 Dec W	Went through White Hill again. Only got 10 ph[easants]. John came.
24 Dec Th	Shot Riverton &c. Fine bright day, but did not find the birds expected. Got 31[.]
25 Dec F	S[t]. Aldwyn came. Have a decided cold. Church am. Milder.
26 Dec S	Shot Wood House Bray Temple & Long Walk. Shot very badly[.] Feeling like flue [*sic*]. Fine after wet night.
27 Dec <u>Sunday</u>	Church am only. Very wet in ev[ening].
28 Dec M	Shot Park Punchbowl & past Bremridge till 2.50 when heavy rain drove us home. Shot pretty well.
29 Dec T	<u>To Exeter</u> & on to Newton Abbot to give away badges.
30 Dec W	<u>To London.</u> CFO. Econ. CMC. Dined with Michael.
31 Dec Th	Com[mi]^{tee} at Econ. [T]hen Local Gov[ernment] Board about Bailey. Board meeting of CFO. CMC. Home by 4.15 after a glimpse of Hugh.

1915

1 Jan F <u>Castle Hill</u>	Motored to Exeter with P. Floods out & we could not get back to Crediton by the high road. Hugh arrived at 6.

2 Jan
S

Hugh & I shot Tilery Burden wood[43] &c. Found 8–10 woodcock but not much else. Got 9 ph[easants] 2 woodc[ocks] 1 snipe 14 rab[bits]. Showers.

3 Jan
Sunday

Church twice remained for Sacram[en]ᵗ . Wet pm.

4 Jan
M

Moved to Exmoor with S[myth] R[ichards] & rode to Malsmead[44] Farleigh and Cheriton. Nice day. Sandie F s came [*sic*].

5 Jan
T

Hugh Hill 3) Sandie & I shot Smal[l]dons Bottom, Higher Beer &c & got 59 ph[easants]. 50 of them cocks.
I shot pretty fairly. Hugh left by 3.40.

6 Jan
W

To Paignton for recruiting meeting. A long day.

7 Jan
Th

Wet nearly all day. Walked with Wallace pm.

8 Jan
F

Shot Longwalk Temple &c with Sandie. [G]ot 21 cocks 4 hens [pheasants] & 8 rab[bits].
Showery. Shot pretty well.

9 Jan
S

Fine after a wild night. Water in all directions. Rode with S[myth] R[ichards] am.
The Sandies left.

10 Jan
Sunday

Rain all day. Church twice.

11 Jan
M

Shot Higher Beer before lunch with Dick & Buttle. Got 12 ph[easants] & 3 rab[bits].
Cold & heavy showers till 12. [T]hen fine.

12 Jan
T

Fine. To Exeter all day. Recruiting Com[mi]ᵗᵉᵉ.

13 Jan
W

To London for CFO Com[mi]ᵗᵉᵉ. Econ & CMC. Travelled up with a Staff Officer of the Indian Div[ision] who said that we had a man to a yard of front. Enough for defence but not for attack that the French were doing well. The Indians rather a disappointment. The native officers were useless, & they had lost very heavily in British off[ensives]. The Germans reckoned the British as the best & the Indians as the worst troops against them. Our new Army & T F were probably quite equal to the new German troops. It was then that we were capturing men about 40 now but their young fellows were not younger than ours.

14 Jan
Th

Com[mi]ᵗᵉᵉ at Econ.
Back to Castle Hill by the 1.30 stopping at S[outh] Molton to see at tea the 3ʳᵈ Devon men who have been route marching for recruits.

---

43   This could refer to the wood next to Bydown House.
44   This refers to the medieval village of Malsmead.

15 Jan F	With P to Exeter for the day. Windy with showers. The Route March has secured 48 – 60 recruits.
16 Jan S	Had a short day through Cawsis Barton,[45] Bradbury Bottom Temple wood & Long walk. [G]ot 15 cocks & a hen. Nester [*sic*] saw a woodcock. Cold N[orth] W[est] wind.
17 Jan Sunday	Church twice. Cold wind. Fine except some short showers.
18 Jan M	Frost in night. Wind dropped. A cold ride with Wallace to the E[ast] Buckland cover.
19 Jan T <u>Castle Hill</u>	To Exeter with P. Col[onel]. Western's Staff Officer told me that he had it from a G.P.O. man that the Germans on the outbreak of war cut over 30 of the telephone & telegraph cables to France: the only 4 that escaped going through Exeter. We however had a cable ship at Plymouth at the time which proceeded to grapple the only direct cable the Germans have to USA wh[ich]. lands at Emden. They picked up 180 miles of it & forthwith relaid [*sic*] it between this & France. The German cable is of extraordinary good quality & worth 50% more than ours. Say 30/ a yard against 20/ ~~so we have~~: so we are using against them £ 500 000 of their own capital & have stopped between 7 & 8 mill[ion]. from earning anything.
20 Jan W	Walked with P pm. The Fullers came. Mild & inclined to rain.
21 Jan Th	About the place.
22 Jan F	To Exeter[.]
23 Jan S	To N[orth] Aller am. Walk with P pm. Fullers left. Gleichens[46] came. Some snow. [A] good deal on Exmoor.
24 Jan <u>Sunday</u>	Church twice. Fine & Bright. Gleichen interesting about the war. He fears a stalemate. Though the Germans have lost so heavily in officers their troops are well led & show no lack of initiative or resource. [B]ut there is no doubt they are putting both elderly men & young ones into the field. He spoke highly of the fighting qualities of the French, though he too had found them unpunctual & difficult to work with. This corroborated by Mrs Fuller story of her relation who patrols daily from Dover to meet a French torpedo boat & rarely finds it where he sh[oul]ᵈ. There is 1 par [*sic*] no doubt there has been signalling to German submarines & sale of petrol on our S[outh]. Coast.

---

[45]   This is presumably Cawsey's Barton.

[46]   Lord Albert Edward Wilfred Gleichen (1863–1937). He was a Count von Gleichen and a major-general in the British army. Gleichen served in both the Second Boer War from 1899 to 1901 and the First World War. He was the military attaché in Berlin from 1903 to 1906 and in Washington from 1906 to 1907; Sylvia Gay Edwardes (1880–1942). She was married to Lord Edward Gleichen and was the Maid of Honour to Queen Victoria from 1897 to 1901. From 1901 to 1910, she was the Maid of Honour to Queen Alexandra.

Our P.O. & Admiralty combined did a smart thing in Aug[ust]. Lifting & cutting off 180 M[iles] of the only cable that went direct from Germany to USA, which was promptly used to improve communication with France, for the Germans had cut 33 out of the 37 wires across the Channel.

25 Jan M <u>C. Hill</u>	To Exeter. The Gleichens left.
26 [Jan] " [T]	To Exeter & then to Tavistock for recruiting meeting. Stayed the night <u>in Exeter</u>
27 Jan W	<u>To London</u>. Economic & CMC. Dined with S[t]. Aldwyns. Heard of Admiral Troubridge[']s[47] approaching departure for Serbia. Cold.
28 Jan Th	To Exeter for special meeting of Chairmen about Bailey. All present but Tremlett & Watson. Agreed he must go. <u>Home after.</u>
29 Jan F	To Exeter for the day. Sharpish frost, but still.
30 Jan S	Sharp frost, but no wind. Motored to Morte[48] for Convalescence Home meeting, & went to Poole Little Woollacombe & onaborough [*sic*].[49]
31 Jan <u>Sunday</u>	Wind changed to N[orth] W[est] & there was rain in night. Bright & fine. Church twice.
1 Feb M	<u>To Exeter</u> & slept there.
2 Feb T	Work till 4. Then to London. The 3rd Devons have sent out 1800 men as drafts: of the original 1st Batt[alion] only the C.O. & 70 men are doing duty.
3 Feb W	C.F.O. War Office. L°[rd] Lieut[enants] meeting & H[ouse] of Lords. Dined with the S[t]. Aldwyns.
4 Feb Th	H[ouse] of Lords. Dined with Dartmouth.[50] Long Timber Co. Meeting[.]
5 Feb F <u>London</u>	CFO & CMC. The Ryles & Mr Buxton dined. There is less crime in London, partly because sundry criminals enlisted with a view to plundering dead & wounded. Some caught at this game have been shot or given long terms of penal servitude. There is reason to suppose, judging from the interest gov[ernment]. are taking in a diving bell invention[,] that we sunk a German submarine some time ago in the Forth & another at Scapa Flow.

[47] Sir Ernest Charles Thomas Troubridge (1862–1926). He was an admiral in the Royal Navy and had served as the Naval Attaché in Vienna, Madrid and Tokyo. Troubridge was the Chief of the War Staff at the Admiralty from 1911 to 1912 and the Head of the British Naval Mission to Serbia in 1915.

[48] This is presumably Mortehoe or Morte Point.

[49] This is presumably Putsborough.

[50] William Heneage Legge (1851–1936). He was the sixth Earl of Dartmouth and the Lord Lieutenant for Staffordshire from 1891 to 1927. He was the Conservative MP for West Kent from 1878 to 1885 and the MP for Lewisham from 1885 to 1891. He was an Alderman of Staffordshire County Council and the Vice-Chamberlain of the Household both from 1885 to January 1886 and August 1886 to 1892.

6 Feb S	John & Peggy dined. She went in to dinner recently with Sir F Hopwood[51] who told her that Winston[52] [Churchill] insisted on his own on sending the Indomitable & Invincible to the Falklands before they were out of dock yard hands, the happy result of which was that they got there the day before Von Spee.[53] Who it is supposed would have gone on thence to the Cape[54] & made himself unpleasant there.
7 Feb <u>Sunday</u>	Miss Carney lunched. Went to Holy Trin[ity] am.
8 Feb M	A good deal of work. Den[zil] came up & Maggie.
9 Feb T	Den[zil] went back in ev[ening]. Fine.
10 Feb W	CFO. Econ & H[ouse] of Lords.
11 Feb Th	Econ. Long afternoon at CMC.
12 Feb F <u>C.H</u>	To Barnstaple for a Recruiting Meeting & back to <u>Castle Hill</u>[.]
13 Feb S	Some heavy showers. Rode am with S[myth] Richards.
14 Feb <u>Sunday</u>	Church twice. Walk pm with Dick[.]
15 Feb M	S[myth] R[ichards] sent me to Molton R[oa]^d at 8.36 in his car. Exeter all day to <u>London</u> by 4.17. Den[zil] up.

[51] Francis John Stephens Hopwood (1860–1947). He was the first Baron Southborough and a prominent civil servant. He was the Permanent Secretary for the Board of Trade from 1901 to 1907 and the Permanent Under-Secretary of State for the Colonies from 1907 to 1911. He was a Civil Lord of the Admiralty from 1912 to 1917 and the Chairman of the Grand Committee on War Trade during War. Southborough was also the Honorary Secretary on the Irish Convention from 1917 to 1918.

[52] Sir Winston Spencer Churchill (1874–1965). He was the Conservative MP for Oldham from 1900 to 1904. He moved from the Conservative party to the Liberals and was the Liberal MP for Oldham from 1904 to 1906. He was the Liberal MP for North West Manchester from 1906 to 1908, an MP for Dundee from 1908 to 1922 and the MP for Epping from 1924 to 1931. He moved back to the Conservatives from the Liberal party and he was the Conservative MP for Epping from 1931 to 1945. He was the Conservative MP for Woodford from 1945 to 1964 and Father of the House from 1959 to 1964. Churchill was the President of the Board of Trade from 1908 to 1910 and Home Secretary from 1910 to 1911. He was the First Lord of the Admiralty from 1911 to 1915 and the Minister of Munitions from 1917 to 1919. He was the Secretary of State for both War and Air from 1919 to 1921. Later, Churchill served as Prime Minister from 1940 to 1945 and from 1951 to 1955.

[53] Maximilian von Spee (1861–1914). He was a Vice-Admiral in the Imperial German Navy and commanded the German East Asia Squadron. He died in action at the Battle of the Falkland Islands in December 1914.

[54] This refers to Cape Horn.

16 Feb
T
London

Fine but cold. H[ouse] of Lords pm.
A small dinner.

17 Feb
W

Florence Corkram came.

18 Feb
Th

P seedy with influenza[.]

19 Feb
F

CFO & CMC[.]

20 Feb
S

P better but still in bed. Fine[.]

21 Feb
Sunday

Church am. P improving.

22 Feb
M

Wire from Hugh early to say he had a slight wound in his foot. rec[ieve]^d
19th 2am. Went to see Sue in ev[ening]. CFO.

23 Feb
T

A good deal of work. C. C agr[iculture] form [sic]. P down stairs. Cold.

24 Feb
W

Economic. (CFO first) then by 3.30 to Exeter.

25 Feb
Th

S. J. Com[mi]^{tee} am. D P F & other work pm.

26 [Feb]
F

Finance Com[mi]'[tee] am. Recruiting pm.
Back to London by the 5.27. Cold.

27 [Feb]
S

P is about well again. Rain in night. Fine but coldish there after [sic].
Dined with the Ryles.

28 Feb
Sunday

Church am. Lunched with Censis Hope [sic].

1 Mar
M

Com[mi]^{tee} at C.F.O. Christens & the Amorys dined. P had her eye cist [sic]
removed[.]

2 Mar
T

H[ouse] of Lords pm to introduce Michael S^t. Aldwyn.[55] CMC after.

3 Mar
W

C.F.O[.] am. Greig & Hancock came to luncheon. Long talk about stag
hounds. Den[zil] up too.

---

[55] Michael Hicks Beach (1837–1916). He was the first Earl St Aldwyn and was the fourth Earl
Fortescue's brother-in-law. He was the Conservative MP for East Gloucestershire from 1864 to 1885
and the MP for West Bristol from 1885 to 1906. He was the Chancellor of Exchequer from 1885 to
1886 and 1895 to 1902. He was the President of the Board of Trade from 1888 to 1892.

4 Mar Th	Had a small dinner in ev[ening]. Den[zil] came back from Oxford late.
5 Mar F	C[.]F.O. M. Von Swinderen.[56] The Dutch Ambassador called. He said he was with Lychnowsky[57] [*sic*] on the afternoon of Mon[day] 3 Aug[ust] & he said while Grey[58] actually was speaking in the House[59] "I do not believe I shall have to pack my things yet". Von S[winderen]. thought Grey should have warned the Germans more plainly as to the consequence of their violating Belgian neutrality. [B]ut Lichnowsky pooh poohed our fleet[,] said they could not aggravate the injury to commerce that would ensue from war with France & all they could do would be to burn a few villages on the German coast. While as to the Expeditionary Force, "The days of Wellington[60] are over, & the English will do no fighting on the Continent". He also told P before I came in that the Queen of Holland had desired him to tell people that she was no partisan of Germany's & that à Court Repington[61] had told him that Russia's failure to make a successful advance was a disappointment. He Von S[winderen]. expected the end to be stalemate.
6 Mar S	Nothing particular. Seymour & Lady Allendale[62] dined. We have got 11–17 submarines.
7 Mar Sunday	Church am. Lunch with Lucy. Den[zil] up en route from Badminton to Clacton. The Danish Minister[63] called & took different views to the Dutchman.
8 Mar M	Very cold. Dined with May Egerton. CFO am.
9 Mar T	Economic. H[ouse] of Lords pm.
10 Mar W	CFO & Economic. Dinner at home.

---

[56] Jonkheer Reneke (René) de Marees van Swinderen (1860–1955). He was an experienced and distinguished Dutch diplomat. He was the Minister of Foreign Affairs at the Hague from 1908 to 1913. Van Swinderen was the Envoy Extraordinary and Minister Plenipotentiary of the Netherlands in London or the Dutch Ambassador to the Court of St James's from 1913 to 1937.

[57] Prince Karl Max von Lichnowsky (1860–1928). He was a German diplomat who served as the Envoy Extraordinary and Minister Plenipotentiary of Imperial Germany in London or the German Ambassador to the Court of St James's from 1912 to 1914.

[58] Sir Edward Grey (1862–1933). He was the first Viscount Grey of Fallodon and he was the Liberal MP for Berwick-on-Tweed from 1885 to 1916. He was the Under-Secretary for Foreign Affairs from 1892 to 1895 and the Secretary of State for Foreign Affairs from 1905 to 1916.

[59] This refers to the House of Commons.

[60] Arthur Wellesley (1769–1852). He was the first Duke of Wellington and was a celebrated general in the British army during the Napoleonic Wars. Wellington was the Lord Lieutenant of Hampshire from 1820 to 1852 and the Lord Lieutenant of the Tower Hamlets from 1827 to 1852.

[61] Charles à Court Repington (1858–1925). He was a lieutenant-colonel in the British army and a military correspondent for newspapers including The Times and the Army Review. Repington was a key figure in the reporting of the shells scandal of 1915.

[62] Alexandra Louisa Maud Vane-Tempest (1863–1945). She was the Lady Allendale or Viscountess Allendale.

[63] Henrik de Grevenkop-Castenskiold (1862–1921). He was a Danish count and law professor. He also held a number of diplomatic appointments in St Petersburg, Berlin and London. From 1912 to 1921, he was the Envoy Extraordinary and Minister Plenipotentiary of Denmark in London or the Danish Ambassador to the Court of St James's. He was also a chamberlain to the king of Denmark.

11 Mar
Th

Com[mi]tee at Economic. H[ouse] of Lords after. Warmer. Lady Poltimore[64] dined.

12 Mar
F

More work over this d[amn]. Belgian Com[mi]tee. CFO in the ev[ening] to Clacton on Sea.

13 Mar
S
Clacton

Went out am to see a Composite squadron, made up of recruits &c drilling. They worked very well.
In afternoon motored with drag near Tendring[.]

14 Mar
Sunday

Parade service at 10 & went round Stables & billets after.
P.m. Motored to St Osyth[s] Priory.[65] A beautiful ~~place~~ old house. Lovely day. R[oyal] 1st Yeom[anry] there.[66]

15 Mar
M

Back to London am
& on to Exeter by the 1.30. Belgian Com[mittee] 5-7.

16 Mar
T

S. J. Com[mi]tee am & Advisory as D. J. P. pm.

17 Mar
W

T F A am. Recruiting meeting at Newton [Abbot] pm.
[T]hen C.C[.] agenda.

18 Mar
Th

County Council till 3[.] [T]hen
T.F[.] work.

19 Mar
F

Work of sorts till 3.
[T]hen back to London.
Fine but chilly. Dined w[ith]. Bentincks.

20 Mar
S

Walked with P. pm.

21 Mar
Sunday
London

Church am. 5 to luncheon. John [Fortescue][67] came in ev[ening]. He returned on Thurs[day]. from the front. Whither he had been as to writing an account of the Oct[ober]–Nov[ember] battle of Ypres.
To his enquiries why our men were there at all, no reply was given or perhaps can be. So the matter stands adjourned for the present. He inclines to think that the flank extension was dictated by political considerations. Why having been left centre we were transferred to extreme left, with infinite complications of supply did not appear. He reports all in excellent spirits, notwithstanding the heavy losses at Neuve Chapelle &c (14 000 – 15 000 altogether) as we got value for our money, bucked up the Troops, & anticipated a big attack prepared by the Germans on St Eloi. They were however disappointed secretly at not having got on to the Aubers Ridge.

---

[64] Margaret Harriet Beaumont (1856–1931). She was the Lady Poltimore or the Baroness Poltimore.
[65] This refers to St Osyth's Priory in Essex.
[66] Fortescue added this observation in pencil.
[67] Sir John William Fortescue (1859–1933). He was a prolific military historian and the fifth son of the third Earl Fortescue. He was the Royal Librarian and Archivist for Windsor Castle from 1905 to 1926 and he was an Honorary Fellow of Trinity College at the University of Cambridge.

half way to Lille. This due partly to Rawlinson[68] who did not throw his reserve Brigade into the fight, & partly to lack of cooperation by the French. To make attacks effective it is necessary they should be simultaneous over say 25 miles[,] or adjoining sections re inforces [*sic*] the threatened one. Charley[69] is being sent home. The 28th & 29 Div[isions] have not been a success. They have been sickly & have run away. He has not shewn want of competence, but his low spirits have been infectious, & to pull their fellows together they need a man with push and cherry confidences.

The complaints of slackness among the men in armament work are not all justified. Many of them are stale from over time.[70]

Manoury[71] [*sic*] saved the situation at the end of the retreat, & enabled an advance to be substituted. The Germans thought that he & we were done, & they could take the troops on our left in flank: but M[aunoury] had brought up fresh troops from Paris & though our men could not have retreated another 5 miles they cheerfully advanced 15.

22 Mar Comm[i]^te[e] as. Econ & CFO.
M   The fine weather of last week on Mon[day] turned to rain after 1.
        Dined with Seymour.

23 Mar Fine. BCWS work. Dined with Christine.
T

24 Mar CFO & Econ. Went to a lecture on Russia in ev[ening].[72] Disappointing.
W

25 Mar Wet. A good deal of work. Dined with Hyltons.[73]
Th

26 Mar Com[mi]^tee at Economic. CFO.
F   A small dinner.
London

27 Mar A lot of work. Fine but cold.
S

---

[68] Henry Seymour Rawlinson (1864–1925). He was the first Baron Rawlinson and a general in the British army. He commanded the 4th Corps from August 1914 to 1916 and was given command of the Fourth Army in January 1916. He was the British representative on the Executive War Board or the Supreme War Council.

[69] This is presumably Charles Granville Fortescue (1861–1951). He was a brigadier-general in the British army and a former private secretary of the Secretary of State for War. He served in both the Second Boer War and the First World War.

[70] This short paragraph is written in the left-hand margin and the text is aligned downward.

[71] Michel-Joseph Maunoury (1847–1923). He was a general in the French army who had served in both the Franco-Prussian War and the First World War.

[72] This refers probably to a lecture given by Sir Charles Theodore Hagberg Wright (1862–1940). He was the Secretary and Librarian of the London Library from 1893 to 1940. He was previously the Assistant Librarian of the National Library of Ireland from 1890 to 1893.

[73] Hylton Jolliffe (1862–1945). He was the third Baron Hylton and the Conservative MP for Wells from 1895 to 1899. He was Lord-in-Waiting from 1915 to 1918 and the Joint Chief Government Whip in the House of Lords from 1916 to 1922.

28 Mar
Sunday
Saw Charles who was Stellenbosched[74] back on Friday. He seems to have been made a scapegoat. Longley lost the trenches at S[t]. Eloi. McFarlane failed to recover them. Charles recovered some. He & McF are removed. There is no lack of nerve or of competence alleged.

29 Mar
M
To Exeter for S.J. Com[mi]tee &c. Cold.

30 Mar
T
Work all morning. John lectured to the Devons pm.
Went back to London with him after, to meet Hugh who arrived unexpectedly yesterday.

31 Mar
W
About with Hugh who is remarkably well. Den[zil] came.

1 Apr
Th
Boys went to Petty France[75] for a hunt.

2 Apr
Good Fri
Chapel Royal am. Boys returned.

3 Apr
S
Hugh hunted with Cottesmore.[76]
About with Den[zil] am. Wet.

4 Apr
Sunday
We all went to early service at Marlboro[ugh] House chapel. Lunch with Aunt Blanche. Den[zil] went back.

5 Apr
M
Saw Hugh off by 8.30 from Victoria.[77] P left by the 1.30. Had lunch with Sue & Mary. Dined with Bentinck.[78]

6 Apr
T
Raw & Cold. CMC work pm.

7 Apr
W
CFO & Economic. By the 3.30 to Exeter[,]
picked up P[,] then to Castle Hill about 9.30. Car refractory.

8 Apr
Th
Blustering wind. Walk pm.

9 Apr
F
Walk with Wallace am. Bella Seeks came.

10 Apr
S
To Dulverton for Hunt finances.
The Strongs came. Warmer[.]

---

[74] This refers to the town of Stellenbosch in South Africa; the expression 'Stellenbosched' was used to describe when English officers were reprimanded and sent to Stellenbosch.

[75] This is presumably Petty France in Gloucestershire.

[76] This refers to the Cottesmore Hunt.

[77] This refers to London Victoria railway station.

[78] Henry Aldenburg Bentinck (1852–1938). He was lord of the manor at Bovey Tracey and a DL and JP of Devon. In 1918, Bentinck was appointed as the High Sheriff of Devon.

11 Apr Sunday	Church twice. Walk pm. Fine but chilly.
12 Apr M	Rode with S[myth] R[ichards] am. Strongs went.
13 Apr T Castle Hill	To Exeter. Left at 7.30 & got back at 6.50. 1[.]
14 Apr W	Walk with P am & pm. Warmer.
15 Apr Th	Nice day. Rode to Middlecot[79] am & walked with Wallace pm[.]
16 Apr F	To Exeter left 7.25 back 6.50. Warmer.
17 Apr S	W. Prout drove S[myth] R[ichards] & me in our car to Exmoor. Rode to Malsmead, Tippacott & Shilston.[80] Motored back from Scob Hill gate. Fine & bright, but a bite in the air.
18 Apr Sunday	Church twice. Walked with S[myth] R[ichards] to High Down &c pm.
19 Apr M	To Weare Gifford, I went to all the farms, but not to the cottages at Allspill[81] [sic], on East of the church. Fine.
20 Apr T London	Nice wet morning[.] [B]y the 9 to Com[mi]^tee at Econ. H[ouse] of Lords after.
21 Apr W	CFO & Econ. Also CMC & War Office as to 3rd Yeomanry sq[uadron].
22 Apr Th	CMC Com[mi]^tee. Lunched with Susan & Mary.
23 Apr F	Econ & C.F.O. To War Office about doctors. only 200 now in ~~admissions~~ hospital for enteric in ~~the whole war so far~~ admissions. 20 in last fortnight. Casualties (? to England only [sic]) 58 000 sick 46 000 wounded. [N]early all the former go back & 60% of the latter.
24 Apr S	By the 11 to Salisbury. Lunch & talk with Gen[eral]. Campbell[.] [T]here about 3rd Line Yeo[manry]. [T]hen to Castle Hill arriving 9.45. A little rain.
25 Apr Sunday	Fine. Church twice. Walk with S[myth] R[ichards] to beyond White hill pm.

---

[79] This is presumably Middlecott Hill.
[80] This is presumably Shilstone cottage.
[81] This refers to Hallspill.

26 Apr   Rode with S[myth] R[ichards] am.
M   P.M. went [to] Exmouth, to Clinton [sic] & the 2/RNDH[.]

27 Apr   Work in Exeter till 4.30[.]
T   [T]hen to C. Hill.
            Fine, but still N[orth] E[ast] wind.

28 Apr   To Challacombe with S[myth] R[ichards] & rode to most of the farms &
W   cottages. Quite hot out of the wind.

29 Apr   To Exeter by the 8.36 & back by the 5.30. Went over the new Hospital &
Th   saw all the men in No 1. Men cheerful than they were before Xmas.
            Warmer. W[est]. wind. The King told P yesterday that we had 2,015,000
            troops under arms.

30 Apr   Small Holdings & Recruiting at Barnstaple. Den[zil] came back.
F

1 May   At Taunton most of the day for Hunt & Horse Show Com[mit]^tee.
S   P came back.

2 May   Church twice. Warmer.
Sunday

3 May   To Exmoor with S[myth] R[ichards] & rode to Malsmead. Some rain in
M   ev[ening].

4 May   To Exeter for the day[.]
T

5 May   To London by the 9. Economic. H[ouse] of Lords after. It seems quite
W   possible that we may have to take to poisonous gas also. Marjoribanks.[82][,]
            partner at Coutts[83][,] told me that Italy agreed last week to join the Allies.
            Quite hot.

6 May   A lot of CMC business[.]
Th

7 May   Com[mi]^tee at Econ. [T]hen CFO[.]
F   [B]ack to Castle Hill by the 4.15. [T]he Bentincks there.

8 May   Motored to Knightshayes for luncheon. Jock came in ev[ening].
S

9 May   Church twice. Walk pm.
Sunday

10 May   Our guests left. Rode the new horse with S[myth]. R[ichards] pm. [T]o
M   Bideford pm.

[82] Sir George John Marjoribanks (1856–1931). He was a partner and later Chairman of the Board of Directors of Coutts & Co., Bank. Marjoribanks was also a member of the Board of Directors of the National Provincial and Union Bank of England, Ltd.
[83] This refers to the bank Coutts & Co.

11 May   To Exeter with P.
T

12 May   Walked to Higher Beer am with P. [R]ode to Acland Barton pm.
W

13 May   Wet[.] Rode am to Whitsford[84] Bushton[85] & Leary Barton.
Th

14 May   To Exeter by the 8.36.
F

15 May   P & I went to Exmoor with S[myth] R[ichards] in his car. Rode about there.
S   [Q]uite cold though wind southerly.

16 May   Wet am. Church twice. Walked to Fullabrook. P's car came.
Sunday

17 May   Rode am.
M

18 May   Motored to Bideford pm for recruiting meeting. Lovely day.
T

19 May   To London. CFO. Econ. Exmoor Mining. All the talk about the Coalition
W   gov[ernment].[86] Michael says Winston [Churchill] is in a highly nervy
           state. He gave the Pall Mall their information yesterday. Apparently it is
           Kitchener's fault we are short of shell & have few high explosives ones.[87]
           He was told months ago what the French were doing but thought he knew
           better. Relations between A[squith] & Sir J[ohn] French are strained. Hot[.]

20 May   Dentist early. then Econ. CMC pm. Dined with the sisters.
Th   Sat next F[rancis]. Acland[88] at luncheon at the Travellers.[89] I gather that
           he at any rate does not think Kitchener at all a success even on the A.G.[90]

---

[84]   This could refer to Whitsford Farm.
[85]   This is presumably Bushton Wood.
[86]   This refers to the Asquith Coalition government which was later formed on 25 May 1915.
[87]   This refers to the shell crisis of 1915 that led to the creation of a Ministry of Munitions that was
led by David Lloyd George, who was the Minister of Munitions from May 1915 to July 1916.
[88]   Sir Francis Dyke Acland (1874–1939). He was the fourteenth Baron Acland of Columb Major
and the Liberal MP for Richmond from 1906 to January 1910. After this, he was the Liberal MP
for Camborne from 1910 to 1922 and the MP for Tiverton from 1922 to 1924. He was the Under-
Secretary of State for Foreign Affairs from 1911 to 1915 and he was the Financial Secretary to the
Treasury from February 1915 to May 1915. He was the Parliamentary Secretary to the Board of
Agriculture and Fisheries from 1915 to 1915. He was also a Deputy Lieutenant and a JP for Devon.
Acland returned to constituency politics in 1932 and was the Liberal MP for North Cornwall from
1932 to 1939.
[89]   This refers to the Travellers Club which was one of the clubs that the fourth Earl Fortescue
frequented while he stayed in London.
[90]   This was Sir Henry Crichton Sclater (1855–1923). He was a general in the British army and
served in the Second Boer War. He was the Director of Artillery at the War Office from 1903 to
1904 and Quarter-Master General in India from 1904 to 1908. He was the Adjutant-General to the
Forces and a Member of His Majesty's Army Council from 1914 to 1916. He was the General Officer
Commanding-in-Chief for Southern Command from 1916 to 1919.

side & his Q.M.G.[91] work has certainly left much to be desired.
F[rancis] A[cland] spoke of Balfour[92] & Haldane[93] as the two men to whom the country owed most.

21 May F	Com[mi]^{tee} at Econ. CFO. [T]hen to <u>Castle Hill</u> by the 1.30. [O]nly 20 minutes late. Polly Stucley came by it too.
22 May S	Quite hot. Rode pm with S[myth]. R[ichards].
23 May Sunday	Church twice.
24 May M	Took S[myth] R[ichards] to Exmoor. Rode to Honeymead Tomshill[94] Oare Malsmead Barton Wood & Hallslake & motored back by Challacombe (. [sic] Twitchen[95] on[.]
25 May T	To Exeter. Fine & hot.
26 May W	Rode with P pm.
[27 May] [Th]	[No entry]
28 May F	To Exeter. [B]right but chilly.
29 May S	To Exmoor with S[myth] R[ichards] & rode to Exford & thence ~~to~~ home by North Molton to meet Hancock about Hunt affairs. [B]right but chilly.
30 May <u>Sunday</u>	Church twice. Walked with S[myth] R[ichards] pm. P has a cold.
31 May M	Rode with S[myth] R[ichards] pm to Heddon Little Riverton, Illers Leary & Middlecot. [B]right but chilly.

[91] Sir John Steven Cowans (1862–1921). He was a general in the British army and the Director-General of the Territorial Forces from 1910 to 1912. He was the Quartermaster-General of the Forces at the War Office from 1912 to 1919 and a member of His Majesty's Army Council from 1914 to 1919.

[92] Arthur James Balfour (1848–1930). He was the first Earl of Balfour and the Conservative MP for Hertford from 1874 to 1885 and Manchester East from 1885 to 1906. He was an MP for the City of London from February 1906 to 1922. Balfour was leader of the Conservative party from 1902 to 1911 and Prime Minister from 1902 to 1905. He was the First Lord of the Admiralty from 1915 to 1916 and was the Secretary of State for the Foreign Office from 1916 to 1919.

[93] It is possible that the reason why Haldane was mentioned in this conversation was due to the fact that Haldane was dismissed from Asquith's Cabinet on 20 May 1915. Haldane's dismissal was one of the conditions insisted upon by the Conservatives in order to form a coalition with Asquith's Liberals which was formed on 25 May 1915. See Edward David, ed., *Inside Asquith's Cabinet: From the Diaries of CHARLES HOBHOUSE* (London: John Murray, 1977), p. 246.

[94] This refers to Tom's Hill.

[95] This refers to Twitchen.

1 June T	Exeter all day. Sue came.
2 June W	Rode[.]
3 June Th	Met Recruiting March at Chittlehampton & went on with them to Swimbridge & Land Key. Lots of food &c, but no men.
4 June F	Exeter all day. Den[zil] came & Sandie[.]
5 June S	Rode with Den[zil] pm. Hugh came very well.
6 June Sunday	Church am & we all stopped for 2nd Service. Den[zil] left in ev[ening].
7 June M	To Exmoor when had a nice ride with Hugh to Badgery, Tomshill & Orchard Combe.
8 June T	Went with Hugh as far as Exeter by 1 [,] & stayed there for Belgian work &c. Hot.
9 June W	To Barnstaple pm for Law Trust.
10 June Th	Rode with Sandy.
11 June F	In Exeter by 8.36. [S]topped at Eggesford to see the saw mills &c on way back. P & Sandy went.
12 June S	To Tiverton with Sue to open a range. [B]ack by Dulverton station when saw Hancock.
13 June Sunday	Church twice. Walk with S[myth] Richards pm.
14 June M	In Exeter all day.
15 June T	To London. Com[mi]tee at Econ. H[ouse] of Lords.
16 June W London	Economic. H[ouse] of Lords after. Meeting at B[oar]d of Trade. Gov[ernment] are keen to get food supply increased. Dined with Eva Quin.[96]

---

[96] Eva Constance Aline Wyndham-Quin (1885–1940). She was the Countess of Dunraven and Mount-Earl.

17 June Th	CMC p.m. BCWS a.m.
18 June F	Econ Com[mi]^{tee} & CFO.
19 June S	Back to C. Hill by the 10.30. Very hot there. Rode with G C S[myth] R[ichards].
20 June Sunday	Church twice. Walk pm.
21 June M	Motored to Exmoor & rode back via South Molton. A little rain.
22 June T	About the place.
23 June W	To Exeter by the 8.36. T.FA am then to Woodbury & see the Yeo[manry]. Cool & pleasant after rain.
24 June Th	County Council. Then to Ugbrooke to see Clifford.[97]
25 June F	Various jobs including Recruiting Com[mi]^{tee} till 4.30. Some heavy rain am.
26 June S	Rode with S[myth] Richards am & walked to Bremridge & Higher Beer with Wallace pm. Muggy with showers.
27 June Sunday	Church am. Rode to Exmoor pm to meet the Pole Carews[98] who arrived there 4.30. Foggy. Some rain.
28 June M	To London by the 9, joining P in Lowndes S[treet]. CFO & CMC.
29 June T	Den[zil] came up. CFO & Econ. Saw Bethune at W.O. Unless the Turkish opposition crumbles, we have a very tough job in the Dardanelles.[99] He said that Churchill had bought all the Turkish CO^s of forts the first time the fleet went there, but the Germans got wind of it, & replaced them all the day before.
30 June W	CFO & Econ. H[ouse] of Lords after.

---

[97] Lewis Henry Hugh Clifford (1851–1916). He was the ninth Baron Clifford of Chudleigh and a count of the Holy Roman Empire. He was a barrister and the ADC to both King Edward VII and King George V. He was the vice-Chairman of the Devon Territorial Force Association.

[98] Sir Reginald Pole-Carew (1849–1924). He was the ADC to Sir Frederick Roberts both during the Anglo-Afghan war from 1879 to 1880 and in South Africa in 1881. He was the Liberal Unionist MP for Bodmin from December 1910 to 1916. Pole-Carew was appointed the Inspector General of Territorials in 1914; Lady Beatrice Frances Elizabeth Pole-Carew (1876–1952).

[99] This refers to the Allied campaign at Gallipoli.

1 July Th	Com[mi]ᵗᵉᵉ at Econ. Lunch with Dartmouth. H[ouse] of Lords & CMC work after.
2 July F	To Exeter by the 11 & on to <u>Castle Hill</u> by the 5.30[.]
3 July S	Rode with S[myth] R[ichards]. Fine but close.
4 July <u>Sunday</u>	Church twice. Thunder all round but we had none.
5 July M	Motored S[myth] R[ichards] to Exmoor & rode about there. Lovely day.
6 July T	Exeter all day. Conference with Davis & I[an] Amory about Red x [Cross] finance.
7 July W	Showers. Gave away prizes at W[est] Buckland.
8 July Th	Fine following wet night.
9 July F	<u>To London</u> by the 9. CFO.
10 July S	CMC am & long talk about the situation. Hot. Dined with the Sandie F's _ & to a play after "the man who stayed at home"[100] [:] v[ery]. good.
11 July <u>Sunday</u>	Church am. Went to Windsor pm to see John[.]
12 July M	Nothing particular ⎫ ⎬ various jobs
13 July T	D[itto] ⎭ H[ouse] of Lords pm[.]
14 July W	Economic. H[ouse] of Lords after. Heavy rain pm.
15 July Th	One wedding day. Went to Intercession service at the Abbey[101] with P then to Economic for Com[mi]ᵗᵉᵉ & to <u>Castle Hill</u> afterwards by the 1.30.
16 July F	To Exeter by the 8.36. County Meeting to advocate thrift. Wet.

[100] This refers to 'The Man Who Stayed at Home', a play by J. E. Harold Terry and Lechmere Worrall.
[101] This refers to Westminster Abbey.

17 July S	About the place & to Small Holdings Meeting at S[outh] Molton.
18 July Sunday	Church twice[.] [B]eautiful day.
19 July M	Motored S[myth] R[ichards] to Exmoor. Thick fog then with rain till the afternoon. P returned.
20 July T	At Exeter all day. Wet am.
21 July W	Helped make hay pm & got very tired.
22 July Th	To S[outh] Molton am about Registration bill.[102] Wet till lunch then fine.
23 July F Castle Hill	To Barnstaple for Small Holdings Com[mi]^{tee}. Rode back & to Middlecot pm. Fine pm.
24 July S	To Exeter. Mostly to see Valletort about Farmers Batt[alion]. Wet am. [F]ine in ev[ening].
25 July Sunday	Showers am but fine pm. Church twice[.]
26 July M	Exeter. Rode home for Umberleigh.
27 July T	A really fine day[.]
28 July W	To London by the 9. Economic & H[ouse] of Lords after.
29 July Th	To War Office am about Officers for the Farmers Batt[alion] they want me to raise. No encouragement from Mil[itary] Sec[retary], who is down to bed rock. [T]o Salisbury by 3.30 to see Campbell thereon & then to Exeter.
30 July F	Work all day till 4.30 when went with P & Christine to Clovelly.
31 July S	Went to Mouth Mill pm.
1 Aug Sunday	Church am. A good many showers.

[102] This refers to the National Registration Bill of 1915 which introduced the creation of a register of eligible men for the purposes of voluntary recruitment. This registration scheme was otherwise known as the Derby Scheme.

2 Aug M	To Hartland pm. Walked back with Dag dale[.]
3 Aug T	To Exeter by the 10 & back to <u>Castle Hill</u> in ev[ening]. Ribblesdale[103] said at Clovelly that no one was stronger against compulsory service than Long[104] & Lansdowne.[105] Harding told me that from instructions given them by W.O. he thought it was coming in Sept[ember].
4 Aug W	Hounds at Cuzzicombe. Sydney laid up by a fall. Found in Lincombe & after a ring at the end of wh[ich]. they fresh found him went away as if for Willingford bridge but turned back to Sandyway & Long Wood. Up by Filedon Bentus taken to Yards & Higher Molland wood. Holewater & East Down Wood. Here there was another deer & there was little done for near an hour. When they stopped them off a young stag in the water under Lydcott. I had already started for home. I got back very tired though before 3. Lovely day. P came back.
5 Aug Th	Overcast. Walk with P am. Mr James & Rawlings came to luncheon. Mr Campbell pm.
6 Aug F	Rode pm. Showery.
7 Aug S	Rode am with S[myth] R[ichards]. Finer.
8 Aug <u>Sunday</u>	Church twice. [R]ode to Middlecot pm. Old Woolacott is supposed to be dying at last in his 98th ye[ar].
9 Aug M	Hounds at Scob Hill gate. Found 2 pony deer in Farley. [T]hen two big ones. [T]he best went down round Church combe. Nearly to Pig Hill Ford. [T]hen by Dry bridges[106] & wet ground to Badgery. [S]ecuring two fresh deer en route [sic]. Hit his line however out of deer park to Stowford bottom & down Chalk Water for ¾ mile. [U]p over Mill Hill & along the cleave past

[103] Thomas Lister (1854–1925). He was the fourth Baron Ribblesdale and a Lord-in-Waiting to Queen Victoria from 1880 to 1885. He was the Master of the Buckhounds from 1892 to 1895 and the Liberal Chief Whip in the House of Lords from 1895 to 1911.
[104] Walter Hume Long (1854–1924). He was the first Viscount Long and the Lord Lieutenant of Wiltshire from 1920 to 1924. He was a Conservative MP for North Wiltshire from 1880 to 1885 and the MP for Devizes from 1885 to 1892. He was then MP for the West Derby division of Liverpool from 1893 to 1900 and MP for South Bristol from 1900 to 1906, MP for South County Dublin from 1906 to 1910, MP for the Strand from January 1910 to 1918 and MP for St George's division of Westminster from 1918 to 1921. Long was the President of the Board of Agriculture from 1895 to 1900 and the Chief Secretary for Ireland from 1905 to 1906. He was President of the Local Government Board from 1900 to 1905 and from 1915 to 1916 and the Secretary of State for the Colonies from 1916 to 1918. Long was the Leader of the Irish Unionist Party (Irish Unionist Alliance) from 1905 to 1910.
[105] Henry Charles Keith Petty-Fitzmaurice (1845–1927). He was the fifth Marquess Lansdowne and the Lord Lieutenant for Wiltshire from 1896 to 1920. He served as the fifth Governor General of Canada from 1883 to 1888 and he was the Governor General of India from 1888 to 1893. He was the Secretary of State for War from 1895 to 1900 and the Secretary of State for Foreign Affairs from 1900 to 1905. Lansdowne was the leader of the Unionist Peers in the House of Lords from 1903 to 1916.
[106] This refers to Dry Bridge.

Black barrow & over Acmead to Alderman's Barrow; beyond this Ernest saw by the shot he was a young one, whose line we must have crossed on Mill Hill, so stopped there at the Porlock Road; about 1 ¾ from the find. Fine but close.
Got back to Simonsbath at 4.

10 Aug
T
To London. Econ Comm[it]^tee & CMC.

11 Aug
W
CFO & Econ & War Office.

12 Aug
Th
CFO. Hugh arrived.
[B]ack to Castle Hill by the 1.30.

13 Aug
F
To Exeter. Hugh came in ev[ening].

14 Aug
[S]
Castle Hill
Den[zil] came early & he &
Hugh hunted. I rode with S[myth] Richards.

15 Aug
Sunday
We all went to Clovelly for the day. Den[zil] back to Aldershot after dinner.
No rain but chilly.

16 Aug
M
Hounds at Nadrid X [Cross]. Found 4 stags in White hill. [A]ll young. [R]an the best by Bremridge to Brayford. Partly by hunting partly by holloa.[107] Down mostly on the E[ast] Bray to near Rockshead. Up again & by Beera Cross & Little Comfort to Bray Common. At the top of which we had two deer in front of us. Were not sure either was right & only had 4 couple to hunt withal. So gave it up about 3.30. Beautiful day.

17 Aug
T
Petty Sess[ions] am. Motored & walked pm with P & Hugh[.]

18 Aug
W
To London with Hugh. CFO & then walked with him & saw him off at 5.40.

19 Aug
Th
Econ & CMC.

20 Aug
F
Econ & CFO. To C[astle]. Hill in ev[ening].

21 Aug
S
Rode with S[myth] R[ichards] am. Mr Harper & Mrs Bampflyde to tea.

22 Aug
Sunday
Church twice.

---

[107] 'Holloa' refers to a very loud cry.

23 Aug M	P went to Windsor. Hounds at Larkbarrow. [K]illed a 3 legged deer from Deer Park. Only small stiff there. Went to Plantations & could do nothing for lack of scent.
24 Aug T	To Exeter for work & on to <u>Salisbury</u> in ev[ening]. Met Valletort there.
25 Aug W	Conference with Campbell about Farmers Batt[alion]'[.] [T]hen to <u>London</u>. Economic.
26 Aug Th	Econ Com[mit]ᵗᵉᵉ & CMC. <u>Home</u> after.
27 Aug F <u>C[astle]. Hill</u>	To Tavistock & see the 3ʳᵈ Line of 4ᵗʰ & 6ᵗʰ. Both badly below strength. Den[zil] came.
28 Aug S	Hounds at Yarde [Yard] Down. Found nothing but hinds &c in Molland Wood &c till past 2. Then went to Dean wood, & West wood. Found there. [U]p to Leworthy bridge & back again. Lain on about 4. Crossed to East Down & round Beera to the open. Down White ladders to Ricksy Ball¹⁰⁸ fence. [B]eside that to the back & up to drive & over 100 acres to Chains. Which was the last most of us saw, as we nearly all made a wrong last to Exhead & Cheriton ridge. Got back about 7.55 & Den[zil] left at 8.20 to go back.
29 Aug <u>Sunday</u>	Church twice. Walk pm. A little rain.
30 Aug M	Exeter all day.
31 Aug T	D[itto][.]
1 Sept W	Hounds at Two gates. Found in Woolhanger. ran to Hoar Oak Buscombe Manor Allot[ment]". Hawkcombe H[ea]ᵈ Shillets. Fresh found & to see above Porlock Weir. A good hunt, but they ran away from us between Benjamy & Manor Allot[ment]" & we ran hinds for an hour in Shillets. RNDH ordered to Mediterranean[.]
2 Sept Th	<u>To London</u> by the 1 after shooting two hours with Francis on Park.
3 Sept F	To Windsor early to see P & Stamfordsham [*sic*].¹⁰⁹ [T]hen CFO. [T]hen <u>Castle Hill</u> via Exeter.

---

¹⁰⁸ Both White Ladder and Ricksy Ball are locations on Exmoor.
¹⁰⁹ This refers to Lieutenant-Colonel Arthur John Bigge (1849–1931). He was the first Baron Stamfordham and an officer in the British army. He was the Aide-de-Cour to Major-General Sir Evelyn Wood in 1879 and the Private Secretary to Queen Victoria from 1895 to 1901. Stamfordham served as the Private Secretary to King George V from 1910 to 1931.

4 Sept S <u>Castle Hill</u>	Hounds at North Molton. Found in cover E[ast] of Berwell ran to West Molland low down. Back to Syndercombe & broke between Whitecott & Bickingcott. The tufters slipped us, but bracy stopped most of them in the combe E[ast] of Higher Willingford lane. Got so far more by riding than hunting 20 min[ute]s to the bad. Hunted it to new Hawkridge planting, Lords & by Westwater to the Barle (the two tufters ahead rejoined [*sic*] in Lords)[.] Went to holloa up the water & above Batsome,[110] ran round that side of Withypool Common & come to a stand still [*sic*] at between the head of Westwater Combe & Porchester Post. Tried Lords & all round in rain. [T]hen the new planting[.] Fresh found there & raced into him under Knaplock about 4.20 about 4 hours from the original find. A big stag with a moderate head BT2.[111] Got home. Meeting car at N[orth] Molton at 7.15. Beautiful day.
5 Sept Sunday	Church twice. Walked with G C S[myth] R[ichards] pm.
6 Sept M	Shot a little. [T]hen a receipt of wire from Hugh[.] [W]ent to <u>London</u> by the 3.40.
7 Sept T	<u>To Exeter</u> by the 10.30 to see as to Kings visit.
8 Sept W	Met the King at S[t] Davids at 11. He went to two Hospitals. [S]aw all the wounded & left at 1. [A]pparently pleased[.] [H]e was well received. Back to <u>Castle Hill</u> by the 4.30. Heard of Gren[ville] F[ortescue] being killed[112][.]
9 Sept Th <u>C. Hill</u>	I should have written before that the King had told Pussy on on [*sic*] about 3rd that we had 1,500,000 men fighting. Hugh told me on 6th that "Grandmother" had been knocked out by a direct hit, & that the American made shells had burst some of our guns. Motored to Challacombe with Wallace & went through the woods there. Lovely day. Den[zil] & P came back.
10 Sept F	Exeter all day. Very unsatisfactory meeting about Economy campaign.
11 Sept S	Shot with Den[zil] over Blackpool & got 11½ brace before lunch. Went to Townhouse & Hill & did not do so well. 17½ altogether. Sh[oul]d have been 20.
12 Sept <u>Sunday</u>	Went to early service all 3 together. Motored to Sheddon to see the Harfords & back to tea with Astons.

[110] This refers to Batsom.

[111] The stag hunting entries in these diaries contain the following B.T or B. B. T. These abbreviations refer to the appearance of the head of the stag when it was killed. The singular B stands for Brow and the abbreviation B. B. T. is for Brow, Bay or Trey. These are accompanied with a number classification that refers to the number of points on top. See John Fortescue, *Records of Stag-Hunting on Exmoor* (London: Chapman and Hall, 1887), p. 287.

[112] This short statement was added in pencil and refers to the death of Grenville Fortescue (1887–1915). He was a captain in the British army and the fourth Earl Fortescue's nephew. He died on 4 September 1915.

13 Sept M	Hounds at Larkbarrow. Found in Badgery Wood. Went out round facing Cloud & back by Withycombe ridge to North Forest. Laid on above Turners path & ran to Trouthill. Manor Allot[men]ts. Kittuck. Black Barrow, Colley Head, Lucott Common. Left handed as if for Bury castle there doubled back down Blackford Combe to the water. Up it out to Poole Plain, Langcombe, Bagley Sweet Tree & lost him among hinds. Fine & hot. Den[zil] & I did not see it well.
14 Sept T	Shot over Bradbury with Den[zil] from 8 – 10.30 in steady rain. Got 5 brace.[113] He left by the 1.
15 Sept W	Hounds at Cuzzicombe Post. Found in Lee Wood. [C]rossed Syndercombe to W[est] Molland valley. Laid on under the House & ran all up to White Post, Lyshwell on under Anstey Barrow to White Rocks & the Barle by Mountsey Castle. All up the valley to Batsome. [T]hen up through Upton brake to Bradley Pond when I left for home. Fog all day with drizzling rain. Hounds ran fast.
16 Sept Th	Shot over Leary p.m. Saw a good many birds, but they were wild & we only got 5 brace. Very stuffy.
17 Sept F	Exeter all day[.]
18 Sept S	P left for London. Exeter & on to Woodbury for Yeomanry Brigade Parade. Good show in lovely weather.
19 Sept Sunday	Fine. Walk pm with S[myth] R[ichards].
20 Sept M	H[oun]d[s] at Hawkcombe H[ea]d. Laid on deer who had crossed from Bury Castle near Colley Head. Ran to ~~Alderman Barro~~ Hurdle Down. When the three jumped up. Away to Acmead & Mill Hill Divided there. Ran one to Chalk water & up Stowford bottom to Deer Park. Fresh found near Water slide. [T]urned left above cottage to Trout hill Pinford Warren farm Reds Hill & top of Hoar Oak. [T]here leading hounds vanished & we never hit the line with the others. Went back to Deer Park & waited till 3.30 then home. Lovely day.
21 Sept T	To Clacton & saw the 1st Devon[s] on parade at St Osyth on arrival.
22 Sept W	Saw RNDH on parade at 8 & said goodbye. They entrain at 1 tonight. Then to London & went to Economic, BCWS & CMC. Benson gave a lamentable account of the dissensions between AG & QMG in W[ar] Office.
23 Sept Th	Com[mit]tee at Economic. To B[oar]d of Agri[culture] about our Small Holdings. [T]hen CMC & H[ouse] of Lords till 7.30.

---

[113] Brace is the description for a pair of pheasants killed in the hunt.

24 Sept   Com[mittee]' at Economic. Caught the 10.30 to Exeter.
F   Business till 4.30[,] then <u>Castle Hill.</u> P driving me up from S[outh]
    M[olton] R[oa]ᵈ

25 Sept   Hounds at Cloutsham. Found quickly in Aller Combe & had a very
S   uninteresting hunt by Codsend, Bincombe, Annicombe¹¹⁴ Ford & Burrow
    to Stovey Wood;¹¹⁵ fresh found there & killed behind Knowle.
    A fine stag & a lovely day.

26 Sept   Church twice[.]
<u>Sunday</u>

27 Sept   Shot with Buttle on Bradbury Conl [*sic*] & got 6 brace.
M   Mr Aston &c came to lunch. Cooler & rain pm.

28 Sept   To Exeter by the 10.26 & rode back from Umberleigh. Cold[.]
T

29 Sept   <u>To Exeter</u> by the 8.39 for T F &c[,]
W   & stayed the night there.
    Went to Hawkmoor with Buckingham pm.

30 Sept   County Council. Back by 4.30. Tired Luke came.
Th
<u>Castle Hill</u>.

1 Oct   Shot Blackpool to S[outh] Aller with 4 guns. 43 ph[easants] before lunch &
F   10 part[ridge]s. 10 more ph[easants] only & 3 more part[ridges]s after lunch.
    Fine & pleasant.

2 Oct   Hounds at Cloutsham.
S   Sport spoilt by fog. Got home at 7.

3 Oct   Church twice. Sacrament am. Motored to Ebberly pm.
Sunday
<u>C Hill</u>

4 Oct   Went out with Buttle & Dick on Sandy Park,¹¹⁶ Middlecott &c pm[.]
M   1.30 – 4.30 got 29 ph[easants] & 3 part[ridges].
    Very nice day. Heard of Ai gerton [*sic*] killed.

5 Oct   Exeter all day[.]
T

6 Oct   <u>To London</u>. CFO & Econ[.] CMC & H[ouse] of Lords after.
W

---

¹¹⁴ This could refer to Hanny Combe.
¹¹⁵ This could refer to Stowey Wood.
¹¹⁶ This refers to Sandypark farm.

7 Oct Th	Com[mit]ᵗᶜᵉ at Econ. Saw Gen[eral] Long[117] at War Office & went to Board of Agriculture. Dined with John.
8 Oct F	Saw Susan & Mary am. CFO. [T]hen to <u>Castle Hill</u> by the 4.15. Mrs Fuller there.
9 Oct S	Hounds at Hawkcombe Head. Found in Lillycombe 12.15. Ran the plantations with bad scent for over an hour. Then got him away by Deddycombe Hollowcombe & Withycombe to Deer Park & Manor Allotment. Touched Trout Hill, then backed it over Manor Allotm[en]ᵗ to Deer Park. Down the valley & killed just above the Flebs Cott[age]. at 2.15. [A] good stag & better sport than the beginning promised.
10 Oct <u>Sunday</u>	Church twice. Weather still very fine & pleasant[.]
11 Oct M	Rode with S[myth] R[ichards] am. Mrs Fuller left.
12 Oct T	Exeter all day.
13 Oct W	Exeter again. Home by Exe Valley[.]
14 Oct Th	Shot with Mr Francis & Buttle over Leary &c. [B]rought in 70 ph[easants] & 4 part[ridges]. [G]ood day. Dampish.
15 Oct F	Exeter all day.
16 Oct S	Rode with S[myth] Richards am. Walked with P pm.
17 Oct Sunday	Church twice. Walked with P to Clatworthy pm. Fine but alull [sic].
18 Oct M	Hounds at Poltimore Arms. Found at 12 in Lydcott wood. Went down & crossed below the farm to East Down. Laid on & went all up the valley & by Muxworthy combe to Duckypool & left handed over Acland allotm[ent]ᵗ. Saw stag there going over Goat Hill. Stopped leader & got hounds together. On over 100 acres to Chains. [R]ight handed to Hoar Oak. Along the E[xe] cleeve. [T]o Cheriton ridge. Crossed Farleigh water[118] below Clannon Ball & over Brendon Common to Langcombe & Badgery. Another stag there but got on ours up Woodcock Combe & by Old hay heath to Chalk water.

---

[117] Sidney Selden Long (1866–1941). He was a major-general in the British army and served in the Second Boer War from 1899 to 1902. He was Assistant Director of Supplies from 1909 to 1912 and the Director of Supplies and Quartering from 1913 to 1914. From 1914 to 1916, Long was the Director of Supplies and Transport at the War Office.

[118] This refers to Farley Water.

After a check up the water to Mill Hill Black Barrow Colley Water. Scent more & Blackford. Barked it from there to the combe above Nutscale. Fresh found & all down the water killing him at 2.10 half a mile below the brake. A good deer BBT 2 long points. A good hunt in delightful weather.

19 Oct
T
Plymouth

Shot with Francis & Buttle on Park & Brayley 9 – 11.30[.]
[G]ot 50 ph[easants]. [T]hen with P to Plymouth for a Red x [Cross] show. Stayed with L[or]d M[oun]t E[dgcumbe].
Admiral & Lady Egerton at dinner. She said that no one was surprised when the Hawke &c were torpedoed & it was Winston's order that they were to do sentry go at half speed.
The German submarines are still pushful. One at the Nab[119] & another in the Thaners [sic] now. The Admiral thought it quite possible for ships with loss to run the gauntlet in the Narrows.[120] The Destroyers are being very hard worked. Sometimes on duty 10 & even 17 nights on end[,] & every ship that comes in is escorted the last 340 m[iles].

20 Oct
W

To London by the 8.30.
CFO. Econ. War Office CMC & H[ouse] of Lords. The Zeppelin damage was considerable, though of no military importance. They hit Woolwich once at least tho[ugh] with little effect. Fine.

21 Oct
Th

Econ & CMC.
Then by 1.30 to Castle Hill. Chilly with drizzle.

22 Oct
[F]

Exeter all day[.]

23 Oct
S

Shot about West Buckland in a keen E[ast] wind. Got 40 ph[easants] but powder not over straight.

24 Oct
Sunday

Church twice. Fine but cold.

25 Oct
M

Shot about E[ast] & W[est] Buckland[.]
[G]ot about 30 ph[easants][.]

26 Oct
T

Exeter all day. Heard of Greig being killed 17th [October][.]

27 Oct
W

Recruiting meeting at South Molton.

28 Oct
Th

To London to meet Derby[121] on Recruiting matters.

---

[119] This could refer to Nab rocks on the Isle of Wight.

[120] This could refer to the Dover narrows.

[121] Edward George Villiers Stanley (1865–1948). He was the seventeenth Earl of Derby and the Lord Lieutenant of Lancashire from 1928 to 1948. He was the Conservative MP for West Houghton from 1892 to 1906 and the Postmaster-General from 1903 to 1905. Derby was the Director-General of Recruiting from 1915 to 1916 and Under-Secretary for War in 1916. He was then Secretary of State for War from 1916 to 1918 and from 1922 to 1924.

29 Oct F	CMC am. <u>Home</u> by the 1.30.
30 Oct S	Shot over the Bradbury's[.] [G]ot 46 wh[ich]. should have been 60.
31 Oct Sunday	Church am. To Exford after luncheon for memorial service to Greig. Many there. Very wet.
1 Nov M	Shot over Bushton & only got 26. Fine after wet night
2 Nov T	[A]t Exeter. Hunt Com[mit]ᵗᵉᵉ at Dulverton on way back.
3 Nov W	Shot over Clatworthy & S[outh] Aller from 11 – 1.30. [G]ot 28 & did pretty well. Beautiful day.
4 Nov Th <u>C. Hill</u>	~~Shot over Clatworthy am.~~ Meeting at S[outh]. Molton pm & am.
5 Nov F	Exeter all day.
6 Nov S	Shot from E[ast] Buckland to Middlecott & back. Got 41 ph[easants][.]
7 Nov Sunday	Church twice. Some rain in ev[ening]. [A]fter a fine week[.]
8 Nov M	To Exmoor with S[myth] Richards. Rode to Horsen Warren &c fine.
9 Nov T	Shot at Pixton. Weather till 1·30 very bad. Fine after. Shot moderately.
10 Nov W	Shot over Litchaton[122] &c pm.
11 Nov Th	To Exeter & Plymouth &c back <u>to Exeter for</u> the night. Did two recruiting meetings. Very wet.
12 Nov F	Ceremony of reception of German guns a.m. Meeting about War Service for women pm. Back <u>to Castle Hill</u>[.]
13 Nov S	To Exmoor & went round most of the woods with Wallace. 30 trees down in Cornham brake.

---

[122] This refers to Litchaton farm.

14 Nov Sunday	Church twice. Walk pm. Frosty & cold.
15 Nov M	Bright frosty morning which turned to cold rain pm. Rode to W[est] Buckland am.
16 Nov T	To London with P. Com[mit]ᵗᵉᵉ at Economic. BCWS. H[ouse] of Lords.
17 Nov W	A long morning at CMC. Economic. War Office afterwards.
18 Nov Th	Com[mit]ᵗᵉᵉ at Economic. Then by the 11 to Honiton for Recruiting. Thence to Tiverton & back to Exeter by 8.
19 Nov F	To Torquay & Newton [Abbot] for recruiting[.] [C]atching the 4.30 home.
20 Nov S	Left at 10.15 & went to Sᵒ[uth] Molton Torrington & Bideford for recruiting meetings. [B]ack at 6.45. Fine but cold.
21 Nov Sunday C. Hill	Church am. Walk with S[myth]. R[ichards] pm. Hugh came & S Levan.
22 Nov M	Shot Dark Lane Wood, past Lower Beer & Higher Beer with 4 guns & Buttle. This took us 10 – 1.30 after lunch did Smalldons bottom &c & a bit more of Lower Beer. Got 106 in the morning, but only made 130 of it. Fine but cold. Sandie came.
23 Nov T	Shot Cawsis Barton[123] before with 4 guns & Buttle. [T]hen Bray wood & Long Walk. Got 125. I shot well at times & at others missed very early chances.
24 Nov W	In Exeter all day[.]
25 Nov Th	Lecke came. Shot White hill &c & got near 140 ph[easants].
26 Nov F	Shot Lower Beer & Goulders[124] Moors & Tilery. Disappointing[,] only got 44[.]
27 Nov S	About the place.
28 Nov Sunday	Warmer. Walk pm with S[myth] R[ichards] & the 2 Australian Officers[.]

[123] This is Cawsey's Barton.
[124] This refers to Gould's Leary.

29 Nov M	Exeter. Sandie F, went.
30 Nov T	Shot Yollacombe,[125] Heddon Bottom, Spa wood &c with Francis Dick & Buttle. Got near 40 ph[easants]. [T]ho[ough] I shot poorly.
1 Dec W	To London. Econ & CMC.
2 Dec Th	Econ. [A] Red x [Cross] meeting. War Office[,] & back to Exeter by 3.30.
3 Dec F	T.F[.]a[.] C.C. Finance & to Tavistock for Recruiting. [B]ack at Castle Hill at 8.
4 Dec S	Very wet am. Rode with S[myth] R[ichards] to W[est] Buckland. M. Stucley came.
5 Dec Sunday	Church twice. Sacrament am. [M]ore rain.
6 Dec M	Fine. Shot Ashen Copse &c with Mr Francis. Shooting indifferent.
7 Dec T	Exeter all day. A good deal of rain both by day & night.
8 Dec W C. Hill	Very nice day. Rode to South Molton am[,] with Capt[ain] Cuthbert.
9 Dec Th	Went out with keepers over Litchaton &c. Very wet. [H]ome for luncheon[.]
10 Dec F	Exeter. Mostly fine.
11 Dec S	Rode to Riverton & Higher Beer am. Rain near all day.
12 Dec Sunday	A little snow. Fine. Church twice.
13 Dec M	Shot with Buttle & hit little.
14 Dec T	Shot White hill & High Bray in steady rain. Only got about 25. Shot pretty well.

[125] This refers to Yollacombe plantations.

15 Dec   Went to London for meeting of dissatisfied peers.
W   S[t]. Aldwyn in the chair. Present Peel[126] Midleton[127] Loreburn[128]
          Bedford Portsmouth Strachie[129] Donoughmore[130] Dysart[131] Sydenham[132]
          Barrymore[133] Foiley[134] [sic] St Davids[135] Parmo[o]r[136] Milner[137] Harries[138]

[126] Sir William Robert Wellesley Peel (1867–1925). He was the first Earl Peel and the Chancellor of the Duchy of Lancaster from 1921 to 1922. He was the Conservative MP for Manchester South from 1900 to 1906 and MP for Taunton from 1909 to 1912. Peel was a lieutenant-colonel of the Bedfordshire Yeomanry and served in the First World War from 1914 to 1915.

[127] William St John Fremantle Brodrick (1856–1942). He was the first Earl of Midleton and a Conservative MP for West Surrey from 1880 to 1885. He was then Conservative MP for Guildford from 1885 to 1906. He was Secretary of State for War from 1900 to 1903 and the Secretary of State for India from 1903 to 1905. Brodrick moved from the Conservatives to the Irish Unionist Alliance and he was the Leader of the Irish Unionist Alliance from 1910 to 1919.

[128] Robert Threshie Reid (1846–1923). He was the first Earl of Loreburn. He was the Liberal MP for Hereford from 1880 to 1885 and the MP for Dumfries from 1886 to 1905. He was appointed as Solicitor General in 1894 and Attorney General in October 1894. He was the Lord Chancellor from 1905 to 1912.

[129] Edward Strachey (1858–1936). He was the first Baron Strachie and the Liberal MP for South Somerset from 1892 to 1911. He was the Parliamentary Secretary for the Board of Agriculture from 1909 to 1911 and Paymaster General from 1912 to 1915.

[130] Richard Hely-Hutchinson (1875–1948). He was the sixth Earl of Donoughmore and the Private Secretary to the Governor of Hong Kong from 1898 to 1900. He was the Under-Secretary of State for War from 1903 to 1905 and the Chairman of Committees in the House of Lords from 1911 to 1931. Hutchinson was a prominent freemason and the Grand Master of the Grand Lodge of Ireland from 1913 to 1948.

[131] William Tollemache (1859–1935). He was the ninth Earl of Dysart and the Lord Lieutenant of Rutland from 1881 to 1906.

[132] George Sydenham Clarke (1848–1933). He was the first Baron Sydenham of Combe and the tenth Governor of Victoria from 1901 to 1903. He was the sixteenth Governor of Bombay from 1907 to 1913. Sydenham was the Chairman of the Central Appeal Tribunal from 1915 to 1916 and a member of the Air Board from 1916 to 1917.

[133] Arthur Hugh Smith-Barry (1843–1925). He was the first Baron Barrymore and he was the Liberal MP for County Cork from 1867 to 1874. He later moved from the Liberals to the Conservative Party and was the Conservative MP for Huntington from 1886 to 1900. He was the Vice President of the Irish Landowners Convention.

[134] This is presumably Fitzalan Charles John Foley (1852–1918). He was the sixth Baron Foley of Kidderminster and a major in the Sherwood Foresters. He was a DL of Surrey.

[135] John Wynford Philipps (1860–1938). He was the first Viscount St Davids and the Lord Lieutenant of Pembrokeshire from 1911 to 1932. He was the Liberal MP for Mid-Lanarkshire from 1888 to 1894 and the MP for Pembrokeshire from 1898 to 1908.

[136] Charles Alfred Cripps (1852–1941). He was the first Baron Parmoor and was Attorney-General to the Prince of Wales in 1895. He was the Conservative MP for Stroud from 1895 to 1900 and the MP for Stretford from 1901 to 1906. After this, he was the Conservative MP for Wycombe from 1910 to 1914. Cripps was the Vicar-General of Canterbury from 1902 to 1924. He moved from the Conservatives to the Labour Party. He was Lord President of the Council from January 1924 to November 1924 and from 1929 to 1931. He was the Leader of the House of Lords with Viscount Haldane from 1929 to 1931.

[137] Alfred Milner (1854–1925). He was the first Viscount Milner and he was the Governor of the Cape of Good Hope from 1897 to 1901. He was the Governor of the Transvaal and the Orange River Colony from 1901 to 1905 and the High Commissioner for South Africa from 1897 to 1905. He was Minister without Portfolio in Lloyd George's War Cabinet from December 1916 to April 1918. After this, he was the Secretary of State for War from April 1918 to January 1919.

[138] George Robert Canning Harris (1851–1932). He was the fourth Baron Harris and a former England cricket captain. He was the Under-Secretary of State for India from 1885 to 1886 and the Under-Secretary of State for War from 1886 to 1890. He was the Governor of Bombay from 1890 to 1895 and a Lord-in-Waiting to Queen Victoria from 1895 to 1900.

Meeth[139] Marlborough[140] Ancaster[141] Devonport[142] Halsbury[143] Lichfield[144] Weardale[145] B of Burleigh[146] & self.

Grey's eyes are very bad[,] he is broken down, & he has never taken long views. Kitchener who is unequal to his responsibilities tries to do everything himself & interferes with his subordinates.[147] Asquith[148] is always "waiting to see" & there is a general lack of decision & failure to grasp the situation. We have gone to Salonica[149] against the advice of our soldiers & against our own better judgement because the French were very insistent. Townshend[150] was ordered to advance on Baghdad with only 8000 men though he only went under protest.

[139] This could refer to Reginald Brabazon (1841–1929). He was the twelfth Earl of Meath and an Honorary Colonel of the 5th Battalion of the Royal Dublin Fusiliers. He was also an experienced diplomat and held appointments in Berlin and Paris. Meath founded the Lads' Drill Association and was also an alderman of London County Council.

[140] Charles Spencer-Churchill (1871–1934). He was the ninth Duke of Marlborough and the Lord Lieutenant of Oxfordshire from 1915 to 1934. He had served in the Second Boer War with the Yeomanry Cavalry and was ADC to Lieutenant-General Ian Hamilton. Spencer-Churchill was the Paymaster-General from 1899 to 1902 and the Under-Secretary of State for Colonies from 1903 to 1905. He was a Parliamentary Secretary to the Board of Agriculture and Fisheries from 1917 to 1918.

[141] Gilbert Heathcoate-Drummond-Willoughby (1867–1951). He was the second Earl of Ancaster and the Lord Lieutenant of Rutland from 1921 to 1951. He was the Conservative MP for Horncastle from 1894 to 1910. He was the Parliamentary Secretary to the Ministry of Agriculture from 1921 to 1923.

[142] Hudson Ewbanke Kearly (1856–1934). He was the first Viscount Devonport and a Liberal MP for Devonport from 1892 to January 1910. He was the Parliamentary Secretary to the Board of Trade from 1905 to 1909 and the Chairman of Port of London Authority from 1909 to 1925. In the Lloyd George War Cabinet, he was the Minister of Food Control, otherwise known as the Food Controller, from 1916 to 1917. Kearly was the Chairman of Royal Commission on Sugar Supplies from 1916 to 1917.

[143] Hardinge Stanley Giffard (1823–1921). He was the first Earl of Halsbury and the Solicitor-General for England and Wales from 1875 to 1880. He was the Conservative MP for Launceston from 1877 to 1885. Giffard served as the Lord Chancellor three times from 1885 to January 1886, August 1886 to 1892, and 1895 to 1905.

[144] Thomas Francis Anson (1856–1918). He was the third Earl of Lichfield. He was the director of the National Provincial Bank of England and the Bank of Australasia.

[145] Philip James Stanhope (1847–1923). He was the first Baron Weardale. He was the Liberal MP for Wednesbury from 1886 to 1892 and the MP for Burnley from 1893 to 1900. He was the MP for Harborough from 1904 to 1906. Stanhope was the President of the Inter-Parliamentary Union in 1906.

[146] Alexander Bruce (1849–1921). He was the sixth Lord Balfour of Burleigh and a Lord-in-Waiting to Queen Victoria from 1888 to 1889. He was the Parliamentary Secretary to the Board of Trade from 1889 to 1892 and the Secretary for Scotland from 1895 to 1903. He was the Chairman of the Committee on Commercial and Industrial Policy after the War from 1916 to 1917.

[147] It is interesting to note that this view of Kitchener was shared by David Lindsay, the twenty-seventh Earl of Crawford, in his diary entry for 11 October 1914. See John Vincent, ed., *The Crawford Papers: The Journals of David Lindsay Twenty-seventh Earl of Crawford and Tenth Earl of Balcarres 1871–1940 during the Years 1892 to 1940* (Manchester: Manchester University Press, 1984), pp. 343–344.

[148] Herbert Henry Asquith (1852–1928). He was the first Earl of Oxford and Asquith. He was the Liberal MP for East Fife from 1886 to 1918 and the MP for Paisley from 1920 to 1924. Asquith was the Chancellor of the Exchequer from 1905 to 1908. After the death of the Prime Minister, Henry Campbell-Bannerman, Asquith became Prime Minister and First Lord of the Treasury in 1908. He held the premiership from 1908 to his resignation in December 1916.

[149] This refers to the Macedonian front which was a military campaign by the Allied armies to assist Serbia against the Central Powers.

[150] Sir Charles Vere Ferrers Townshend (1861–1924). He was a major-general in the British Army and served in the Second Boer War and the First World War. Townshend led the defence of Kut al-Amara with British and Indian troops against the army of the Ottoman Empire from 1915 to 1916. The siege finished when Townsend surrendered to Ottoman forces in April 1916. Townshend was also the Independent Conservative MP for The Wrekin from 1920 to 1922.

Cromer[151] wrote from a sick bed advocating an address to the King. Milner was for throwing out the Parl[iamen]ᵗ act amendment bill[,] as contact with their constituencies would be very healthy for Ministers & MPˢ alike. Morley[152] wrote much dissatisfied with the want of sense in the conduct of the war. The difficulty was the impossibility of candid debate. Decided ultimately to do nothing but tell Lansdowne what we had been saying, as it was clear Gov[ernment]. would consent to limit the prolongation of Parl[iamen]ᵗ to six months at most.

No one spoke more strongly than Loreburn & Devonport, except perhaps Milner, who as usual was for the most drastic action.

Back to Exeter by the 5 50[.]

16 Dec Th	A short County Council. Then War Agric[ulture] Comm[it]ᵗᵉᵉ & home[.]
17 Dec F	Exeter again for recruiting work & Timber Co.
18 Dec S	Shot Cawsis Barton Temple & Long walk. Very nice day. [G]ot 37 ph[easants].
19 Dec Sunday	Fine but cold. Church twice.
20 Dec M	To Exmoor with S[myth] R[ichards]. Looked at site for Cottage near Black Pits.
21 Dec T	Exeter all day. Wet[.]
22 Dec W	Shot round Stoodleigh. Did pretty well am, but got next to nothing pm. Capt[ain]. Cuthbert left.
23 Dec Th	Showery. About with Wallace[.]
24 Dec F	Hugh arrived 2.45 a.m. Very well. Shot Park & Bremridge. Got 22 ph[easants] & 14 rab[bits] 1 w[ood]c[ock]. Showers after wet night.
25 Dec S Xmas day	Very wet night & some heavy showers p.m. Church am. Walked to Fullabrook pm. Heard of Georgie's death.
26 Dec Sunday	Fline & Polly came over for Church & luncheon. Fair[.]

---

[151] Evelyn Baring (1841–1917). He was the first Earl of Cromer and the Private Secretary to the Viceroy of India from 1872 to 1876. He was the first Controller-General in Egypt from 1878 to 1879 and the first Consul-General of Egypt from 1883 to 1907.

[152] Edmund Robert Parker (1877–1951). He was the fourth Earl of Morley and a Liberal Unionist peer in the House of Lords. He was a captain in the Royal 1st Devon Yeomanry Cavalry. He was President of the Plymouth Chamber of Commerce and a JP for Devon.

| 27 Dec M | Violent gale from W[est]. Motored with Hugh to Knightshayes for luncheon & on to Exeter for Lodge 39. |

28 Dec
T
C. Hill

Shot Higher & Lower Beer &c.
[G]ot 32 ph[easants] & 3 H[ares]. Hugh had to go back by 3.40. Fine & pleasant.

29 Dec
W

<u>To London</u> for Economic &c[.]

30 Dec
Th

CMC. Dined with the Bentincks. No particular news.

31 Dec
F

Very wet. Saw Bevans about investments. Com[mit]^tee
at Econ. C[.]F.O[.,] <u>& home</u> by 3.30.

1916

1 Jan
S
<u>Castle Hill</u>

Blowing hard though little rain with it.
Rode with S[myth] R[ichards] to E[ast] Buckland am; to Bradbury & Black
post pm. A good many scattered trees down, but no
serious damage f[r]om the gales.

2 Jan
<u>Sunday</u>

Wet. Church twice.

3 Jan
M

Exeter 10.30 – 4.30. Motor went wrong on our return & we did not get home till 8.30.

4 Jan
T

Shot with Dick & Buttle through Long Walk & on to Fullabrook[.]
[T]hen up the water to Bradbury.
Got 20 ph[easants] by 1. Rather good.

5 Jan
W

Shot till luncheon over the Allers & Clatworthy. Only got 7 ph[easants].
Very pleasant day.

6 Jan
Th

Rode around with S[myth]. R[ichards][.]

7 Jan
F

Shot about Heddon till lunch.
Got about 12. Fine after wet night[.]

8 Jan
S

To Weare Gifford with S[myth]. R[ichards] & inspected Smayes Moor[153] &
Weare wood. [T]hen on to Holoworthy [sic] to look at Saw Mill there. Fine.

9 Jan
<u>Sunday</u>

Church twice[.] [F]ine.

10 Jan
M

With Wallace am. [W]ork pm.

---

[153] This refers to Smaye's Moor Plantation.

11 Jan To Exeter by early train
T   & on to <u>London</u> by the 5.27[.]

12 Jan CFO. Econ & H[ouse] of Lords[.]
W

13 Jan Econ. CMC. H[ouse] of Lords. Lunched
Th   with Sandie. Dined with Sue. Cold.

14 Jan Econ. CFO & <u>back home</u>[.]
F

15 Jan Hounds at North Molton.
S   Went with them to Burwell where they found 2 male deer.
<u>C Hill</u> Home for luncheon[.]

16 Jan Church am. Fine[.]
[Sunday]

17 Jan With S[myth] R[ichards] to Exmoor & Challacombe. [D]rizzle all day.
M

18 Jan Rode pm to Middle Hill.
T   Miss Hamlyn[154] came.

19 Jan Shot Cawsis Barton past & about Bradbury. No scent, & we lost 3 birds[.]
W   [G]ot 8 & 10 rab[bits].

20 Jan Meeting at S[outh] Molton pm
Th   about getting women to work. Coldish[.]

21 Jan To Exeter with P. Milder.
F

22 Jan By the 11 <u>to Petty France</u>.[155] Fine[.]
S

23 Jan Church at Badminton[156] am. Walk with Sandie Kinglake pm.
<u>Sunday</u> Mrs Harford said that a man high in the intelligence dep[artment] had told
        her that Peace would be signed by Aug[ust]. Asquith told Mrs Graham
        Smith[157] who passed it on that all was going well & that there really was
        internal trouble in Germany.

---

[154] Mary Sylvia Calmady-Hamlyn, MBE (1881–1962). She was a travelling inspector for the Board
of Agriculture and Fisheries during the First World War. She was an important figure in Devon from
1914 to 1918 as she sat on the Devon Military Appeals Tribunal and the Devon Agricultural Wages
Board. From 1920 to 1940, Calmady-Hamlyn was a Governor of Seal Hayne Agricultural College.
[155] This is Petty France in Gloucestershire.
[156] This is Badminton in Gloucestershire.
[157] Lucy Katharine Graham-Smith (1860–1942). She was the sister of Margot Asquith, the Countess
of Oxford and Asquith.

24 Jan
M
To Shirehampton to see the Remount Depot.[158] Tiresome journey but interesting. [T]o London after[.]

25 Jan
T
Lowndes S
Went to W.O. pm & later to Memorial Service to Uncle John Leslie.[159] A funny show.

26 Jan
W
Economic. CMC & several other jobs[.]

27 Jan
Th
Com[mit]tee at Economic: BCWS. &c[.]

28 Jan
F
Went to C.O.S. Conference[160] am about settling discharged solders on land. [T]hen C.F.O. [T]o Raemakers[161] [sic] cartoons with P after. Well drawn & very striking.

29 Jan
S
Lunch at Apsley House.[162] Were shewn the plate after & Napoleon's & the great Duke's travelling dressing cases. The former as big as a footbath. The latter about 12 x 6 x 8. Fine & mild.

30 Jan
Sunday
P rather seedy & stayed at home. Went to Holy Trin[ity] am.

31 Jan
M
Comm[it]tee at CFO.

1 Feb
T
Patriotic Fund meeting at Local Gov[ernment] Board. Prince of Wales[163] read a good speech. [M]arred by his not emphasizing any of it. Crewe[164] said he really had not heard what damage had been done by the Zepp[elin]s last night. Mary Eg[erton]. came.

2 Feb
W
CMC[,] CFO & Silver Com[mit]tee. Ftine [sic] dined.

[158] The Remount Depot at Shirehampton was a horse remount depot.

[159] Sir John Leslie (1822–1916). He was the first Baron of Glaslough and a Conservative MP for County Monaghan from 1871 to 1880. He was previously a lieutenant in the 1st Life Guards.

[160] This conference took place at Denison House from 28 January 1916 to 29 January 1916. See 'The Winter Conference', Charity Organisation Review, New Series, Vol. 39, 230 (February 1916), pp. 62–93.

[161] This is presumably the exhibition of Louis Raemaekers (1869–1956) at the Fine Art Society on Bond Street. Raemaekers was a celebrated Dutch artist whose anti-German illustrations during the First World War were employed as Allied propaganda. He was an Honorary Member of the Royal Society of Miniature Painters in 1915.

[162] This refers to Apsley House in London.

[163] Edward VIII (1894–1972). He was the Prince of Wales during the First World War. Edward was king of the United Kingdom and the Dominions of the British Empire from January to December 1936. He abdicated the throne in 1936 and became the Duke of Windsor.

[164] Robert Offley Ashburton Crewe-Milnes (1858–1945). He was the first Marquess of Crewe and Lord-in-Waiting to the Queen in 1886. He was the Lord Lieutenant of Ireland from 1892 to 1895 and Secretary of State for the Colonies from 1908 to 1910. He was Lord President of the Council from 1905 to 1908 and 1915 to 1916. He was the Secretary of State for India from 1910 to 1915 and President of the Board of Education in 1916. Crewe served as Leader of the House of Lords from 1908 to 1916 and Chairman of London County Council from 1917 to 1918.

3 Feb
Th
> To Exeter by the 10.30. A good
> deal to do. Wet pm.

4 Feb
F
> Public Health Com[mit]ᵗᵉᵉ & struggle over
> the nursing scheme 12– 2. Got off to Castle Hill by the 4.30.

5 Feb
S
> Rode the mule with S[myth] Richards.
> A lovely day after slight frost.

6 Feb
Sunday
> Rain am. Fine after. Church
> twice. Walk pm to Spa Wood &c.

7 Feb
M
London
> To London via Barnstaple.
> Peacock & Lady Harewood[165] dined.
> Former said that Munitions people were giving over £130 for machine
> pens which the much abused W.O[.] had been buying for £100 & suggested
> corruption.

8 Feb
T
> Various jobs. Bright but cold.

9 Feb
W
> CMC. CFO. Economic.

10 Feb
Th
> Com[mit]ᵗᵉᵉ at Economic. Dined with Christine.

11 Feb
F
> Wet. Camden Brewery meeting.
> CFO. [D]ined with G[eorge]. Harlech.[166]

12 Feb
S
> Admiral Fanshawe[167] came to
> luncheon. Dined with Ryles.

13 Feb
Sunday
> Church am. Major Kendall
> & two NZ OTC men lunched[.]

14 Feb
M
> CFO.

15 Feb
T
> Hugh arrived for breakfast[.]
> [V]ery well. H[ouse] of Lords.

[165] Florence Katharine Bridgeman (1859–1943). She was Lady Harewood or the Countess of Harewood.

[166] George Ormsby-Gore (1855–1938). He was the third Baron Harlech and the Conservative MP for Oswestry from 1901 to 1904. He was the Lord Lieutenant for Leitrim from 1904 to 1922 and the Lord Lieutenant for Merionethshire from 1927 to 1938. He was the Constable of Harlech Castle from 1927 to 1938.

[167] Sir Arthur Dalrymple Fanshawe (1847–1936). He was an admiral in the Royal Navy and was appointed the Admiral of the Fleet in April 1910. He was ADC to Queen Victoria from 1895 to 1897 and Commander-in-Chief of the Australian Station from 1902 to 1905. He was the President of the Royal Naval College at Greenwich from 1906 to 1908 and the Commander-in-Chief at Portsmouth from 1908 to 1910.

16 Feb W	CFO. Dined with L[or]d Stanmore.[168] Gale from N[orth] W[est][.]
17 Feb Th	H[ouse] of Lords _ [sic] Fine but cool. Small dinner. Bevan said that Scotland & Liverpool had declined to sell their American securities to the Gov[ernment] & that the Gov[ernment] had not yet sought to purchase them in Ireland though the amount held there is very large.
18 Feb F	Wet. CFO. Den[zil] got to Royal Free Hospital about 9 pm.
19 Feb S	Den[zil] arrived after breakfast. Looking well & practically recovered not very soft.
20 Feb Sunday	P in bed. About with the boys most of the day.
21 Feb M	Walk with the boys am.
22 Feb T	Com[mit]tee at Econ. H[ouse] of Lords in ev[ening].
23 Feb W	Saw Hugh off by 9.15 train. CMC. [W]here it really seems settled the Gov[ernment] will take the show over. Economic & then to Exeter by the 3.30. Cold.
24 Feb Th	Snowy & cold. Much business.
25 Feb F	D[itto] D[itto] to Castle Hill in ev[ening.]
26 Feb S	Snowing hard. Felt very seedy & hardly went out[.] [B]y 3.40 to London[.] Train late & no cabs.
27 Feb Sunday	Influenza & temp of 102. Spent the week in bed.

[No entries from 27 Feb to 5 Mar]

5 Mar Sunday	Allowed down stairs [sic] for first time this afternoon. Never felt so tired as I did last Tuesday.
6 Mar M	Allowed to drive a bit with Lucy & enjoyed it much.

---

[168] George Hamilton-Gordon (1871–1957). He was the second Baron Stanmore and was Lord-in-Waiting to King George V from 1914 to 1922. He was appointed Deputy Speaker in the House of Lords in 1915 and was the Chief Whip for the Liberal Party in the House of Lords from 1923 to 1944.

7 Mar
T

Snowy. Did not go out.

8 Mar
W

Went to the Economic & to the
Travellers after. [R]ather tired.

9 Mar
Th

Saw Ryle[169] am about Exmoor Living. Tried to walk home from Victoria &
could not stick it. Den[zil] discharged from hospital & has six weeks leave[.]

10 Mar
F

Went to CFO & to the Travellers
after. [G]etting on [sic] [.]

11 Mar
S

Went to see Aunt Cam pm & to Brooks on 12th[.]

12 Mar
Sunday

Church am. Warmer.

[No entry for 13 Mar]

14 Mar
T

To Exeter by the 10.30. Went to S[oldiers] & S[ailors] Help meeting & to
T F office after. Tired by 6.

15 Mar
W

DPF & TF Quarterly am.
Interesting lecture by Professor Pollard[170] pm. Warmer.

16 Mar
Th

Avoided the County Council where many nice things were said of me. [T]o
Knightshayes pm.
Ian told me he had seen one Walcott, an American of Bonbrights[171] fine
[sic] who had been to Poland on relief work. [T]he Russians burned all
buildings & removed all stock but could not get the people away[,] who are
starving on a ration of 30 gramme[s] a head. [T]yphus & other diseases are
rife. [I]f they go into Germany & work they give them 50 gr[ammes]. The
feeding of the Belgians is the only thing that prevents their labour being
exploited by the Germans.
The bankers told him that Germany was beat. The generals that she would
not win the victory they had hoped. The populace however still believed in
complete success. The food riots 4 – 6 weeks ago were mostly imaginary.

17 Mar
F

Hunt Finance Meeting at the Palmerston at 9.45. [T]hen to
Exeter. Timber Co. Meeting at 2.30 & then to London.

---

[169] Rt Rev. Herbert Edward Ryle (1856–1925). He was the Dean of Westminster from 1911 to 1925.
Previously, Ryle was the Bishop of Exeter from 1901 to 1903 and the Bishop of Winchester from
1903 to 1911.

[170] This was a lecture on 'Britain's Navy' and it was delivered by Albert Frederick Pollard (1869–
1948). He was a British historian and a fellow of All Souls College at the University of Oxford
from 1908 to 1936. Pollard was Professor of Constitutional History at the University of London
from 1903 to 1931. He was one of the founders of the Historical Association in 1906. Pollard was a
founder of the Institute of Historical Research and he was a Chairman of the Institute from 1920 to
1939.

[171] Mr Bonbright was a tenant of the Heathcoat-Amory's Scottish Lodge, Glenfernate, in Perthshire.
See Roderick Heathcoat-Amory, Reminiscences (n.p: privately published, 1989), pp. 11–12.

18 Mar   Nothing particular.
S

19 Mar   Church a.m. Mild spring day.
Sunday

20 Mar   Lunched with Sue.
M

21 Mar   P left for CH. Wet[.]
T

22 Mar   Lynton Railway meeting.[172] CMC.
W   Econ. H[ouse] of Lords. Cold & Wet.

23 Mar   Com[mit]^tee at Econ. Meeting of
Th   L[or]^d L[ie]^u[tenants] at H[ouse] of Lords. [T]hen by 1.30 to <u>Castle Hill</u> to
            join P & Den[zil]. [C]old.

24 Mar   Some snow early. Not bad day
F   after, but cold N[orth] W[est] wind. Rode[.]

25 Mar   Snow in night. Rode[.]
S

26 Mar   Snow am, but cleared after 10.
Sunday   Church am. Cold but less wind.

27 Mar   Den[zil] & I motored with S[myth] R[ichards] to Poltimore Arms & rode on
M   to Simonsbath. Half Yards Down Hill is full of snow & all Emmetts
            plain,[173] though the worst of the fall was five weeks ago.
            The wind shifted pm from W[est] S[outh] W[est] to E[ast] & it began to
            snow again. Some sheep reported drowned.

28 Mar   A good deal of snow about
T   but it was melting fast. Motored
<u>C. Hill</u>   to Barnstaple with Den[zil] pm.

29 Mar   Rode to North Molton to meet
W   the Stag H[oun]^ds but they could not get there.

30 Mar   Den[zil] went to Exford by Simonsbath & had great difficulties the other
Th   side of that. [R]ode with him to beyond Poltimore Arms & back round
            Brayford.

31 Mar   Rode with Den[zil] am & walked
F   with Wallace pm. Spring like at last.

---

[172] The fourth Earl Fortescue was a director of the Lynton and Barnstaple Railway Company.
He was a director until 27 March 1918 when he resigned due to his appointment as a Member of
the Council of the Duchy of Cornwall. See TNA: RAIL 446/1, Lynton and Barnstaple Railway
Company, Proprietors' minutes, 1895–1923 and TNA: RAIL 446/2, Lynton and Barnstaple Railway
Company, Board of Director's minutes, 1895–1922.
[173] This is probably Exe Plain.

1 Apr S	Alice Seymour & Mrs Bampflyde came. Went to Exmoor with G C S[myth] R[ichards]. Bright & pleasant. Much snow still.
2 Apr Sunday	Church am & remained for HC. Walk pm. Bright & fine.
3 Apr M	Misty am but bright & fine pm. Rode to S[outh] Molton am. Den[zil] went to London.
4 Apr T	Rode pm to Blakewell &c.
5 Apr W	Walked to Woodhouse am. Motored to Poltimore Arms pm to bring Den[zil] back from hunting. Fine but chilly.
6 Apr Th	Den[zil] went to Bristol to hunt tomorrow with the Duke's.[174]
7 Apr F	Nothing particular. Fine but chilly.
8 Apr S	Den[zil] came back[.]
9 Apr Sunday	Church am. Walk pm. [T]he Baylys lunched.
10 Apr M	Stag H[oun]ds at North Molton. Found 11 stags big & small, if not more. Got one away from Longwood about 1230 & ran to Willingford & down the valley to Hawkridge where many fresh deer. Rode home by 6. Mr Rees & Mr James came.
11 Apr T C. Hill	Took Mr Rees to Exmoor. partly motor. There walked then tragen [sic]. He was pleased with the place luckily. Den[zil] left for Tidworth.
12 Apr 15 ---	Cold but fine. Mr Ralli & Susan here. Hugh arrived on 14th. I was at Exeter 12 & 13th. Gen[eral] Western returning with me. He left 15th.
16 Apr Sunday	Wet all day but milder. Walk with Hugh pm.
17 Apr M	To London. CFO & Com[mit]tee at Econ. Hugh dined with me & we went to the Empire.[175] [D]ull show. C M C.

[174] This refers to the Duke of Beaufort's Hunt, a fox hunting pack that frequently hunted in the countryside of Gloucestershire.
[175] This presumably refers to the The Empire variety theatre in Leicester Square in London.

18 Apr   Hugh left by 7 o [clock] train. I went by the 10.20 to Ebrington[176] & all
T   round the place there with Knowles. Notes filed in letter to him dated
            20th. Showery. Got back for dinner.

19 Apr   CMC am. [T]hen CFO & Econ & H[ouse] of Lords. Asquith[']s statement
W   wh[ich]. I heard first in the Commons was little cheered except below the
            gangway on his side. Lloyd George[177] is for a forward policy. Robertson[178]
            & the Army Council have it is said tendered their resignations. Kitchener
            did too, according to Fleetwood Wilson,[179] but withdrew it on learning he
            would lose his pay. Dined at Lady Northcote's[180]
            R Benson[181] there. Very critical of the Gov[ernmen]t's Finance, though
            it may not work badly if we come out on top. All are desponding about
            Townshend who has only 3000 left according to Seymour.[182]

20 Apr   Back to C. Hill. Den[zil] came in ev[ening].
Th

21 Apr   Good Friday. Church am.
F   Walk with Den[zil] to Riverton pm.

22 Apr   Stag H[oun]ds at North Molton.
S   Found directly in Leigh wood & crossed by Veraby to Redlands. Laid
            on opposite W[est] Molland & ran by Cuzzicombe Hill & White Post to
            Lyshell.[183]
            Molland moor gate & along the ride. Down over to Barham[184] & down the
            valley.
            I rode home from the Ridge by 4.20. Hounds went on to Bridgtown.[185]
            Nice day.

[176] This is Ebrington in Gloucestershire.
[177] David Lloyd George (1863–1945). He was the first Earl Lloyd-George of Dwyfor and the Liberal
MP for Caernarvon from 1890 to 1931. He was the President of the Board of Trade from 1905 to
1908 and was the Chancellor of the Exchequer from 1908 to 1915. Following the munitions crisis, he
was appointed the Minister of Munitions from 1915 to 1916. After Asquith resigned in December
1916, Lloyd George was Prime Minister and First Lord of the Treasury. He held the premiership
from December 1916 until 1922.
[178] Sir William Robert Robertson (1860–1933). He was the first Baron of Beaconsfield and a field
marshall in the British army. He was the Quartermaster-General of the British Expeditionary Force
in 1914 and the Chief of General Staff of the British Expeditionary Force in 1915. He was the
Chief of Imperial General Staff from 1915 to 1918 and the General Officer Commanding-in-Chief
of Eastern Command in 1918.
[179] Sir Guy Douglas Arthur Fleetwood Wilson (1851–1940). He was an experienced civil servant
in both Britain and India. He was a Finance Member of the Supreme Council of India from 1908
to 1913 and the Vice-President of the Legislative Council of India from 1911 to 1913. He was the
Commissioner of the Special Government Enquiry in Dublin in 1916 and a Director of the Imperial
Continental Gas Association.
[180] Alice Northcote (1853–1934). She was the Lady Northcote or Baroness Northcote.
[181] This is presumably Robert Henry Benson (1850–1929). He was a senior partner of the merchant
bank Robert Benson & Co., and a Trustee of the National Gallery.
[182] This is presumably Sir Seymour John Fortescue (1856–1942). He was a captain in the Royal Navy
and was a member of the Naval Intelligence Department from 1891 to 1893. He was Naval ADC
to the Commander-in-Chief in South Africa from 1899 to 1900 and Equerry-in-Waiting to King
Edward VII from 1893 to 1910. Fortescue also served as the Serjeant-at-Arms in the House of Lords
from 1910 to 1936.
[183] This is presumably Lyshwell.
[184] This is probably Barham Hill.
[185] This is probably Bridgetown.

| 23 Apr | Church twice & walked |
| Sunday | pm with S[myth] Richards. |

| 24 Apr | Rode to Bydown with |
| M | Den[zil] am. |

25 Apr To London by the 9 for the secret session, wh[ich]. was opened by a bill to
T   reverse the Cobham attainder.[186] [T]he House was full only a few vacant
        spots being visible even on the Gov[ernment] side, & there were quite 20
        peers in khaki.[187]
        Crewe's opening statement lasted over an hour. [H]e had got it all typed so
        delivered it with pleasant & unusual fluency.
        The number of men under arms & of recruits is much larger than I supposed,
        & a very respectable % of pop[ulation]. Russia has still large resources in
        men, but lacks equipment. Italy cannot use near all her men on a narrow
        front in difficult country & has lots of men to spare & abundant equipment.
        The Allies really do depend on us largely for supplies. The men of military
        age in Munitions is not so very large, but the proportion of Mercantile
        Marine[188] taken up is substantial. The losses are not negligible, but there is
        enough under construction[,] given labour to take their place. All the same
        the Germans are hitting us hard in this department.
        The men in the Navy are ~~small~~ few compared to the Army, but each needs 2
        if not three in navies dockyards & supply ships to keep him going.
        Asked by Middleton[189] [sic] whether the army council thought the proposals
        adequate Kitchener who spoke fluently without notes said that bar
        accidents they were.
        Derby approved the programme said that little time had been lost from
        the Compulsory Service point of view as Registration & Mil[itary] Service
        acts[190] had paved the way; he fully endorsed all Crewe had said of the way
        Henderson[191] & the Labour leaders had played up, & of the danger there
        would have been in rushing compulsion.

[186] This refers to when the Cobham attainder was removed and the abeyance was ended by an Act
of Parliament in September 1916. See 'Barony of Cobham', The Times, 9 September 1916, p. 3.
[187] Khaki was the description of the military uniform that was worn by the British army during the
First World War.
[188] This refers to the Merchant Navy.
[189] This presumably refers to Lord Midleton.
[190] The Military Service Act of 1916 replaced the voluntary system of recruitment with a system of
conscription.
[191] Arthur Henderson (1863–1935). He was the Labour MP for Barnard Castle from 1903 to 1918
and the MP for Widnes from 1919 to 1922. From January 1923 to December 1923, he was the Labour
MP for Newcastle upon Tyne. He was the Labour MP for Burnley from 1924 to 1931 and the MP
for Clay Cross from 1933 to 1935. Henderson was the leader of the Labour Party from 1908 to 1910,
from 1914 to 1917, and from 1931 to 1932. In the Asquith Coalition, Henderson was the advisor on
labour matters to the government. He was also the President of the Board of Education from 1915 to
1916 and the Paymaster-General in 1916. After Asquith's resignation and the formation of the Lloyd
George Coalition, Henderson was a member of the five-man war cabinet with his appointment as
the Minister without Portfolio from 1916 to 1917 and he advised the war cabinet on labour matters.
In August 1917, Henderson was forced to resign from the war cabinet. This was due to the fact
that Henderson and his Labour Party colleagues were unable to attend a proposed conference of
European socialist parties at Stockholm after the Cabinet had refused to issue passports for them.

Little beyond rumours about Ireland.[192] They are nervous about the E[ast] Coast. Lovat[193] told me that he & all other officers from there had to be brought back tonight.

Heard at 11pm that Micky Beach[194] had been killed in the fighting at Katia.

26 Apr W	Went to see Lucy[195] after breakfast. Poor thing Michael gets no better & her well beloved son is gone. Back <u>by 1.30 to C. Hill.</u>
27 Apr Th	Very pleasant but not so warm. To S[outh] Molton pm for War Agri[culture].
28 Apr F	To Exeter with P. Had very successful meeting about endowing the Palace with furniture. Warm.
29 Apr S <u>Castle Hill</u>	Rode am. Walk with Sue pm. Mary came. Warm. Heard of fall of Kut.[196]
30 Apr <u>Sunday</u>	Church. Walk with S[myth] R[ichards] pm.
1 May M	To Exeter. Riding back from Umberleigh. Showers[.]
2 May T	<u>To London.</u> CMC & H[ouse] of Lords.
3 May W	Walked with Sue Beach am. Econ. H[ouse] of Lords after.
4 May Th	With Susan Mary & John by 9.50 to Coln [St. Aldwyns] for S[t]. Aldwyn's funeral. Lucy very brave. Dined with Sue on return which was not till near 8. [R]ather tired.
5 May F	Com[mit]ᵗᵉᵉ at Econ. CFO. Saw Ryle about Exeter divren [sic][.] Left for <u>Castle Hill</u> by 3.30. Miss Leash & Addie there.

[192] This refers to the Easter Rising of 1916 which was an armed uprising that took place in Dublin on 24 April 1916 (Easter Monday) by Irish Republicans against British rule and who sought to establish an independent Irish republic. See Andrew Thorpe and Richard Toye, eds, *Parliament and Politics in the Age of Asquith and Lloyd George: The Diaries of Cecil Harmsworth, MP, 1909–1922* (Cambridge: Cambridge University Press, 2016), p. 216.

[193] Simon Joseph Fraser (1871–1933). He was the fourteenth Lord Lovat and the third Baron Lovat. He was chairman of the Inverness Territorial Force Association in 1908. Lovat was the Parliamentary Under-Secretary of State for Dominion Affairs from 1927 to 1928 and chairman of the Overseas Settlement Committee from 1928 to 1929. He was the forty-first MacShimidh, chief of the clan Fraser, from 1887 to 1933.

[194] Michael Hicks Beach (1877–1916). He was the Viscount Quenington and the Unionist MP for Tewkesbury from 1906 to 1916. He was the Assistant Private Secretary to the Chancellor of the Exchequer from 1901 to 1902 and the Assistant Private Secretary to the Chief Unionist Whip from 1904 to 1905. After the outbreak of war, he joined the 1st Royal Gloucestershire Hussars and he died as a result of his wounds at Katia in Egypt in April 1916.

[195] Lucy Catherine Fortescue (1851–1940). She was the Countess St Aldwyn or Viscountess St Aldwyn and daughter of the third Earl Fortescue.

[196] This refers to the end of the siege of Kut al-Amara.

6 May S	~~Did not do much~~ Hunt Com[mit]ᵗᵉᵉ at Taunton
7 May <u>Sunday</u>	Church am. Walk with S[myth] R[ichards] pm. Some rain.
8 May M	Rode with Addie to Stoodleigh am.
9 May T	Rode with Addie pm. Cold
10 May W	Rode with Dick to Bale-water & Simonsbath & back by Pray way. Titchcombe Moles Chamber & Brayford. Warmer.
11 May Th	Walked through White hill am with P & Wallace. To Barum[197] pm & walked most of the way back. Warmer.
12 May F	To Exeter by early train & rode back from Umberleigh. Den[zil] came & Miss Hamlyn.
13 May S	Rode with Den[zil] am. Jock came.
14 May <u>Sunday</u>	Church twice. Walk with S[myth] R[ichards] & Jock pm. Showery.
15 May M	Rode with S[myth] R[ichards] to West Buckland &c am.
16 May T	To Exeter ~~with P~~ via Barnstaple[.]
17 May W	<u>To London</u>. Economic. Warmer.
18 May Th	CMC back to <u>C[astle]. Hill[.]</u> Seymour Gore[198] came.
19 May F <u>Castle Hill</u>	To Exeter with P. Lovely day.
20 May S	Rode.

---

[197] This refers to Barnstaple which was historically referred to as Barum.
[198] Seymour Fitzroy Ormsby-Gore (1863–1950). He was the Conservative MP for Gainsborough from 1900 to 1906 and a senior partner in the stockbrokers, Gore & Co.

21 May Sunday	Church twice. Walked with Seymour pm. Hot.
22 May M	Seymour went. Rode with S[myth]. R[ichards]. pm. Cooler.
23 May T	Rode am. P at Exeter all day. Mrs Mildmay &c came.
24 May W	P & her party went to Saunton to botanic. I rode at home.
25 May Th	P &c went to Hartland. I motored to Simonsbath & rode round the Brendon Tenants. A nice day.
26 May F	Walked am. Motored pm to Molland station to find a wild lily. Found it close by to N[orth].
27 May S	To the Demonstration of women's work at Killerton. Fine day & successful expedition.
28 May Sunday	Church a.m. Walk with S[myth] R[ichards] pm[.]
29 May M	P went to London. Rode am & pm with S[myth]. R[ichards].
30 May T	To Exeter for S.J. Com[mit]^tee &c[,] & on to London by the 3.12.
31 May W	CMC & Economic. H[ouse]. of Lords after. Warm.
1 Jun Th	Den[zil] left to take up ADC work with Hoare in Kent. Com[mit]^tee at Econ. H[ouse] of Lords. Almost cold.
2 Jun F	Walk with P am. [T]hen CFO to Coln St Aldwyn by the 4.55 train.
3 Jun S	Rode with Sue Beach over all the Northern part of the Estate. Crops looking well.
4 Jun Sunday	Church am. Cold & showery. Walk after tea.
5 Jun M	Rode with the girls am. Heavyish [sic] rain at lunch time. Walked in ev[ening].

6 Jun T	Motored with the girls to Fittleton & Salisbury & back round Salisbury. Beautiful drive from the later to Marlboro[ugh]. A long day – 9.45–7.45 but did a good deal.
7 Jun W	<u>To London</u> by the 9.10 train. CMC & CFO. Walk with P pm.
8 Jun Th	Econ & CFO am. [B]y 3.25 to <u>Exeter[.]</u>Fine & warmer.
9 Jun F <u>C. Hill</u>	A long day. Finance Com[mit]^{tee}. Memorial Service. DPF. Timber Co & TF. [G]ot away by <u>5.30 to CH[.]</u>
10 Jun S	Rode. P came down.
11 Jun Sunday	Church twice & walked to Fullabrook pm.
12 Jun M	Rode am to West Buckland.
13 Jun T	A long day in Exeter[.]
14 Jun W	W Leeks & Lillo came to luncheon. Told us something of this sea fight.[199] Beatty[200] did not know he was going into action till 1½ h[ours] before. The midshipman behaved very well & the destroyers were most gallant. Hugh came.
15 Jun Th	Fine but not warm[.]
16 Jun F	Exeter.
17 Jun S	Miss Beaumont left & Den[zil] came. Weather v[ery] nice. Began hay.[201]
18 Jun <u>Sunday</u>	Church am. Walk with the boys pm. Fine & pleasant. S[myth]. Richards seedy.

[199] This refers to the Battle of Jutland which was a naval battle from 31 May to 1 June 1916 between the Royal Navy and the German Imperial Navy in the North Sea. See Lawrence Sondhaus, *The Great War at Sea: A Naval History of the First World War* (Cambridge: Cambridge University Press, 2014), pp. 213–227.

[200] David Beatty (1871–1936). He was the first Earl Beatty and an admiral in the Royal Navy. He was the Naval Secretary to the First Lord of the Admiralty in 1912 and served in the First World War. He commanded the Grand Fleet from 1916 to 1919 and was First Sea Lord from 1919 to 1927. Beatty was appointed Admiral of the Fleet in April 1919.

[201] This refers to haymaking.

19 Jun M	Boys left. Rode to Exmoor after which rather tired me.
20 Jun T	Petty Sess[ions]" Worked at hay pm. Heard about H & DB.
21 Jun W	To Exeter for TFA. Went to Ugbrooke to see Clifford. Better but seriously ill.
22 Jun Th	County Council. Long & Tedious. Got home by the 3.15.
23 Jun F C. Hill	Nothing particular[.] Den[zil] came.
24 Jun S	To Bideford to confer with Bartlett about Timber Co. ~~Den[zil] came.~~
25 Jun Sunday	Church am. Walk with Den[zil] pm.
26 Jun M	Den[zil] left. Rode. Showers. Barnstaple pm for Law Trust.
27 Jun T	Exeter. Showers.
28 Jun W	Went with P to Bideford to look at Mr Heavers things. Fine.
29 Jun Th	To London. Com[mit]tee at Econ. H[ouse] of Lords after. Discussion on Ireland where our only choice seems to be between rival perils. Wet in ev[ening].
30 Jun F	To the City to endorse dollar shares for Henry & Seymour. Saw Hyslop about Timber Co affairs. Econ. CFO. CMC & dined with the Allendale[s]. CMC are sending to EFC ⅙ of the ASC stores & their business at home & abroad is equal to the gross of all the home canteens put together.
1 Jul S	Back to Castle Hill by the 10.30. Rain am & no hay making. Good news of the beginning of the push.[202]
2 Jul Sunday	Church twice & made hay pm. We saved about 12 tons.
3 Jul M	Rode with S[myth] Richards. Showers pm.
4 Jul T	Rode am. Heavy rain pm.

[202] This presumably refers to the first day of the Battle of the Somme on 1 July 1916.

5 Jul
W

Rode. Astons came to luncheon.

6 Jul
Th

Showery.

7 Jul
F

To Exeter. Made hay in ev[ening].

8 Jul
S

Rode am. Made hay pm.

9 Jul
Sunday

Church twice. Helped Rowland with hay pm

10 Jul
M

Showery. Rode am.

11 Jul
T

Exeter with P. Mostly fine.

12 Jul
W
Castle Hill

Showery. Rode pm with S[myth] R[ichards]. ~~Walk with~~ P saw 5 stags in White hill.

13 Jul
Th

To London by the 9 with P. Com[mit]tee at Econ. CMC after.

14 July
F

CMC & CFO. P went to Chilton. Fine after wet night.

15 July
S

Went Windsor to see the timber work there. At the first mile a Coral man is giving 8^u a foot all round & is reselling Scots pine sleepers at 6/-. It takes 5 cut ft. in the round to produce a sleeper of 3 cut ft. & there is a lot of waste. 14'' diameter is the most economical tree to cut sleepers from. This man is under contract to make everything possible into sleepers. All goes to France, including the hit wood. The mill is mostly manned by boys who are earning 18/6- 25/-. [N]o special accidents among them. Working with 3 hands at a Tiverton bench they can turn out 200 sleepers in a 10 ½ hours day.

At the Canadian Mill near the Wheats Leaf all work was being done 10^{ft} off the ground. They were dealing there with 20 000 board feet equivalent to about 14 000 cut ft. per day.

Noticeable tools were lance head saws for felling which made the minimum of sawdust M M[.][203]

[A] Jacobs ladder for removing sawdust & a machine which gave straight edges to any board of any width or thickness. Adjusted in a minute by an expert with an accurate eye.

Nice day. Den[zil] came up.

---

[203] At this point Fortescue illustrates the blade pattern of the saw.

16 July Sunday London	Church am. Wet pm. Saw Nev[ille]. Lyttelton[204] who had met Robertson at dinner last night at Lady E[va] Quin's. He was very well pleased with our progress. Whine Q[uin].[205] asked him when the war would be over. He said he could not promise by Xmas.
17 July M	Beautiful day. [T]o <u>Castle Hill</u> by the 10.30. Rode a little with S[myth] R[ichards].
18 July T	To Exeter via Barnstaple. Fine[.]
19 July W	Fine. Rode to Barnstaple & on to <u>Clovelly</u>. Charles & Ethel there.
20 July Th	Quite Hot. Walked in West woods pm.
21 July F	<u>To Exeter</u> & stayed the night[.]
22 July S	To Cliffords funeral at Ugbrooke. Long & not impressive. [O]n to <u>Castle Hill</u> by the 1.17. Hot.

Notes
What the horrors of war are no one can imagine. They are not bounds & blood & fever & dysentery, and cold & heat & famine.

They are intoxication, drunken brutality[,] demoralisation & disorder on the part of the inferior; jealousness, meanness, indifference[,] selfish brutality on the part of the superior

23 July Sunday C. Hill	Church twice. Walked to Bremridge with S[myth] R[ichards] pm. Very hot.
24 July M London	<u>To London</u> by the 9. o [clock]. P decidedly better. Dined with Ryles. The archbishop said that an American friend of his of German origin, a Pacifist who wants to stop fighting was with him on 18th having come from Berlin via the Hague. The tone in Berlin is quite different to what it was. They are distinctly chastened, & have told the public nothing of our successes on the Somme. He ascertained however at the Hague that they would not hear of giving back Alsace a Lorraine [sic]. The extracts from German papers in ours do not truly represent the information they give their public. It is both fuller & more accurate.

[204] Rt Hon. Sir Neville Gerald Lyttelton (1845–1931). He was a general in the British army and served in the Second Boer War. He was the Chief of the General Staff and First Military Member of the Army Council from 1904 to 1908. He was the General Officer Commanding-in-Chief to the Forces in Ireland from 1908 to 1912. Lyttleton was the Governor of the Royal Hospital at Chelsea from 1912 to 1931.
[205] This is presumably Windham Henry Wyndham-Quin (1857–1952). He was the fifth Earl of Dunraven and Mount-Earl and the Conservative MP for South Glamorganshire from 1895 to 1906. He had previously commanded the Glamorgan Imperial Yeomanry and he was the High Sheriff of County Kilkenny in 1914.

24 July
M
London

Dined with the Ryles. The Archbishop there. He told me that an American friend, a bona fide [*sic*] pacificist who came to him last week from Berlin via the Hague said that the Germans were chastened now, & had not told their public the truth about the Somme fighting. They have no notion however of giving up Alsace a Lorraine [*sic*] yet.

25 July
T

House of Lords pm.

26 July
W

Economic & CFO. Com[mit]^tees.
Lunch with Allendales in ev[ening] to <u>Leeds</u>. Hot journey.

27 July
Th

Inspecting Economic property at Hillam with Kentish
& got t[o] <u>Lowndes St</u> home again for dinner.
Sir A[lfred] Keogh[206] told P at a hospital today that we were treating now 210 000 sick & wounded here & 47 000 in France & he had beds for 30 000 more. Very hot.

28 July
F
London

Economic & CFO. Den[zil] came up.
Again very hot.

29 July
S

Den[zil] went to Cambridge for Staff course. Went with P to See A[un]^t. Blanche at Wimbledon pm.

30 July
Sunday

Very hot. Church in ev[ening].

31 July
M

Went to Hursley[207] to see the TF Reserve Units,
& on by late train to <u>Exeter</u>. A long day, but interesting. Met Hardings at Winchester who told me that his brother & Robertson expected the end in October.
That he had enlisted 76 000 men at the Rifle Depot in the last two years including a man with a cork leg & a boy of 12.

1 Aug
T

Work till past 2. Caught the 3.17
& joining P at Dulverton[.] [G]ot to <u>Castle Hill</u> about 6.30. Train, very late.

2 Aug
W

Rode to Tossells Barton & <u>moved to Simonsbath</u>.

3 Aug
Th

Rode out pm. Leading sweetheart[.]
A very hot ride[.]

4 Aug
F
Exmoor

Rode to Picked Stones am[.]
[G]etting straight pm[.]

---

[206] Sir Alfred Henry Keogh (1857–1936). He was a former army medical officer and a lieutenant-general in the British army. He was the Director-General Army Medical Services from 1905 to 1910 and from 1914 to 1918.
[207] This refers to Hursley Park.

5 Aug   Hounds at Hawkcombe H[ea]ᵈ.
S   4 stags below the stables. 6 or 8 above, 20 in deer park. Up to 1.30 only
           found a hind & a m.d. [T]hen got on a one horned deer. No scent in cover
           & very hot. Left at 2 & rode home by Oare.

6 Aug   Church am. Tea party pm.
Sunday

7 Aug   Rode to Red Deer Warren &c with S[myth] R[ichards].
M

8 Aug   With P to S[outh] Molton R[oad] ? [sic] and Exeter. Cooler am.
T

9 Aug   Rode pm[.]
W

10 Aug   To London. Com[mit]ᵗᵉᵉ at Econ. Saw Benson after.
Th

11 Aug   Econ & CFO.
F   Back by 3.30 to Exmoor[.] Still hot.

12 Aug   Stag H[oun]ᵈ[s] at Two gates. Drew Badgworthy Wood blank. Found in Deer
S   Park & laid on at 1.15 on Hoccombe. Up the combe to near the wall, then
           crossed the forest to Black Pits, Little chains combe & by Pinkery Pond[208]
           to Challacombe common. Here they were stopped for 15 min[utes] to let
           Sydney & others who had gone right of hounds over the Chains come up.
           [O]n to Swincombe combe [sic], up beside the Plantation & through the
           enclosure to Withycombe.
           Fresh found near the boundary W[est] of house, & went back over
           Chapmans Barrows to Woodbarrow hangings. Up there. Left handed to
           Ruckham Combe. Fresh found a little below the wall. [O]n to Hoar Oak
           water & killed a little below the cottage at 3.15.
           A young deer who ran very weak for except from Withycombe to
           Woodbarrow he never was pressed.
           Cooler. Rain in ev[ening].

13 Aug   Church am. Took it easy.
Sunday
Exmoor

14 Aug   Rode with young Spearman to Horner &c pm.
M   Showery.

15 Aug   To Exeter by S[outh] Molton R[oa]ᵈ. A good deal of rain[.]
T

16 Aug   Hounds at Cloutsham.
W   Found in Horner Wood. He went up, crossed to Stoke & then by
           Cloutsham Enclosure to Sweet Tree & Dunkery. Laid on there.

208 This is otherwise known as Pinkworthy pond.

Up by Rowbarrow. Right handed by Snows path to Chetsford Water by Little Hill downward. Up over Lucot[t] Common & pointed for Wear water but Turned to the right to Hawkcombe H[ea]ᵈ & crossed the Shillets to the cover below White Stones. Left there at 2 making for Porlock. Wet before 8.30 & after 3. Rode Florence who carried me very pleasantly.

17 Aug Th	The Le Bas[209] came to luncheon. Rode to Exford after on Hunt business.
18 Aug F	Rode with Molland am to Badgworthy & Cheriton Ridge.
19 Aug S	Hounds at North Molton. Found in South Wood. Transferred pack from that deer to two lying on Barkham Heath. Ran round that, up & down South Wood. All up Long Wood & away by Sandyway to Cloggs Lish[w]ell & Hawkridge following the water all the way. Left hounds in Barle valley.[210] Very pretty. Fine.
20 Aug Sunday	Church am. Quite hot. Walk with Dick in ev[ening].
21 Aug M	Hounds at Hawkcombe H[ea]ᵈ. Hot & no scent. Left hounds at 4.30 running in Plantations having been round <u>Exmoor</u> by Worthy Combe Parks Peep out[211] Shillets & Wear Wood.
22 Aug T	To Exeter with P by the 9 from Dulverton.
23 Aug W	Steady rain.
24 Aug Th	Rode with Wallace to Pinkery. Wet[.]
25 Aug F	To Barnstaple for Small Holdings & Dulverton for Hunt Com[mit]ᵗᵉᵉ.
26 Aug S	Hounds at Larkbarrow. After an hours fruitless work in Deer Park, found low down in Buscombe. He crossed Trouthill to Pinford Crossing. Black Pits & Cheriton Ridge. When laid on. Down to the enclosures. Fresh found to Farleigh, Bridge bale,[212] Combe Park, Myrtleberry Cliff. Fresh found & killed soon after opposite Lynton Station. A fine stag BT4. Fine.
27 Aug Sunday	Went to luncheon with the Astons. Some showers.

[209] This refers to Mr. R. V. Le Bas who was a member of the Devon and Somerset Stag Hounds.
[210] This is a valley of the River Barle.
[211] This is referred to as Peep-out.
[212] This refers to the bridge over the River Bale.

28 Aug M	Hounds at Cuzzicombe. Found in Veraby. Crossed to West Molland. up under Cuzzicombe to White Post Lysh[w]ell. Slade. White rocks. [B]ack round to Hyneham[213] [sic] & New Invention. Up the valley. Fresh found below Three waters & killed a bit further down. Lovely day. P went to Windsor.
29 Aug T	To Exeter & stayed there the night.
30 Aug W	Fine after much rain in last 24 hours. [T]o Castle Hill[.]
31 Aug Th	To Taunton for Hunt meeting[.] [T]o Exmoor after. Fine.
1 Sept F	Rode with Molland am[.] [T]o C. Hill pm to meet Den[zil][.]
2 Sept S	Shot about Proutworthy[214] for about 3 hours am. [G]ot 5 brace. Did not see much. [T]o Exmoor in ev[ening].
3 Sept Sunday Exmoor	Church am. [T]o Exford pm to tea with Astons. Rain most of the day.
4 Sept M	Rode with Den[zil] nearly to Hele bridge on chance meeting the hounds. Fine till 4. [T]hen wet.
5 Sept T	Exeter[.]
6 Sept W	Shot over the Barton with Den[zil] am. Amusing morning though the bay was small. Drove to Cornham p.m.
7 Sept Th	To London. Com[mit]tee at Econ.
8 Sept F	C.M.C. Econ & CFO. [T]o Castle Hill[.]
9 Sept S	Hounds at North Molton. Found in Red land[215] after some very pretty hound work. Ran along, S[outh] side Molland Common. Then to Lish[w]ell & down to Slade bridge. [U]p to Anstey Barrows. Left by devious course to 5 ways,[216] Durham & the Danesbrook.[217] Along the side & in the water to Shircombe. Slade. All up to Tarr steps. [H]alf way to Ashway. [A]cross by Knaplock ball up to Well.

213 This possibly refers to Hinam.
214 This is probably Proutworthy Brake near Filleigh.
215 This refers to Redland Wood.
216 This refers to Five Cross Ways or Five Ways Cross.
217 This refers to the Dane's Brook River.

[B]roke out left handed by Westwater to Cloggs. All down nearly to Castle bridge crossed to the Barle & killed below three waters. A tough stray who ran over 3 hours from laying on this he had 3 & 2 on top. Did not get to Exmoor till 8.

10 Sept
Sunday

Church am. Walked to Gallon H⁰[use] pm & to take back a stray hound.

11 Sept
M

Hounds at Yarde Down.[218] Found in Wort wood 12.50. Laid on at Leworthy bridge half an hour later & never made anything of it.
Wet after 3.

12 Sept
T

To Exeter & on to Plymouth for a very ill attended meeting about the Bishop.

13 Sept
W

Back to Exmoor via Exeter.
Met Den[zil] & we shot for 2 hours on Bradbury & got 2 brace. Showers & fog.

14 Sept
Th

Bullock & Wreford of Devon Reg[iment] came to luncheon. Rode pm.

15 Sept
F
Exmoor

Hunted with the Harrier at Kitnor Heath. Did little.

16 Sept
S

Hounds at Aldermans Barrow.
Nothing on the forest. One young stag at Badgworthy. Went to Culbone Stables. [G]ot away at W[est] end about 1.45. Ran to County gate down over & Eastward. [B]ack again & by Old Barrow to the Cliffs under Desolate when they drove the Stag over. 4 hounds killed. Nice weather.

17 Sept
Sunday

Church am. Walked to Gallon H⁰[use] pm.

18 Sept
M

Hounds at Hawkridge. Found a young deer in Webbers Plant[ation]"[219] who went up Danesbrook. Laid on above Slade bridge. Ran nearly to White Post where encountered two better stags. [P]ut the pack on in view & raced over Humber Ball[220] to Hawkridge Plan'[ation] & West water & the Barle. After some time lost on the water ran down to Castle Bridge & beyond, up round Durham. Down to Dulverton almost & killed ½ mile above. A good stag. Fine day after heavy rain.

19 Sept
T

Walked a good many miles over Duredon & Cornham with Den[zil] for 1 Landrail[221] & 4 rab[bits]. Fine[.]

20 Sept
W

To London by the 9. CFO. Econ.[,]
& saw Mr Davis about Minerals.

[218] This refers to Yarde Down that is located below the Poltimore Arms.
[219] This is now known as Luscombe plantation.
[220] This refers to Humber's Ball.
[221] This is another name for a corncrake bird.

21 Sept Th	Econ & CMC. Lunch with Sue. Took Daisy to the Scala.[222]

| 22 Sept
F | Econ & CFO. [A]lso Belgian Com[mit]^tee[.]
[T]o <u>Castle Hill</u> by the 3.31. |

| 23 Sept
S | Hounds at Two gates. Found at Woolhanger. Crossed Chapmans Barrow to Swincombe & went down the valley to Embercombe where they killed. I saw nothing. Den[zil] left for France in ev[ening]. Fine. |

| 24 Sept
Sunday
<u>Exmoor</u> | Church am. Walked with P
to Winstitchin[223] pm. |

| 25 Sept
M | S[myth] Richards out. Rode with him pm. |

| 26 Sept
T | Harriers at Honeymead.
Went out till lunch. Lovely day.
Walked to Lime combe in ev[ening]. |

| 27 Sept
W | With P <u>to Exeter</u>. Work there all day. P to Hestercombe[224] in ev[ening]. |

| 28 Sept
Th | County Council. Hepburn[225] seedy[,]
so I had to take the chair. Got it done by 2, but was Tired. Back to <u>Exmoor</u> by Dulverton & Filleigh[.] |

| 29 Sept
F | Wet morning. Many letters.
Rode to Challacombe pm.
<u>Twitch</u>en. Mr Sany asks for larder to be made back kitchen, & for front kitchen & stairs to be coloured.
<u>Ring of</u> Belles nil.
<u>Bick f</u>ont. Mr Dullyn. West wall takes wet.
<u>C</u>ottage near nil (unoccupied) my side)[.]
<u>Swincombe</u> E[ast]. [S]aw Mr ~~Huxtable~~ Ridd. [N]il.
<u>Swincombe</u> W[est]. [S]aw Miss Huxtable[,]
when will Trap house be done ?
<u>Barton ga</u>te. W[est]. [C]amp's door on smithy premises want repair. Some windows supposed shaky but not produced.
<u>Barton gate</u> E[ast]. [N]il.
<u>Black gate</u> Cott[age]. [N]il.
<u>Black gate.</u> [C]owards. Outs labs [*sic*] wanted to repair shippen & some plank to repair door.
<u>Home place</u> no one at home. |

[222] This refers to the Scala Club in London.
[223] This refers to Winstitchen.
[224] This refers to Hestercombe House and Gardens in Cheddon Fitzpaine.
[225] Sir Thomas Henry Hepburn (1840–1917). He was an alderman of Devon County Council and was appointed Chairman of the County Council in 1916. He was the JP for Devon.

30 Sept S	Hounds at Cloutsham. Found in Sweet Tree. Got away at 2 over Dunkery to Higher House. Fresh found & away through Codsend Moors to Hoar Moor Post. Chetsford Water. Nutscale. Old Wood. All down the valley. Fresh found above Horner Mill & killed at Selworthy about 3.15. Cold East Wind all the morning & visibility v[ery] bad. Sandie F & May came.
1 Oct Sunday <u>Exmoor</u>	Church am. Sandie Kinglake & B Harford came to lunch. Walk pm.
2 Oct M	To Barnstaple seeing S[myth] R[ichards] on the way for Lynton Railway meeting. Wet & foggy.
3 Oct T	Harriers at Driver. Had a Cheery moving between the Barle & Chains farm.
4 Oct W	<u>To London</u>. CFO Econ & CMC. Dined with Sue.
5 Oct Th	Econ. Exmoor Mines[226] & CFO.
6 Oct F	CFO & Econ. Caught the 1.30 to <u>Exmoor[.]</u> D. Beaumont coming too.
7 Oct S	Hounds at Poltimore Arms. Found in Molland Wood crossed to W[est] Bray. Laid on there. [R]an to Bremridge. White Hill Fullabrook Longwalk. Huds[c]ott at Warkleigh Parsonage & down to the Taw between Umberleigh & Portsmouth Arms where the water was so high that the deer had the best of it. Left them there at 4.15 & rode back with DB to C.H. Left horses there & motored back to Exmoor by 7.30. Fine but windy. A big stag.
8 Oct <u>Sunday</u>	Church am. Walk with DB pm.
9 Oct M	To Cornham with Molland am. Walk with DB pm. Wet am.
10 Oct T	Harriers at Cow Castle. Ran about Horsen Hill & Spooners Allot^m[ent]. Some rain am. Fine pm.
11 Oct W Exmoor	DB went. Rode round Challacombe. <u>Withycombe.</u> No complaints. <u>Whitefield.</u> 3 sons at home. N[orth] Barton. [P]romised board for tallet 10 x 14. He to put it in. He wants 2 gates 8 shutter[s] 2 top bars.

[226] In 1916, Earl Fortescue purchased the Exmoor Mining Syndicate, a company which up until 1916 had focused its operations in Somerset. Fortescue intended to expand the company's operations into north Devon's iron fields on Exmoor. Yet, despite Fortescue's best efforts, the ambitious venture was ultimately not successful. See DHC: 1262M/o/E/5/16, Correspondence with J. M. Lester, Bennerley Furnances, Exmoor Mining Syndicate and others with catalogue of sale 1913, concerning Exmoor Minerals, 2 files: 1917 (45) 1917–1919 (92), 1917–1919.

Barton Town Roof of trap house has slipped down a bit. Shuting of dwelling H°[use] & barn wants fixing.
He asks for some glars slate in roof over Shippen in lower yard.
Cottages there & at Chall[acombe] Mill nothing. [N]or at the Mill.
Buscombe. [F]rame wanted for Pip House door 6' x 3' outside measurement. The ~~damn~~ Timbers being about 2½. Sheet of iron on cart shed ~~i sheets~~ fixing.
Showlsbury nil.
Horte foot nil. Tar next year both S[outh] & E[ast] End.
Yelland Cot[tage]'. One vacant the other all right.
Still windy & overcast.

12 Oct Th	Hounds at Hawkcombe H[ea]ᵈ. Following a gale from S[outh] W[est] but the rain held off between 10.30 & 3.30. Found in Parks. Changed on to a one all deer & did no good. Found again in Shillets. Went down the valley & I left the[m] at 3.45. An unpleasant ride home.
13 Oct F	To Exeter. [R]eturning in ev[ening] to Castle Hill[,] to which we moved [sic].
14 Oct S	Various jobs am. Shot on Tower & Heddon pm & did pretty well. May F came.
15 Oct Sunday	Church am. Walked with P to Fullabrook pm.
16 Oct M	To Molton am & round the stock pm. Showery[.]
17 Oct T	To Exeter. Wet most of day.
18 Oct W	To London. CFO & Econ. Dined with John[.]
19 Oct Th London	CFO & CMC. Saw Gerard Wallop[227] who told me a Councillor of the Roumanian[228] legation told him they were pledged to join us as long ago as Oct 14 (Query to neutrality then & to cooperation in May 15)[.] [T]hat being unable to fight for more than C[irca]. 8 months they had chosen their time to begin in consultation with the Allies. [T]hat they had gone into Transylvania lest Russia – unless they were there first should keep it at the peace. [T]hat Russia was late[,] they were outgunned, & short of medical staff &c. [B]ut things would be better in a fortnight.

---

[227] This is presumably Gerard Vernon Wallop (1898–1984). He was the ninth Earl of Portsmouth and the Conservative MP for Basingstoke from 1929 to 1934. He was the Vice-Chairman of the Hampshire War Agricultural Committee from 1939 to 1947.
[228] Romanian.

20 Oct
F
CFO & Econ.
Back by 4.15 to <u>Castle Hill</u>[.] Fine but chilly.

21 Oct
S
Shot on Tower & Heddon &c 11–3. Found little. [S]hot ill.
Jock came. Fine but cold E[ast] wind.

22 Oct
<u>Sunday</u>
Church am. Walked to Fullabrook pm.

23 Oct
M
About the ~~place~~ house & rode round the stock pm. Wet.

24 Oct
T
Exeter, from which Motty Seeks came back with me.

25 Oct
W
Shot with Seeke about West Buckland. Got 37 ph[easants] and 9 part[ridge]s.
Fine.

26 Oct
Th
Shot with Seeke on Bradbury 10 – 2.30[.] [G]ot 25 ph[easants] 4 part[ridges]
3 rab[bits].
To S[outh]. Molton after for a War Agric[ultural] Com[mit]ᵗᵉᵉ.

27 Oct
F
To Exeter. Trains very late both ways. Wild & stormy[.]

28 Oct
S
Wild night & morning but fine after 12. To Taunton with P for Crawfords[229]
meeting. He spoke well though he told us little that was new.

29 Oct
<u>Sunday</u>
Wet & windy. Did not go to Church p.m.

30 Oct
M
Windy, but no rain after midday. Went to Exmoor with S[myth]. R[ichards].
& back by Challacombe Mill.

31 Oct
T
To Exeter. Tiring day.

1 Nov
W
<u>To London</u>[,] CMC & saw Davis about the mines.

2 Nov
Th
With Daisy to the Star & Garter[230] at Richmond am. Econ at 3. CMC 4–6 &
took Daisy to a play in ev[ening]. Fine.

3 Nov
F
CMC 10–12.
[T]hen Econ.[,] & to <u>Castle Hill</u> by the 1.30.

4 Nov
S
Shot with Ganett over Crossbury &c. [G]ot 28 ph[easants] & 2 part[ridge]s.
Shooting moderate. Nice weather.

---

[229] David Alexander Edward Lindsay (1871–1940). He was the twenty-seventh Earl of Crawford and
the tenth Earl of Balcarres. He was the Conservative MP for Chorley from 1895 to 1913 and Junior
Lord of the Treasury from 1903 to 1905. Crawford served as the President of Board of Agriculture
from July 1916 to December 1916 and Lord Privy Seal from 1916 to 1918.
[230] This refers to the Star and Garter hotel in Richmond.

5 Nov Sunday	Church am. Sacrament. Wet pm & stayed home.
6 Nov M	Walked with P to Bremridge am & Rode to W[est]. Buckland farms pm.
7 Nov T	Exeter. Showers. [R]ivers v[ery]. high.
8 Nov W	Exeter for Dio[cesan]. Conference. Shot from Clapworthy bridge to Fullabrook on way home. Got little. Heavy showers[.]
9 Nov Th	Windy with showers all the morning. Shot with Ganett over Leary & Gubbs[231][.] [G]ot 19 ph[easants] & 6 part[ridge]s[.] [W]ould have been 30 ph[easants] on a better day.
10 Nov F	To London. CFO[,] Econ & the CMC from 4.15 till near 7.
11 Nov S	Back by 10.30 to Castle Hill[.]
12 Nov Sunday	Church twice. Walked to Bremridge with P p.m. Nice day.
13 Nov M	Lovely bright sun after white frost. Rode with S[myth] R[ichards] am & pm[.]
14 Nov T	Walk with Wallace am.
15 Nov W	P went to London. Shot over the Stoodleighs with Mr Pike & his son. Hard walk & poor results. The son said that our push on 1st July was really a disappointment.[232] The 10th Corps failed at Theipval [sic] [Thiepval] & all the staff were sent home &c.
16 Nov Th	Shot with Francis at Bradbury & Fullabrook. Sporting day. 13 ph[easants] 9 part[ridges] 7 rab[bits] 1 snipe. Cold E[ast] Wind.
17 Nov F	Exeter. Windy with heavy rain pm.
18 Nov S	Exeter & accompanied Colonel Golightly in inspection of Test mobilisation of volunteers for guarding the railways &c. Trains out of Exeter very late & did not get home till 8.

[231] This refers to Gubbs Farm near West Buckland.

[232] This refers to the causalities inflicted on the first day of the Battle of the Somme which was the worst day in the history of the British army. See Robin Prior and Trevor Wilson, *The Somme* (New Haven, CT: Yale University Press, 2005) and William Philpott, *Bloody Victory: The Sacrifice on the Somme* (London: Abacus, 2010).

19 Nov Sunday	Wind westerly. Milder with rain. Church am.
20 Nov M	Rode with S[myth] Richards pm & on to South Molton[.]
21 Nov T	Exeter[.]
22 Nov W	Rode to Bishops Tawton for lunch with Davis & on to Barnstaple. Fine[.] [B]elieve I saw a black cock on Codden Hill.
23 Nov Th	Walked with a gun pm round Hill & S[outh] Aller. Wet in ev[ening].
24 Nov F	Exeter. DPF Meeting &c.
25 Nov S	Rode to Blackpool am. Bartlett out from about Timber Coi Balham Nut [*sic*][.]
26 Nov Sun[day]	Church twice. Walk pm with S[myth] R[ichards]. [N]ice day.
27 Nov M	Shot in & about Tilery for 3 or 4 hours pm. Weather very nice. Got a few ph[easants] & 1 woodc[ock].
28 Nov T	To Exeter & on to London by the 5.27 after Timber Co meeting.
29 Nov W	CMC business till 9.30 till near 1. Back to Castle Hill by the 1.30. Hugh & Daisy there.
30 Nov Th	Shot Higher & Lower Beer. Lovely day. I as usual there shot ill. We brought in 70 ph[easants] 5 woodc[ocks] & 4 hares. We have used up 666 aeroplanes since 1 July. It took us 1½ hours to do the H[igher]. Beer valley & rather more to do Smalldon's bottom.
1 Dec F	About the place. Walk pm.
2 Dec S	Shot Cawsis Barton Temple & Long Walk & had quite a nice day. Cawsis Barton took just 3 hours. 93 ph[easants] 4 wood[cocks] 9 H[ares].
3 Dec Sunday	Church am. Hugh & Daisy[233] & Lady A.[234] [R]emained with us for second service. Walk pm.

[233] This is presumably Margaret Helen Beaumont (1892–1958) who was the daughter of Lord Allendale. She was the wife of the fifth Earl Fortescue and the Countess Fortescue.
[234] This is presumably Lady Allendale.

4 Dec M <u>C. Hill</u>	The Allendales & Hugh left. Went out with a gun pm & got 2 cock ph[easants]. Fine & frosty.

5 Dec T	To Exeter <u>& London</u>. Dined with M[ary]. Egerton. Cold.

6 Dec W	Various jobs. Asquith has resigned. Bonar Law[235] cannot form a ministry[,] presumably for want of radical support & Lloyd George is sent for.[236] Dined with the Allendales. L[or]d Carnock[237] is delighted that A[squith] is out & that Grey will leave F.O.

7 Dec Th	Saw Hugh off by 10.35 from Charing X [Cross][238] & took Daisy out after. CMC p.m. H[ouse] of Lords for 10 minutes. Dined with Sue.

8 Dec F	Com[mit]tee at Econ. CFO & back to <u>Castle Hill</u> by the 4.15.

9 Dec S	A cold thaw. Rode with S[myth] R[ichards] pm. School Com[mit]tee in ev[ening].

10 Dec <u>Sunday</u>	Fine. Church twice.

11 Dec M	To Exmoor with S[myth] R[ichards]. Foggy & cold. A little snow on ground.

12 Dec T	Shot Tilery Cover &c. 16 ph[easants] 4 woodc[ocks] 7 rab[bits]. Sharp frost. Still.

13 Dec W	<u>To Exeter[.]</u> T F Ag [sic] DPF &c. Cold but fine.

14 Dec Th	County Council[.] [T]o <u>London</u> after.

15 Dec F	Walked with Daisy am. Econ. CFO. Volunteer meeting & returned to <u>Castle Hill</u> by 4.15

[235] Andrew Bonar Law (1858–1923). He was the Conservative MP for Blackfriars and Hutchesontown Division of Glasgow from 1900 to 1906 and the MP for Dulwich from 1906 to December 1910. He was the MP for Bootle from 1911 to 1918 and the MP for Glasgow Central from 1918 to 1923. Bonar Law was the leader of the Conservative Party from 1911 to 1921. He served as Prime Minister from 1922 to 1923. Bonar Law was the Secretary of State for the Colonies from 1915 to 1916 and the Chancellor of the Exchequer from 1916 to 1918. He was also the Leader of the House of Commons from 1916 to 1921.

[236] See John Vincent, ed., *The Crawford Papers: The Journals of David Lindsay Twenty-seventh Earl of Crawford and Tenth Earl of Balcarres 1871–1940 during the Years 1892 to 1940* (Manchester: Manchester University Press, 1984), pp. 373–376.

[237] Sir Arthur Nicolson (1849–1928). He was the first Baron Carnock and a veteran British diplomat. He served as His Majesty's Ambassador Extraordinary and Plenipotentiary at Madrid from 1904 to 1905. He was the British Ambassador to Russia from 1905 to 1910. Nicolson was the Permanent Under-Secretary for Foreign Affairs from 1910 to 1916.

[238] This refers to Charing Cross railway station.

16 Dec S	With S[myth] Richards & Molland am.
17 Dec Sunday	Church twice. Walk with Capt[ain]. Moore pm. Sharp frost
18 Dec M	A good deal of work. Walk with S[myth] R[ichards] & Moore pm to see stock.
19 Dec T	By early train to Exeter. A little snow.
20 Dec W	Shot about Clatworthy & S[outh]. Aller till lunch. Heavy rain 12.30–1. Bella Seeke came. Thaw
21 Dec Th	Shot Spa wood & there abouts am. Farmers Union Meeting at Molton pm.
22 Dec F	Shot the Stoodleigh cover &c. Did not get much. Bright & fine after a heavy shower about 10. [R]oads a sheet of ice.
23 Dec S	Rain am. Walk with P pm in cold N[orth] W[est] wind.
24 Dec Sunday	Fine but cold. Church am. Walk with P pm.
25 Dec M	Xmas day. Church am. Walk pm.
26 Dec T	Motored to Simonsbath am. Roads there mostly ice.
27 Dec W	Shot Park & Bremridge. Got about 35 ph[easants] & 5 woodc[cocks]. Beautiful bright day with sharp frost.
28 Dec Th	To London. Thaw in ev[ening][.]
29 Dec F	CMC. Took Daisy for a walk. Econ & CFO. Home by 4.15[.]
30 Dec S C. Hill	Rode am & pm with S[myth] Richards[.]
31 Dec Sunday	Church twice. Wet pm.

1917

1 Jan
M
<u>C. Hill</u>

Shot between the ponds & Heddon till lunch with Dick & Buttle. Got 9 ph[easants] 1 duck 1 woodc[ock] 2 hares 1 rab[bit]. Misty.

2 Jan
T

<u>To Exeter</u> with P for War Pensions &c[.]
Stayed there the night.

3 Jan
W

Enthronement of the Bishop.[239] A long & tedious service. Child welfare com[mit]tee pm & then conference about getting more out of the land. Motored back with P & Ftime [sic]. tired.

4 Jan
Th

Two Hancocks & Thorton & we shot Higher & Lower Beer. Very disappointing. [O]nly 25 ph[easants]. Lovely day. Very tired in ev[ening].

5 Jan
F

Walked a bit am & pm. Wet pm.

[6 Jan]
[S]

[No entry]

7 Jan
S[unday]

Church twice.

8 Jan
M

~~Out with a gun but did not do much~~
Exeter. P to Plymouth.

9 Jan
T

Exeter. Pretty busy about food production.

10 Jan
W

Shot Whitehill but got very little. Fine[.]

11 Jan
Th

<u>To London</u>. Econ & CMC. Wet[.]

12 Jan
F

Econ & CFO. Saw Davis[.]

13 Jan
S

Back <u>to Castle Hill</u>[.]
[T]aking a War Agri[culture] Com[mit]tee at S[outh] Molton on the way.

14 Jan
<u>Sunday</u>

Church twice.

15 Jan
M

Rode to Park Crossbury H[igher]. Beer & Bradbury to ask if they had too many hen pheasants. Only the two holts suggested that a few more might be killed. Coln stirred up Lock at Indicombe[.]

[239] This refers to the new Bishop of Exeter who was Rt Rev. Lord William Gascoyne-Cecil (1863–1936). He was the Bishop of Exeter from 1916 to 1936. He was previously the Rector of Bishops Hatfield from 1888 to 1916 and the Rural Dean of Hertford from 1904 to 1916.

16 Jan T	Exeter[.]
17 Jan W	About the place[.]
18 Jan Th	Shot Cawsis Barton & Long Walk[.] [A] nice day. 34 ph[easants] & woodc[ocks]. Went to Curlins[240] lecture in Barnstaple in ev[ening]. [D]ecidedly interesting.
19 Jan F	Two meetings at Barnstaple & then two at Exeter. Left at 9.30. [G]ot home after 8.
20 Jan S	Motored pm with S[myth] R[ichards] to Weare Giffard when called at Huxwill[241] Park Vinton[242] & Salternes,[243] & on to Torrington for Food Production.
21 Jan Sunday	Church am. Mrs Bampfylde came to tea & dinner. Walked to Fullabrook pm[.]
22 Jan M	Shot over Higher Beer Indiwell &c but got little. 3 duck the' [sic] in L[ower] Beer.
23 Jan T	Exeter[.]
24 Jan W	To London by the 9. CFO & Econ[,] & went to see Allendales in ev[ening].
25 Jan Th	Econ. Lunched with Sue. B[oar]d of Agriculture pm. Dined at home.
26 Jan F	Econ & CFO. Conference of TFA chairmen pm. P came up.
27 Jan [S]	Various jobs. Very cold.
28 Jan Sunday	Church at Holy Trinity. George came to luncheon.
29 Jan M	Busy various job[s][.]
30 Jan T	Took Daisy to see about marriage licence.

---

[240] Daniel Thomas Curtin (1886–1963). He was an American author and a special correspondent for The Times and The Daily Mail.
[241] This is presumably Huxhill.
[242] This probably refers to Venton.
[243] This is presumably Salterns.

| 31 Jan
W | CMC pm. Long meeting. |

| 1 Feb
Th | To Exeter[,] busy all p.m. |

| 2 Feb
F | Busy all day.
~~Back to London[.]~~ |

| 3 Feb
S | Back to London[.] |

| 4 Feb
Sunday | With P to S¹ Pauls Cathedral
& walked back. Snow in ev[ening]. |

| 5 Feb
M | With P am to Harrods[244] & Maples[245] to choose table for Hugh. Snow & slush but warmer in ev[ening]. Hugh came. |

| 6 Feb
T | Fine & bright but slushy.
Econ Com[mit]ᵗᵉᵉ am. ~~with Jock pm about seed potatoes~~. Wedding feast at home[.] |

| 7 Feb
W | Den[zil] came home. Big spread at Allendales in ev[ening]. Went with P to opening of Parl[iamen]ᵗ. Curzon very eloquent on the losses the House had sustained. |

| 8 Feb
Th | Hugh's wedding at S[t] Peters at 1.30.[246] They were both very composed and the ceremony was reverent & well done. A lot of friends.
Dick doing duty as footman on the box of Thean [sic] brides car! Went with Den[zil] & Billy Corkran to a music hall. |

| 9 Feb
F | Walked to City with Den[zil] am. Econ & CFO. The Caters dined & we went to a rotten Music Hall. |

| 10 Feb
S | Den[zil] dined out. |

| 11 Feb
Sunday | Lunched with Polly Stucley. |

| 12 Feb
M | Saw Den[zil] off at 12.40. CFO. |

| 13 Feb
T | Various jobs. H[ouse] of Lords in ev[ening].
Freight across channel is 45/6 & before the war it was 9/16 to gib [sic].
We are sending 65 000 tons of hay monthly to France. |

| 14 Feb
W | To Exeter by the 10.15. Food production work. P came also to Exeter. |

244 This refers to the Harrods department store in London.
245 This refers to the Maples and Company which was a furniture retailer.
246 This refers to the marriage of the fifth Earl Fortescue and Margaret Helen Beaumont.

15 Feb   TF& Child Welfare. Met Hugh & Daisy at 11.40. Went with H[ugh] to
Th   Lodge 39[247] & we lunched together.

16 Feb   Food production. D.P.F. & War Agric[ulture].
F   Caught the 4.29 & got home. Began to thaw pm with a little rain. The Taw
Castle Hill frozen all over except in spots from Lapford to S[outh] Molton R[oa]ᵈ.

17 Feb   A lovely spring like day.
S   Walked with Wallace am to Bremridge & Punch Bowl & with S[myth]
           R[ichards] pm to Woodhouse farm which was burned on Thurs[day].
           He brought news of Hartland wireless station having been shelled yesterday.[248]

18 Feb   Still thawing but raw & chilly.
Sunday   Church twice. Walk pm with S[myth] R[ichards].

19 Feb   To London by the 11. Nelly Seymour came.
M

20 Feb   Econom[ic]. Com[mit]ᵗᵉᵉ am. Claude Seymour,[249] Capt[ain] R N dined. He
T   said the Germans did well in the Jutland fight, & we could not call it a
           victory. Had Jellicoe[250] closed & fought a night action it might have been,
           but the risk would have been very great, & he thought he was bound to get
           them next day: but they with courage & skill counter marched & got passed
           under Jellicoe's stern, our destroyers were in rear & picked up some as they
           passed, but we did not sink very more than we claimed.

21 Feb   Econ. Com.ᵗᵉᵉ. H[ouse] of Lords pm. Lansdowne interesting on land.
W   Chaplin[251] the reverse.

22 Feb   H[ouse] of Lords pm.
Th

23 Feb   Econ & CFO[,] & War Office[.]
F

24 Feb   CMC a.m. Fine & warmer.
S

---

[247] This refers to Lodge 39 which was the St John the Baptist Lodge of the Freemasons in Exeter.

[248] Although there is no evidence to suggest that Hartland wireless station was shelled on 16 February 1917, this could in fact refer to the sinking of the Merchant Ship Greenwood on 16 February which was sunk by gunfire six miles to the southwest of Hartland Point. See A. J. Tennant, *British Merchant Ships Sunk by U-Boats in World War One* (Penzance: Periscope Publishing Ltd, 2006), p. 51.

[249] Claude Seymour (1876–1941). He was a vice-admiral in the Royal Navy and served in the First World War. He commanded HMS Royal Oak from 1925 to 1926.

[250] John Rushworth Jellicoe (1859–1935). He was the first Earl Jellicoe and an admiral in the Royal Navy. He was the Second Sea Lord of the Admiralty from 1912 to 1914 and he commanded the Grand Fleet from 1914 to 1916. Jellicoe was the First Sea Lord from 1916 to 1918 and was Chief of the Naval Staff in 1917. He was appointed the Admiral of the Fleet in April 1919 and was later the Governor-General of New Zealand from 1920 to 1924.

[251] Henry Chaplin (1840–1923). He was the first Viscount Chaplin and he was a Conservative MP for Mid Lincolnshire from 1868 to 1885. He was the Conservative MP for Sleaford from 1885 to 1906 and the MP for Wimbledon from 1907 to 1916. Chaplin was the President of the Board of Agriculture from 1889 to 1892 and the President of the Local Government Board from 1895 to 1900.

25 Feb Sunday	Went with P to S[t] Pauls for sermon & H.C. [A] beautiful service[.]
26 Feb M	CFO. John dined.
27 Feb T	Econ. H[ouse] of Lords.
28 Feb W	CFO.
1 March Th	To Exeter[.] Child Welfare &c.
2 March F	A long day[.] [G]etting back to Lowndes S[t] little before midnight.
3 March S London	With P to the Scala pm. Dinner in ev[ening].
4 March Sunday	Took Daisy to the Temple Church am. Beautiful music. Lunched then with L[or]d Parmoor after.
5 March M	A little snow & much slush. CFO am.
6 March T	Lynton Railway Meeting am. Conference about Nat[ional] Service pm. House of Lords after. Dinner in ev[ening].
7 March W	Very cold. CFO. H[ouse] of Lords.
8 March Th	Very cold again.
9 March F	Econ & CFO. [T]o Exeter after.
10 March S	[A]t it from 10 till 4[.] [T]o Castle Hill by the 4.29. Milder.
11 March Sunday	Church am. Rode round the stock with S[myth] R[ichards] pm in cold rain.
12 March M	Fine & pleasant. [T]o Exmoor & rode to Picked Stone & back by Prayway & Duredon. Motored home via Wistland P[oun]d.
13 March T	To Woodhouse with Garland am to see about rebuilding. To Barnstaple pm for Food Production: then Exeter.
14 March W	Work all day. Fine & mild.

15 March Th	County Council & other work all day.
16 March F	Food production 10 – 12[.] [T]hen to Topsham barracks to get horses. [T]o <u>London</u> by the 2.5 [*sic*]. Lucy in Lowndes St.
17 Mar S	Running about half the day after seed potatoes &c &c. Mild[.] Called at W.O. about horses for farmers. Could not get much help from Birkbeck[252] who however showed me some of his figures. To 31.12.16 we sent 170,000 horses to France. He is now sending over 1000 – 1200 a week. The mud on the Somme was very hard on the H.O. horses, & in one army 900 got punctures in one month. Shell fragments & packing case nails.
18 Mar <u>Sunday</u>	The Czar's[253] abdication confirmed. General opinion is that it is a good thing.
19 Mar M	Very busy hunting various Gov[ernment] Departments, mostly on agric[ultural] matters.
20 Mar T	Econ. Saw Chilston[254] about Davis' & G. Buller's ructions. He told me that Weardale, who had only subscribed £20 to their Kentish hospital fund asked him to put him on a Committee that he might be able to get petrol. Dysart told me he heard on good authority the sailors were pretty well satisfied with their successes against submarines. Some rain.
21 Mar W	CFO. Saw Sir A Keogh pm about G. Buller. Dysart told me he was in the gallery next Fisher[255] yesterday when Asquith spoke about the Dardanelles. Fisher said he has not said anything untrue & he has not concealed much but he has given quite a misleading impression of what happened. S[256] kept the War Council waiting 80 minutes while I tried to dissuade Asquith from the Dardanelles show. How can they say I did not dissent when K[itchener] took me aside & said we are all agreed but you"[.] If these were his views why did not Fisher send in his resignation. Cold & raw. Some rain & sleet.

[252] William Henry Birkbeck (1863–1929). He was a major-general in British army and served in South Africa from 1899 to 1902. In 1905, he was attached to the Japanese 3rd Army in Manchuria. Birkbeck was the Director of Remounts at Army Headquarters from 1912 to 1920.

[253] Tsar Nicholas II (1868–1918). He was the last emperor or tsar (czar) of Russia from 1894 to 1917.

[254] Aretas Akers-Douglas (1851–1926). He was the first Viscount Chilston and was a Conservative MP for East Kent from 1880 to 1885. The East Kent constituency was restructured with the Redistribution of Seats Act of 1885 and he was the Conservative MP for St Augustine's from 1885 to 1911. Chilston served as the Chief Whip to the Conservative Party in the House of Commons from 1883 to 1895. He was the First Commissioner of Works from 1895 to 1902 and the Secretary of State for the Home Office from 1902 to 1906.

[255] John Arbuthnot Fisher (1841–1920). He was the first Baron Fisher and an admiral in the Royal Navy. He was appointed as the Admiral of the Fleet in December 1905. Fisher served as the First Sea Lord of the Admiralty from 1904 to 1910 and from 1914 to 1915.

[256] This is probably Sir Mark Sykes (1879–1919). He was the sixth Baron of Sledmere and a lieutenant-colonel in the British army. He was the Conservative MP for Central Hull from 1911 to 1919; it is noted in the minutes of the War Cabinet meeting on 21 March that Sir Mark Sykes was absent for Minutes 4 to 10 of the meeting and he was present for Minutes 2, 3, 11, 12 and 13. See TNA: CAB-23-2, War Cabinet minutes, 100, p. 109, http://filestore.nationalarchives.gov.uk/pdfs/large/cab-23-2.pdf (accessed 5 February 2018).

22 Mar Th	Went with P pm to see the furniture lent L[ady], D[uke] of Devonshire[257] & other to S[outh] Kensington. Cold. Lynton rail meeting & Econ.

23 Mar
F
London

Army Canteen meeting. [T]hen Econ & CFO. At the first we learned that the Gov[ernment] had forgotten all about the army when settling how much there should be brewed[,] which made a difference of 1 000 000 extra 36 gal[lon]. barrels.

Saw Benson also afterwards who showed me figures as to EFC takings in France. There have doubled since last April & from 1 Ap[ril] [19]16 – 28 Feb[ruary] [19]17 exceed £ 5 000 000. The number of men we have there is less than is supposed under 1 300 000 British, about 117 000 Australians & 100 000 Canadians.

Just about 1½ mil[lion].

L[or]^d Carnock at the Travellers is depressed about Russia. Does not believe in the Empress[258] being pro German & the Emperor certainly was not that way at all. Before the war he said once "My Cousin Wil[l]iam[259] thinks he is going to run this country but he is damnably mistaken".

24 Mar
S

Nothing particular[.]

25 Mar
Sunday

To S[t] Pauls am with P to hear Preb[endary]. Carlile[260] who talked rot. Got seedy in ev[ening].

26 Mar
M

Spent the day in bed[.]

27 Mar
T

Downstairs again.

28 Mar
W

Went out a little. Dined with Lady Northcote. Pleasant. Milner & Revelstoke[261] came back from Russia without any idea that the revolution was so near. Sir R[obert] Borden[262] said they had some 8000 men in the Canadian forces who gave an address in USA for their next of kin & there would be all 2000 more in the French flying Corps, Foreign Legion &c.

---

[257] Victor Christian William Cavendish (1868–1938). He was the ninth Duke of Devonshire and the Liberal Unionist MP for West Derbyshire from 1891 to 1908. Devonshire also served as the Lord Lieutenant of Derbyshire from 1908 to 1938. He was the Treasurer of His Majesty's Household from 1900 to 1903 and Financial Secretary to the Treasury from 1903 to 1905. He was the Civil Lord of the Admiralty from 1915 to 1916 and the Governor-General of Canada from 1916 to 1921. Devonshire was the Secretary of State for the Colonies from 1922 to 1924.

[258] Empress Alexandra [Aleksandra] Feodorovna (1872–1918). She was the last empress of Russia and the wife of Tsar Nicholas II of Russia.

[259] Kaiser Wilhelm II (1859–1941). He was the last emperor or kaiser of Germany and the king of Prussia from 1888 to 1918.

[260] Reverend Wilson Carlile (1847–1942). He was appointed the Prebendary of St Pauls Cathedral in 1906. He was the founder of the Church Army in 1882 and was the organisation's Honorary Chief Secretary.

[261] John Baring (1863–1929). He was the second Baron Revelstoke and he was the Lord Lieutenant of Middlesex from 1926 to 1929. He was the head of Barings Bank and a director of the Bank of England. He was Receiver-General of the Duchy of Cornwall from 1908 to 1929. Revelstoke also acted as the London financial agent for the Russian Imperial government during the Great War and was a member of the Committee of Experts for Settlement of Repatriations in 1929.

[262] Sir Robert Laird Borden (1854–1937). He was the Canadian Member of Parliament for Carleton from 1905 to 1909 and the eighth Prime Minister of Canada from 1911 to 1920.

29 Mar Th	Dentist a.m. Took Daisy to Permit Office pm. (19 Bedford sq[uare]). Showery, but pleasant between.
30 Mar F	Annual meeting of CFO at wh[ich]. I took the chair for Kinnaird.[263] Did Woollcombe's day at Econ.
31 Mar S	With Daisy about her passport a.m. The whole place very slushy in consequence of early snow.
1 Apr Sunday	Chapel Royal am. Some calls p.m. Snow fell early.
2 Apr M	Snowed hard till near 1. [T]hen a beautiful afternoon. Dined w[ith] Bentinck.
3 Apr T	Com[mi]^{tee} at Econ. H[ouse] of Lords pm. Dinned with G[eorge] Harlech.
4 Apr W	CFO rota & Econ. [T]hen by 3.25 to Exeter[.] Cold & raw[.]
5 Apr Th	Food Production nearly all the time from 10 – 4. [T]hen to C[astle]. Hill[.]
6 Apr F	Good Friday. Church am. Walk with P pm.
7 Apr S	Rode to Tossells Barton am with S[myth] R[ichards] & with him to Woodhouses & Townhouse pm.
8 Apr Easter Sunday	Church am. Walk with P & Mrs Bampfylde pm.
9 Apr M	Slader drew Bremridge with his mixed pack & found 6 stags. Got one away northward about 12 & laid on. Hounds promptly doubled back to Bremridge & we missed them. Slader ultimately killed a deer with 3 hounds at Brayford. Cold N[orth] W[est] wind with hail stones. I came home for luncheon.
10 Apr T	Rode to Clockhay am & walked to Townhouse marshes with Wallace pm. Mrs B[ampfylde]. left.
11 Apr W	Exeter all day. Some snow. Susan came.
12 Apr Th	Everything white when we got up, but most of it was gone by noon. Rode to Morris & Dennis Ten[emen]'[s] a.m. Walked with Sue & P pm.

[263] Arthur FitzGerald Kinnaird (1847–1923). He was the eleventh Lord Kinnaird of Inchture and third Baron Kinnaird of Rossie. He was a keen footballer and was the President of the Football Association. He was a Director of Barclay's Bank Ltd and the President of the YMCA. He was Lord High Commissioner to the General Assembly of the Church of Scotland from 1907 to 1909.

13 Apr F	Exeter by the 8.39. Stag Hunt Com[mit]^{tee} at Dulverton on the way back.
14 Apr S	Rode to Exmoor. Wind & some rain. Road nearly blocked in places by snow. The sheep pinched for want of keep but the lambs looking well.
15 Apr Sunday	A little warmer. Church twice & walk pm.
16 Apr M	About the place am & went to Whitechapel with P & Sue pm.
17 Apr T	To Exeter by the 8.39.
18 Apr W	To London for B[oar]^d of Agriculture conference. We are eating corn faster than we can import it[,] & a large area of grass is to be broken for 1918 harvest.
19 Apr Th	About Gov[ernment]. Offices all the morning. [T]o Exeter by the 3.25.
20 Apr F	Work 9.30 – 4.30. Very tired. [B]ack to C. Hill.
21 Apr S C. Hill	Lovely spring day. [D]ecidedly warmer. Rode with S[myth]. R[ichards]. pm.
22 Apr Sunday	Church twice. Warmer.
23 Apr M	About the place. Burnt ferns &c in the park with Sue pm.
24 Apr T	Exeter by early train.
25 Apr W	Really warm. With Wallace am to Higher Beer &c.
26 Apr Th	About the place: took Cecil firls [sic] for a walk pm.
27 Apr F	Exeter all day.
28 Apr S	To North Molton pm with P.
29 Apr Sunday	To Exeter by the Volunteer Special for French's Inspection.[264] Went on to London with him afterwards.

---

[264] See 'Lord French', 1917, British Pathé, https://www.britishpathe.com/video/lord-french/query/Devon (accessed 14 December 2017).

30 Apr M	Various jobs am. Saw Fellowes[265] & Strutt[266] at B[oar]ᵈ of Agric[ulture]. pm, & went to <u>Exeter</u> by the 5.50.
1 May T <u>C. Hill</u>	A long day[']s work. [G]ot home at 7.45. Beautiful weather now.
2 May W	Rode[.]
3 May Th	With P. to S[outh] Molton pm to a Nati[onal] Service Meeting.
4 May F	Exeter. Quite hot.
5 May S	To Taunton for Hunt Meeting. We got near £2600 in Sub[scription]ˢ. which is extraordinary considering.
6 May [Sunday]	Church twice. [H]ot rather cold wind.
7 May M	Rode with S[myth] R[ichards] am. Walk with P pm.
8 May T <u>C. Hill</u>	Exeter all day. Bright but wind chilly.
9 May W	Rode to Molton am. Walk with P pm.
10 May Th	Rode am. Cut wig [*sic*] pm. Some rain.
11 May F	Div[isiona]ˡ Meeting for Food Production at Barnstaple pm.
12 May S	Rode am. Motored S[myth] R[ichards] pm to North Barton & Wistland P[oun]ᵈ & walked over farms. Good rain pm.
13 May <u>Sunday</u>	Church twice. Walked to Saw Mills & down Long walk with P pm. Looked lovely.

---

[265] Ailwyn Edward Fellowes (1855–1924). He was the first Baron Ailwyn and the Conservative MP for Ramsey from 1887 to 1906. He was Vice-Chamberlain of Queen Victoria's Household from 1895 to 1900 and the President of the Board of Agriculture from 1905 to 1906. Ailwyn was the Chairman of Norfolk County Council and he was also a DL and JP for Norfolk.

[266] Hon. Edward Gerald Strutt (1854–1930). He was an experienced farmer and served as an agricultural advisor to the Board of Agriculture. He was the chairman of the Essex War Agricultural Committee and President of the Central Association of Dairy Farmers. Strutt was an alderman of Essex County Council and a director of the Yorkshire Insurance Company, Ltd.

14 May   To London by the 9. Econ & sat with Daisy after.
M

15 May   Econ. War Refugee business. Disabled Men & H[ouse] of Lords. Dinner
T   there to Smuts[267] who made an interesting speech.
          Much colder. We have got a grain convoy across safe from USA.

16 May   Econ & Food Production am. [B]y 1.40 to Oxford to see Bishop Robertson[268]
W   & on to Coln S. Aldwyn. House full & cold[.]

17 May   Rain all day. Dedication service in ev[ening] for the memorial they have put
Th   up to Michael & Micky. Very well done. The arch bishop giving an
          admirable address.

18 May   Left at 8 for Swindon. To London from there.
F   Econ & CFO[,] & on to Exeter by 3.25.

19 May   Did a little at FP Office
S   & went to Castle Hill by the 11. Walked to Townhouse with P pm. Stuffy
          after some rain.

20 May   Mr Bate came over, via Francis on duty at Aldershot & gave us a moving
Sunday   service.

21 May   Exeter[.]
M

22 May   To ~~Torrington~~ Bideford pm for FP work.
T   Rain in ev[ening].

23 May   Rode am. Daisy came. Wet pm.
W

24 May   Rode to Molton pm for Food Production meeting.
Th

25 May   To Exeter by the 8.30. Motored at 1 to Barnstaple for Food Production
F   meeting.

26 May   Motored with Daisy & P to Wear[e] Gifford & Torrington for F.P.
          meeting.
S   Very tired in ev[ening].
C. Hill   Rain all night. Mrs Bampfylde came.

27 May   Church in evening only.
Sunday   Very pleasant arrangement.

---

[267] Jan Christiaan Smuts (1870–1950). He was a field marshal in the British army and commanded the British army in the East Africa campaign. He was a South African representative on the Imperial War Cabinet from 1917 to 1918 and the Plenipotentiary, alongside General Botha, for South Africa at the Peace Conference at Versailles in 1919.

[268] Rt Rev. Archibald Robertson (1853–1931). He was the Bishop of Exeter from 1903 to 1916. He had previously served as the Principal of King's College London from 1897 to 1903 and the Vice-Chancellor of the University of London from 1902 to 1903.

28 May M	Rode with Daisy pm.
29 May T	To Exeter by the 8.30 & on to <u>London</u> by the 4.17. Some rain.
30 May W	B[oar]^d of Agriculture am. C.F[.]O. Dined with Sue.
31 May Th	An Early day. Went to see Daisy in ev[ening].
1 June F	Econ & CFO. [T]hen by 3.25 to <u>Exeter</u> Some rain.
2 June S	Work till 2. [T]hen to <u>Castle Hill</u> More rain.
3 June Sunday	Church & Sacrament am. Fine[.]
4 June M	Rode[.]
5 June T	Exeter all day[.]
6 June W	Fine following a thunderstorm. Den[zil] arrived 2.56.
7 June Th	Rode with Den[zil].
8 June F	Exeter all day. Some showers.
9 June S	Rode with Den[zil] am & with S[myth]. Richards pm.
10 June <u>Sunday</u>	Hot. Church in ev[ening].
11 June M	Rode with Den[zil] to C Slader's pm. Very hot[.]
12 June T	Exeter all day. P to London.
13 June W	Rode to Exmoor to see Mr Congreve about poor Rees' affairs.
14 June Th	To Barnstaple am for Timber Co &c. Rode pm with S[myth] Richards & found Hugh & Daisy arrived when we came in.

15 June F	Exeter all day.
16 June S	To Melbury to see the motor ploughing & on to Torrington with S[myth] R[ichards] for District FP meeting. Hot with thunder in ev[ening].
17 June Sunday	Church am. Hot.
18 June M C. Hill	To Exmoor with the couple at 11. Had a lovely ride pm to Exe Head & back to Holewater where had tea & motored home by 7.30.
19 June T	To Exeter by the 10.30. Rainy.
20 June W	To Exeter for TFA &c and stayed there.
21 June Th	County Council. Went to Seal Hayne college after.
22 June F	Food Production till 1. Prothero's meeting after. Got to Castle Hill again by the 4.30.
23 June S	Rode pm with S[myth] R[ichards]. Cloudy with a very little rain. [B]ut we have begun cutting hay.
24 June Sunday	Walked to Higher Beer with S[myth] R[ichards] & Wallace am. Church in ev[ening].
25 June M	To London by the 9. Com[mittee] at Economic.
26 June T London	Various jobs. Dined with the Allendales. H[ouse] of Lords pm.
27 June W	Lunch with Sue. H[ouse] of Lords.
28 June Th	Com[mit]tee at Economic. Sir A Lawley[269] came in after dinner. We have a very qualified superiority in the air now. Our Tanks downed 3 of our observation balloons in one day recently. One poor boy has had to clear out in a parachute four times in 5 weeks & has lost his nerve. [N]o wonder. The Mesopotamia report[270] hardly does justice to the mismanagement. At one time the troops were short of solar topees & quinine. Some rain pm.

[269] Sir Arthur Lawley (1860–1932). He was the sixth Baron Wenlock and a former captain of the 10th Hussars. He was the Administrator of Matabeleland from 1897 to 1901 and the Governor of Western Australia from 1901 to 1902. Wenlock was the Lieutenant-Governor of the Transvaal from 1902 to 1906 and the Governor of Madras from 1906 to 1911.
[270] This refers to the Report of the Mesopotamia Commission.

29 June F	Econ & CFO. Went to the Academy after with P. Daisy dined. Drizzle all day.
30 June S	Long talk with Benson about acc. am. <u>To Castle Hill</u> by the 1[.]
1 July <u>Sunday</u> <u>C. Hill</u>	Church am. Walked to Town house with S[myth] R[ichards] pm. Hot. All crops look well.
2 July M	Rode pm.
3 July T	Exeter all day. P came back. Rain pm.
4 July W	Drove with P to W[est] Buckland pm. Fine but dull.
5 July Th	Exeter. Fine & Warm.
6 July F	Barnstaple for Divisional Food Prod[uction]. Com[mit]ᵗᵉᵉ & Small Holdings[.]
7 July S	Rode am. Haymaking pm. Rain at night fall.
8 July <u>Sunday</u>	Heavy rain p.m. Walked am with S[myth] Richards.
9 July M	Beautiful day. Rode am. Haymaking pm.
10 July T	To Exeter & <u>on to London.</u>
11 July W	CFO. H[ouse] of Lords. ~~Mesopotamia~~ debate uninteresting. Dined with C[laude]. Seymour.
12 July Th	Lunch with Allendales. Took Daisy to H[ouse] of Lords for Mesopotamia debate. Lansdowne much down on Sir B. Duff.[271] CMC work in ev[ening].
13 July F	Econ & CFO. Back by 3.25 to <u>Castle Hill</u>[.] Hot all the week.
14 July S	To Exeter with P. for her Red X [Cross] Meeting. A[rthur] Lawley spoke very well. Frannie & Joyce came.
15 July <u>Sunday</u>	Long walk with Frannie pm.

[271] Sir Beauchamp Duff (1855–1918). He was a general in the British army and served in the Second Anglo-Afghan War. He was the Chief of the General Staff in India from 1906 to 1909 and he was appointed Military Secretary to the India Office in 1907. Duff was the ADC General to King George V in 1914 and the Commander-in-Chief in India from 1913 to 1916.

16 July M	P left for London & the other for Clovelly. To Exmoor with S[myth] R[ichards]. Some heavy rain there but a beautiful afternoon. Bartlett came at 4 about transfer of Timber Co to Gov.
17 July T	Exeter all day. Rode back fr[om]. Umberleigh. Rain in ev[ening].
18 July W	Heavy rain[,] all the morning. Rode pm.
19 July Th	Exeter. Fine[.]
20 July F	Rode am. To Barnstaple pm for Divisional Meeting F.P. Fine.
21 July S	To Exmoor at 10.30 with S[myth] R[ichards]. Rode round there & returned by 2.30. Rode to S[outh] Molton after[.]
22 July Sunday	Beautiful day, but hot. Walked to Townhouse am. Church pm.
23 July M	Rode to W[est]. Buckland am. Col[onel] Allen &c came to lunch. Motored to K[ing]'[s] Nympton pm. Horne stayed the night.
24 July T	To Exeter by 10.26 & stayed there the night. Rain after dark.
25 July W	Various jobs. Went to Torquay pm to look at "Larchmont"[.]
26 July Th	FP work till 4. [T]hen to London[.]
27 July F	Econ & CFO[,] & L M C. Talk also with Benson about A[rmy]. Canteen Com[mit]^tee[.]
28 July S Mytchett Place,	To Aldershot by 1 train. Spent the afternoon with P. & went for dinner & bed to the Ellisons[272] Farnborough. Interesting evening with him. He thought the German General Staff could still claim something like victory, for though we could turn them out of positions we could not get after them. Our generals have never had the chance of learning how to handle men in the hundred thousand in the open. There are a lot of Conscientious Objectors here. Mostly feminine & they give little trouble. There are more officers now than there were men in 1915. We have got corn in store for 8 months.

---

[272] This could refer to Sir Gerald Francis Ellison (1861–1947). He was a colonel in the British army
and Major-General of the General Staff from 1914 to 1915. He was Deputy Quartermaster General
at Gallipoli in 1915 and the Major-General in Charge of Administration at Aldershot from 1916 to
1917. Ellison was the Deputy Quartermaster General at the War Office and Inspector-General of
Communication from 1917 to 1923.

29 July Sunday	Stayed at home all the morning. [J]oined P after lunch & had tea at the Roy[al] Pavilion. T.M. very gracious & the parrot very amusing at Sir W[illiam]. Robertson's expense. Wet pm.
30 July M	Back <u>to London early</u>. Econ am & various jobs after.
31 July T	ACC am. Long Timber Co meeting. Very wet.
1 Aug W	Very wet. Economic am. [T]hen saw Benson. [T]hen caught the 1 from Paddington with Daisy for <u>Castle Hill</u>[.] [A]rriving an hour late.
2 Aug Th	Exeter but got away by the 4.29 & went on from C.H. to <u>Exmoor</u> with Daisy[.]
3 Aug F	Rode with Daisy to Lark Barrow & Tomshill.[273] P came[.]
4 Aug S	D[274] & I hunted at Cuzzicombe. Found near Molland Station came all up the valley to White Post. Then to Lyshwell & down the water to the Barle & down that. Rode home Hawkridge. Nice day.
5 Aug <u>Sunday</u>	Church am. Walked to 60 acres & Reds Hill pm.
6 Aug M	S[myth] Richards out. Rode with him p.m. Showery am.
7 Aug T	P & D drove to Lynton & I rode there. Lovely day. Heard Louis Egerton[275] was killed.
8 Aug W	Very wet all day. Walked pm to Balewater & Halscombe.
9 Aug Th	Rode pm to Drive[,] & Showlsbarrow Castle.[276]
10 Aug F	Rode am to Lanacre Common & Red Deer.[277] Wet pm.
11 Aug S	Showers all day. Hounds at two gates. Found in Farleigh & got away over Cheriton ridge to Black pits. Down Buscombe to Manor Allotm[ent]s & Deer Park & they killed about Oare Ford. Rode Mollands pony & saw a fair amount.

[273] This presumably is Great Tom's Hill.
[274] This presumably refers to Daisy.
[275] Louis Edwin William Egerton (1880–1917). He was a captain in the Royal Buckinghamshire Hussars and was attached XIVth Corps Heavy Artillery. Egerton was killed in action in August 1917.
[276] This probably refer to Shoulsbury Castle.
[277] This is probably Red Deer Farm.

12 Aug Sunday	Showery. Church am. Walked pm.
13 Aug M	Rain off & on all day. Mr Surtees came to luncheon.
14 Aug T	Rode with Daisy to Emmetts Wintershead[278] & Horsen.
15 Aug W Exmoor	Fine day. Hounds at Sandyway. Did not find in Southwood till past 2. [T]hen went right up by Tabor Hill to the head of Long wood & crossed to Brooks' Allotm[ent]t. Up the water. [A]cross Horsen Hill to Feney Ball[279] & by Sherdon Hutch broke out over the hill towards Worth & we came home. Very pretty so far[,] & weather pleasant.
16 Aug Th	Left at 8 for Exeter & got back at 8.15. Daisy went. .
17 Aug F	To Barnstaple pm for FP Div[isional]" Com[mit]ᵗᵉᵉ. Showery[.]
18 Aug S	Hounds at Hawkcombe H[ea]ᵈ. 3 good stags harboured, but could only find a young one & hinds. About 3 when we were on our way home they got away after something up Weir water & we joined in. Crossed Mill Hill high up. Turned by N[orth] corner of Kittuck to Porlock common. [O]ver that, dodging about to the head of Acmead boy. Right handed nearly to Hayes Allotm[ent]ᵗ then left & crossed at the N[orth] E[ast] corner of that into the enclosures & ran there to near Wellshead when we came home. Nice spin. Weather pleasant. They killed at Riscombe a nott stag.[280]
19 Aug Sunday	Church am. Fine.
20 Aug M	S[myth] Richards out & the Le Bas came to Luncheon[.]
21 Aug T	Rode with P to Showlboro[281] & Buscombe farms & back by the Castle. Beautiful day.
22 Aug W	Rode with P to Withypool & hearing there that Hounds some drawing in Lanacre Valley[.] [R]eturned home by Litton's & Sherdon. Heavy rain after 5. Very nice between 11 & 4.
23 Aug Th Exmoor	Rode with Dick to Challacombe & visited most farms. Heavy rain before 12 & after 6. Fine & pleasant between.

---

[278] This refers to Wintershead Farm.
[279] This presumably refers to Ferny Ball.
[280] This is a description of a hornless stag.
[281] This refers to Showlsbarrow or Showlsbarrow Castle.

24 Aug F	Very rough day. Rode with Molland am to Emmetts & Flexbarrow about Timber[,] & motored with P to Challacombe pm to see the remaining farms & cottages. Little needed.
25 Aug S	Hounds at Larkbarrow. Ran a herd from Manor Allotm[en]^{ts} to near Two gates & took a good stag[.] [T]hen by Farleigh water back to Badgworthy wood & Cloud Common. Laid on on [sic] Oldhay heath & ran over Mill Hill to Weir Wood. Two deer there one of which had gone into Plantations & the others to Porlock Hill. Followed the later & got on hinds in the Shillets. Went back to Culbone Stables & tufted. We left for home soon after 3.30 & got back very tired before 6. Very wet in evening.
26 Aug Sunday	Church am. Wild weather.
27 Aug M	To S[outh]. Molton to hear from some Boro[ugh]' cases of getting sugar improperly. Very heavy rain after 2.
28 Aug T	Another wild day. Front meadow flooded. Exeter all day.
29 Aug W	Neither better. Went with the Harriers on Red's Hill &c for an hour am. Walked to Clover Rocks & Flexbarrow pm.
30 Aug Th	Left for Exeter 8 a.m.[,] & got back 8 p.m. Still rainy.
31 Aug F	Beautiful day! P left for London & Windsor. Rode am[.]
1 Sept S Exmoor	Hounds at Cloutsham. Westerly gale all day with heavy rain till 11.30. Found above Horner Mill on Luckham side. Laid on just after 1 beyond Luckham[282] Allers. Ran to Cousincombe. After checks out at top of that & above N[orth] side of Dunkery to Bagley[,] Old Wood & water near Blackford. Up[,] out through Nutscale to Lucot Moor.[283] Colley Head Blackbarrow & Mill Hill. Killing at Oare. I saw nothing after Blackbarrow being out paced [sic].
2 Sept Sunday	Drove to Castle Hill with Dick after breakfast. Walk with S[myth] R[ichards] pm. Fine after 9am.
3 Sept M	Shot over Park with Buttle 10–1. Saw our cover, & got 3 Birds in corn. Fine day & much carrying. Rode with S[myth] R[ichards] to Townhouse pm.

---

[282] This presumably refers to Luckham Alders.
[283] This refers to Luccombe.

4 Sept   To Exeter by the 8.39
T   & on to <u>London</u> by the 3. Fine & pleasant.

5 Sept   Air raid last night.
W   I heard the first part but slept through the second. The aeroplane sounded
              just over the house. Though the bombs it dropped landed in the Strand on
              Edgware R[oa]d. Not much damage done.
              'Planes are practically invisible at night. We have been raiding the Germans
              constantly for 5 weeks with only one casualty.
              The way in wh[ich]. the neighbourhood of Charing X [Cross] has been hit
              repeatedly looks as if they were working up the river to get the War Office
              & Admiralty, miscounted the bridges & fired too soon.
              Heavy thunderstorm 9–11.

6 Sept   Meeting with Davis am about Exmoor Minerals.
Th   Sat to Shannon[284] pm. Den[zil] came & we dined & went to a Hall together.
<u>London</u>

7 Sept   Den[zil] went to Windsor early. Saw Bonbrights about income tax on U.S.
F   securities. Econ & CFO & went back with Den[zil] to <u>Exmoor</u> by the 3.25[,]
              arriving 11.20.

8 Sept   Hounds at Two Gates. Found in Farley Wood. Up the valley to Peg Hill[285]
S   & left to Dry bridges. Laid on, ran to Badgery & by Prince of Wales bog to
              Chalk Water over Mill Hill. Up weir water to N[orth] Colley Head.
              To Shillets & crossed by Broadway to Parks & the sea.
              Very nice run in lovely weather.

9 Sept   Walked to Red's Hill & Picked Moor am. Church pm. Fine.
<u>Sunday</u>

10 Sept   Hounds at Cuzzicombe. They went to Whitechapel to draw & when the
M   pack was taken there to lay on I rode Molland's 4 ye[a]r old pony to North
              Molton Common & on home by 3, without seeing anything, as they ran
              parallel to the rail to W[est] Molland. Then to Cuzzicombe Hawkridge &
              Dulverton & killed. Den[zil] not back till 8.30.

11 Sept   To Exeter by the 10.36. Back by the 1.10 & brought P & Den[zil] who had
T   been shooting back from C[astle]. Hill.

12 Sept   Hounds at Cutcombe. Did not good though it was fine & pleasant.
W   No scent in cover.

13 Sept   To Exeter via Dulverton.
Th   Wet evening.

14 Sept   To Exeter by the S[outh]. M[olton]. Road.
F   Den[zil] stopping at CH to shoot.
              Wet am.

---

[284] Sir James Jebusa Shannon (1862–1923). He was an Anglo-American portrait painter and a
founder of the Society of Portrait Painters. From 1910 to 1923, he was the President of the Society
of Portrait Painters.
[285] This could refer to Pig Hill.

15 Sept
S
Exmoor

Nice morning. Hounds at Two Gates. Too many deer about. Tufters ran from Brendon Road to Longstone bay & brought back three deer. Laid on near Tomshill & ran to Deer Park. More deer there. Ran on to Hollowcombe & out by Deddycombe to Yannery & then Cliffs & to sea. Unsatisfactory day.

16 Sept
Sunday

Walk to Prayway & Flexbro am.[286]
Church pm.

17 Sept
M

Moved to Castle Hill[.]

18 ⎤
19 ⎬ Exeter
20 ⎦

Showery &c
unsettled.
Finer

21 Sept
F

Shot am over Bradbury.
Saw very little. Got 3 part[ridge]s 1 duck & some rabbits. Beautiful day.

22 Sept
S

Hounds at Yarde Down.
Found in West Wood, but did not get away till past 1 when he broke 5 of gratters [sic] & crossed by Natsleigh[287] to Muxworthy. Down the valley. [T]hen up under Beera & up Sherracombe to the right at the top of this & by Five Barrows to Hangley Cleave & S[outh] Forest, crossing below Wintershead to the Barle at Cow Castle. All but a very few were a long way behind, & saw very little of hounds till they were held up here. Tried up the Barle to Halscombe Plant[ation]" leaving Flexbarrow on the left. Went back & made good the bend on S[outh] of that & carried a faint line into Little Woolcombe. Presently they spoke on it & fresh found him. A very pretty bit of hunting.
Back to the river & ran him in view to Simonsbath. Then down to below Flexbarrow. Up again & down again & at last killed near 4. A very good stag.

23 Sept
Sunday
C. Hill

Church am. Walked pm with P & G C S[myth] R[ichards] to Townhouse.
Fine.

24 Sept
M

Worked the ground from County School to Easter close 11–3. Got 6 shots & killed 5 birds. Hot.

25 ⎤
26 ⎬
27 ⎦

Stayed in Exeter returning
on 27th after the C.C to
Castle Hill[.]

28 Sept
F

To North Molton with P. pm & onto Sandyway to S Tucker.

[286] This is presumably Flexbarrow.
[287] This refers to Natsley.

29 Sept S	Left at 8 for L[or]ᵈ M[ount] Edgcumbe's funeral with P & got back at 7. Fine weather. Lunch with the Admiral – Sir A[lexander] Bethell.[288] We have got the upper hand of the Submarines. We shall not cease to suffer from them, but they will not defeat us. We have had the microphene [*sic*] the French are now burning for months past.
30 Sept Sunday	Beautiful day. [Q]uite hot. Walk am. Church in ev[ening].
1 Oct M	Shot about S[outh] Aller 10–2.30. Fair sport but shooting moderate.
2 Oct T	Exeter. Hugh & D[enzil] came & went to Exmoor[.]
3 Oct W	<u>To London</u> to meet Davis about minerals & Seymour & Addie about Dupob & ODE [*sic*].
4 Oct Th	Sat to Shannon most of the day.
5 Oct F	Econ & CFO[,] & went by 3.25 to <u>Castle Hill</u>[.] Fine
6 Oct S	Motored early to <u>Exmoor</u>. Showers till 11. Fine after. Hounds at Larkbarrow. Found near Warren & ran with 4 couple to Buscombe. Badgery Deer Park Mill Hill Colley Water. Bronham. Up Broadway, & down Porlock Hill into the covers by Holmbush & we left then going down. Hugh had to rejoin [*sic*].
7 Oct Sunday <u>Exmoor</u>	Rainy nearly all day. Went to Church pm.
8 Oct M	Heavy rain all day. So our return <u>to Castle Hill</u> was rather difficult & uncomfortable.
9 10 11	Exeter. The last a very long day.
12 Oct F	Shot 11 – 2.30 on Tower & Heddon with Buttle. Steady rain wh[ich]. spoiled sport. 10 ph[easants] 2 R[abbits].
13 Oct S	Rode with S[myth] R[ichards] & Daisy. Raw & chilly. Mrs Bampfylde came.

[288] Hon. Sir Alexander Edward Bethell (1855–1932). He was an admiral in the Royal Navy and Director of Naval Intelligence from 1909 to 1912. He commanded the battleships of the 3rd Fleet in 1914 and was the Commander of the Channel Fleet in 1915. From 1916 to 1918, Bethell was the Commander-in-Chief at Plymouth.

14 Oct Sunday	Church am. Sacrament. Walk with S[myth] R[ichards] pm. Fine[.]
15 Oct M	Beautiful day. [T]o London. CFO & Econ.
16 Oct T	Econ & Food Production. Sat to Shannon. Wet.
17 Oct W	Food Production. L[or]ᵈ Lieut[enant]s meeting. Lunched with the sisters. CFO.
18 Oct Th	To see Strany am about Hepburn's picture. Sat to Shannon pm. Tea with John.
19 Oct F	Food Production. Econ. CFO & to Taunton after by the 6.30.
20 Oct S	To Castle Hill by the 7.56. Shot with Hugh on Leary farm. Got 14 ph[easants]. Fine[.]
21 Oct Sunday	Church in ev[ening]. P sprained her ankle badly.
22 Oct M	Shot with Hugh on Blackpool &c. [G]ot very little pm. Fine[.]
23 Oct T	To Exeter by the 10.56 & on to London.
24 Oct W	Meeting with Prothero pm where he spoke very strongly of the certainty of scarcity & possibility of worse. [T]o Exeter by 5.50.
25 Oct Th	A long day on Food Production. J[ohn]. Wallop[289] very tiresome. Back to Castle Hill by the 4.29. Showers[.]
26 Oct F	To Barnstaple pm for War Aims[290] meeting. Fine mostly.
27 Oct S C. Hill	Shot with the Australian Officers on Clatworthy &c pm.
28 Oct Sunday	Church am. Rode with S[myth] R[ichards] to Townhouse pm.

[289] John Fellowes Wallop (1859–1925). He was the seventh Earl of Portsmouth and a Vice-Lieutenant for Devon. He was previously a private secretary to the Governor of Tasmania and the chairman of the Liberal Party in the South Molton division. Portsmouth was Vice-Chairman of Devon County Council and Chairman of the Devon Education Committee.

[290] This refers to the National War Aims Committee which was a government-backed initative created by the Lloyd George war cabinet that sought to remobilise the British population to continue to support the war effort.

29 Oct M	Shot on Tower &c. Were pretty lucky am but got little pm.
30 Oct T	
31 Oct W	Exeter each day. Food meeting at Newton Abbot on 31st[.]
1 Nov Th	
2 Nov F	Rode to Barum for Small Holdings meeting. Mild with drizzle.
3 Nov [S]	Showery. Col[onel] Thompson went[.]
4 Nov Sunday	Drove with P to Swymbridge[291] for Church am.
5 Nov M	Rode with S[myth] Richards & Mr Conwell to Bremridge. Pitt & Riverton. Some corn out still & 3 or 4 acres on Blakewell uncut.
6 Nov T	Exeter & on to Barnstaple for Div[ision] FP meeting. Conwell left.
7 Nov W	Shot on Bradbury &c. [R]oughish day. [U]nlucky with the birds & shot poorly.
8 Nov Th	Exeter[.]
9 Nov F	
10 Nov S	Shot on the Cleve & Clatworthy from 11–3 Windy with heavy showers. Got 14 ph[easants] 2 part[ridges] 1 woodcock 4 rab[bits].
11 Nov Sunday	Church am. Walk with P. pm.
12 Nov M	To London by the 9. CFO & Econ. Fine & Coldish[.]
13 Nov T	P came up. Went to Econ.
14 Nov W	Sat to Shannon am… C[.]F.O.
15 Nov Th	Various jobs. Went to Econ. Daisy dined.

[291] This refers to Swimbridge.

16 Nov F	Econ & CFO. [A]fter that to Exeter.
17 Nov S	TF & FP work till 12 then meeting at Guildhall for Sailors Fund.[292] [T]hen to Honiton for F.P. meeting. [T]hen to C H[.] I picked up the following from sure sources in London. An aeroplane is worn out in about three months active service, & is out of date in 4 months. After 100 hours flying (equivalent after all probably to 10 000 miles) the engines have to be literally reconstructed. In the last four months[,] we have destroyed as many German submarines as in all the previous period of the war. The Admiralty know that the Huns have had to shoot men who refused to serve in Sub[marine]s. Our authorities agree that ups & downs are inscribable in sub[marine]. losses.
18 Nov Sunday	Walk with S[myth] R[ichards] am. Church in ev[ening]. Fine but dull.
19 Nov M	Barnstaple for FP work.
20 Nov T	To Exeter. DPF Meeting &c.
21 Nov W	To Kingsbridge to speak on FP[.] Lovely day.
22 Nov Th	Work till 2.30. [T]hen back to Castle Hill[.] Dull. Some rain.
23 Nov F	Went with Mr Somers Cocks to see the Tractor ploughing at Morte[-Hoe] a.m.[,] & spoke at Barum on Food Prod[uction] pm. Foggy.
24 Nov S	Fine day after a rough night. Shot Cawsis Barton &c with 4 guns & got near 80 head.
25 Nov Sunday	Church am. Walk with S[myth] R[ichards] pm. Fine but blowing hard fr[om]. N[orth].
26 Nov M	A long day at FP in Barnstaple.
27 Nov T	Shot on Bradbury &c with Dick & Buttle. Got 13 ph[easants].
28 Nov W	To Exeter for Standing Joint & on to Thorney Wood W Christchurch to stay with Mrs. Gren[ville]. F[ortescue].[293]

---

[292] This refers to the King George's Fund for Sailors.
[293] This refers to Adelaide Jephson (1885–1977).

29 Nov Th	Addie drove me all through the Forest. A beautiful trip to Nathook[294] [*sic*] which I explored thoro'ly [thoroughly] & on to Lyndhurst R[oa]ᵈ whence I took train to London.
30 Nov F <u>London</u>	Exmoor Minerals meeting at 10.30. No clear proposals yet from King Hiller.[295] [T]hen Econ & CFO[,] & saw about my passport. Many formalities.
1 Dec S	Completed the passport formalities & then sat to Shannon 11–1. Dined with Sue.
2 Dec Sunday	Went with P to Holy Communion at Sᵗ Pauls & to see Sir W. Young pm & Aunt came.
3 Dec M	Left for France & got to <u>Cassel</u> about 8.30[.]
4 Dec T	To Messines Ridge, Wytschaet[e] & Ypres.[296]
5 Dec W	Went round Devon units. 1ˢᵗ & 2ⁿᵈ Wes[tern]. F.A. 2ⁿᵈ Devons 5 6 7" RE[.]
6 Dec Th	Saw Devon Cas[ualty]. Clearing Station 47". Then to Laventie[297] to find Gren[ville]. F[ortescue]'s grave.
7 Dec F	Motored to <u>Brai sur Somme</u> & put up with Hugh & 2ᵘ Cav[alry]. Brigade.
8 Dec S	Motored with Hugh round S[outh]. part of the Somme battle field. Lunch with Den[zil] at HQ VII Corps & back through Peronne.
9 Dec Sunday	Drizzling morning after a fine week. Rode with Hugh to Maricourt & on part of the battle field, & left after lunch for <u>Boulogne</u>, seeing Dorothy Greig on the way. Got in about 8.15.
10 Dec M	Round the EFC till lunch with Capt[ain]. Brightman. Harper came to lunch. Boat left 2.15 2[.] I got to <u>Lowndes St</u> by 7. Daisy & Mrs Harford dined.
11 Dec T	To <u>Castle Hill</u> by the 10.15. A lot of amass of letters & work.
12 Dec W	To <u>Exeter</u> for TFA etc.
13 Dec Th	County Council &c[.] [B]ack <u>to C.H[.]</u>

---

[294] This refers to Nat Hook.

[295] Henry King Hiller (1866–1946). He was a British engineer who was a member of both the Institute of Mechanical Engineers and the Institute of Gas Engineers.

[296] All three of these battlefields are located in the area around Ypres.

[297] This refers to Laventie military cemetery.

14 Dec F	Exeter again for Timber Co &c.
15 Dec S	Shot with Buttle & Dick on Heddon Spa Wood &c. 18 ph[easants] 2 part[ridges] 3 rab[bits]. Beautiful day. 2 Canadian off[icers]. came[.]
16 Dec Sunday <u>C. Hill</u>	Very wet & raw. Walked to Bremridge Wood with S[myth] R[ichards] am. Church in ev[ening].
17 Dec M	Barnstaple all day. Rode out in ev[ening]. Sharpish frost.
18 Dec T	Shot Temple High Bray & Wood house. Got with pick up 61 ph[easants]. [M]ostly on Temple side.
19 Dec W	To Exeter & on to Newton [Abbot] for War aims meeting. Did not get home till 8.
20 Dec Th	Exeter[.]
21 Dec F	Shot Burdens Wood & part Tilery. 20 ph[easants] 14 rab[bits] 3 woodcock of which we saw 10. East wind but not much thaw with it.
22 Dec S	Exeter to hear about scheme for employing prisoners of war. Train back an hour later.
23 Dec <u>Sunday</u>	Church am. Walked with Wallace to Park Wood & Bremridge pm, to see what trees sh[oul]^d not be sold to Gov[ernment]'.
24 Dec M	Thaw, but no rain. Thornton came from Dulverton & we shot Whitehill. Brought in 39 ph[easants] 1 part[ridge] 7 wood[cocks] 3 duck[s] 2 rab[bits]. Shooting not very good especially by our Canadian officers. Den[zil] arrived.
25 Dec T	Church & HC. a.m. Walked to Clatworthy & Woodhouse pm. Nice day.
26 Dec W	Mr Pike & his son came up & we shot Higher Beer Smalldon's & Lower Beer in beautiful weather. The shooting was distinctly poor but we got 83 ph[easants] 3 wood[cocks] 2 H[ares] 4 rab[bits].
27 Dec Th	Picked up with Den[zil] & Buttle did Heddon bottom &c. 24 ph[easants].
28 Dec F	Shot Bremridge till lunch. 33 ph[easants][.] [T]hen to Barnstaple for F.P.
29 Dec S	Den[zil] & Capt[ain] Porton left. Rode with Molland to Townhouse am. [C]old.

30 Dec Sunday	Walk with S[myth] R[ichards] am. To church at E[ast] Buckland pm.
31 Dec M	To Barnstaple for FP. Rode home.

1918

1 Jan T <u>Castle Hill</u>	Shot from Goodwills Head[298] by Stoodleigh & Gubbs[299] to bottom of Ashen Copse with young Pike, in a bitter East wind. Only got 15 ph[easants].
2 Jan W	A beautiful bright day with slight frost. Shot from County School & Mays Leary 11–2[,] & got 17 ph[easants]. Dick & Buttle made it up to 30 [pheasants] pm.
3 Jan Th	Exeter for FP 11.30–4.30[.] [T]wo Amory boys came.
4 Jan F	Shot White hill Woodhouse & High Bray. Got 33 ph[easants] mostly cocks[.] 7 woodc[ocks] 3 duck[s] 15 rab[bits]. I shot poorly. Sharp frost, but still.
5 Jan S	Walk with P am & over Townhouse with S[myth] R[ichards] pm.
6 Jan <u>Sunday</u>	Church & HC am. A raw & wet thaw.
7 Jan M	Shot with Buttle & Dick about Bradbury &c.
8 Jan T	Exeter some snow[.]
9 Jan W	Cold thaw. Some rain. Killed 4 ph[easants]. with Dick pm.
10 Jan Th	Shot pm in Lower Beer with with [sic] Sir C Coke[300] & his party. Not an efficient lot.
11 Jan F	Hunt Com[mit]tee at Taunton. An hours work. Left at 11 & got back at 7.
12 Jan S	Drove with P pm to ask after Miss Mould at Warkleigh. Mr Harper & Alice Seymour came.

---

[298] This is presumably Goodwells Head.
[299] This refers to Gubbs Farm near West Buckland.
[300] Sir Charles Henry Coke (1854–1945). He was an admiral in the Royal Navy and had served in the Third Anglo-Ashanti War. He was the ADC to King Edward VII in 1907 and Commander-in-Chief of the Coast of Ireland Station from 1911 to 1915.

13 Jan Sunday	Very nice day. Walk with S[myth] R[ichards] am & to E[ast] B[uckland] church pm.
14 Jan M	Snow. Work all day in Barnstaple.
15 Jan T	Rain[.]
16 Jan W	Shot over Bradbury & Cawsi[s] Barton with Capt Pike Dick & Buttle. A very sporting day[.] 38 head 7 sorts [*sic*].
17 Jan Th	Exeter. F time came.
18 Jan F	Exeter. The Bishop came.
19 Jan S	Fine after much heavy rain. Shot Ashen Copse[,] Birchen Copse &c[.] 15 ph[easants]. 13 rab[bits] 2 woodc[ocks].
20 Jan Sunday	Church am. Walk with S[myth] R[ichards] pm. Blowing hard.
21 Jan M	Not a bad day. Shot in Bremridge till 3. Got a few ph[easants] but only saw 1 or 2 woodcock.
22 Jan T	To London. H[ouse] of Lords for Proport[ional]" [*sic*] Representation.[301]
23 Jan W	Various jobs. CMC. H[ouse] of Lords pm.
24 Jan Th	Went to meeting about Kut prisoners.[302] A pitiful affair. H[ouse] of Lords after. P came up.
25 Jan F	Econ & CFO.
26 Jan S	Den[zil] came up from Cambridge. Lady Allendale & Sandie lunched[.]
27 Jan Sunday	Church in Sloane S[treet]. am. Daisy & Betty later dined. Fine.
28 Jan M Lowndes S[t]	Com[mi]tee at Econ & CFO. H[ouse] of Lords. Got back for dinner just as Air raid began. It lasted 8 – 10.30 & began again for half hour about 12.30. Much noise.

[301] This refers to the discussion in the House of Lords surrounding the Representation of the People Bill of 1918 which extended the franchise to all men over the age of 21 and women over the age of 30 who personally held property to value of no less than £5.

[302] See 'Prisoners of the Turks', *The Daily Mail*, 25 January 1918, p. 5.

29 Jan   To Food Production Office pm. [T]hen H[ouse] of Lords. Another air raid.
T

30 Jan   Thick fog am. Dentist pm.
W

31 Jan   Went to Shannon's am with P & Daisy, but the light was too bad for painting.
Th

1 Feb   Went to Canteen Board am & to Brit[ish] Museum pm. Less fog.
F

2 Feb   Hugh Bampfylde[303] who is just invalided back from E[ast] Africa came to
S   luncheon. He was nearly 3 months en route [*sic*] from Nairobi via the Cape.
           He says that the war might have been over in 1916 if the Portuguese had
           not sold them munitions, if Pegasus had not been sunk, if the Germans
           had not got a store ship through & if the Dutch had fought; but they were
           only out to see the country, & when Smuts had the Germans cornered
           they would open out & let them through, & for political reasons Smuts
           dared not let them in for casualties. The Germans fought clean & had
           treated prisoners well as a rule. They would have about 300 whites & 2000
           natives left, of whom they have made very good soldiers, & it might take
           six months to round them up. They had made a very fine fight of it & the
           natives had stuck to them.
           [P]artly because Smuts instead of letting native deserters go home had
           insisted on putting them into our Army.
           Sydney Clive[304] told me lately that the Germans we take prisoner in France
           are well nourished & their canteens are full of food.

3 Feb   Fine but dull after rain.
Sunday   Went to service at the Temple am. Daisy & her sister dined[.]
London

4 Feb   To Exeter by the 11. Food Production & TF[.]
M

5 Feb   Child Welfare Com[mit]ᵗᵉᵉ & Comrades of the gr[eat]. War.
T   Back by the 3 to Lowndes Sᵗ[.] Fine but dull.

6 Feb   Sat to Shannon am. To Ministry of Food &c pm. We have only ½ the
W   feeding stuffs for animals we used in 1917 & ⅓ of what we used in 1916.

7 Feb   Lunched with Davis & decided to close down Exmoor mines. Dined with
Th   Lady Northcote. [P]leasant.

[303] Hugh De Burgh Warwick Bampfylde (1888–1978). He was the sixth Baron Poltimore and a
county councillor of Wiltshire from 1937 to 1945. During the First World War, he had served in East
Africa with the King's African Rifles.
[304] Sir (George) Sidney Clive (1874–1959). He was a lieutenant-general in the British army and
served in the Second Boer War and the First World War. He was the Military Governor at Cologne
in 1919 and the British Military Representative to the League of Nations at Geneva from 1920 to
1922. He was the Military Attaché to Paris from 1924 to 1927 and the Director of Personal Services
at the War Office from 1928 to 1930. Clive was the Military Secretary to the Secretary of State for
War from 1930 to 1934.

8 Feb F	Wet. Econ & CFO.
9 Feb S	<u>To Castle Hill</u> by the 10.15. Went for a short ride.
10 Feb Sunday	Took S[myth] R[ichards] to Exmoor am. Church in ev[ening]. Rather windy.
11 Feb M	At Barnstaple on Food Production all day.
12 Feb T	To Exeter, & rode back over Townhouse on the way home.
13 Feb W	Shot in Tilery &c with Hugh Bampfylde. Only got 3 ph[easants] & 20 rab[bits]. Saw 5 woodcock.
14 Feb Th	To Exeter for F.P.[,] & on by the 4.20 to <u>London</u>[.] Den[zil] up for the night.
15 Feb F	Did Com[mit][tee] work at Econ & CFO. Reggie Seymour,[305] just back from Palestine came to luncheon.
16 Feb S	Cold but still. Danish Minister dined. Air Raid.
17 Feb Sunday	Church at S[t] Peters am. Good sermon. Air raid.
18 Feb M	Econ & CFO Com[mit][tee]. Tea with John. Air Raid.
19 Feb T	Statement in H[ouse] of Lords about Robertson &c. Gov[ernment] have a pretty good case, & would not have made so bad an impression in the Commons last week if Ll[oyd] George had spoken straight. Derby having resigned at least once remains in office.
20 Feb W Lowndes S[t]	Sat to Shannon am. Some rain. Went to the 13th Chair[306] in ev[ening]. Desart[307] told me last night that a few weeks ago 75% of the Irish Convention were in favour of what seemed a workable scheme. [B]ut influences had been brought to bear & it would do little more than command a majority now.

---

[305] Sir Reginald Henry Seymour (1878–1938). He was a lieutenant-colonel in the British army and served in both the Second Boer War and the First World War. He was equerry to King George V from 1916 to 1936 and equerry to Queen Mary from 1936 to 1938.

[306] This refers to 'The Thirteenth Chair' which was a play by Bayard Veiller.

[307] Hamilton John Cuffe (1848–1934). He was the fifth Earl of Desart and the Lord Lieutenant of Kilkenny from 1920 to 1922. He was the Queen's Proctor from 1894 to 1909 and the Director of Public Prosecutions from 1894 to 1908. Desart was a Unionist member on the Irish Convention from 1917 to 1918.

21 Feb Th	Winding up Meeting of the C.M.C. pm. In 22 years the turnover rose from £5500 to £2 000 000 p'er an[num]. Not bad for an amateur crowd.
22 Feb F	Econ & CFO.
23 Feb S	Made some calls with P pm. Dined with Manner's. Pleasant.
24 Feb Sunday	Church at St Peters am. To Exeter by 2.40 train & stayed at the club.
25 Feb M	To Barnstaple by early train for Food Production[.] [T]o Castle Hill in ev[ening].
26 Feb T	To Exeter.
27 Feb W	Wet all day. Rode with S[myth] R[ichards] to Leary Long Walk & Townhouse.
28 Feb Th	To Exeter for FP & on by 4.20 to Lowndes Street. Den[zil] up for two nights – snow.
1 Mar F	Fine. Walk with Den[zil] am. N[avy] & A[rmy] Canteen Board at 11.30. They have opened a canteen for 20 000 men at Medros [sic]. Com[mit]^{tee} at Econ & CFO.
2 Mar S	Mrs Bentinck went away. Very cold.
3 Mar Sunday	Went to St Pauls for HC am.
4 Mar M	Com[mit]^{tee} at Econ & CFO. Charlie came to lunch.
5 Mar T	To Mulbery Walk[308] am when many ladies including P are making surgical boots &c.
6 Mar W	Stayed in all day having I think a touch of flu. Rall's & Florence Corkram dined.
7 Mar Th London	Went to Charing X [Cross] to see Charles off to Salonica. [B]ut hardly left the house else. A pleasant dinner. Then Roselyn Benyon. Ellisons. Jarstin & Polly Strucley. Benyon Jarstin & Ellison agreed that but for our Allies we should be all right. The French are gallant fighters on the day, but expect other people to do the spade work. Very parochial in their views & very exacting, far more difficult to deal with than Germans.

---

[308] This refers to Mulbery Walk in Chelsea.

8 Mar F	Econ & CFO[,] & final meeting of CMC. Rather tired.
9 Mar S	Stayed in till after tea then went to Aunt Blanche to escape from doing duty at a little Jane. P. had for Helen Duff[.]
10 Mar Sunday	Stayed in all day.
11 Mar M	Duchy of Cornwall Council a.m.[309] S camped a lot of business in 40 min[s]. The Ryles came to luncheon.
12 Mar T	To Exeter by the 1 0 [clock][.]
13 Mar W	TFA & FP meeting. [A]t work fr[om] 10 till 5 nearly. Very tired.
14 Mar Th	County Council & then Timber Co Meeting. Back by the 4.15 to Castle Hill P & Den[zil] also came.
15 Mar F	Rode with Den[zil] a.m. Fine but cold.
16 Mar S	Rode to Whitechapel for lunch.
17 Mar Sunday	Den[zil] left at 11.40 for Crediton & London. Walked to Church at E[ast] Buckland with P pm.
18 Mar M	Spent the whole day going to Broomford & back for poor old White Thomson's[310] funeral.
19 Mar T	The wind has changed to W[est] & the long spell of fine E[ast] wind weather has changed to rain. Petty Sess[ions]" at Molton.
20 Mar W Castle Hill	Walked to Acland Barton & Higher Beer pm. P to Flete [sic].
21 Mar Th	Rode with S[myth] R[ichards] to Townhouse am. [T]o gardens p.m. Warm[.]
22 Mar F	Walked to Higher Beer am & to Bradbury pm. P returned.

[309] In 1918, the fourth Earl Fortescue was appointed the Office of Member of the Council of the Duchy of Cornwall.

[310] Sir Robert Thomas White-Thomson (1831–1918). He was a colonel in the British army and commanded the Devon Militia. At the House of Laymen, White-Thomson represented the Diocese of Exeter. He was an alderman of Devon County Council and a DL and JP for Devon.

23 Mar S	About the place[.]
24 Mar Sunday	To Church at Swymbridge. Walk pm[.]
25 Mar M	Hugh worid [*sic*] [worried] he had ~~recalled~~ gone back to France. Grave news from there.[311] At Barnstaple most of day for FP.
26 Mar T	To Exeter by the 12.50. Explosion heard about 4.30.
27 Mar W	Rode with S[myth] R[ichards] am. Bad war news.
28 Mar Th	To Exeter. Steady rain in forenoon. Bright & fine after.
29 Mar F	Good Friday. Church at 11. Cold N[orth] W[est] wind.
30 Mar S	About the place am. To West Buckland School in ev[ening] & talked to boys about the war.
31 Mar Sunday	Church am. H.C. Walk pm.
1 April M	Had a look at Sladers Hounds who ran a hind up the valley from Bremridge. Rode with S[myth] R[ichards] pm.
2 April T	To South Molton for policing am. Rode with P. to Stoodleigh pm.
3 Apr W	To Exeter for Child Welfare &c. [T]hen by 2.56 to Tavistock & on with Peacock to Princetown. Walked to Tor Royal after tea & looked at the house & horses. Clinton came late.
4 Apr Th	Tor Royal again to inspect horses & young stock. [T]hen rode to the land they are reclaiming. Very misty which spoiled one's enjoyment, though one could see the effect of M. Bendelmann's work in the deep peat. After lunch motored to Brimpts.[312] Saw the plantation there. Walked. Missing our way. [T]o Laughter Hall. [G]ot the car again there & went on to the farm in hand at Belliver when we saw all the stock. Their best Dartmoor ran cut 31 [16] cuts of wool. Back at 7. [P]retty tired.
5 Apr F	Left about 9.20 via Tavistock for Kit Hill when we inspected the Wolfram mine[,] which has great possibilities; though nearly all the work done so far is exploration & installation of plant & there will be no great action for a time. Went on to the model farm at Stoke Climsland. Very good buildings

---

[311] This refers to the Spring Offensive of 1918.
[312] This refers to Brimpts Farm at Dartsmeet.

which must have cost ten years purchase of the land. A lot of fashionable short horses of all ages, very plump, which at present prices pay well & some good Devons.
Caught the 4.40 at Tavistock & got to <u>Castle Hill</u> at 7.45. Beautiful day & splendid view from top of Kit Hill.

6 Apr S	About the place. P & M Stucley came.
7 Apr Sunday	Fine. Walk am. Church in ev[ening].
8 Apr M	Barnstaple for FP. Fine.
9 Apr T	Exeter for Red X [Cross] etc. Very tired after[.]
10 Apr W	Drive to S[outh] Molton pm & walked after. Raw & dull.
11 Apr Th	To Exeter by the 8.30 & came back by Exe Valley arriving 6 40. [N]ot tired considering.
12 Apr F	Rode to Townhouse am. Walk with P pm. Thornton Hancock & Badge came about Hunt affairs.
13 Apr S	Motored with P & S[myth] R[ichards] to Exmoor & Challacombe where saw new tenants at Westland etc. Beautiful day, but grave news from France.
14 Apr Sunday	Church am. Cold wind. Better news fr[om]. France[.] [T]hank god.
15 Apr M	Rode with S[myth] R[ichards] to see new tenants at ~~Brayley~~ Park to E[ast] B[uckland] Mill Bushton Tower & Bradbury.
16 Apr T <u>Castle Hill</u>	Some nice birthday letters, including one of 12" from Hugh. Rode pm with Dick to see stock in heavy rain.
17 Apr W	To Plymouth to present OBE medals. Ceremony went off well though it was chilly work. To <u>Bidlake Veau</u> pm to stay with Miss Hamlyn & had much useful talk.
18 Apr Th <u>London</u>	Fine after a wet night. Walked over whole farm, including what I had not seen last night. To by 12.50 train arriving 5.40. Sat next L°[rd] Carnock at dinner. He holds strongly that the Kaiser did not want war with us a bit[,] & was rather let in for it by Austria. Feeling seems to be that we are past the crisis.

19 Apr F	Various jobs & went to CFO for annual meeting.
20 Apr S	Back <u>to Castle Hill</u> by the 10.15. Very wet 3 – 7[.]
21 Apr <u>Sunday</u>	Church at Swymbridge am & came back by Riverton to see the barn etc that was burned. Cold.
22 Apr M	To Barnstaple at FP all day.

[No entry for 23 April]

24 Apr W	Rode with P. to Blackpool pm. Lovely day.
25 Apr Th	To Exeter by early train back by Exe Valley. Quite warm.
26 Apr F	Exeter again with P. who had to open a sale there for Prisoners.
27 Apr S	P went to London. Rode with S[myth] R[ichards] to Townhouse Riverton etc. 10.30 – 4. Lovely warm day.
28 Apr <u>Sunday</u>	Beautiful day, but less warm. Church am. Walk pm.
29 Apr M	<u>To London</u> by the 9. CFO[.] Dined with Mary Egerton[.]
30 Apr T	Various jobs. B[oar]ᵈ of Agric[ulture].[,] etc. [C]old.
1 May W	CFO. Busy day between F.P. & W.O. P left for Windsor.
2 May Th	To Exeter for FP Com[mit]tee.[,] & on to <u>Castle Hill</u>[.] Warmer.
3 May F <u>Castle Hill</u>	Rode with Dick am to Townhouse Hill S[outh] Aller &c. Some mild rain in ev[ening].
4 May S	To Taunton for Hunt Com[mit]ᵗᵉᵉ & to give S Tucker the £485 subscribed for him. Woollcombe came back with me.
5 May <u>Sunday</u>	Walked with Woollcombe to Brayley bridge am. Church in ev[ening].
6 May M	Barnstaple 10.30 – 4.30 for F.P.

7 May T	Exeter, for presentation of DCM & Mil[itary]. Medals by Sir H Sclater. Lunched with him first, some rain.
8 May W	Rode with Woollcombe to Exmoor. Lovely day.
9 May Th	All day on exemptions at Barnstaple. Very tired.
10 May F	Ditto. Ditto.
11 May S	Rode with S[myth] R[ichards] to Townhouse am & motored him to Challacombe pm to look at the two Barton gate holdings.
12 May Sunday	Chilly. N[orth] W[est] wind. Church am. Walk with S[myth] R[ichards] pm.
13 May M	Fine & pleasant after some much desired rain. To Barnstaple all day on F.P.
14 May T	Rode to Tossells Barton am & went back through woods. Some rain pm.
15 May W	To Exeter for Presentation to City of Colonial Flags.[313] Good function. Stayed at Club.
16 May Th	Work from 10–4. Back to Castle Hill by the 4.35. Lovely day.
17 May F	Rode to Riverton, where there has been another fire am & went to Barum pm go to finish work on exemptions.
18 May S Castle Hill	Beale Browns came over for the day. He caught no fish but we rode together after lunch & we had some interesting talk about the German push. The Hun success at end of March seems to have been due to three things. They got across the marshes which was not expected. We were holding too much line for our strength. Though some of our men fought well, especially the Australians some fought very badly. The 16th Irish Nationalist Div[ision] were deserting in dozens on the eve of the push & bolted wholesale when it began. The 14th were so shaky that he had to post the 4th D.G. behind them with drawn swords to keep them in their trenches in front of Amiens. Another Div[ision] under Gough's late chief of Staff[314] was no better: & many M[achine]. G[un]. men bolted.

---

[313] See 'Australians at Exeter', 1914–1918, British Pathé, https://www.britishpathe.com/video/australians-at-exeter/query/Devon, (accessed 14 December 2017).

[314] This refers to Sir Neill Malcolm (1869–1953) who was General Gough's Chief of Staff until 21 December 1917 and this would then mean that the division to which Earl Fortescue was referring was the 66th Division.

The infantry hated Gough[315] & thought he sacrificed them. We lost very heavily in material.

The scenes in the retreat were as pitiful as in 1914[,][316] & the feeling among the French civilians unpleasantly strong. Our collapse was a complete surprise to ourselves. In the north the Portuguese[317] gave us away. [T]hey had been kept in the line though they had told the natives they did not mean to stand.

The bombardment before the attack was the heaviest he had ever known & the very thick fog helped the Huns too.

Hugh had arrived back from leave just in the nick of time & had done very well. He had rec[ommende]ᵈ him for D.S[.]O. & if he did not get it now he would later.

The Australians had fought very well. Our MGC not.

19 May Sunday C. Hill	Church am. H.C. In pm walked to Huxtable with S[myth] R[ichards].
20 May M	At Barnstaple for FP.
21 May T	To S[outh] Molton for Petty Sess[ions]. A thunderstorm with welcome rain between 1 & 2.
22 May W	Rode to Townhouse am. More thunder pm. P returned. Rain at night[.]
23 May Th	Exeter for FP etc.
24 May F	Exeter again for Women's Recruiting Rally! DPF &c.
25 May S	Motored with P & S[myth] R[ichards] to Exmoor & rode about there in pleasant weather. All well there.
26 May Sunday	Church am. Walked up the river with P pm.
27 May M	A lot of work. Hardly went out.
28 May T	With P to Exeter.
29 May W	Exeter for S. J. Com[mit]ᵗᵉᵉ &c[.]

---

[315] Sir Hubert de la Poer Gough (1870–1963). He was a general in the British army who served in both the Second Boer War and the First World War. He commanded the 5th Army at the Battles of Pozieres, Thiepval and Beaumont-Hamel.

[316] This refers to the retreat at Mons in 1914.

[317] This refers to the Portuguese Expeditionary Force.

30 May Th	Spent the morning with Horne & S[myth] R[ichards] on F.P. work. Rode in ev[ening] with S[myth] R[ichards].
31 May F	Rode with P pm to Cowst Hall[.]
1 June S	To Torrington to meet RSM Brooks who gave me some news of the Reg[iment]. but train was so late. I had only about 40 min[utes] with him.
2 June Sunday	Went to Church at E[ast] Buck[lan]ᵈ pm.
3 June M	Long day at Barnstaple. The Fullers came.
4 June T	Barnstaple in afternoon[.]
5 June W	Barnstaple all day[.]
6 June Th	To Exeter by ~~early~~ 10 [o clock] train. Some rain.
7 June F	To Exeter by 8.30 train. Hugh Neville came[.]
8 June S	Barnstaple all day. Den[zil] came & Jock.
9 June Sunday	Church am. Nice rain. Den[zil] got fever pm.
10 June M	A very long day at Barnstaple on exemptions. Fine but cool.
11 June T	Cleaned up arrears of work & rode pm. Den[zil] better. Fine.
12 June W	Rode with Neville pm.
13 June Th	To Exeter for War Pensions Com[mit]ᵗᵉᵉ &c. Susan & Mary came[.] C. Hill
14 June F	Long day at Barnstaple on exemptions. Nice rain.
15 June S	Rode with Den[zil] am. He went to Clovelly pm. Timber Co meeting at Barnstaple. Cold.

16 June Sunday	Walked with P to Church at E[ast] Buckland pm. Fresh wind.

17 June M	A long day in Barnstaple. P went to London.

18 June T	Steady rain from S[outh] E[ast]. Rode to Molton to see Bank am.

19 June W	To Exeter for TFA etc.

20 June Th	County Council. Back by 4.35 to Castle Hill[.] Rain in ev[ening][.]

21 June F	Rain all day. Hardly went out.

22 June S	Fine but blowing fresh from N[orth]. W[est]. Barnstaple for FP pm.

23 June Sunday	Church am. Went with the sisters to High Down pm.

24 June M	To London. CFO. Dined with Allendales. Daisy seedy.

25 June T	Various jobs. H[ouse] of Lords in ev[ening].

26 June W	CFO & Econ. H[ouse] of Lords.

27 June Th	Econ. Went to Hampstead to see Lucy. H[ouse] of Lords.

28 June F	Econ & CFO. Dined with Mary Egerton.

29 June S	By the 10.15 to Castle Hill. Rode in ev[ening].

30 June Sunday	Walk with Dick am. Church in ev[ening]. [H]ot.

1 July M	Barnstaple all day. P returned.

2 July T	Rode to Charles am.

3 July W	To Exmoor with S[myth] R[ichards] & P. Had a good ride.

4 July Th	Exeter all day.
5 July F	Ditto[.]
6 July S	Rode with S[myth] R[ichards] & Molland to Townhouse etc. Still fine & hot.
7 July Sunday	Church am & HC. Walk with P pm.
8 July M Castle Hill	Rode to Molton am about Prisoners of War etc.
9 July T	P went to Plymouth. Some welcome showers though all Sandywalk field is down.
10 July W	To Newton Abbot to meet P & see the hospital for neurasthenics at Seale Hayne under Major Hurst. Most interesting. A good deal of rain.
11 July Th	Showers at short intervals all day. Went out little.
12 July F	P to Exeter. Rode to Whitsford & back by Stoodleigh & Indicombe. Showers[.]
13 July S	About the place. Rain in ev[ening].
14 July Sunday	A good deal of rain till 4. [T]hen fine. Church in ev[ening].
15 July M	P to London. At Barnstaple all day. S[mith] Rewse came.
16 July T	Walked with S[mith] Rewse am after it cleared up & drove him to Molton pm.
17 July W	Rode to Townhouse am with S[myth] R[ichards] & motored pm to Challacombe & Bridwick.[318] Showery.
18 July Th	Exeter all day. Showers.
19 July F	Rode with Dick am. Still muggy with drizzles.
20 July S	To Coln S[t]. Aldwyn. A tedious journey & train very full.

[318] This probably refers to Bridwick Farm near Kentisbury.

21 July
Sunday

Church am. Walk with Sue Beach to Swire farm pm.

22 July
M

To London by the 9.15.
CFO.[,] & Home Office after. Showers.
Palmer has gone off kokey [sic] morning & there is no servant of any sort in
Lowndes St but Kearsly, wh[ich]. is sd [sic] uncomfortable.

23 July
T

Went to Ebrington with Daisy. It rained nearly all the way but cleared just
before we arrived at 1. Went to Longmoor first. He complains the roof leaks
but there was no sign of it in the main part of the house. Wet is coming in
however on the ridge of the centre gable that in n [sic] N[orth].[,] & some of
the rafters are rotten. The roof of the annex at N[orth] E[ast] corner (over
dairy I think) is also defective. Purlins have sagged & slates have slipped.
The chimney top of kitchen chimney is cracked & I authorised him to get a
new one put up.
Shuting is badly wanted along W[est] side as it soaks in through kitchen
walls. Some skirting sh[oul]d be put there after shuting is fixed.
Inside they have done up most of the bedrooms but the kitchen range is in
bad order. Bagshaun says he could not get a new one fixed even if one were
procurable.
The woodwork of the windows etc needs paint, & of the outbuildings[.]
Far. B. speaks well of tar or corrugated iron.
The Pigs have gnawn the partitions of the pig styes [sic] & some sleepers
APX as skirting would be desirable.
The tenant & his son made a good impression on us both. He has 20 or 21
milking cows & supplies the Birmingham Fever Hospital. All are tested for
Tube[r]cul[osis]. 9 calves which I did not see. No sheep. Three good horses
& a lab[rador].
He had not got heavy crops of hay. A very good crop of wheat in part of
153. 12 – 16 acres probably roots & beans beyond. Mainly corn he had
was oats in 157. Not much over half a crop, & not too clean. 143 had been
cultivated across & above. There are a lot of gates wanted.
Went there to the Oakham Cottages & saw old Woodward.
All seemed well in the rood except leakage in the roof by Suttons Chimney.
[T]he Western house.
Had only time after that for a short visit to the Hall & caught with an effort
the 4.3 home.

24 July
W

CFO & other jobs. Charlie & I lunched together at Travellers.
He is very strong about the grasping of the French in all matters financial.
Showers.
Went from H[ouse] of Lords to hear Mr Hughes speak about the Pacific
Islands. He was clear & knew his mind, but was disappointing.

25 July
Th

To see the Naval photos am with P & Daisy. Excellent. [T]hen C.F.O.
H[ouse] of Lords pm. Heavy showers.

26 July
F

Back to Castle Hill by Exeter.
Saw Inspector of Police there.
He said the Gov[ernment]. were not frightened of the aeroplane men striking.
They could spare them for a month: but if the Electric engineers struck all
the cold storage works might go wrong. Showers.

27 July S	Rode with S[myth] R[ichards] to Townhouse am. Fine & pleasant[.]
28 July Sunday	Walk with S[myth] R[ichards] am & to Acland Barton pm[.] [B]efore church[,] hot.
29 July M	Barnstaple all day.
30 July T	Rode to Exmoor with Dick. Hot but not unpleasant.
31 July W	Rode a little am. P returned.
1 Aug Th	Exeter all day. [B]ack by Exe valley. Rain. [H]eavy at night doing damage.
2 Aug F	Exeter again. More rain.
3 Aug S	Moved out to Exmoor[.] Fine luckily[.]
4 Aug Sunday	Church am. Surtees[319] did the War Anniversary service well & did not preach a sermon. Walk pm. Fine.
5 Aug M	Wet morning so did not ride out on chance of seeing hounds till after lunch. Met them coming home from a hill at Badgery after a nice run from Cloutsham. More rain in ev[ening].
6 Aug T	Rode to Cornham & Wintershead pm. Fine after a very wet night.
7 Aug W	Rode with Molland pm to Warren & Larkbarrow. Fine[.]
8 Aug Th	Stag H[oun][ds] at Cuzzicombe. Waited on the top till 2 when there being no signs of life rode home by Litton F[erny Bal][l] and Horsen.
9 Aug F	Rode with P to Hoar Oak pm. Fine but windy.
10 Aug S	Stag H[oun][ds] at Hawkcombe Head. Found between Silcom[b]e & Twitchin Combe & after a little got him away over North Common. Laid on. [C]rossed Deddycombe to Yannery Common[320] & went down over toward Glenthorne when we came home. Fine & warm.

[319] This refers to the Reverend George. W. Surtees.
[320] This is probably Yenworthy Common.

11 Aug Sunday	Church am. Walked pm to Wintershead.
12 Aug M	Barnstaple for Ag[ricultural] Exec[utive].[321]
13 Aug T	Busy with the ponies pm[,] first driving in & then sorting. Fine.
14 Aug W Exmoor	Rode pm to Buscombe. E[ast] side of roof of Woodhouse off porch takes wet. Showlsbury.[322] [N]il. Chall[acombe]. Mill. How about the wire fence? A little plastering some above porch. Wants grate instead of decayed bodley in parlour. Barton. Tenant of No 2 cot[tage]. wants some land. Whitefield Tennesleigh the oats are poor & rode home by Woodbarrow & Pinkery Cot[tage]. A good round. Fine.
15 Aug Th	To Exeter for the day. Heard Hugh had arrived in London last evening. Wound doing well.
16 Aug F	A short ride with Dick pm.
17 Aug S	Hounds at Two gates. Found 3 stags in Combe W[est] of Hoar Oak Tree who presently joined about 12 more on the Chains. Played about there for an hour. We could see little for the driving mist. About 1.30 laid on near Woolhanger & ran down the Combe & by Ilkerton to the W[est] Lyn above Barbrook Mill. Went to a holloa toward New Mill & after some patient hunting fresh found in the clear. [R]aced him back the way he had come to Ilkerton & over the open to Ruckham Combe & Hoar Oak Water. Down that across by Cheriton & killed at bridge under Farleigh. The pace was too good for us & we went home from Hoare Oak. [A] 5 or 6 y[ear] old stag. BT.2. [F]at.
18 Aug Sunday	Church am. Walked to Duredon pm & back through Cornham Brake.
19 Aug M	S[myth] Richards out. Rode with him & Molland p.m. Driving mist nearly all day.
20 Aug T	Lovely day. Rode with P. pm to Brendon & Ashton.
21 Aug W	To Exeter for presentation of my picture to P. Everybody very nice about it. Beautiful weather & harvest progressing fast.
22 Aug Th Exmoor	Rode with Dick am to Driver after a stray pony. Gen & Mr Burnett Stewart came to luncheon. Our disasters in March & April were due to our holding more lines than we could defend. This was enforced by our politicians under pressure from

---

[321] This refers to the Devon War Agricultural Executive Committee.
[322] This probably refers to Shoulsbury.

the French, who wanted to rest & train their divisions. They rested them,
but did not train them, they never do in billets, hence their own disasters
soon after in Champagne. We knew we were taking grave risks[,] & we lost
something like 100 000 prisoners. The prisoners we took the other day were
well clothed & well fed, but unfeignedly glad to be captured. [T]hey did not
know of their defeat on the Marne.[323]

23 Aug F	Rode with Dick to Acland allot^m[ents] am & back by Emmetts.

23 Aug
F

Rode with Dick to Acland allot^m[ents] am & back by Emmetts.

24 Aug
S

Hounds at Hawkcombe H[ea]^d.
Found in the Plantations & ran by Deddycombe & Yannery Common &
the Cliffs. Lovely day. Hugh & Daisy came.
He little the worse now for the wound he got on 9th.

25 Aug
Sunday

Much rain. Church twice.

26 Aug
M

Rode with Hugh am with S[myth] R[ichards] pm. Fine.

27 Aug
T

To Exeter with P. [R]ain most of the day.

28 Aug
W

Fine. Rode with Hugh pm.

29 Aug
Th

Exeter. Fine.

30 Aug
F

Fine am. Rain pm. Walked about woods with Mr Crossfield.

31 Aug
S

Hounds at Larkbarrow. Laid on near Two Gates. Fresh found near Elson
Barrow. Ran to Woolhanger. A ring to near Martinhoe x [Cross] & by
Woolhanger Common back & to the Plantations there & over Butter hill
to Woodbarrow hangings. The Chains, Buscombe & Tom's hill killed at
Robbers bridge.
A good hunt in pleasant weather. We saw the first part well.

1 Sept
Sunday

Church am. Walked with Molland about the woods pm.

2 Sept
M

Barnstaple all day.

3 Sept
T

Rode with Hugh to Challacombe pm. Twitchen no complaints. Ring of bells
pump received by frost. Cottage. [T]he thatch on Ridd's half lets in wet on
dividing wall. Withycombe nil. Swincombe E[ast] nil. Swincombe W[est].
Roof of Milking shippen [sic] very bad. Some window frames need repair.
Lovely day.

---

[323] The events in both Champagne and the Marne refer to the second Battle of the Marne that took
place from 15 July 1918 to 6 August 1918.

4 Sept W	To London by the 9.10. CFO & saw Aunt Blanche.
5 Sept Th	Long interview at Central Prisoners of War Com[mi]^{tee} & went to Ministry of Pensions pm & Local Gov[ernment]. Board twice. Heavy rain between 6 & 7.
6 Sept F	B[oar]^d of Agriculture. [T]hen Econ & CFO.
7 Sept S	Back to Castle Hill & home to Exmoor by the 10.15. Showery.
8 Sept Sunday	Church am. Showers.
9 Sept M	Much rain pm. Motored to Minehead.
10 Sept T	Di[tto]. [W]ent to Barnstaple for Timber Co meeting.
11 Sept W	Shot with Hugh on Wintershead & Horsen am. Bag[ged] 1 hen ph[easant] & 1 rab[bit]. Windy with showers.
12 Sept Th	Hounds at Cuzzicombe. Found directly in Syndercombe & crossed to Redlands. Laid on above the lane a full half hour behind. Up the valley & over Cuzzicombe braking near White Post to Moor house Ridge[324] & Lish[w]ell went up near by the fence & along S[outh] side of Anstey Common to Race Course & down over by White Rocks to Castle Bridge. Could not hit him downward. [T]ried up the Danesbrook & had a time in Church wood. When I came home. Windy but pretty fine till 2.30 then heavy showers.
13 Sept F	With Hugh & Daisy to Dulverton. They thence to London. I to Exeter.
14 Sept S	Stag H[oun]^{ds} at Two Gates. Wind rain & mist, which continued more or less all day had made harbouring very difficult. There had been stags at Farleigh, but they had moved & we had a blank day.
15 Sept Sunday	Church am. Walked with P to Driver cot[tage] pm.
16 Sept M	To Barnstaple & back in ev[ening] to Castle Hill[.] Showers[.]
17 Sept T	To Exeter. P came down.

---

[324] This refers to Moorhouse Ridge.

18 Sept W	About the place. Fine am but heavy showers pm.
19 Sept Th	To Exeter. Finer.
20 Sept F	Walked with Wallace to Park Wood & rode after with GC S[myth] R[ichards].
21 Sept S	To Indio & went pm to rather a dismal concert at Seale Hayne Hospital.
22 Sept Sunday	Church am at Bovey [Tracey]. [A] beautiful building. Stormy pm.
23 Sept M	Walked to Hawkmoor pm & went over the place. Showers.
24 Sept T	The Bentincks took us to Exeter[.] [S]ome small jobs there.
25 Sept W Exeter	Housing Conference & TFA. Hayes Fisher[325] very good at the former. Fine.
26 Sept Th	County Council. [O]ver by 1. [B]ut the train's so late owing to the strike that I did not get home till 6.30. Everyone[,] thank god[,] condemns the railway strikers unjustifiable conduct. Wet pm.
27 Sept F	Walked to Townhouse with P pm.
28 Sept S	Slader at W[est] Buckland. Found in Collythorne[326] & ran by Stoodleigh & Tossells Barton to Little Bray & up the valley. We then rode home. Hounds went on to Acland Allot[ments]". Lovely day with fresh N[orth]. W[est]. wind.
29 Sept Sunday	Church am. Very wet.
30 Sept M	Barnstaple for Agric[ulture] Exec[utive]. Fine.
1 Oct T Castle Hill	Shot with Col. Worall[327] over Blackpools & Townhouse. Got 36 ph[easants] 5 rab[bits] 2 part[ridge]s – only saw about 10 part[ridge]s. Lovely day.

[325] William Hayes Fisher (1853–1920). He was the first Baron Downham and the Conservative MP for Fulham from 1885 to 1906 and January 1910 to 1918. Downham was the President of the Local Government Board from 1917 to 1918 and Chancellor of the Duchy of Lancaster from November 1918 to January 1919.
[326] This refers to Collythorn Wood.
[327] This could be Percy Reginald Worrall (1880–1940). He was a colonel in the British army with the Devonshire Regiment and served in the Second Boer War and First World War.

| 2 Oct
W | Shot with Buttle on past Heddon & Tower 10.30 – 1.
Got 14 ph[easants] 2 part[ridges] 1 H[are] 1 rab[bit].
Cloudy with showers[.] |

3 Oct
Th

Exeter. Pretty fine.

4 Oct
F

Shot with C. Slader & Buttle over S[outh]. Aller & Hill. 42 ph[easants] 4 part[ridge]s 5 rab[bits].
A beautiful day.

5 Oct
S

A wet night & dull day.
Corn still out.

6 Oct
Sunday

Church am. High wind.
Walk with P pm.

7 Oct
M

Rode with S[myth] R[ichards] am. It rains most nights, but not much by day.

8 Oct
T

Shot with Buttle on Knightsbray Hill &c. [O]nly got 15 ph[easant], 1 part[ridge] 1 pig[eon]. I shot badly & we had bad luck with the birds.

9 Oct
W
C. Hill

To Exeter with P for a speech by Gen[eral] Biddle[328] of USA.
[N]ot a great speech but he & Surg[eon]. Gen[eral] Winter[329] who came back with us were very pleasant.

10 Oct
Th

Shot with Reg[inald]. Seymour & Buttle at Leary. We shot poorly & had bad luck & only got 27 ph[easants].
Fine but dull. Strong W[est] wind.

11 Oct
F

Rode with P to County School pm.

12 Oct
S

Rode to Townhouse am. Walked with P to Combe pm. Fine.

13 Oct
Sunday

White frost & bright sun.
Church am. Walk with P pm.

14 Oct
M

To London by the 9. CFO. Fine[.]

15 Oct
T

To Trinity House to enquire about K.G. Fund.[330] [T]hen Econ. [L]unched with Sue. H[ouse] of Lords. Dined wi[th] Daisy.

[328] John Biddle (1859–1936). He was a distinguished major-general of the United States army. Biddle was Acting Chief of Staff in Washington from October 1917 to November 1917 and from January 1918 to March 1918. From March 1918 to June 1919, he was the commander of the American forces that were stationed in Great Britain and France.

[329] Francis Anderson Winter (1867–1931). He was appointed Chief Surgeon of the American Expeditionary Force stationed in the United Kingdom from May 1918 to October 1918. Winter also served as the Director of the American Medical Library from 1918 to 1919.

[330] This refers to the King George's Fund for Sailors that was set up in March 1917 at Trinity House to aid sailors of all the services, their widows and dependants.

| 16 Oct
W | Econ & CFO Com[mit]^{tee}. Meetings of L[or]^d Lieut[enant]s & of Unionist Peers. |
| | Reports that have some foundation that the Germans are making a humble response to Wilson's[331] uncompromising statement[332] as to the conditions on wh[ich]. he will recommend an armistice. Newton[333] told me that he knew for a fact that Ludendorf [f][334] was ready to make peace last July, knowing he had made false moves & could not win. The people who will not accept the situation are not the soldiers, who doubt if they can rely on their Army, but the Reventlows[335] & Pan Germans. |

17 Oct
Th   Dined with the sisters.

18 Oct
F   Econ & CFO. [T]ea with Daisy.

19 Oct
S   Back to <u>Castle Hill</u> stopping at Taunton 1–5 for Hunt Finance.

20 Oct
<u>Sunday</u>   Rather cold & raw. Walked with S[myth] R[ichards] to station am.

21 Oct
M   With S[myth] R[ichards] to Eggesford to meet Horne re Forestry.

22 Oct
T
<u>Castle Hill</u>   To Exeter with P by early train for DPF. Showers[.]

23 Oct
W   Shot over Crossbury & Brayley with Mr Snell till 2.30. [G]ot 22 ph[easants] & I left him to go on.
Beautiful day.

24 Oct
Th   Exeter all day.

25 Oct
F   Shot with Buttle over Knightsbray & Blackpost.
Shooting indifferent by best.

26 Oct
S   Rode to North Molton with P. p.m.

---

[331] Thomas Woodrow Wilson (1856–1924). He was the twenty-eighth President of the United States of America from 1913 to 1921.

[332] This 'uncompromising statement' refers to the address that President Wilson made to both houses of Congress on 8 January 1918 which was also known as Wilson's Fourteen Points.

[333] Thomas Wodehouse Legh (1857–1942). He was the second Baron Newton and the Conservative MP for Newton from 1886 to 1898. He was the Paymaster-General from 1915 to 1916 and the Assistant Under-Secretary of State for Foreign Affairs from 1916 to 1919.

[334] Eric Ludendorff (1865–1937). He was a general in the Imperial German Army and he was quartermaster in the Second German Army. He was the First Quartermaster-General of the German General Staff from 1916 to 1918.

[335] This is presumably a reference to Ernst Graf zu Count Reventow (1869–1943). He was a captain in the German Navy, newspaper columnist and author who was renowned for his anglophobia and his zealous assaults against Germany's leaders including Chancellor Bethman-Hollweg.

27 Oct   Motored to Bow by 10.30 & went on thence to Devonport where the
Sunday   Admiral put me up. Prince Arthur[336] & suite arrived in ev[ening].[,] & there
           was a big dinner.
           Did not hear much of interest except that the German U Boats have gone
           north – probably to lay mines. Flu[337] is so bad that they can hardly man
           the Destroyers who are out five nights of seven. For convoy work they use
           about 1 destroyer to 4 ships. Wilson spoke too much without consultation
           in his recent notes & both Clemenceau[338] & Ll[oyd] George had to protest.
           Pershing tries to ken his whole force that are at the front, over 1,000,000
           men him self [sic] with chaotic results.

28 Oct   Helped to receive Prince Fushimi[339] in the dockyard.
M   A dull function. Then to 3rd Devon Barracks & after lunch
           to Exeter.

29 Oct   Celebration of Ralegh[340] Tercentenary. Fine sermon from the Dean.[341]
T   Meeting after went off pretty well, but it is a gamble to ask for a whole
           University as a memorial.

30 Oct   Shot with Buttle & Snell on Fullabrook & Bradbury. Shot poorly.
W
Castle Hill

31 Oct   To Exeter for F.P.[,]
Th   & on to Princetown to meet Peacock[.]

1 Nov   Walked over Brimpts[342] & Fernworthy in steady rain.
F   Motored with Horne from Chagford to Exeter & back to
           Castle Hill by Exe Valley.

2 Nov   P went to London. Rode with S[myth]. Richards, am & pm.
S

3 Nov   Walk with Wallace am.
Sunday   Church in ev[ening]. Nice day.

4 Nov   To Exeter for interesting meeting about Church Finance.
M

---

[336] Prince Arthur of Connaught (1883–1938). He was a lieutenant in the British army and served
in the First World War. He was the Governor-General and Commander-in-Chief of the Union of
South Africa and High Commissioner for South Africa from 1920 to 1923.

[337] This refers to the Spanish flu pandemic of 1918 to 1920.

[338] Georges Benjamin Clemenceau (1841–1929). He was a distinguished French statesman and the
Prime Minister of France from November 1917 to January 1920.

[339] Prince Yorihito Fushimi [東伏見宮依仁親王] (1867–1922). He was the Prince Yorihito of Higashi
Fushimi or Prince Higashifushimi Yorihito and a member of the Japanese Imperial Royal family. He
was an admiral of the Imperial Japanese Navy and served in both the First Sino-Japanese War from
1894 to 1895 and the Russo-Japanese War from 1904 to 1905.

[340] Sir Walter Ralegh [Raleigh] (1554–1618). He was a Devonian soldier and explorer who was an
important figure in the courts of both Elizabeth I and James I.

[341] Very Rev. Henry Reginald Gamble (1859–1931). He was the Dean of Exeter from 1918 to 1931.
Previously, Gamble was the Rural Dean of Chelsea from 1906 to 1916 and the Honorary Chaplain
to the King from 1910 to 1918.

[342] This refers to Brimpts Farm near Dartsmeet.

5 Nov T	Beautiful morning after a very rough night. Shot till luncheon with Dick & Buttle on Haddon.
6 Nov W	Rode to North Molton for memorial service to Poltimore.[343] Fine bright day after sharp frost[.]
7 Nov Th	Shot over Gubbs etc. Did not find much, but it was a beautiful bright day after white frost.
8 Nov F	To Exeter for DPF Com[mit]ᵗᵉᵉ at which we did nothing.
9 Nov S	To London by the 11.0i [clock] & joined P in Lowndes S[t].
10 Nov Sunday	The War is practically over & we have won a great victory but everybody though happy is quiet & there is no outward difference. The small boys are having the time of their lives with the captured guns that are packed the whole length of the Mall & on the Horse Guards parade etc.
11 Nov M	Began the day by rubbing up the boots & gaiters I shall want for the Investiture tomorrow.[344] Then went to Truslove's[345] in Sloane St[reet]. to pay for some books. Got there just at 11, when 2 or 3 maroons were let off in the Park & people all began to go out from the shops into the street, & took for granted it was all right: but one girl asked with a shudder whether it was an air raid & there was nothing to show what the maroons meant. Going on thence to Buck[ingham] Palace to deliver a letter for P. [T]he scent grew hotter & flags were coming out. At the Palace a bit of a crowd. I delivered my letter & learned that the Armistice was signed at 5 am & that the King had just gone in from the balcony.[346] Went on to SW P[ost]. Office to get a License for Den[zil], & after calling at Food Production Office wh[ich]. was beginning to get out of hand went on to Atkins[347] to order cartridges for Den[zil]. By this time the rejoicings were in full swing[,] the most popular form was to overfill a taxi or motor lorry, the crew for choice to include a soldier or two & drive along waving flags & cheering. Flags were now all over the place. Out there was no horse play that I noticed. Went to a short service at 12.30 at S[t]. James's, Piccadilly for I felt I wanted to thank God _ [sic] and to cry.[348] Coming out met Polly Stucley & walked with her eastward a little way. Then she remembered she had left a parcel in the church. A precious bit of cheese she had managed to buy

[343] Coplestone Richard George Warwick Bampfylde (1859–1918). He was the third Baron Poltimore. He was a lieutenant in the 1st Life Guards and a captain in the North Devon Yeomanry from 1881 to 1889. He was a DL and JP for Devon.

[344] The fourth Earl Fortescue was on duty as ADC to King George V.

[345] Truslove's was an independent publishing business.

[346] Fortescue added in the printed version of the typescript: 'After the crowd had given him an unequalled reception.'

[347] Atkins was located in Jermyn Street.

[348] 'For I felt I wanted to thank God and to cry' is crossed out in pencil. This short statement was omitted from the transcript of this diary entry that Fortescue included as part of the printed version of the typescript in A Chronicle of Castle Hill.

from Fortnums,[349] so we went back & recovered it from the pew opener
who said he had smelt it before he found it. Lunch at the Travellers' &
then rota work at CFO. [G]oing on to H[ouse] of Lords where they were
scraping up peers to follow the Chancellor to an impromptu service at S[t].
Margaret's. As no one had had notice we were but few[,] but the H[ouse]
of Commons mustered strong & the nave was well filled. [T]he service
was very simple, but just right. The old hundredth, a few prayers, one the
Psalm. 61st Isiah as the lesson, read by the Primate & the Te Deum & God
save the King to finish up. By 3.15 it had begun to rain. Walked back with
P to the House, where after statement of the terms of the Armistice – very
ill delivered by Crawford, we went on with the agenda,[350] the first item in it
was Reconstruction.
Middleton[351] told me that we have in fact been playing our last cards
lately: our losses from Aug[ust] to middle of Oct[ober] were 240000 & the
Americans 160000 (about 30%. I suppose in their case) and since then our
casualties have been 4000 a day. A rate at which no Army could go on.
Walked home between 6 & 7 in steady rain wh[ich]. had returned
demonstration almost to vanishing point, though Victoria S[treet]. was full
of people.
We dined quietly together sampling a new cook![,] & so ended a great day.

12 Nov T <u>London</u>	Investiture at Buck[ingham]. Palace at 10.30. Very dull affair. [T]hen to Education Office to present deputation about S[outh] W[est] University. Fisher[352] kept us waiting 45 mins & then turned all our proposals down. This prevented my going to the service at S[t] Pauls which P went to with H. M. [M]ost impressive. H[ouse] of Lords after & dined with Marion Stucley.
13 Nov W	CFO am. H[ouse] of Lords pm & dined with Sue.
14 Nov Th	Rota at Economic. H[ouse] of Lords[.]
15 Nov F	Econ & CFO. We went to Twelfth Night[353] at the Court. Pretty Good.
16 Nov S	Investiture after breakfast. Caught the 1 & went <u>to Castle Hill</u>.
17 Nov <u>Sunday</u>	To early service & again at 6.30. Good congregations at both. Rode with S[myth] R[ichards] to Townhouse am. Fine but cold.

---

[349] This refers to the department store of Fortnum and Masons.

[350] In the transcript of the diary entry included with the printed version of the typescript, Fortescue added a footnote: 'The House of Commons adjourned.'

[351] This refers to Earl Midleton. Fortescue added a footnote in the transcript of the diary entry included with the printed version of the typescript that stated: 'A former Secretary of State for War.'

[352] Herbert Albert Laurens Fisher (1865–1940). He was the Liberal MP for Sheffield Hallam from 1916 to 1918 and a National Liberal MP for the Combined English Universities from 1918 to 1926. Fisher served on the Bryce Commission on alleged German atrocities and was the President of the Board of Education from 1916 to 1922.

[353] This refers to the play 'Twelfth Night', a comedy by the celebrated playwright William Shakespeare.

18 Nov M	Rode with S[myth] R[ichards] to Blakewell Shome's & Riverton. Many letters.
19 Nov T	To Exeter by the 8.38 returning by the 5.40. Long day.
20 Nov W	Rode to Brayford & back by Middle Hill am.
21 Nov Th	Walked to Fullabrook am. Blowing hard from E[ast].
22 Nov F	Exeter for DPF. Less wind & milder.
23 Nov S	Walked with Wallace pm. Milder.
24 Nov Sunday	Church am. Walked with Dick pm. Milder. Some rain.
25 Nov M	Motored S[myth] R[ichards] to Exmoor. Rode to Sherdon Linhay etc. Fine & pleasant. Mr Davis came.
26 Nov T	Shot in & about Tilery Cover. Got 19 ph[easants] & 2 woodc[ocks]. Saw about 10 w[ood]c[ocks]. Den[zil] came.
27 Nov W	Exeter all day.
28 Nov Th	Ditto. Had to go by 8.30 train & got home at 8.

MOBILISING THE COUNTY FOR WAR (1914)

DHC: 1262M/0/O/LD/113/135

LETTER WRITTEN BY EMILY COUNTESS FORTESCUE

August 14, 1914

CASTLE HILL.

SOUTH MOLTON.

DEVON.

Dear Sir,

Everyone is anxious to do their best to help in our National Emergency & everything is a help so long as it is done on systematic lines. ~~Every~~ From countless villages I receive letters asking to the formation of working parties & I should be much obliged if you w[oul]ᵈ. kindly inform people thro[ugh]' your columns that a list of garments required by the troops & articles needed for hospitals can be obtained by applying to the

V.A. Linen League.

Young Men's Christian Ass[o]ᶜ[iation].

Kings Alley. High Sᵗ. Exeter

& patterns of the garments will also be supplied from the same service.

Would you kindly let the other Devon newspapers have a copy of this letter

Yours

F[aith]f[ull]y,

E[mily] Fortescue

DHC: 1262M/o/O/LD/136/3

NEWSPAPER CUTTING OF AN ARTICLE COMPARING RECRUITMENT IN DEVONSHIRE FOR THE FIRST WORLD WAR WITH THAT OF A RECRUITMENT DRIVE IN 1794

The Barracks of Barnstaple -- 1794 to 1807.[1]

The call made by Lord Kitchener for 100,000 men through the Lord Lieutenants of the Counties, as also the appeal of the Lord Lieutenant of Devon for funds, recalls a similar appeal made by the present Earl Fortescue's grandfather acting as Lord Lieutenant of Devon in 1794.

At a meeting held in Exeter April 22nd, 1794, convened by Earl Fortescue, it was resolved that Volunteer troops of Fencible [sic] Cavalry and Infantry Companies be formed in defence of the King and country against the threatened invasion of England by the great Napoleon, with his 50,000 "caps of liberty."

The result of that meeting was the receipt of over £14,053 to the fund and the formation in this county of a wonderful Volunteer service. The population of the county at that time was 343,000, and the total number of Volunteers amounted to 16,663, so that one in twenty of the whole population was a Volunteer. Under Colonel Rolle the First Devon Cavalry Regiment was formed, with 618 men, pledged to march to any part of the Western district on actual invasion, and if required to assist Civil Magistrates within the district to suppress riot or tumult.

Another result was the formation in Barnstaple of an infantry troop of 493 men, under a then well-known military man, Lieut[enant].-Col[onel]. Henry Beavis, and his Adjutant, Captain Nott. The troop drilled every Sunday morning in the Square—a place adorned with lofty elm trees, which were cut down in the thirties or forties of 1800. The Recorder (Mr. Robert Newton Incledon of Pilton House and Yeo Town) also succeeded in the formation of "Volunteer Horse," clothed and equipped at their own expense, including the principal county family representatives and the wealthy merchants of the town, whilst Mr. Tanner, an attorney, and Mr. Bowhay, a grocer, formed a Company of tradesmen, which some mischievous people designated "Goldfinches" because of the rich dresses, bedizened with lace and gold, in which they appeared.

Colonel Beavis, however, was the prominent soldier to whom all looked for orders. He had been in early life a commissioned officer in the German Wars in the early time of the Third King George,[2] and would occasionally recount the reminiscences of the Prussian Prices and Generals of the then (not now) allied Armies. It was Colonel Beavis who was instrumental in getting the Government to build Barracks on the now secluded and peaceful spot so well-known to us

---

[1]   This newspaper article was taken from the *North Devon Journal*, 13 August 1914, p. 6.
[2]   King George III (1738–1820). He was the king of Great Britain and king of Ireland from 1760 to 1820 and was the king of Hannover from 1814 to 1820.

as Ebberley Lawn, then known as Bear-street Meadow, belonging to Colonel Beavis himself. The meadow adjoined the "Great Fort," which had played such an important part in the military history of our town.

It is not, perhaps, generally known that at the termination of the war with France in the early part of the 19th Century the Barracks were sold to Mr. Henry Hole, of Ebberley, Torrington, who converted it into the present row of houses known as Ebberley Terrace—the same Mr. Henry Hole being the gentleman who, at his own expense, made the first footpath from Ebberley Lawn through Bear-street to the town. A painting showing the Barracks is in the possession of Mrs. F. Symons. Similar Barracks were at that time erected throughout the county, and troops were constantly coming in and out, giving the town quite a military importance in North Devon.

We have been able to judge a little of what happened at that time by what we have seen during the past week, the town being aroused to great excitement by the preparation of the Market as a temporary Barracks by our well-known townsman, Major Charles Lock. After all arrangements, however, he had been made to accommodate a Battalion of five or six hundred, much to the disappointment of thousands of people who had congregated awaiting the arrival of the troops until midnight, news was received to the effect that the order had been cancelled, and the 6th Devons had been ordered to Plymouth and Devonport. The Yeomanry, however, had been billeted in the town, and Barnstaple has also been made a centre by the Government for the purchase of horses, many having been sent from our stations to different parts of the country during the past few days.

The Barracks in Bear-street Meadow were built for quite a limited number of men and horses, accommodating less than a hundred of each. There were 6 rooms and a large mess room for the officers and the same for the non-commissioned officers and privates. Four large cellars were built, which contained the wine and 76 barrels of ale.

Besides the Barracks, there were also built a farriers' shop with forge, a fire engine house, a guard room, stables, granary, coal yard, and a salting house, which I have found out meant a canteen. Owing to sickness, however, the canteen was converted into a hospital fitted up with beds (filed with 12lbs. of straw), and suitable conveniences, including 24 rugs used as extra coverings, there being no other means of heating the rooms. The yearly coal bill averaged about £80, the price being at that time from 1s. 6d. to 2s. per cwt., supplied chiefly by a merchant of the town, a Mr. Metheral. The quantity of candles supplied in one year by Mr. G. Wickey and Mr. Nicholas Glass, amounted to 1,388 lbs, 502 lbs. described as moulds and 886 lbs. as dipped candles, the moulds costing from 10¼ d. to 1s. per lb. and the dips from 9½ d. to 10½ d. per lb. Great difficulty was experienced in getting the supply of candles owing to the high price of tallow. The rations for the horses varied, from the 1st March to 30th September 12lbs. of hay, 8lbs. of straw, and 10lbs. of oats were allowed each horse, but from September to February 12lbs. of hay, 8lbs. of straw, and 7lbs. of oats. The price of oats varied from 2s. 6d. to 3s. 6d. per bushel and hay from £3 to £5 per ton.

The building of the Barracks was carried out under the superintendence of Barrack Master Samuel Ford Bashleigh, a native of Honiton, appointed at a salary of £91 a year, £25 a year being allowed him in lieu of a house. He was also, after serving six years, given a commission and uniform. It is from his journal, commending 1794 and ending 7th October, 1807, I have been able to give the above information. This journal was kindly given me (for the town) by the late Mrs. William Gammon. It contains over 1,000 letters and copies of letters which passed between the Barrack Master and the Barrack Master General in London on every conceivable matter in respect to the building and its working. Hanging in the Hall at Castle Hill is the head of a stag which ran into the Barracks and was killed there in 1806.

My reason for sending this communication is that many of our townsmen who have nobly come forward to their country's calls, and are far away from us, will be receiving from their friends the local papers, which will be so acceptable to them in their loneliness, and will feel interested in reading the doings of their worthy forefathers in days of old.

SYDNEY HARPER.

High-street, Barnstaple, August 10th, 1914.

THE BARRACKS OF BARNSTAPLE --
1794 TO 1807.[3]

(CONTINUED)

The recent finding of the Barnstaple Barrack Master's Journal has opened up quite a few chapters in the history of Barnstaple which will be useful to future historians in filling up the pages during the last decade of the 18th century and the first decade of the 19th century, of which period, owing to the loss of the records of that time, we know so little.

A very valuable description is recorded in the Journal of the Isle of Lundy bringing out many features of the island, and recognising its importance as a military station. The barrack-master received an order from the barrack-master-general to proceed to the island from Barnstaple, taking an experienced surveyor with him to report without delay on the suitability of the island as a Government station. The barrack-master's account of his visit and the voyage from Ilfracombe is of the greatest interest, and will, I hope, with your permission, form a subject for another article at no very distant date.

I have also been able to gather a full list of the names of the different regiments which, during this period, visited the town which must have caused Barnstaple to have had busy and exciting times. The arrival of these troops would be the means of also hearing from those who had taken part in them of the victories and defeats which were at the time passing in rapid succession. Mention is made of the following regiments in the Barrack Master's book and in the Parish Registers:–The Glamorgan Militia, Surrey Cavalry, North Devon Militia, 2nd Yorkshire Foot, Wiltshire Militia, Royal Artillery, Duke of York Fencibles, South Devon Militia, North Hants Militia, Devon and Cornwall Fencibles, Norfolk 28th Regiment of Foot, 2nd Somerset Militia, and an Essex Regiment. It is of interest here to note that no less than 80 soldiers of the above-named regiments were married at the Parish Church in Barnstaple.

A very bad outbreak of sickness occurred in 1799 among the regiment of the Duke of Yorks Fencibles, commanded by Colonel Hay, stationed in the town, who made an urgent appeal to the Barrack Master for 24 beds, 24 blankets, and 24 rugs for his sick soldiers. This at first was refused, but upon a second application made by him stating that the men would perish unless granted, the Barrack Master was ordered to supply the necessary articles under protest, because "it was the duty of the surgeons of the regiment to supply." When we consider the time it must have taken to get the necessary permission, we do not wonder at the long list of deaths we find recorded in our Parish Registers from this regiment: the bodies were laid to rest around our old Parish Church, and the

---

[3]   This second article was published in the *North Devon Journal*, 20 August 1914, p. 6.

solemn service was conducted by the Vicar (the Rev. William Marshall), whose portrait has been recently presented to the Church.

Another very interesting incident happened in Barnstaple showing the patriotism and spirit of the Mayor. Great difficulty arose in consequence of the lack of recruits for the Navy, and the Mayor, Mr. John Servante (whose ancestors were Huguenots), a retired Lieutenant of the Navy, immediately volunteered for active service, it being the only occasion we know of a resignation of a Mayor in such circumstances. He was accepted, and at once issued a notice making a sporting offer to give to the first six men who came forward fifteen guineas each. The following is taken from the Barnstaple Session book of 1795:–"That in consequence of His Majesty's command signified to him by the Right Hon. Earl of Chesterfield,[4] he, the said John Servante, had thought fit to remove with his family to the town of Falmouth, County Cornwall, for the remainder of the year, and therefore begged to be removed from the said office of Mayor, and that the same office of Mayor be declared vacant." The vacancy was duly filled by a brother-in-law of the Mayor, Mr. George Greek, an uncle of the late John Leworthy Greek, of this town.

It was at this time an embargo was laid on all British shipping for furnishing able-bodied seamen for the Navy, and a call was made on the seventy-three shipowners [sic] of Barnstaple to send from each vessel one able-bodied seamen and two able-bodied men, which meant that at least two hundred men from our town and district went to serve their King and country on the seas. Two worthies of Barnstaple who represented the borough for several years in Parliament were doing fine service for their country, viz :–Sir Edward Pellew[5] (afterwards Lord Exmouth) and Sir Eyre Coote,[6] Knight. Sir Edward Pellew was knighted after the war with France, and his action with the "Cleopatra" when in command of the "Nymphe," which was one of the most desperate battles ever fought, ended with the defeat of the French ships. He was the appointed to the "Arethusa." His action in the rescue of the crew of the "Dutton" at Plymouth in 1796 was an act of heroism never surpassed; he swam out in evening dress with a rope to the distressed ship and thus became the means of saving between 500 or 600 lives. For this gallant act he was created a baronet and the Corporation of Plymouth voted him the freedom of the town, which he richly deserved. After serving Barnstaple in Parliament for several years he was sent with a fleet to punish the Dey of Algiers[7] and inflicted such damage that the Dey agreed to his demand and liberated 3 000 Christians he had taken captive. (Bravo, Sir Edward !) When Sir Edward was M.P. for Barnstaple great distress prevailed in the town. Wheat was sold at 22s. to 24s. per bushel. Meat was so dear that it was impossible for

---

[4]   Philip Stanhope (1755–1815). He was the fifth Earl of Chesterfield and the Lord Lieutenant of Buckinghamshire from 1781 to 1782. He was the Master of the Mint from 1789 to 1790 and Master of the Horse from 1798 to 1804.

[5]   Sir Edward Pellew (1757–1833). He was the first Viscount Exmouth and an officer in the Royal Navy. He was Vice-Admiral of the United Kingdom from 1832 to 1833 and was one of the MPs for Barnstaple from 1802 to 1804.

[6]   Sir Eyre Coote, KCB (1762–1823). He was a general in the British army and served during both the American War of Independence and the French Revolutionary Wars. He was also the Governor of Jamaica from 1806 to 1808 and was one of the MPs for Barnstaple from 1812 to 1818.

[7]   This refers to the Regency of Algeria.

the poor to buy. Sir Edward came forth nobly, distributing bread and flour and causing two fat oxen to be slaughtered and their carcases given away to the poor of the town.

The other worthy M.P. for the Borough at this period was a distinguished soldier who did fine service for his County and King. He was born in Ireland in 1762, the son of Dr. Coote, Dean of Kilfenora, and was the brother of the last Baron Castle Coote. At the early age of thirteen he carried the colours of the 37th Regiment at the battle of Long Island in 1775, and served all through the American War till York Town, where he was made a prisoner with the Army under Lord Cornwallis.[8] Then after serving in the West Indies he was in command at Bandor, in Ireland, where he was relieved by General Moore[9] (afterwards of Corunna) in 1798 was 2nd in command in Egypt (after Abercrombie[10] was killed) under General Hutchinson[11] in 1801, was appointed Governor General of Jamaica 1805 and going out to take up his command passed Nelson's[12] body on its return from Trafalgar and the squadron in escort.

This for the present must suffice of the past history of the town and its worthies during the period Barnstaple had its Barracks.

SYDNEY HARPER,

High-street, Barnstaple, August 18th, 1914.

[8]   Charles Cornwallis (1738–1805). He was the first Marquess Cornwallis and an officer in the British army who served during the American War of Independence. He was also the Lord Lieutenant of Ireland from 1798 to 1801. During the period when the East India Company administered over India, Cornwallis was the Viceroy of India from 1786 to 1793 and in 1805.

[9]   Sir John Moore (1761–1809). He was an officer in the British army and was known as Moore of Corunna. He was the MP for Lanark Burghs from 1784 to 1790 and the colonel of the 52nd Regiment of Foot from 1801 to 1809.

[10]   Sir Ralph Abercromby (1734–1801). He was the Governor of Trinidad in February 1797. Abercromby was also the MP for Clackmannshire from 1774 to 1780 and 1796 to 1798.

[11]   John Hely-Hutchinson (1757–1832). He was the second Earl of Donoughmore and a general in the British army with a distinguished career. He was a Member of the Parliament of Ireland from 1776 to 1801: he was an MP for Lanesborough from 1776 to 1783, an MP for Taghmon from 1789 to 1790, and an MP for Cork City from 1790 to 1801. After the Act of Union in 1801, Donoughmore was an MP for Cork City from 1801 to 1802 in the UK Parliament. He was the Lord Lieutenant of Tipperary from 1831 to 1832.

[12]   Horatio Nelson (1758–1805). He was the first Viscount Nelson and a celebrated admiral in the Royal Navy.

DHC: 1262M/o/O/LD/129/7

LETTER FROM FORTESCUE TO THE MR ASQUITH AND LLOYD GEORGE REFERRING TO THE SEPARATION ALLOWANCE AND RECRUITMENT

**Territorial Force Association
of the
County of Devon.**

57, HIGH STREET, EXETER.

14th September 1914.

Dear ⎰ Mr Asquith

     ⎱ Lloyd George

I rather gather from the newspapers that the Government are preparing to reconsider the question of [the] separation allowance with a view to increasing it materially. Up to date as far as my knowledge goes in this county we have been very successful in recruiting men of the labouring class, earning less than £1 a week, and men of the middle class who have, in the majority of cases, joined from motives of patriotism without regard to the pay or allowance.

But I think there is no doubt that we have not tapped here and I doubt if recruiters have tapped anywhere the superior wage class men who are earning anything from 30/- to 50/- a week.

There is no doubt that [to] increase [the] separation allowance which would enable their wives to live as they had been doing previous to the enlistment of their husbands would appeal to this class, but if the separation allowance is raised to anything like £1 a week or reward it has been suggested in some quarters you will put the wives of all the less affluent men in a better position by reason of the war than they were in before, and equally when the war is over and their husbands revert to their former jobs they will be less well off than during the continuance of hostilities.

I am disposed to doubt whether this would be desirable.

I can give you instances from my own knowledge of various cases where even on the present separation allowance women are better off than they were before their husbands enlisted.

It is an exceedingly difficult problem and I have no doubt that you are looking at it from every point of view.

Meanwhile I venture to enclose a copy of a Memorandum which the Patriotic Fund Committee of this county had prepared for the guidance of their local representative committees.

     F[ortescue].

RECRUITMENT
(1914–1915)

DHC: 1262M/o/O/LD/153/3

MEMORANDA ON RECRUITING

The Secretary,

Devonshire T. F. Association.

The accompanying copy of remarks of the Director of Recruiting on the results obtained for the Army (excluding Territorials) between 4th August and 10th October, and Analysis, for your information.

Exeter	W. Western	Colonel
9/11/14.	Commanding No 8 District.	

Officer Commanding

Recruiting Area.   23569

The following remarks of the Director of Recruiting on the results obtained up to October 10th, and also figures of ~~No. 8 District~~ the Southern Command, are forwarded for information.

Exeter	Godman	Captain
8/11/14.	Staff Captain	No 8 District.

Remarks on analysis of the yield of Recruits for the Army (exclusive of Territorials) between 4th August and 10th October.

Towns and Mining localities give far the best results, probably because it is the easiest to get at people where the population is most dense. It follows that we should endeavour to work the country districts more thoroughly.

The percentage stated are of recruits to population.

SCOTTISH COMMAND. The whole north of Scotland down to the recruiting areas of Edinburgh, Perth, Stirling, and Glasgow show under .5 per cent, except the town of Dundee which is just over that figure.

WESTERN COMMAND. Results fairly level, Cumberland and Westmorland and North Wales the worst. Lancashire 1.65 the best.

NORTHERN COMMAND. Nottinghamshire and Derbyshire 1.77 per cent the best. Lincolnshire only .74 per cent.

SOUTHERN COMMAND. Birmingham 3.35 per cent, the best, but Warwickshire .89 per cent has no doubt ~~hepl~~ helped to raise Birmingham's figure. Worcestershire, Berkshire, Devonshire, Hampshire and Cornwall are all below .75 per cent, the figure for the last named county being particularly low.

EASTERN COMMAND. No very high result. Essex, Kent and Middlesex (outside London) are all below 1 per cent.

IRISH COMMAND. Cork 2.12 per cent, shows the best result. Belfast gives 1.85 per cent, and Dublin 1.3 per cent. Otherwise the figures are very poor, going down for Clare, Limerick, Cork County and Kerry to .11 per cent.

13/10/14

Table 1. Analysis of recruiting by War Office up to 10/10/1914

Rect[ruitin]g Area.		Population.	Recruits raised,	Percentage.
11th Area.	Devon	701,944	4,414	.62
13th Area.	Somerset	388,847	3,194	.82
32nd Area.	Cornwall	328,098	922	.28
37th Area.	Hants	1,003,590	6,965	.69
39th Area.	Dorset	223,266	3,219	1.44
62nd Area	Wilts	286,822	3,196	1.11
6th Area	Warwick	173,039	7,044	4.07
28th Area	Gloster	736,097	10,292	1.39
29th Area	Worcester	562,409	2,920	.51
43rd Area.	Oxford	397,655	3,842	.96
49th Area	Berks	280,794	2,060	.73
Birmingham		850,947	28,521	3.35

DHC: 1262M/o/O/LD/153/5

SPEECH (INCOMPLETE)

Tiverton

1/12/14

Ladies and Gentlemen,

I need not spend much time in telling you the object of this Meeting. You will all recollect that very soon after this war was thrust upon us by the deliberate action of Germany the Government announced that they wanted more men.

I then put myself in communication with all the local authorities, and begged them to use all the influence that as representative bodies they possessed to stimulate recruiting.

The <u>results were disappointing</u>. For a few weeks recruiting was brisk here as it was everywhere else, but our totals at the end of two months compared badly with those of our neighbours. Somerset and Dorset together are nearly 100,000 less in population than we are: but where we raised 4,000 recruits they raised 6,000. There are 5000 sound single men and 4000 sound married ones in our rural districts alone who might have enlisted but have not.[1]

However as far as the first call was concerned our deficiencies were made up by other people's superior patriotism. Now more men are needed and it is for us now to make up for what we failed to do before.

I am bound to add that the figures for this neighbourhood are better than they are in some parts, and I am looking to you now to give a lead to the districts that have been backward.

I have studied such figures as are available with a good deal of care, and as far as I can make out it is rare that there is any group of parishes, such a group for instances as a County Council constituency, with a population of about 5000, in which you cannot find one parish at least that shows up well.

What is wanted/ is to bring every <u>parish up to a good standard</u>: and the District and Parish Councils having in many cases failed to do so, we are going to try what the <u>political organizations</u> can effect.

In ordinary circumstances each party spends its time in counteracting the mischief the other is doing. Now laying aside party politics they are going to work together. Though in politics men are generally confident that their opponents are wrong, yet sometimes they have secret misgivings that their own friends may either be going too far or not far enough.

In this recruiting campaign each side is sure that the other is right: there are no doubts and no misgivings anywhere. We all alike believe our cause is just. We all alike know that the crisis is a very grave one. We all alike long to do our best to serve our country and to get others to do the same, each in place for which he is best fitted.

I am not going to try to teach you your business. Political committees generally know pretty well how to impress the people they want to influence in any particular

---

[1]   Fortescue added this sentence in pen.

locality. There may be places where ignorance still prevails about the War and where meetings at which trusted speakers can emphasize the righteousness, the necessity, the life and death character for us of the struggle may be of value.

But I do not think meetings are going to be of much use. People go to them as to a form of entertainment and do not realize that if we allow ourselves to beaten our Empire is gone and with it our prosperity, our prestige, our power for good.

Everyone regards the idea of accepting defeat as an impossible one: but unless our Armies are kept up to strength, they cannot whatever their heroism resist for ever, and unless they are reinforced they cannot turn the tables on the enemy, and by carrying the war into his country compels him to sue for peace.

The war is not going badly for us just now, but the striking successes in it have not been won by us but by our Allies, and they have been won by sacrifices ; and it is by sacrifice only that our ends can be obtained: sacrifices in which we must all join, which no selfishness must tempt us to shirk; sacrifices in which those have influence must set an example.

I said something the other day at Exeter about farmers sons not having joined as freely as some. There are notable and honourable exceptions. I accuse no man: none need put the cap on unless it fits them.

My farmer friends can plead and plead with truth that they have already made sacrifices. In various cases their sons have gone, many of their horses are gone, many of their men are gone, and many a soldier's wife is living rent free in the cottage which her husband occupied before he enlisted and which his employer still generously lets her have. I do not suppose there is a farmer in the County who has not subscribed according to his means to one or more of the War funds. Many a farmer too is taking his share of the extra public work imposed on most of us by the war, and they ask how if the land is to be cultivated, how if business is to go on as usual, can we spare more labour, whether it be that of our sons or our labourers. Women & boys[2]

My answer is that the life is more than meat. If we cannot get men without injury to business the business must be let go. Unless we find enough men and find them quickly we shall not win, and if we fail to win our fate will be as the fate of Belgium, business will disappear, there will be no farms to till and many a family now in comfortable circumstances will be wandering homeless and ruined, suppliant for food and shelter.

We have all read of what has happened to that gallant people and to their sorely tried country: some of us have seen those pitiful families of refugees who are dispersed over nearly every County in England: but somehow it was all brought home to me more vividly by a few words from my son than by anything I had seen or read myself.

He has been serving with his Regiment, the [Scots] Greys, abroad and has been in all the fighting from the beginning of the war, while his brother has been doing duty with the Yeomanry on the East coast. Two or three weeks ago Lord Ebrington had to go to Hospital; when he was fit to travel they sent him back here for a week to pick up.

Well of course we talked about the war. Last August like every other young soldier he had been wild to go and thought the war the finest thing in the world.

---

[2]   The words 'Women & boys' were added in pencil by Fortescue.

Three months of active service have shown him the other side of the medal, but what seemed to have made more impression on him then the losses among our people or the hardships they had all, officers and men alike, sustained, was <u>the terrible fate of the unoffending non-combatants,</u> the farmers and village folk in the country they had been fighting over.

The sort of thing that happened time and again was this. The Regiment would be billeted in a farm as it might be this evening, where the inhabitants would make them welcome; next day the enemy learning their position would start shelling the place. The fire would be answered; an engagement would ensue and the inhabitants would clear out with what possessions they could, old people, women[,] children[,] babies, their good[s] packed hastily in such farms carts as were left, or on wheelbarrows or perambulators, piled up with anything and everything they could remove from a harmonium to a feeding bottle.

And the sorrowful procession would disappear among the troops, going they know not where, to live they know not how, fleeing always from the deadly shells which meanwhile were killing their stock[3] setting alight their stacks and reducing the old home to a heap of ruins.

I think scenes like that which he had witnessed many times had made more impression on my son than the actual bloodshed of the battles; and if we would avoid <u>such scenes in England we must break the power</u> of Germany abroad. That our Generals can do if we provide them with enough men of like courage and discipline, with those gallant troops of whose deeds the whole Empire is proud.

But be sure of this, unless <u>we break the Germans they will</u> break us. This is a matter which concerns every one of us from the least to the greatest. Let none say it is no affair of mine, let no class give another the chance of saying my landlord or my master or my employer is keeping his son at home, why <u>should mine go if his does not</u>. Rather let there be a generous emulation between us all as to which shall show the best example of self sacrifice and patriotism and let us make haste to fill up the ranks of our County Regiment. Though they have suffered less than some their casualties have not been small for they have been maintaining the reputation they won in South Africa.

I saw a letter in a newspaper last week saying how they had hold their trenches on one ~~day~~ occasion a month ago for over 24 hours in spite of heavy attack. Not a man left his post. When they were relieved hundreds of Germans dead were lying in front of their position. As they marched back to their billets all the troops they passed cheered them and Sir H. Smith Dorrien[4] paid them the compliment of a special telegram of commendation.

That is not more perhaps than might have been expected from the Battalion that made the charge at Wagon Hill[5] and received for that exploit the special thanks of Queen Victoria,[6] but it is another reason for our keeping their ranks well filled with Devonshire men.

---

[3]   Fortescue added 'killing their stock' in pen.

[4]   Sir Horace Lockwood Smith-Dorrien, GCB (1858–1930). He had a distinguished and prolific career in the British Army. Smith-Dorrien had served in the Zulu war and was the ADC General to the king in 1910.

[5]   This refers to the Battle of Wagon Hill which took place during the Second Boer War.

[6]   Queen Victoria (1819–1901). She was the queen of the United Kingdom and Ireland from 1837 to 1901 and was the empress of India from 1878 to 1901.

DHC: 1262M/0/O/LD/120/30

THE WAR: AN APPEAL TO DEVON MEN AND WOMEN ISSUED BY THE DEVON PARLIAMENTARY RECRUITING COMMITTEE.

Figure 1. Front cover of 'The War: An Appeal to Devon Men and Women, issued by The Devon Parliamentary Recruiting Committee'. Reproduced with the kind permission of Devon Archives and Local Studies Service.

MEN OF DEVON!

You are called to help your country in an hour of very great need.

In past time, England has often called to her men for help, and the Men of Devon have never been deaf to her call. They sailed with Drake[7] against the Armada,[8] they went with Marlborough[9] into Flanders,[10] with Wellington to the Peninsula[11] and Waterloo[12], with Roberts[13] to Afghanistan,[14] and with Buller[15] to Africa.[16] Wherever in the world their country has wanted them, Men of Devon have ever been to the fore.

But, Men of Devon !–your country never needed you more than she needs you now. **Never in all the mighty story of the English people has the Motherland been faced by a more tremendous task or threatened with dangers so terrible.** Never has she been more confident than she is now that she can accomplish the task and win through her trial hour.

But why is England confident? It is simply because she has a Mother's faith– that her sons will not desert her, that they will prove the love they owe her, that they will see her through. She says to them, "I am strong because you are brave and true. Come and help me!"

Our Country fills many a splendid page in history. **We believe you will write Devon's name large across the pages in which will be told the history of the great war.**

You have read how the Army in Belgium cheered the Devons when they filed out of the trenches in Ypres. Those cheers call us–every one of us who is able–to prepare ourselves at once to go and aid those gallant men in their great work and share in their great glory.

---

[7]   Sir Francis Drake (1540–1596). He was an Elizabethan privateer and legendary Devonian sea explorer who played a key role in the defeat of the Spanish Armada of 1588.

[8]   This refers to the Spanish Armada of 1588.

[9]   General John Churchill (1650–1722). He was the first Duke of Marlborough and an MP for Newtown in 1679. Marlborough was an experienced soldier and military commander; he was Commander-in-Chief of the Forces from 1690 to 1691 and 1702 to 1708. During the War of the Spanish Succession, he commanded the English, Dutch and German forces in Flanders. He was the first Lord of the Treasury from 1702 to 1710.

[10]   This refers to the Flanders campaign during the War of the Spanish Succession of 1701 to 1714.

[11]   This refers to the Peninsula War of 1807 to 1814.

[12]   This refers to the Battle of Waterloo of 18 June 1815 in which the armies of the Seventh Coalition led by the Duke of Wellington and Gebhard Leberecht von Blücher achieved a victory against the armies of Napoléon Bonaparte.

[13]   This refers to Sir Frederick Roberts.

[14]   This refers to the Second Anglo-Afghan War.

[15]   This refers to Sir Redvers Buller.

[16]   This refers to the Second Boer War.

You cannot resist that call. It is a call to the heart and conscience of every man.

Think of what the British Army is doing, and why it is doing it :

It is fighting to save the honour of England and the very life of Belgium.

It is fighting to save civilisation itself from perishing by the sword or being crushed under the heel of a cruel military despotism.

It is fighting so that by its victory it may endure the sacredness of Treaties, so that in the future as in the past the world may rely upon a nation's plighted word.

All this it is fighting for, but much more also. **It is fighting on the Continent of Europe in order to keep the horrors of war away from our own land.**

Men of Devon! Already German guns have spoken on our shores. German shells have burst in our streets. The blood of English women and of English children has been shed by Germans.

Surely this concerns you!

No man can picture in his mind what happened in Scarborough,[17] when peaceful citizens going about their business were killed or wounded, when helpless women were slaughtered in their beds, when the postman on his rounds and the maidservant at her work and the innocent children walking to school were suddenly hurled into another world or dreadfully maimed by the shells from the German ships—no man can realise all this without feeling that **it is the duty of all who have not enlisted to join at once and avenge them.**

The bombardment of our unfortified sea-coast towns was the act of an inhuman and a ruthless enemy. It is a monstrous crime that cries to heaven for punishment. The enemy may attempt to repeat it. Give him the best warning you can by coming to the colours now.

This crime does not stand alone. You have read of the terrible things that have befallen brave, unhappy Belgium—of the ravages of fire and sword, the ruined towns, the blighted fields, the massacred people, of all the hellish deeds that have turned a fair and prosperous little land into a dismal desert, and driven from their homes to shelter among strangers the survivors of these horrors.

Men of Devon!–Your country is calling you to come now, quickly, to her assistance, so that all these things and worse may not befall the English countryside, that our streams may never be tinged with the blood of innocent children, that our women may never pass through the bitter valley of shame and woe as the women of Belgium have passed, that our towns and villages may never be put to the sword and the torch, that our churches may never be desecrated, and our fields may never be ploughed into trenches and sown with death.

This is England's call to you: "Come and help quickly, men of Devon! Let us put it at once beyond a shadow of doubt that these things shall never be!"

---

[17] This refers to the bombardment of Scarborough by the German navy on 16 December 1914.

Our men in the trenches are asking how long before those left at home are coming to join them. No many who can read the signs of the times will dispute the reality of our dangers. No man can have realised how deeply England is hated by her enemy without feeling that, if there be any weakness on our part, if we do not resolve to go on to the end and provide the Government with all the men it needs, Belgium's fate will be ours, and, indeed that our suffering and humiliation will be even greater and deeper than hers.

We must win this war, and win it well–so well that the enemy which threatens us shall have no power left to make his threats good.

Men of Devon!–join up at once to defend the just and righteous cause of your country, and to save it from the worst woes of war.

It is a just cause. We are not in this war because we wanted war. We wanted Peace. Our Foreign Minister[18] strove for peace to the last minute of the eleventh hour.[19] The war was forced upon us by an enemy determined to have war, and to have it at the time which best suited its selfish plans.

That enemy contemplated war a year before. The plan broke down. But Germany was ready last July, and as soon as she was ready she rushed into war with Russia and France, and marched through Belgium, trampling on her own honour as she went. She had signed with us a Treaty guaranteeing the neutrality of Belgium. She ridiculed it as "a scrap of paper."[20] But we kept our plighted word.

Who will deny that it is a just cause?

It is a righteous cause. In resisting the military tyranny of Germany, we are resisting a diabolical influence and fighting against an anti-Christian principle. The world is in flames, set on fire by an incendiary nation. To dominate Europe, to Germanise Europe, to break down the independence of small nations, to convert all peoples of the Western world into vassals of Germany–that is the aim of the German military caste.

They boldly declare that Might is Right, that the strongest must rule, and that it is their mission to make every other nation bow down before their power.

Against this conception of the relations between the nations of the earth, we English protest with all our might, and fight with all our strength. We believe it to be the very denial of all the precepts of justice, mercy, and tolerance which Christianity teaches us. It is a barbarous conception which, if it come to fruit, will shake civilisation to its foundations, and undo the work of centuries.

---

[18]   This refers to the Foreign Secretary at the outbreak of war, Sir Edward Grey.

[19]   This refers to the ultimatum that the British government sent to Germany to demand the withdrawal of the German army from Belgium that expired on 4 August 1914 at 11 pm GMT.

[20]   This refers to the Treaty of London of 1839 which upheld the neutrality of Belgium to which both Great Britain and Germany were co-signatories. The statement dismissing the significance of the treaty was made by the German Chancellor Theobald von Bethmann Hollweg (1856–1921), who concluded that in his view Britain would not declare war against Germany over a 'scrap of paper'.

We fight, then, for liberty, for tolerance, for self-government, and for deliverance from the apostles of moral barbarism and political slavery.

Who will deny that our cause is a righteous cause?

Finally, in the truest sense of the word, we are fighting a defensive war. We defend our ideas of justice as between man and man and between nation and nation. We defend our honour. We defend the little kingdom whose independence we have sworn to protect. **We defend our own shores, our own cities, our own homesteads against the bitterest, the most relentless foe that has ever appeared in the world in arms.**

Already there is mourning in many English homes, but the Belgians have no homes to mourn in. Bismarck[21] said that a German army should leave the inhabitants of an invaded country nothing but their eyes to weep with. You have read how that devilish principle of war has been carried out in Louvain and Termonde and Malines and a hundred villages of Flanders and France. We ask you to help to keep these horrors from our Motherland by joining the khaki line which is adding so many undying laurels to the crown of English glory. There lies our defence. **By beating Germany on the Continent we prevent her from crossing the Channel.**

MEN OF DEVON!

We appeal to you to strengthen our defence, to come forward now in such numbers and with such a spirit as to hasten the day of final victory, when the hateful yoke will be removed from the neck of Belgium, when the soil of France will be purified of the plague that now afflicts it, and when our beloved England will be no longer in danger of its very existence.

WOMEN OF DEVON!

We appeal to you to help the great and sacred cause by giving your consent and your blessing to the men who are willing to go, and to show in this vital matter the same patriotism and the same fine self-denial that you have shown in succouring the wounded and distressed.

---

[21] Otto von Bismarck (1815–1898). He was the Chancellor of Germany from 1871 to 1890 and the Prince of Bismarck from 1871 to 1898.

1st February, 1915.

FORTESCUE,	Lord Lieutenant, Castle Hill.
HENRY Y. B. LOPES,	Sheriff of Devon, Maristow.
C. THOMAS DYKE ACLAND,	Killerton.
GERTRUDE ACLAND,	Killerton.
IAN H. AMORY,	Hensleigh, Tiverton.
ARTHUR AXE,	Chairman, Devon Congregational Union.
E. J. BRAILSFORD,	Chairman, Exeter Wesleyan Methodist District.
AUDREY BULLER,	Newton House, Newton St. Cyres.
A. EXON,[22]	Bishop of Exeter.
T. T. BUCKNILL,	Hylands House, Epsom.
T. BAKER,	Mayor of Plymouth.
CLIFFORD,	Ugbrooke, Chudleigh.
CLINTON,	Heanton, Satchville.
COLERIDGE,	The Chanter's House, Ottery St. Mary.
HENRY CURNOW,	Chairman, Plymouth & Devonport Wesleyan Methodist District.
EMILY FORTESCUE,	Castle Hill.
THOS. H. HEPBURN,	Dunmore, Bradninch.
J. H. KENNAWAY,[23]	Escot.
GEORGE LAMBERT,[24]	Spreyton.
FRANCIS LAYLAND-BARRATT,[25]	Manor House, Torquay.
A. MARLBOROUGH,	Dean of Exeter.
JAMES G. OWEN,	Mayor of Exeter.
J. KIRK G. OWEN,	Mayoress of Exeter.
D. J. ROUNSEFELL,	Chairman, United Methodists, Exeter and Shebbear District.
JOHN W. SPEAR,[26]	Venn, Tavistock.
W. TREMLETT,	Chairman, Devon Farmers' Union.
JOHN WALLOP,	Barton House, Morchard Bishop.

[22] This refers to Archibald Robertson who as the Bishop of Exeter from 1903 to 1916 was referred to as A. Exon.

[23] John Henry Kennaway (1837–1919). He was the third Baronet Kennaway of Hyderabad and was the Conservative MP for East Devon from 1870 to 1885. After the constituency was abolished, he was the MP for the Honiton Division from 1885 to January 1910. Kennaway was also appointed Father of the House of Commons from 1908 to 1910.

[24] George Lambert (1866–1958). He was the first Viscount Lambert and a prominent Devon agriculturalist. He was a member of Devon County Council from 1889 to 1952. He served as the Liberal MP for South Molton from 1891 to 1924 and from 1929 to 1931. Lambert was the Civil Lord of the Admiralty from 1905 to 1915. After the introduction of the National Liberal Party, he became the National Liberal MP for South Molton from 1931 to 1945.

[25] Sir Francis Layland-Barratt (1860–1933). He was the first Baron Layland-Barratt and he was a JP in both Devon and Cornwall. Layland-Barratt was the Liberal MP for Torquay from 1900 to December 1910 and the MP for St Austell from 1915 to 1918.

[26] Sir John Ward Spear (1848–1921). He was the Liberal Unionist MP for Tavistock from 1900 to 1906 and December 1910 to 1918. Spear was President of the Poor Law Union Association for England and Wales and he was a member of Devon County Council.

5 Questions to Men who have <u>not</u> enlisted.

1.–If you are physically fit and between 19 and 38 years of age, are you really satisfied with what you are doing to-day?

2.–Do you feel happy as you walk along the streets and see *other* men wearing the King's uniform?

3.–What will you say in years to come when people ask you– "Where did *you* serve" in the great War ?

4.–What will you answer when your children grow up and say, "Father, why weren't you a soldier, too?"

5.–What would happen to the Empire if every man stayed at home *like you?*

––––––––––

Your King and Country Need You

ENLIST TO-DAY.

––––––––––

At any Post Office you can obtain the address of the nearest Recruiting Office.

GOD SAVE THE KING.

DHC: 1262M/o/O/LD/116/42

NEWSPAPER CUTTING – THE GREAT CANVASS

THE GREAT CANVASS.[27]

LORD FORTESCUE DEALS WITH
POINTS AT TORQUAY.

PAIGNTON BACKWARD.

BRIXHAM FISHERMEN AVERSE
TO THE ARMY.

Earl Fortescue, Lord-Lieutenant of Devon, attended a meeting of the Torquay Division Parliamentary Recruiting Committee at Torquay yesterday, Capt. Phillpotts, R.N., presiding, and there being also present the Mayor (Mr. C. T. Towell), Col. G. Stovell, Rev. Stewart Sim, and Messrs. J. C. Chapman, W. J. Ham, W. G. Couldrey, J. Smerdon, F. S. Hex, E. C. Perry, A. Bateman, W. E. Thomas, E. Hutchings, and H. G. Leveson Hallewell and L. G. Peake, hon. secretaries. Apologies for absence were received from Sir F. Layland-Barratt, the Mayor of Dartmouth (Mr. T. Wilton), Mr. J. H. Cooper (chairman of Paignton Urban Council), one of the joint secretaries of the county committee.

RESULTS OF CANVASSING.

The Chairman explained that the committee had met to discuss the question of recruiting so far as it had gone. Up to date the returns had been very satisfactory for the division, the number of cards issued having been 4,883, returned 3,392, recruits promised, 1,200.

In reply to questions, Mr. Hallewell stated that not all the 1,200 had passed; the number was simply promises to the canvassers to come forward. The average for the Torquay office was 40 recruits per day, or 300 a week. Over 200 cards not taken up were accounted for by removals; there were only some 50 cards that had not been taken up by canvassers. It was expected that by to-night every card, including those of removals, would be out.

---

[27]   This newspaper cutting is taken from the *Western Morning News*, 20 November 1915, p. 8.

Earl Fortescue asked if there was any reason to believe that there were any men in the constituency not registered at all.

Mr. Hallewell replied that there might be one or two instances, but the committee had not had any general complaint.

Mr. Couldrey said at Paignton the cards had not been issued very freely. There was room there for more canvassers.

Mr. Hallewell said he had received a report from Paignton that morning showing that there were only 40 cards not issued.

Earl Fortescue asked for a report from each portion of the constituency.

Mr. Hallewell gave, for Torquay, 2,783 cards issue, 2,180 returned, and 846 recruits promised. At Brixham every canvassing card (686) had been taken out, but 100 had come back because it was impossible to get at the men, as they were at Newlyn, Milford Haven, and other places engaged in fishing. 530 cards were returned by the canvassers, and the total promises were only 132. These included eligibles between 18 and 40, but did not include those men at present engaged in his Majesty's service. In regard to Dartmouth and Kingswear (a combined canvass), 491 cards were taken out and 379 returned, and there were 145 promises. For Churston Ferrers 34 cards were issued and 18 returned, with six promises. At Paignton 845 cards were taken out, and there were 469 returned, with only 74 promises. At Stoke Gabriel 44 cards went out and 15 were returned, with seven promises. The only parish not yet dealt with was Marldon, with 46 eligibles, and the cards there were to be got out this afternoon. More than one-third of those canvassed in the whole constituency had promised to enlist.

PAIGNTON SPOILS THE AVERAGE

Earl Fortescue: Yes; but the average is spoiled by Paignton.

Mr. Couldrey said the reasons of this was that unfortunately the recruiting meeting was broken up rather too quickly, before the canvassers had been appointed. People went away, and the result that very few remained to give in their names as canvassers. A request should be made to those who were suitable for canvassers. He did not think Paignton had worked as it ought to be.

Earl Fortescue: But where the work had been done the result has been disappointing. A certain number of canvassers must have been at work, because they have returned 500 cards.

Mr. Ham said one of the canvassers told him that a very large proportion of those left were married men, and that many of these had enlisted since last Saturday. The promises of the married men were included in the 74, and that meant that they would go when they were called. Forty had already enlisted besides the 74.

Mr. Hutchings said he did not think that any fault was attributable to the meeting at Paignton. The whole recruiting scheme was fully explained, as in every other place in the division. The town was divided up into 40 districts and streets, and cards were given out, and if people went away without taking any it was obviously not the fault of the meeting, but that people did not want to canvass.

Earl Fortescue remarked that from the very little result up to date it looked as if the canvassers obtained were unfortunate selections, or else that they had been unfortunate in regard to the people had been up against.

Mr. Couldrey said he took 40 cards, and the results had been unsatisfactory. Out of the 40, only three of the men were unmarried.

Mr. Ham said Paignton had sent 700 already.

Earl Fortescue observed that this was an honourable contribution, but were there no single men left amongst those canvassed?

Mr. Hallewell said recruits had come forward at the rate of 30 a week during the last few days from Paignton.

"SINGLE MEN FIRST."

Earl Fortescue asked if he could help the committee in any way.

Mr. Hutchings said the most important question was that of married men. Canvasers [sic] had met with the response, "You get the single men first," and they had told the married men that they would not be called upon until the unmarried had gone first. During the last few days, however, there had been a considerable amount of complaint, and they did not seem to know exactly where they were in this respect.

Earl Fortescue, in reply, pointed to the explicit statements by Lord Derby and Lord Lansdowne contained in the morning newspapers, and said he thought the positions was clear enough now, or ought to be. What was more to the purpose was that Lord Derby had hinted that if the Government threw him over he would resign; he did not put it in quite those terms, but that was what it amounted to. He (Lord Derby) looked upon the statement as to single men first as a Government pledge.

THE BRIXHAM FISHERMEN.

Rev. Stewart Sim asked what about the Brixham fishermen. A great number of these men between the ages of 18 and 40, were engaged in a very important industry, and a deputation had been sent up to London to see if anything could be done in the matter. He understood with regard to recruits for the navy the group system did not apply.

Earl Fortescue: That is so.

Rev. S. Sim said that interfered considerably with them. It ought to be known that they were not asked to recruit for the Admiralty at all. The group system only referred to the Royal Naval Division. If many of these men were to enlist, it was going to interfere tremendously with the fishing industry, which was of national importance. He was told that a great many of the younger men had volunteered for mine sweeping to avoid being sent into the army, which they said they would not join.

Earl Fortescue said these young fishermen should be told that it did not follow because they had been brought up to the sea that they were not fit for the army. They knew as much about soldiering as 99 recruits out of 100. It was quite natural to them to stick to the sea if they could, and if the navy wanted recruits, that was the place for them, but for those who were not indispensable in their industry, the right line for them to take, if they wanted to carry on that industry was to get attested and be placed under the group system. They could appeal to the local tribunal, who had it in their power to transfer single men of, say, 35 to the group for married men, but there was nothing to prevent a further appeal, if the facts and conditions justified it, when the latter group was called up. What should be aimed at was to get as many men as possible, even of those who thought they were wanted for their business, to be attested and transferred to the B Reserve group.

Mr Chapman asked if there was any authority for saying that the group system, which applied to the Royal Naval Division, did not apply to the Royal Navy itself or the Royal Naval Reserve or to the trawler section of the R.N. Reserve.

Earl Fortescue said that question was raised at South Brent, and he wrote to Lord Derby asking whether the group system applied to fishermen who would not join the army, but were quite ready to join the navy, and the answer was in the negative, and that the group system did not apply in cases of this kind.

FISH SUPPLY IN DANGER.

Rev. S. Sim said the important question was raised of the national food supply. Many of their fishermen had joined the Naval Reserve or the mine sweepers, and the result was that some boats were laid up and others were working short handed [*sic*], and if many others were to go it would mean the stoppage of the fishing industry. It should be remembered that Brixham was one of the main sources of fish supply now that Scarborough and other places on the East Coast were closed.

Earl Fortescue said he quite appreciated the importance of this, and that was why he suggested that the better course for the men asked to go would be to get attested and transferred to the B Reserve group, because in that case, if there was a great national emergency when every man would be wanted, and they were able to do more for the nation by catching fish than by killing Germans, they would be allowed to stick to catching fish.

Rev. S. Sim asked if that would apply to the young men.

Earl Fortescue replied yes. Unmarried men could join the B Reserve, and, when their group was due for calling up, they could go to the local tribunal and ask to be put in another class. An unmarried man of 25 could be placed in the group for married men of the same age.

RIDICULOUS STARRING.

Earl Fortescue went on to ask if the committee had come across many cases in which starring had been improperly done.

Mr. Couldrey and Mr. Hutchings mentioned two cases in the districts of Marldon and Stoke Gabriel.

Earl Fortescue remarked that the way starring had been done was perfectly ridiculous, especially in the agricultural districts. The authorities had promised that there should be further investigation into this matter, and it would be of great assistance if the canvassers would report to the chairmen of their committees with a view to an inquiry into any cases where there had been obvious mistakes. Speaking generally, it was his opinion that men whose presence on their farms was indispensable to the proper conduct of the business should not enlist for service at once, but that they would act rightly if they got attested and were then transferred to the B Reserve, with a view to being called up later if required.

Col. Stovell asked if Lord Derby had not said that starred men could enlist and go into the reserve.

Earl Fortescue answered in the affirmative. Replying to Mr. Smerdon, he said all the District and other Councils had appointed their local tribunals, and that the regulations under which they were to act were ready, but had not yet been received.

Mr. F. G. Hext (town clerk) said the regulations were in course of preparation and would be placed in the hands of the local authorities in a few days.

PROPOSED COUNTY COURT OF APPEAL.

Earl Fortescue said the recruiting officer would have the right to be present when the local tribunals were deciding on cases. He imagined they would be open courts; they ought to be. He believed there was to be a sort of county court of appeal, to which cases in which the decisions of the local tribunals thought unsatisfactory might be taken. He only got this verbally in an interview at the War-office, so that it might be taken for what it was worth, but he was under the impression that something of the kind was contemplated. What he was given to understand was that the War Committee of the County Council would be invited to appoint a committee who would sit as a court of appeal in the county, and that this county court of appeal would have assessors to assist them in their deliberations—for instance, persons cognisant with fishing or agriculture.

APPOINTMENT OF ADVISORY COMMITTEE.

A circular letter from the Parliamentary Committee was read, requesting the appointment of an Advisory Committee of five for the Parliamentary area, whose duty would be to consider cases in co-operation with the recruiting officer for the district, which were to go before the local tribunals.

On the motion of Mr. Hutchings, seconded by Col. Stovell, it was decided that on the committee there should be one representative for Dartmouth and Kingswear, one each for Brixham and Paignton, and two for Torquay. Mr. Chapman and Mr. Hutchings were appointed for Torquay, Mr. Couldrey for Paignton, and Mr. W. J. Sanders for Brixham, the election of a Dartmouth member being left to the local committee.

THE QUESTION OF AGE.

Earl Fortescue said he had written to the authorities on another question which had caused a little difficulty in some places, and that was as to the meaning of the age of recruits. Was it governed by the age written on the canvassing card, or was it the age of the recruit on August 15th, or his actual age? The reply was that a man was 18 until he reached his 19th birthday: and that he was 40 until he attained his 41st birthday. This meant that they must go by the fact and not by the card. His lordship thanked the committee for their kindness in meeting him, and again asked canvassers to make notes and report cases where starring was obviously ridiculous and futile, as the committee were to unstar [sic] men as well as to star them. By making reports of this kind, canvassers might save a great deal of time and add to the valuable services which they were rendering. He desired to thank the canvassers for the way in which they had tackled the work had proved that they at any rate appreciated the gravity of the situation, and, if they could bring home to those whom they had to canvass that the state of affairs was serious, he did not think that any of them need fear but that the country would respond to any demand that might be made upon it. They knew that things were not going quite as they could wish, and that without men and without sacrifices we should not get that victorious peace which the country was determined to have.

During the meeting Mr. Hallewell announced the receipt of an intimation [sic] from a local company that the whole of their 25 employés [sic] would enlist at once in the Army Reserve.

MID-DEVON RESULTS.

Earl Fortescue visited Newton Abbot yesterday and met the Mid-Devon Recruiting Committee. Lord Fortescue went fully into the results of the canvass, which showed that canvassers were at work in 47 out of the 48 parishes in the division. Nearly half of the total of 4,700 blue cards had been returned. The promises, without reservation, obtained up to the present totalled 26 per cent. of the cards returned.

It was decided to call a meeting of the Mid-Devon Parliamentary Recruiting Committee to appoint an advisory committee of five members, as it is the intention that they should co-opt from time to time representatives of both employers and employed.

GOOD NUMBERS AT PLYMOUTH.

Up till nine o'clock last night 74 recruits were attested at the Plymouth Recruiting-office. Thirteen joined the 5th Devon Regt., T.F.

No. 8 DISTRICT RETURNS.

In No. 8 District on Thursday 154 men were enlisted for immediate service, the details being : —Hants, 52; Devon, 43; Wilts, 17; Cornwall, 17; Dorset, 13; Somerset, 12.

FORTY PASS AT TAVISTOCK.

Yesterday 84 recruits presented themselves for medical examination at Tavistock under Lord Derby's scheme, and 40 were passed. Dr Cree was assisted by Dr. Hillyar and Dr. J. Leslie Watt.

DHC: 1262M/o/O/LD/114/2

**TYPED LETTER FROM FORTESCUE TO UNNAMED GENERAL
ABOUT RECRUITMENT SCHEME**

26th. June [191]5.

My dear General,

I have your C.R. S.C. 58600/A.2 of 24th.

The subject of it was brought before me on Thursday by the C. C. 8th. District and on Friday by the Chief Recruiting Officer at Exeter and the Secretary of the T.F. Association.

I can only reply to you as I have to them :-

(1).   It will be perfectly futile to attempt anything until the corn harvest is over.

(2).   There are quite enough farmers' sons staying at home in this County to furnish our proportion of an 8th. District Farmers' Battalion.

(3).   But I do not see why farmers' sons who have hitherto refused to join the Yeomanry should be more willing to join an infantry battalion.

(4).   If however a scheme which the Board of Trade and the Board of Agriculture have in contemplation materialises and additional labour from other sources becomes available for agricultural purposes I do ~~not~~ think[28] that more farmers' sons would enlist and they would be more likely to do so in a class regiment than in one in which they would be mixed up with their own labourers.

(5).   A very great deal however would depend on the Officer selected to raise both the Battalion and the local Companies.

I send you in confidence a copy of the draft letter from the Board of Trade which is to be sent out any day now to the County Councils. If it is properly coordinated with your movement success for both might be much more easily obtained, but the procedure up to date seems to me only one more example of the way in which the public departments ignore each other in matters in which they ought to cooperate.

---

[28]   The word 'not' is crossed out in pencil and was replaced with the word 'think' added in pencil.

DHC: 1262M/o/O/LD/114/4

TYPED LETTER TO FORTESCUE FROM PITCAIRN-CAMPBELL

Head Quarters,
Southern Command

C.R., S.C., 58600. (A.2)   S a l i s b u r y.

12th July, 1915.

My dear Lord Fortescue,

Let me begin by thanking you for your letter of 26th June in which you express the opinion that in Devon there are enough Farmers' sons staying at home to enable the County to furnish its proportion of a Farmers' Battalion provided they will enlist.

As you will see by the enclosed War Office letter (No. 20/Infantry/720 (A.G.1) of 7th July, 1915) the Government are very desirous to attempt to raise such a Battalion or Battalions in my Command, although I reported that the General tenor of the replies to my letter of June 24th was not encouraging.

By this War Office letter discretion is given to me to postpone the formation of such Battalion or Battalions until after Harvest, and I intend to avail myself of such permission, as it would be obviously hopeless to attract the Farmers' sons until the Harvest is gathered. But it may be possible, when the Registration Bill comes into effect, to induce such men to enlist, giving them leave at once to take part in Harvest work.

I feel that no one in the South of England is as competent as yourself to raise (or <u>perhaps I had better say to attempt to raise</u>) such a Unit, and I beg you sincerely to undertake the task, the difficulty of which I do not attempt to minimize.

Your own County and Cornwall seem at present to offer the best prospect of success.

You were kind enough to send me in confidence a copy of a draft letter from the Board of Trade which it was proposed to send out to the County Councils; I agree with you that the scheme therein set out, if properly co-ordinated with recruiting for the Farmers' sons Battalions, might help the movement, but I can find no trace of any such letter having been received in this Office, and therefore I do not know whether it has been issued by the Board of Trade.[29]

The conditions laid down in War Office letter No. 20/Infantry/712 (A.G.1) of 14th June, 1915, (copy herewith) will apply, except that the standard will be the normal one for the Infantry, viz., 5 feet 2 inches; and that recruiting need not be restricted to particular Military Districts.

---

[29] Fortescue added in pen in the margin 'wash out never got beyond "Draft" stage'.

Do you think that the addition of the word (Yeoman) to the Title of the Battalions would be popular – e.g., ____ (Yeoman) Battalion Devonshire Regiment, or would it be considered as impinging on the Yeomanry? If so what title[30] would you suggest?

      Yours sincerely,

      Pitcairn Campbell

The Right Honourable

    The Earl Fortescue.,

      Castle Hill,

        NORTH DEVON.

Reply [from Fortescue] 15/7 15[31]

Would not in any case attempt to raise another Yeoman[ry] class unit till our Yeo[manry]. is complete.

Before replying I want to know [:] Do you ask me to raise a Batt[alion]" or a D[evon] & C[ornwall] Co[mpany]. for a Wessex Battalion

Am I to be C.O? I am not fit for it, but if not who is to be CO & who is to find time?

If only D[evon] & C[ornwall] Co[mpany] how about Officers? Is the Capt[ain]. Com & to be nominated by OC or by me?

Can application be made for a Transfer of a suitable officer from some existing unit? or should we be expected to take the best dug out we can find?

---

[30] Pitcain Campbell added the word 'title' in fountain pen.
[31] This section was written by Fortescue in pen as a first draft reply or initial response to Pitcairn Campbell's letter.

DHC: 1262M/o/O/LD/114/8

TYPED LETTER REF TO PITCAIRN-CAMPBELL FROM FORTESCUE

Castle Hill,
South Molton,
21st. July 1915.[32]

58600
C. R. S. C. 5 A/600/ A 2.

My dear General,

I have carefully considered your letter of 19th.

(1). On paper it ought to be possible to raise a farmers' battalion in the Southern Command. According to the Census there are 23,292 sons of farmers and graziers assisting in the work of the farmer in the your twelve Counties.[32] The establishment of the thirteen Yeomanry Regiments in the same – taking 1st and 2nd Line at 450 and 3rd. Line at 200 – is 14,300. Judging by the Devonshire Regiment not more than one-half of these at the outside are strictly farmers' sons; and if this estimate is correct it would leave 16,000 available. If one-third of these would not pass the Doctor (which is a liberal estimate) there must be 10,000 more or less available for a farmers battalion, exclusive of people like dairymen, manure dealers and the like whose connection with agriculture would qualify them for such a battalion as is proposed. It seems therefore that there ought to be a fair chance of success, and I think a Company could be collected in Devon, Cornwall, and Dorset at any rate.[33]

(2). As to my being the raiser of the Battalion, this would involve conference with other Lords-Lieutenant as I could not do anything outside Devonshire except with their support and approval.

(3). The answer to this would depend on the conference referred to in (2). If, for example, the Lord-Lieutenant of Bucks refused to have anything to do with it, the men who might be found by that County would have to be secured from somewhere else.

(4). I note you would leave the raiser a free hand as to machinery: it is premature to discuss this yet.

(5). Command. I do not think it would be possible for me to undertake this. The C. O. will have to train officers as well as men and I have not the knowledge for this. I might learn perhaps, but in that case I should have to be relieved of all my other duties as Lord-Lieutenant, Chairman of the County Council and

---

[32] These counties are listed in the margin: Berks, Bucks, Gloucter [Gloucester], Oxford, Warwicksh[ire], Worcestersh[ire], Cornwall, Devon, Dorset, Hant, Somerset, Wilts[hire].
[33] The words 'at any rate' were added later by Fortescue in pen.

T.F.A. But if a suitable Commanding Officer could be found I could and would do all in my power to raise men for him, subject however

(6) to a distinct promise of the Authorities of favourable consideration of requests that he or I might make in the matter of Officers. So much depends on the Officers in a matter of sort that I could not touch it nor could I ask any man fit for it to undertake the Command if there was no better prospect in respect to Staff and Company Commanders than scraping together of dug outs and men who have hitherto been unable to find employment.

I will see L[or]ᵈ Lansdowne & if he gives his blessing the rest are pretty sure to come into line & I could then as soon as a C.O. was secured and I got the assurances required as to officers make a start.[34]

F[ortescue].

---

[34] This paragraph was added by Fortescue in pen.

DHC: 1262M/o/O/LD/114/12

TYPED LETTER TO FORTESCUE ABOUT FARMERS' BATTALION

LANSDOWNE HOUSE,

BERKELEY SQUARE, W.

22nd July 1915.

My dear Fortescue,

I shall be delighted to see you next week.

Had we not better meet in the House of Lords on Wednesday evening ?

Meanwhile I may perhaps say that I was approached on the subject of the formation of a Farmers' Battalion and asked for an immediate reply. My answer was to the effect that I did not believe there were many farmers' sons who, if at home, could be spared for military service, although there might be a few here and there. I also said that in my opinion farmers' sons would be more likely to join a mounted unit than a battalion of infantry.

I was afterwards asked if I thought it would be a good thing to call units composed of farmers' sons Yeomen Battalions, and I replied that I thought this would be a mistake and would lead to confusion with the existing Yeomanry.

When we meet, I should be glad if you would tell me what you are doing in your part of the world in regard to Volunteer Training Corps.

Yours sinc[erely]

L[andsowne].

DHC: 1262M/o/O/LD/114/20

TYPED LETTER TO FORTESCUE FROM COLONEL GRETTON

Head Quarters, Southern Command,

Radnor House, Salisbury.

C.R.,S.C., 58600/1. (A.2.)   8th August, 1915.

Dear Lord Fortescue,

The Commander-in-Chief will not be back till Monday afternoon, so I send you a copy of the War Office letter (20/Infantry/720 A. G. 1. of 6-8-15) in reply to his letter of 30-7-15, which enclosed yours of 28-7-15.

As soon as Sir William returns to Salisbury, the letter will be laid before him, but I forward you this copy to show you how anxious the War Office are to raise this Farmers' Battalion.

I hope you have received the copy of Major Champion's letter.

Yours sincerely,

G Leill Gretton.

The Right Honourable The Earl Fortescue.,

Castle Hill,

South Molton,

NORTH DEVON.

DHC: 1262M/o/O/LD/114/22

TYPED LETTER FROM FORTESCUE TO COLONEL GRETTON

Castle Hill,

South Molton.

11th August 1915.

Dear Col[onel] Gretton,

I am much obliged to you for the copy of War Office letter 20/Infantry/720 A.G.I. of 6.8.15.

The Army Council may, as you say, be very anxious to raise a Farmer Battalion, but if so their speech is admirably calculated to conceal their thoughts.

I represented to Sir D. Campbell on 28th July that I had got so little encouragement about Officers at the War Office that I could not undertake the task he wished; the Army Council now simply repeat their communication in official terms. –

Here they both are

Ld. F. to G.O.C. S.C. 28.7.15	A.C. to G.O.C. S.C. 6.8.15
The Military Secretary & Director of Organisation gave me to understand that no promise could be made of favourable consideration of the transfer to the new Battalion of any special officers who might be applied for on the ground of their local connection and influence, but that the Commander of the Battalion and I would have to rely on such officers at present unemployed as we could collect.	It will probably not be possible to provide the full number of specially qualified officers asked for by Lord Fortescue, but I invite you to submit a list and the case of each will be considered on its merits, and an endeavour made to give at least a proportion of those asked for. You should not exclude from your list on the ground of their being unemployed or unfit for active service any who would be useful.

There is not much difference between the right hand column and the left, for they could keep their word to the letter by giving me all the unfits and unemployed (because unemployable) with the addition of a "proportion" of one able bodied serving officer.

The preparation of a full[35] list means local consultation with 2nd[36] Lieutenants and leading Agriculturalists in a dozen counties as to the persons who by reason of County influence and connection would be likely to help recruiting, and[37]

All the assurance I am offered, that all the trouble involved would not be absolutely thrown away, is a vague statement that binds no one to anything.

The Army Council seem to misapprehend my position. I am not out for promotion or decoration or anything of that kind. I am ready to make myself useful if I am provided with the necessary tools. I am not ready to court certain failure by attempting without them, a task, the difficulties of which, Sir D. Campbell himself fully appreciates.[38]

If however the General thinks it worth while [*sic*] to go any further, & to draft a list with such knowledge as he & L[or]d Valletort & I possess without taking the trouble to consult the local people in each County till we see how the W. O. treats his preliminary suggestions, I could meet him on Tuesday afternoon 17" at Exeter or Salisbury or Bristol or in London on 18" or 19". It would be most desirable L[or]d V[alletort]. should be present too.[39]

F[ortescue].

---

[35] The word 'full' was added in pen.
[36] Fortescue added 'Lords?' in the margin in pencil.
[37] The word 'and' was added in pen.
[38] This entire paragraph was crossed out by Fortescue.
[39] This was added by Fortescue in pen.

CHARITIES AND VOLUNTARY AID
(1914–1918)

DHC: 1262M/o/O/LD/113/127

TYPED LETTER FROM FORTESCUE HEADED
DEVONSHIRE PATRIOTIC FUND

Rough Draft

15, High Street,
Exeter.
28th April, 1915

Dear Sir,

I beg to forward an audited Statement of the Receipts and Expenditure to 31st March last.

The Expenditure on Relief of Families would have been infinitely greater but for the changes made by the Government in regard to separation allowance. I may remind you that the Wife of a Seaman, who last August got nothing beyond her Husband's allotment, now receives 6/- a week, provided the Husband makes an allotment of £1 per month; and the Wife of a private Soldier, with three children, now receives 19/6 per week, as against 14/9, in addition to her Husband's minimum allotment of 6d. per day.

Notwithstanding this, the local sub-committees who investigate and report on cases still find that Grants amounting in all to a substantial sum per week are required to keep from want some of the relatives of those who are fighting our battles; and the need for assistance in relieving the sufferings of the sick and wounded cannot, I fear, fail to increase the continued increase of the number of men who are putting into the field.

Under these circumstances, even if we knew how long the War would last, it would be impossible to form any reliable estimate as to the sum likely to remain in hand at the end of it.

The generosity of the public continues, and subscriptions are still coming in, and though they do not keep pace with the expenditure, it is likely that there will be a balance–perhaps a considerable one–unexpended on the termination of hostilities. It is idle to suggest any scheme for the disposal of this yet. All that can usefully be said is that we believe there will be no difficulty in finding good use for any money that remains in supplementing Pensions and Grants to some of the disabled men, widows, etc., for whom the provision made by the necessary inelastic rules of the Government is in their circumstances inadequate.

Yours faithfully,
Fortescue
President

DHC: 1262M/o/O/LD/139/1

PAMPHLET ON THE HISTORY OF
THE DEVON AND CORNWALL WAR REFUGEES COMMITTEE.

The first meeting of the Committee formed in Exeter for the Relief of War Refugees was held in Exeter on the 25th September, 1914, and there were present the Mayoress (Mrs. K. King), Countess Fortescue, Mrs. Gordon, Mrs. Lind, Miss Barnes, Mrs. Worthington, Miss Andrew and Mr. Barnes. At this meeting, the Mayoress was electing President and Lady Fortescue, Vice-President; Miss Andrew, Hon. Secretary; and Mrs. Worthington, Assistant Hon. Secretary; and it was decided to make a public appeal for funds.

At the next meeting of the Committee, held a fortnight later, it was reported that £450 had already been subscribed, and many homes and vacant houses had been offered. At this meeting, the Mayoress, Lady Fortescue, and Miss Andrew were appointed a Sub-Committee, with power to act, for the purpose of receiving Refugees. Acting on this authority, Miss Andrew was sent to London, and returned to Exeter with 120 Refugees, and Exeter became the first provincial centre to receive Refugees, and the first place to provide them with homes. By the end of October, it was reported that over 800 persons had been provided for in the neighbourhood. Local Sub-Committees were formed in many places, Miss Andrew being the leading spirit in these activities.

By February, 1915, 3,000 Refugees had been received, and it was felt that the work had become too big for the Committee as constituted, so the Lord Lieutenant of the County was approached for the purpose of forming a Devon Committee; this he did, and shortly after-wards invited the Lord Lieutenant of Cornwall to join with him in constituting a Committee for Devon and Cornwall; and this was set up accordingly, under the title of the Devon and Cornwall War Refugees Committee.

For a time Exeter retained a separate Committee for the purpose of looking after those within the boundaries of the County of the City of Exeter, but transferred some of its workers to the new Devon and Cornwall Committee. In February, 1916, however, the Exeter Committee amalgamated with the Devon and Cornwall Committee.

The Headquarters of the Devon and Cornwall Committee were throughout fixed at No. 24, West Southernhay, lent free of charge by the Dental Hospital. The first Hon. Secretary of the Committee was Miss Andrew, with Mrs. Worthington as Assistant Hon. Secretary, and Mr. Rybot as Treasurer. Later, Miss Bannatyne, M. B. E., became Hon. Secretary ; after a time, Miss Harrison, M. B. E., was appointed Joint Hon. Secretary, and on Mr. Rybot's leaving Exeter, Mr. F. Walker became Treasurer. Prebendary Buckingham was Chairman, and had throughout the support and assistance of the heads of the Roman Catholic Church in Exeter. Mr. S. Andrew and Mr. T. Snow also gave much valuable help.

The offices were open daily, except Sundays, from 10 a.m. to 5 p.m. continuously, and the work was discharged by a band of voluntary workers; and after office hours, letters and callers were received by one of the ladies living on Southernhay.

For three years the Committee met weekly : afterwards once a fortnight was found to be sufficient.

In the course of 1915 the Government assumed more direct responsibility for the Refugees, and made a grant in respect of their maintenance, which, being supplemented by public generosity and carefully administered, proved quite sufficient for the requirements of the Committee, who, indeed, thanks to the War ending sooner than expected, was able on winding up to return to the Government a substantial sum.

As some evidence of the magnitude and character of the work undertaken, it may be stated that the letters received for some years averaged 50 at least a day, and the persons interviewed often numbered 100 in the 24 hours. Refugees arrived at all hours, and often unannounced, but they were always provided for. On one occasion a telegram was received at 10 o'clock at night, saying that 190–unexpected–had been sent off from London and would arrive in Exeter at 2.15 a.m. On arrival they were found to total 235, but they were met and housed that night, and all ultimately placed. Refugees would sometimes come in blocks of between 200 and 300, and they were met by a line of City trams and taken to one or other of the Hostels. From first to last, over 8,000 Refugees were received and provided for ; many schemes were undertaken for securing their employment, and with much success.

It was not till January, 1919, that conditions made it possible to begin repatriation, and it was nearly six months before the last Refugee was sent back to his home.

The operations of the Committee thus lasted for a period of more than four years and a half; their disbursements at one time amounted to £2,000 a month, and as many as 6,000 persons were at one moment under its charge ; but they never had a salaried official. Every-thing was done by voluntary helpers.

Such a work was only made possible by the extraordinary hospitality offered by the people of our Counties ; and this good-will is more remarkable when it is remembered that the Refugees were not selected specimens ; indeed, sometimes they were not very desirable visitors, and more often than not they were persons with a different standard of living and observance to those who housed them. The arrangements in this regard were made through the Local Sub-Committees, which, as previously stated, were formed throughout Devon and Cornwall; these each undertook to receive a certain number of Refugees from the Central Committee, and raised and administered their own funds.

The following Committee and persons deserve particular mention for valuable services ; but to mention all is impossible :

BARNSTAPLE	-	-	A. F. Seldon, Esq. ; G. Lefroy Esq.
BIDEFORD	-	-	Mayor's Committee.
BODMIN	-	-	Mr. G. S. Bricknell.
BRIXHAM	-	-	Miss Shears.
CAMBORNE	-	-	Mrs. Battishill.
CREDITION	-	-	Mrs. Francis.
DAWLISH	-	-	Mrs. Hildyard.

EXETER	-	-	Till merged in Central Committee.
EXMOUTH	-	-	Miss Worthington ; Miss Landon.
GUNNISLAKE	-	-	J. Blewitt, Esq. ; T. T. Bowhay, Esq.
ILFRACOMBE	-	-	Miss Norton.
LAUNCESTON	-	-	Mrs. Smith Pearse.
NEWTON ABBOT	-	-	Miss Froude.
NEWQUAY	-	-	G. Ockford, Esq.
PAIGNTON	-	-	Mrs. Boyd Thomson.
PENZANCE	-	-	G. Bunt, Esq.
PINHOE	-	-	F. Crooks, Esq.
ST. AUSTELL	-	-	A. Hugh, Esq. ; Miss Hancock.
ST. IVES	-	-	J. Daniel, Jun., Esq.
SIDMOUTH	-	-	Miss Havelaar.
TAVISTOCK	-	-	A. Echalaz, Esq.
TEIGNMOUTH	-	-	Mrs. Jordan.
TIVERTON	-	-	A. Gregory, Esq.
TORQUAY	-	-	R. Lane, Esq.
WADEBRIDGE	-	-	T. Rickard, Esq.

DHC: 1262M/0/O/LD/136/4

Extract from BOOKLET TITLED
'RED CROSS AND VOLUNTARY AID IN DEVONSHIRE DURING THE WAR'

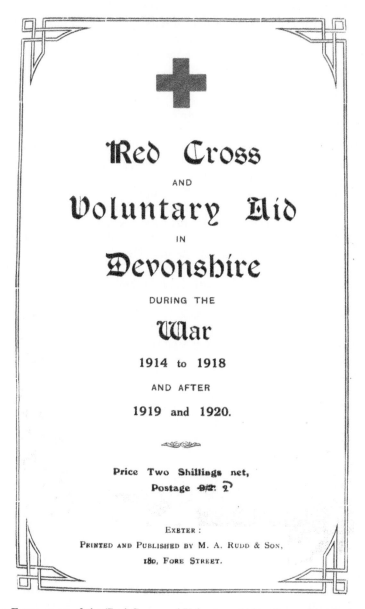

Figure 2. Front cover of the 'Red Cross and Voluntary Aid in Devonshire during the War'. Reproduced with the kind permission of Devon Archives and Local Studies Service.

Close of War Work.—The War Work of the V.A. Detachments was brought to a fitting close on Friday, July 11th, 1919, when a Parade, followed by a Special Service in the Cathedral and an Inspection by the Lord Lieutenant, were held at Exeter. Later in the day a General Meeting of the Devonshire Branch took place. The following account of the proceedings is reproduced, by the kind permission of the Editor, from the *Devon and Exeter Gazette* of July 12th, 1919.

The Castle Yard, Exeter, has been the scene of many notable gatherings in the past. A conspicuous addition to the list was made yesterday, when it formed the parade ground for an assembly of members of the Devonshire Voluntary Aid Organisation, which is shortly to be demobilised as a military auxiliary. The immense value of its work is too well-known to need recapitulation here. Before the war, it was one of those organisations upon which the general public cast only cursory glances, and frequently queried its value. The war had scarcely enveloped the country ere the possibilities of such an organisation were immediately recognised, and, being recognised, were requisitioned for military service, and instantly yielded abundant proof of its value. Throughout the stressful days of hostility its labour in connexion with the organisation of hospitals, equipping beds, tending and caring for the sick and wounded were increasing. Now, it is to reap the reward of its labours in a well-earned rest, so far, at any rate, as martial associations are concerned. Yesterday's concentration was, more or less, in the nature of a "wind up". Brilliant weather prevailed. The muster totalled slightly over a thousand. The mass of navy blue uniforms, relieved here and there with greys and khakis, made a very imposing picture in the Castle Yard, and was framed with the refreshing verdure of the slops under the famous old walls.

The detachments on parade included representatives from Plymouth, Ashburton, Barnstaple, Exeter, Honiton, Torquay, Paignton, Southmolton, Tiverton, Totnes, and Tavistock. A special train was run by the Great Western Railway from South Devon. The various Divisions were commanded by Assistant County Directors as follows:—Divisions 1 and 2, Mrs. Wilmott, O.B.E.; 4, Mr. A. Scott Brown; 5, Admiral Sir Chas. Coke, K.C.V.O.; 6 and 7, Mrs. Rennell Coleridge; 8, Dr. J. Quick ; 9, Mrs. Fuller ; 10, Major W. P. Martin; 12, Mr. W. Brownfield Craig, O.B.E.; 13, Mr. H. V. Soltan. The men's detachments were grouped with their respective Divisions. The St. John Ambulance Brigade was represented by detachments from the Exeter, Newton Abbot, and Torquay Divisions, and officered by Supt. Bowden, Supt. Wyse, and Chief-Officer Rivers. Commandant Harbottle Reed, M.B.E., was in charge of the parade, which, headed by the band of the 1st Battalion Devonshire Regt. (whose attendance was made possible by the kindness of the Officer Commanding, and was under Bandmaster Cox), proceeded by way of Castle Street, High Street, and Broadgate to the Cathedral. The progress was watched by large crowds, and many expressions of admiration at the splendid work done by the Red Cross were heard.

Cathedral Service.—The service in the Cathedral at 12.30 was of an impressive character, and the large congregation included many prominent people of the city and county. The clergy present, in addition to the Dean (Dr. H. R. Gamble), who was the preacher, were the Bishop of Crediton, the Archdeacon of Exeter (the Ven F. A. Sanders), Canon McLaren, Treasurer Jackson, Prebendary Bird, and the Revs. R. W. B. Langhorne (Priest-Vicar), and R. C. B. Llewellyn (Succentor). A special form of service was used. The opening sentences were intoned by the Succentor, and Pslams cxxiv. and cxxv. were sung to familiar chants. The Lesson (taken from 1 Cor. xii. 12–27) was read by the Bishop of Crediton, following which came the anthem, "See that ye love one another with a pure heart fervently" (Wesley). Appropriate prayers were offered by the Rev. R. W. B. Langhorne, special Thanksgivings being said for the generous support given to the funds of the Red Cross, for the work of the hospitals, for the skill and organisation of medicine, surgery, and nursing, and for the health of the Army. Then followed the singing of the hymn "Now thank we all our God." The Dean based his discourse on the words, "It is more blessed to give than to receive" (Acts xx. 35), and "Give, and it shall be given unto you ; good measure pressed down, and shaken together, running over" (St. Luke vi. 38). It was, he said, surely a true instinct which had led them to gather together that day in the House of God. The suggestion for the service came from them ; not from the Church. But it gave the Cathedral body no small pleasure to welcome them. It was a happy occasion, for it marked the completion of their long labourers— labours necessitated by the awful conflict which had come to end at last. In that conflict they, as much as anyone, would give the first place to those men who had fought our battles, and in so many instances, alas, had laid down their lives—those men whom they had specially commemorated belonging to the Devonshire Regiment in the great service which was held a month ago. "But you too," went on the Dean, "have your martyrs, and no small share in the victory belongs to you and such as you, who, for the last four years, have alleviated suffering and done in other ways a work which will not lightly be forgotten, and who have shrunk from no tasks, however humble they may be seemed, which have been laid upon you. The war is ended, and, with it, as I have said, your work is ended, too. To-day we meet to thank God Who has inspired so many women's hearts—for I here address especially, though not exclusively, women this morning—with strength, tenderness, courage, and patience, and who have brought us all through so many perils and anxieties."

"It is more blessed to give than to receive." That, proceeded the preacher, was the thought in most of their minds to-day. The words were Christ's they were told, although they did not occur in any of the Gospels. Yet they seemed to sum up the life of Him Who went about doing good. He was always giving until His hands at last were nailed to the Cross, and even then, as one of their poets sung :—

> "Thy hands to give ; Thou canst not lift,
> Yet will Thy hand still giving be ;
> It gives, but oh! itself the gift ;
> It gives though bound ; though bound 'tis free."

In thus striving, so far as they had striven to follow Christ's example, to give the labours of their hands and their hearts, to forget themselves in their work for others, they had learnt something of the meaning of His words. They had not given in order to receive ; yet as they had given it had been given them. In sacrificing, as many of them had done, some of them accustomed joys and pleasures they had found, perhaps to their surprise, that their lives had not been emptier but fuller ; not duller but brighter. They were, many of them, conscious of a new vitality. Proceeding, the Dean said: In laying down your work to-day, your work of giving and serving is not, I would believe, really over. "Peace," said Milton, "hath her victories no less renowned than war," and Peace has its own opportunities of giving and serving no less great than those of war. The time of war has its own excitements ; it makes its special appeal to the imagination. But though in other ways your country needs you still, needs the gifts of your hands and of your hearts, more than once since the war was ended I have heard girls say, "Now my work is over I don't know what I shall do without it. I feel lost without it." But believe me, there is no occasion for that. We talk much about reconstruction. You must almost be tired of the word ; but depend upon it that in this work of reconstruction during the years—the perilous years—which still lie before us, women will be called upon to play not the smallest part. Opportunities of new kinds of work and service will present themselves to those who are ready to receive them, and besides the new tasks and new opportunities, you must remember there will be the old ones as well—those which existed before the war, and that neither man nor woman was always quite ready to take up. It may be, of course, that some of the tasks will seem to be dull and unexciting, but "Go, work to-day in my vineyard," was the Divine command. No one will grudge you your return to those social pleasures and joys which many of you for a time laid aside entirely or almost altogether. No one, or very few, would wish it otherwise, and if, after the strain of the war there seems to be now an almost excessive passion for pleasure there is no need for the moralist to be too severe. But still, as I have said, no life of merely selfish pleasure can entirely satisfy most of you now. In the streets of our great towns, in our quiet villages, among the poor, among the children, among your sisters, among the falling or the fallen, very near to your own doors it may be, the opportunity of service will be at hand. The State needs you ; the Church needs you ; and as you thank God to-day for the completion of your task—such a task as we trust by the mercy of God will never be laid upon you again, you may still go forward with stronger characters and with larger hearts to tread the common paths, which Christ never disdained to tread, and in one way or another to follow the blessed steps of Him Who loved us and gave Himself for us."

After the singing of "O God, our help in ages past," the Dean pronounced the Blessing and the service ended with a verse of the National Anthem. As the congregation were leaving, the Organist (Dr. Wood) played a Solemn March, by Smart.

Subsequently the members assembled, forming three sides of a square, in the Cloister Garth. Here the Lord-Lieutenant, accompanied by Countess Fortescue, Major-General Sir Harold Tagart, Col. H. Smith-Rewse (of the Devon Territorial Force Association), the Deputy Mayor of Exeter (Mr. T. B. Rowe) and Mrs. Rowe, the Sheriff (Mr. W. Townsend) and Mrs. Townsend, the Dean of Exeter (Canon Gamble), and the Archdeacon (the Ven. F. A. Sanders), inspected the parade, and chatted with several Members. Then, mounting a dais, Earl Fortescue, addressing the parade, said they had been familiar lately with memorial and Thanksgiving services. It was very right. They had their own Roll of Honour. And they had much to be thankful for. None could think it was otherwise than fitting that now, at the close of five years of labour on behalf of the sick and wounded of the Empire, they should meet together for worship in the Cathedral, and, beside it, for a final parade. Their thoughts must go back to the time when they first took up Red Cross service. There had been incidents, some tragic, and some laughable enough, in connexion with their hospital service, and they would be entitled, in future years, to look back with great satisfaction to the time they had given to those duties. They had done very good work. Their patients and the country were grateful to them. In Devonshire they were ahead of a good many counties in organisation when war broke out. There were 62 detachments, and though the personnel was something like 500 under strength, the vacancies were very soon filled. He noticed among those present a good proportion of ladies and gentlemen, whom he hoped would not take it amiss if he called them "Old Contemptibles." (Laughter.) After them, another 1,000 joined up, as their services were required. Since August, 1914, 34 hospitals had been organised, 3,900 beds had been equipped, and more than 45,000 patients had passed through their hands. The figures spoke for themselves, and now, except for a couple of hospitals kept going for special purposes in Exeter, it was all over.

They had shown that the supposedly feebler members of the community were necessary, and could do good work. As necessary as munitions, and as necessary as men for the fighting line, had been the organisation of the medical services, and, if that had failed, disaster must have ensued. But the hospitals did not fail, and they, and such as they in other parts of the county and country, had taken on whatever duty had been required of them, whether it had been interesting work, such as the assisting of surgeons at operations, or the drudgery—though no less necessary—of cooking meals and washing plates. Their services were now no longer necessary in those capacities, but he hoped they would not put their war experience behind them. Other people had been learning to kill and to prepare instruments of death ; they had been learning to cure and save life. Europe had had enough fighting for the present, and, although wars had not yet been made to cease in all the world, he did not think that fighting men would have much opportunity, at least for the next few years, of proving their skill upon each other. But there was the whole civil population upon which the members of the Voluntary Aid Organisations could exercise their skill and experience. The campaign against dirt, disease, and insanitary conditions was a never-ending one, and there was no discharge in that war. They were taking, and deserved, a good holiday, but when that was over he did not think they would want to go back to an aimless and purposeless life. They could find great use for their experience and skill in connexion with such movements as child welfare and nursing organisations. If they could raise the standard of health in the country they would assist in repairing the ravages of war, and thereby increase the obligation the country owed them. The Red Cross Society and the St. John Ambulance Association were not going to be either disbanded or demobilised. He did not like to say good-bye as to people whose occupations had gone, and for whose services there would no longer be a demand, because, while he thanked them most earnestly for what they had done, he hoped, no less earnestly, they would continue to give the country the benefit of the knowledge and experience they had gained.

General Meeting.—A general meeting was held in the afternoon at the Drill Hall, Bedford Circus, and largely attended. Earl Fortescue presided. At the entrance to the hall a pretty little ceremony took place. This consisted of the presentation of a charming bouquet, composed of white and pink carnations, to Countess Fortescue. The presentation was made by Miss Pope (Secretary to the County Director) on behalf of the County and Assistant County Directors. Earl Fortescue, in opening the meeting, said there had, from time to time, been what he termed "stock-taking" gatherings at which accounts were given of the work of the organisation. That day was a rather special occasion. They came to hear of the work that had been done during the last five years, the like of which, please God, would not have to be done again by any of them. The St. John Ambulance Brigade was a very ancient foundation. The Red Cross Society went back to the Geneva Convention held about 50 years ago, but the present British Red Cross only dated from 1905, and the Voluntary Aid Organisation from some 10 years ago. Lord Haldane had builded [sic] better than he knew, when he started that organisation, and he (Earl Fortescue) expected that Mr. Davis hardly foresaw the great task and the importance of his position when, to their great advantage, he accepted the post of County Director. (Applause.) At first he believed there was a feeling that the duties of the V.A.D. were to be limited to nursing, in their own parishes, wounded and sick men of the Territorial Force in the event of an invasion. The public acknowledged that first aid and the elements of sanitary work were great assets whether in military or civil life. The good humoured banter with which the movement was assailed quickly died away. But for untiring and increasing energies of the County Director and his staff, and the guidance of their officers, and the patience and goodwill of their medical instructors, very little could have been accomplished. He trusted the public would learn, from the record of the proceedings, of the work which, although it had not been done in the limelight, was, nevertheless, as necessary and helpful to the success which attended our arms, as any arsenal or factory.

(Applause.)

Mr. J. S. C. Davis, in the course of a resumé of the work performed by the Organisation in Devonshire, extended thanks to the Dean and Chapter for the Cathedral service, the Standing Joint Committee for the use of the Castle Yard, Mr. Harbottle Reed for taking charge of the parade and march, the Territorial Force Association and Major Coleridge for the Drill Hall, the Sergeant-Major and men of the Territorial Force Depôt Staff for arranging and decorating the Drill Hall, Mr. Martin and other proprietors of Bedford Circus for placing the gardens at the disposal of the Association for the luncheon, Major Jenkins and Bandmaster Cox for the band of the 1st Devon Regiment, Chief-Constables of the County and City for policing arrangements and Lord and Lady Fortescue for their constant help and support throughout the war. (Applause.) He recalled the days before the war, from 1910, when the first V.A. Detachments were formed in the county, to 1914. A considerable number of enthusiastic persons underwent a great deal of training in first aid and nursing. In 1914 they held an experimental mobilisation on a considerable scale, which proved that elementary work could be undertaken successfully. All that time their prescribed duties were limited to the performance of odd jobs for the Territorial R.A.M.C. in the event of an invasion. The establishment and maintenance of hospitals on a large scale was never considered. Then came the war, and on the 6th August, 1914, General Donald G.O.C. Wessex Division, asked if hospitals for wounded men could be started at short notice. Assured that that could be done, he directed Mr. Davis to prepare hospitals at Exeter, Torquay, and other places. The first patients were received in October, 1914, and their hospitals were the first hospitals in the country to receive wounded men from overseas. (Applause.) The establishment of those hospitals involved considerable expense. Later, when he reported his action to the County Red Cross Committee, Lord Fortescue, in moving what he had done be approved, said with a smile, that "if Mr. Davis had not undertaken this responsibility he would deserve to be hanged on the nearest lamp-post." (Laughter.) That kindly mode of expressing approval cheered and encouraged him exceedingly, and made him feel that the county wished and demanded that nothing should be permitted to stand in the way of undertaking whatever further responsibility the military authorities might impose. There had been no lack of funds. The county had responded to all calls for money for carrying on the work. No work had ever been stopped or prevented from want of money, nor had men or women ever been wanting. (Applause.) It was no light task to run hospitals continuously for prolonged periods. All kinds of responsibilities, financial and otherwise, were involved. A vast amount of drudgery and subterranean work had to be carried through, bringing with it no public recognition or reward. But all the work had been performed cheerfully and well. The workers in the hospitals had the satisfaction of knowing that healing and comfort were brought to a very large number of sick and wounded men.

They had, of course, occasional difficulties, personal and otherwise. All were overcome. There were practically no difficulties in respect of discipline of members of detachments and hospital staffs. He had throughout taken the view that in a voluntary organisation such as that the first essential of discipline was that those in authority should discipline themselves and should only issue such orders as would commend themselves to those who had to obey them. He regarded any attempts to Prussianise [sic] the Red Cross as an insult to educated and intelligent Red Cross workers. (Hear, hear.) He was deeply grateful to all the officers and members who had worked under him during the war for their ready and prompt acceptance of all the orders which had been issued, and he was well aware that had involved a great deal of self-sacrifice and self-effacement on the part of a great many people. The work had been heavy, but it had been lightened by the kind and willing co-operation of many hundreds of capable and willing helpers. What could he say which would afford anything like an adequate recognition of the work of some of the Assistant Directors (Mr. W. Brownfield Craig, Mrs. Wilmot, Mr. W. P. Martin, and Mrs. Coleridge), or of the devotion of those who had lent their houses for hospital purposes (Colonel and Mrs. Barton, Sir Ian and Lady Amory, Mr. and Mrs. Vereker, Mr. and Mrs Woodroffe, Mr. and Mrs. Yonge, and Mr. and Mrs. Fleming), or of the services of the many capable Commandants and Matrons and other officers and members of hospital staffs? He thanked the members of his office staff. Each and all of them had rendered most unfailing and devoted service. (Applause.) Over £250,000 of receipts and a similar amount of payments had been accounted for methodically and punctually in such a manner as to win the unqualified approval of the Hon. Auditor (Mr. W. W. Beer), to whom the most cordial acknowledgements and thanks were due for his careful supervision of the accounts. When it became necessary to open a large store for the supply of groceries, etc., to the hospitals, the ladies of the office cheerfully undertook the heavy and laborious additional work.

Early in the war the War Office undertook to grant compensation to V.A.D.'s for loss of salary or employment. At that time a considerable number of women of small means, governesses, school teachers, and shopgirls, [*sic*] had given up everything in order to render service to the country in the hospitals. When application was made for small allowances in some typical cases, he received orders intimating that nothing of the kind would be granted, and requesting him not to employ such persons in future. He need hardly say that he did not comply with the latter request. Early this year the financial position of the hospitals gave rise to great anxiety. There were few patients and practically no income from capitation grants. He was losing money at the rate of £1,500 a month. He applied to Plymouth for permission to alter his proposals for closing hospitals, and, in reply, was told that the Red Cross was a wealthy institution, and that the A.D.M.S. did not care whether it lost money or not. The result was a deficit of £4,500 on the working of the hospitals. In other words, a waste of £4,500 was caused by the Military authorities insisting on a large number of hospitals being kept open when there was no need for them. However, they were able to close their war work with funds in hand. (Applause.) They were, in every respect, far stronger than in 1914. They had numbers, enthusiasm, and experience. What the future would bring he could not say precisely. It was hoped that the Red Cross detachments would be used in civil work under the new Ministry of Health. He appealed to them all to wait and see what the future would bring.

(Applause.)

The Deputy Mayor of Exeter (Mr. T. B. Rowe) moved a vote of thanks to Earl and Countess Fortescue, and paid tribute to the great and generous help they had rendered the organisation.

The Sheriff of Devon (Mr. W. P. Martin) seconded, and said that at all times Lord and Lady Fortescue had been of the greatest assistance to the Red Cross movement in the county.

The motion was carried with acclamation.

Earl Fortescue briefly acknowledged the compliment, and said that now the war was over a good many things he had said and done might be brought up in evidence against him. (Laughter.) He asked them to allow for extenuating circumstances. If he had been of some service to the Red Cross organisation it would help in mitigating some of his sentence. His one object had been to help forward the causes that would make for the country's success during the war. (Applause.)

Presentation to Mr. Davis.—The proceedings were closed with the presentation to Mr. Davis of a silver salver appropriately inscribed, together with a motor car and a finely-illuminated volume containing the names of more than 1,400 subscribers. The presentation was made by Countess Fortescue on behalf of Members of the Devonshire Red Cross Branch, the St. John Ambulance Brigade, Members of the V.A. Detachments and other friends.

Food Production and Agriculture (1915–1918)

DHC: 1262M/o/O/LD/112/97

TYPED SHEET – DISTRIBUTION OF AGRICULTURAL LABOUR IN DEVONSHIRE

DISTRIBUTION OF AGRICULTURAL LABOUR IN DEVONSHIRE
11th Dec, 1918

Soldier Labour.

No. of soldiers on the land in Devon   2774 in Somerset 2000[1]

Distributed as follows : -

Eastern Division	1012	
Southern "	752	
Northern "	546	
Western "	464	
Total	2774	

Applications sent to Barracks since last report : -

Eastern Dvn.	Southern Dvn.	Northern Dvn.	Western Dvn.
12	25	21	12

Applications fulfilled since last report : -

60	60	3	35

Total no. of applications waiting : - 27.

56 ploughmen from the 3rd Devons, Plymouth, will arrive in Exeter today and will be attached to the Agricultural Companies. During the 7 months ending 7th December the total number of special applications and received and submitted for agricultural furlough for individual soldiers was 1225. The total number sanctioned was about 120.

As the Metropolitan Police Constables have been recalled the Ploughing School at Exeter will be closed as from the 21st inst.

WAR AGRICULTURAL VOLUNTEERS. The total number of applications received for enrolment was 584, of which 382 were placed and 205 were cancelled. As volunteers are now released from their obligations on giving or receiving customary notice the majority have returned to their civil employment.

---

[1] Fortescue added 'in Somerset 2000' in pencil.

PRISONERS OF WAR.

Eastern Dvn.	Western Dvn.	Southern Dvn.	Nthn Dvn.	Total
222	121	192	80	615

of which under Scheme "B":

| 83 | 24 | 21 | 35 | 163 |

Migratory gangs of 10 prisoners each are working at Kenn,[2] Bondleigh, Sutcombe and Beadon.

Application has been made for 65 additional prisoners have been allotted.

The private Camp at Sir Charles Cave, Sidbury, has finished the work for which it was required and one half of the number of prisoners have been sent to Honiton and the other half are remaining at Sidbury in case they should be needed for local requirements.

H. C. PATERSON.

Labour Officer.

11th Dec. 1918.

[2] 20 gangs in Som[erset] is added in pencil.

DHC: 1262M/o/O/LD/112/154

TYPED SHEET DETAILING ACREAGE OF GRASSLAND PLOUGHED SINCE THE OUTBREAK OF WAR

ACREAGE OF GRASS LAND PLOUGHED IN THE COUNTY OF DEVON TAKEN FOR THE BOARD OF AGRICULTURE RETURNS.

THIS NOTE IS ON THE RETURN:–
"GRASS" means land which has remained continuously under permanent Grass, or under Seeds, Clovers, Sainfoin or Lucerne since the outbreak of War.

DISTRICT	No. of Holdings	No. of Acres Ploughed	Per holding
NORTHERN DIVISION			
Barnstaple	881	11141	
Bideford	420	5408	
Torrington	538	7856	
South Molton	760	10833	
Total for Division	2599	35238	13½
SOUTHERN DIVISION			
Newton Abbot	629	7162½	
Totnes	544	8623½	
Kingsbridge	498	7558	
Plympton	372	4611	
Total for Division	2043	27955	14
EASTERN DIVISION			
St. Thomas	798	7224	
Crediton	556	8143	
Tiverton	993	9112	
Honiton	505	3441	
Axminster	401	2079	
Total for Division	3253	29999	9⅓

WESTERN DIVISION

Okehampton	772	11681½	
Holsworthy	741	9915	
Tavistock	625	6332½	
Total for Division	2138	27929	13⅓
TOTAL FOR COUNTY	10,033	121,121	12$^{A[cres]}$ per holding

My Lord,

I am very sorry I did not mark my Copies A & B.

Will you will tell me if the above is A or B?[3]

To Lord Fortescue

From R. F. W. 12/9/18

---

[3]   This copy is marked A is blue pencil.

DHC: 1262M/o/O/LD/155/9

TYPED RETURN OF TRACTOR PLOUGHING FROM THE DEVON AGRICULTURE EXECUTIVE COMMITTEE

18.1.18

DEVON AGRICULTURAL EXECUTIVE COMMITTEE.

R. F. Woodcock.   50, Queen Street,
  Secretary.   Exeter.

Return of Tractor Ploughing in the County for the week ending 18th January 1918.

Northern Div.	No. of acres Ploughed.	Average per Tractor.	No. of Tractors attached to Unit.
Barnstaple.	13	2.60	5
Torrington	8	.90	9
South Molton.	2	1.00	2
	23		16
Southern Div.			
Newton Abbot.	30	6.00	5
Totnes.	29¼	5.85	5
Plympton.	14½	2.90	5
	73¾		15
Eastern Div.			
Crediton.	10½	1.70	6
Tiverton.	9½	1.90	5
Honiton.	36½	4.50	9
	56½		20
Western Div.			
Holsworthy.	26	4.33	6
Okehampton.	16¾	3.35	5
Tavistock.	8	8.00	1
	50¾		12
Total for County	204	3.24	63

DHC: 1262M/o/O/LD/155/39

TYPED LETTER TO THE RT. HON EARL FORTESCUE FROM H. J. BUTLER, TRACTOR REPRESENTATIVE, STATISTICS, CIRCULAR AND BALANCE SHEET

1, Cross Street,
Barnstaple
North Devon.

May 1st 1918

The Rt. Hon Earl Fortescue,

    Castle Hill,

        SOUTH MOLTON.

My Lord,

Re Trac[t]or Ploughmens Prize Fund.

I beg to hand you an account of the prize winners for the month of April.

For Tractors 2851 30/- and 2848 10/- a cheque payable to Supervisor Clements 40/-.

For Tractors 2853 30/- and 2855 10/- a cheque payable to Supervisor Parnell 40/-.

For Tractors 4579 30/- and 4681 10/- a cheque payable to Engineer Moor 40/-.

Vouchers for winners signatures and addressed envelopes are also enclosed.

The enclosed balance sheet shows cash remaining in hand to amount of £6.17.0. It is improbable that there will be enough work to keep <u>all</u> the Tractors going for the next 4 weeks I shall therefore be glad of instructions as to whether the Competition is to cease for the time being. in [*sic*] accordance with the original circular, or whether you wish it to continue.

The results of some of the tractors, although so comparative[e]ly poor on paper, are largely due to bad luck. Several men have been dismissed as slackers.

    I am,

        Your Lordships obedient Servant,

        H. J. Butler

        TRACTOR REPRESENTATIVE.

NORTH DEVON

Tractor Ploughmens Prize Fund.

For 4 weeks ending April 26th 1918.

BARNSTAPLE.	Apl5	Apl12	Apl19	Apl26	Total	
2847	11½	11¼	5¼	16¾	44¾	2851 1st Prize 30/-
2848	9½	17	5	14¾	46¼	Driver J. Medland
2849	7½	13½	10½	10	41½	Ploughman W. Medland
2850	11½	6½	4½	21¾	44¼	2848 2nd Prize 10/-
2851	13¼	15½	15	13	56¾	Driver Pte Smith
						Ploughman Pte Browning

TORRINGTON						
2852	-	2½	10¼	5¾	16½	2853 1st Prize 30/-
2853	5	8¾	15½	20¾	50	Driver J. Daniel
2854	18½	3	3	10½	35	Ploughman Pte Wright
2855	3	10	13	12¾	38¾	2855 2nd Prize 10/-
2856	6½	5¼	6½	10	28¼	Driver A. Tallen
						Ploughman Pte. Holgate.

S.MOLTON.						
2857	8½	7	9¼	10¾	35½	4679 1st Prize 30/-
3672	5	7½	6	10	28½	Driver Sgt Foister
4679	8½	6	12½	14	41	Ploughman G. Speed
4681	8½	8¼	9	11	36¾	4681 2nd Prize 10/-
5562	6	7½	6½	3	23	Driver Pte Stephenson
						Ploughman Pte. Martin.

A weekly progress account has been delivered to every officer and man and everything possible has been done to stimulate the leaders and hustle the laggards.[4]

---

[4]   This is added vertically on the right-hand side of the document in red ink.

Results of the competition for the Silver Cups presented by Mr. G. W. Brindley of the Barnstaple Motor Coy (Engineer to F.P.D.) covering the period from March 2nd to April 26th (8 weeks) 1918

1	Barnstaple	Tractor	2851	139¼ acres.	Average per week			17.4
2	"	"	2848	109¼ "	"	"	"	13.6
3	S.Molton	"	4679	101 "	"	"	"	12.6
4	Barnstaple	"	2849	98 "	"	"	"	12.2
5	Torrington	"	2854	96¼ "	"	"	"	12.0
6	"	"	2853	94½ "	"	"	"	11.8
7	"	"	2855	91 "	"	"	"	11.4
8	S.Molton	"	4681	88 "	"	"	"	11.0
9	Barnstaple	"	2847	87¾ "	"	"	"	10.9
10	"	"	2850	83 "	"	"	"	10.4
11	S.Molton	"	2857	71½ "	"	"	"	8.9
12	"	"	3672	71½ "	"	"	"	8.9
13	Torrington	"	2856	71¼ "	"	"	"	8.9
14	"	"	2852	54 "	"	"	"	6.8⁵

Tractor 5562 South Molton only worked 6 weeks.

The cups are won outright & retained by the very deserving Champions the brothers W and J Medland of Chittlehamholt. Their average of 17.4 is a Superb performance and of course was only achieved by real hard work and much overtime. Being Grade I and both young men they have left us now to join up – if they serve their country as well in the Army as they have done at the plough we shall expect to see them come hone [sic] [home] covered with glory.

Anyhow we wish them the best of luck and safe return.

Which is going to be our Champion Team for the next period.?

Although Mr. Brindley generously put these Cups up for competition throughout the whole of North Devon it must be ve[r]y gratifying to him to award them to the very men whom he personally engaged when the Barnstaple Unit was first formed in October 1917.

Reckoning that 3 acres of cultivating etc are equal to 1 acre of ploughing the results of the various Units for the 8 weeks are as follows

Barnstaple	5 Tractors	517¼ acres.	Average per Tractor Per week					12.93
S.Molton	4 "	332 "	"	"	"	"	"	10.38
Torrington	5 "	407 "	"	"	"	"	"	10.17
Whole Division	14 "	1256¼ "	"	"	"	"	"	11.21

Signed.

H. J. Butler
TRACTOR REPRESENTATIVE

Copy delivered to each officer and man   The average for all England is about 7.8 per tractor in commission

---

⁵ The following is added in red: 'This team won the 1st prize in March Feb – they are really good men but have had shockingly bad luck ever since'.

Tractor Ploughmen's Prize Fund.

DEVON (NORTHERN DIVISION).

In each Unit the Team which Ploughs the greatest number of Acres every four weeks will receive a First Prize of 30/-.

The Team ploughing the next greatest number will receive 10/-.

CONDITIONS.

No Second Prize will be awarded in any Unit which contains less than 5 Tractors actually working.

In every case bad work will be disqualified.

3 Acres of cultivating, etc., will be reckoned as equal to 1 Acre Ploughing.

In any dispute the decision of the Tractor Representative will be final.

For the 3 months ending April, 26th, the Prizes will be as follows:–

			Barnstaple.		Torrington		South Molton.
March 1st.	1st Prize	...	£1 10s.	...	£1 10s.	...	£1 10s.
	2nd "	...	10s.	...	10s.	...	
" 29th.	1st "	...	£1 10s.	...	£1 10s.	...	£1 10s.
	2nd "	...	10s.	...	10s.	...	10s.
April 26th.	1st "	...	£1 10s.	...	£1 10s.	...	£1 10s.
	2nd "	...	10s.	...	10s.	...	10s.

Full particulars of all the Team's results will be given weekly. In every case in which a Tractor is held up through the neglect or oversight of any Officer, the men should write to me. I will fully investigate each complaint and, if justified, credit the Team with the full number of Acres they have lost through the same. Look out for your results. I mean to get rid of every Slacker, but those who "try" will receive every consideration and appreciation.

Lord Fortescue, who will personally award the Prizes, sends you this message:—

"The Tractor Plough is almost as new a thing as the Aeroplane. Just as our Airmen have done services of untold value by their skilful handling of their new weapon, so can you render immense services if you imitate them and get the utmost possible out of your new implements, and I am sure you will."–FORTESCUE

DONATIONS.

	£ s. d.		£ s. d.
Lord Fortescue	5 5 0	Mr. G. W. Brindley ...	2 2 0
Mr. H. J. Butler	5 0 0	Mr. H. N. G. Stucley ...	2 2 0
Mr. A. N. Heard	5 0 0	Mr. F. W. Moor ...	1 1 0
Miss Chichester	2 2 0	Mr. W. Dunn ...	5 0
		Mr. J. M. Metherell	1 1 0[6]

H. J. BUTLER, Tractor Representative,

1, Cross Street, Barnstaple.

1, Cross Street,

Barnstaple

North Devon.

May 1st 1918

BALANCE SHEET

Tractor Ploughmens Prize Fund.

To cheque book	1 : 0	By subscriptions	23 : 18 : 0
Mar 1 awards	5 : 10 : 0		0
Mar 29 awards	5 : 10 : 0		
Apl 26	6 : 0 : 0		
Bal in hand	6 : 17 : 0		
	23 : 18 : 0		23 : 18 : 0

H. J. Butler

[6] This was added later.

DHC: 1262M/o/O/LD/155/45

TYPED NOTES, ENTITLED – AS TO THE CLEAN CUT IN DEVONSHIRE AND ADDITIONAL HAND WRITTEN NOTES

NOTES as to the Clean Cut in Devonshire. June 1918.

In 1915 the cultivated area of the County was 1,208,000 acres of which 479,000 were arable, and 729,000 permanent grass.

The quota of additional land to be tilled to corn in 1917 was 130,000. This and rather more has been done.

As there are nearly 12,000 farms on the books of the Agricultural Executive it is obvious that the majority of them are small and they are very largely cultivated by family labour.

Recruiting though varying in different parishes had never been very good in our country districts partly for the general reason indicated above, partly because the Rural Tribunals have taken rather a parochial view of the situation, and have given more weight to the needs of agriculture which they thoroughly understood than to the necessities of the Army which they only imperfectly appreciated.

There consequently appeared to be a considerable number of young men "wholly employed on the land" when the clean cut was proclaimed; though the official number of 1257 was reduced by between 50 and 100 when the men of wrong age, grading etc. had been eliminated.

The Committee were severely handicapped by the delay in announcing the County quota and by not being informed till late in the day that deficiencies in the men 19 – 23 could be made up from those between 23 – 31.

We were quite in the dark when we began and as no one knew how many men had to be found we could only guess as to the action needed to meet requirements; but it was soon apparent that after deducting those, mostly skilled horsemen, who were indispensable because there were no soldiers or substitutes at hand to replace them, there were not enough sound men among the 1257 called up to furnish the 800 spoken of as our quota, much less any higher figure.

In due course the official quota of 950 was announced and permission given to utilise the men 23 – 31 towards furnishing it.

The latter were slightly more plentiful than the younger men, numbering 1410: these added to the 1257 men 19 – 23 gave 2667 from which to get 950, and the Central County Committee divided the quota between the four Divisions in proportion to the whole number 19 – 31 called up in each, it being considered that that was fairer than any allotment based on acreage or gross population.

This gave	278	to the	North
	290		South
	253		East
	219		West

Except in the West the men required were provided by 19th. but it was a hard struggle, and though on paper it ought not to require any great effort to find two men from every parish and one from every 12 farms yet the County is in my opinion so depleted now of labour that unless we are freely re-inforced [*sic*] by men from Agricultural Companies, by Prisoners and War volunteers a lot of corn will be spoiled unless the weather is very favourable and[7] it will hardly be possible for us to grow the additional acreage of corn that I understand will be required in 1919.

I can best support this contention by some short details of my own experience of the "Combing out" committee of the N[orth]. Division.

We had 395 19–23 cases under the Proclamation. To one-half we refused leave to appeal, dealing with them much more drastically than any of the other Divisions. In various cases we took the only able bodied man besides the tenant from farms of about 100 acres with 30 acres of corn, leaving the farmer to do the best he could with a boy of 16–17 and such other help as he could procure.

Half the remainder we considered should have been exempted unconditionally being indispensable and irreplaceable, while the remaining quarter could only we thought be spared if replaced by substitutes.

The number of men 23–31 in the Division was 388. Fully a quarter were occupying tenants whom we could not take off their farms except in a few cases where the holdings were quite small or where there was a relative within easy reach.

Nearly a quarter were medically unfit or over-age and about 10% were managing for widowed mothers or infirm fathers or in about a dozen cases belonged to families who had already made heavy sacrifices.

This left us a very small margin to select from, and we had to send in the names of 70 to 80%[8] four-fifths of the remainder.

Rural Population in a county where there are several Boroughs and Urban Districts with scores of farms within their boundaries is difficult to calculate but the number of men 19–31 as compared with the population within the borders of the Local Government "Rural Districts" varied considerably; being in N[orth]. about 1.75%, in S[outh]. & E[ast]. about half that, and in W[est]. 1.55.

I ascribe this partly to more active recruiting in S[outh]. & E[ast]. Politically those areas are more conservative and there is less dissent than in N[orth]. & W[est]., factors, which though no party or creed is more patriotic than another, undoubtedly affect recruiting hereabouts.

Lack of cottages causes a great deal of the farm work to be done by family labour, and as men grow up and marry they are apt to get into farms of their own and to seek other employment so the number of labourers of mature years is limited.

Moreover many men in the prime of life emigrated not long before the war.

Undoubtedly between one thing and another the supply of labour, never too plentiful, is now very short, and machinery will not take the place of men. Tractors have rendered material assistance but a great many fields are too small or too hilly to be ploughed or cultivated by anything but horses. Of our present

[7]   After the document was typed, Fortescue added later in pen 'a lot of corn will be spoiled unless the weather is very favourable and'.

[8]   '70 to 80%' was added later by Earl Fortescue in pen.

cereal area of 89 000 acres barely 3000 were tractor ploughed, and our Tractor Representative does not except to do more than 6000 a[cres]. for 1918–19.[9]

Some farmers have threatened to turn their cattle into their mowing grass; and I am told a few have done it. Unquestionably some are throwing up their farms, and any movement in that direction will be highly contagious, for stock, implements and temporary grazing are all making fancy prices.

I must repeat that I do not think we can stand further depletion and that if the 1900 class has to be called up at least an equivalent number of men must be provided from other sources.

I must repeat that I do not think we can stand further depletion and that if the 1900 class has to be called up at least an equivalent number of men must be provided from other sources.

It is the fashion in some quarters to suggest that farmers' sons are shirkers in every sense of the word : that they evade military service and do not exert themselves over much on the land. There are men in the farming class as in every other who has "taken cover", but my Committee, on which I was the only landowner were unanimous in their desire to be down on any family that had shirked military service. While as to work there is no doubt that in this district the ordinary farmer's son works both longer and harder than the ordinary labourer, and very much longer and harder than the men in khaki who are employed in civilian labour under or on behalf of the military authorities.

A very bad impression has been caused in many quarters by the way in which both time and manpower often appear to be wasted.

F[ortescue].[10]

---

[9] This sentence was added later by Fortescue in pen.
[10] These two paragraphs were added by Fortescue in both pen and pencil after the document had been typed.

DHC: 1262M/o/O/LD/143/37

**DRAFT LETTER FROM CHAIRMAN OF DEVON AGRICULTUAL
EXECUTIVE COMMITTEE DISCUSSING THREAT BY
DISGRUNTLED FARMERS TO PUT CATTLE IN FIELDS LAID UP
FOR HAY. TABLE OF POLICE NUMBERS AND STATIONS ON
BACK OF SHEET.**

50, Queen Street
Exeter
May 30th 1918

It has been reported to me that some farmers who anticipate ~~are apprehensive~~ that they will be severely inconvenienced ~~farmers who resent~~ by the calling up of their sons or labourers under His Majesty[']s Proclamation of 20 April are saying that they will to put their cattle into the fields they had laid up to cut for hay.

People suffering from a sense of grievance ~~I hope these threats are no more than~~ are apt to say more than they mean and I hope there is no occasion to take threats of this kind at all ~~very~~ seriously ; but if there should unfortunately be any farmers in this County who in resentment at steps made necessary by the requirements of ~~the~~ National Defence have forgotten ~~oblivious of~~ their duty to provide all they can for the food of the nation and its fighting men and their animals, I would remind them that under the Powers entrusted to Agr[icultural]. Exec[utive] Com[mit]tee by ~~London~~ the Defence of the Realm Act ~~they are any one who~~ they can be compelled to farm as directed, and are liable to £100 fine and (or) imprisonment if they fail to do so ~~is liable~~

Yours Sin[cerely]

Chairman Devon Ag. Ex. Com.

~~DORA Nov 1917 go co 2 M C Eg~~

	Sup	Sergt	Const	Pop	Acres
			1903		
	I	3	19;	18775	172339
B Division	I	3	5:	5871	34750
			14:	12904	137589

Deduct Station	Sup	Sergt	Const	Pop	Acres
S. Molton	I	I	3	3062	8160
Chulmleigh		I	I	1284	10235
Witheridge		I	I	1525	16355
	I.	3.	5.	5871	34.750

Hence each single Station Constable has a charge on 921 people spread over nearly 10000 acres

Three Police PC' however had only

	Pop	Acres
Chawleigh	695	6648
Molland	560	9264
Rackenford	368	5156
	1623 :	21,068

While two had at

	Pop	Acres
Chittlehampton	1590	11033
Winkleigh	1453	12580
	3043 :	24,613

If the Quota of pop[ulation] per P.C. were varied from 920 to 1200 & already 4 have from 1209 to 1590

3 if not 4 P.C. could be economised; & the area per P.C. to be covered would be increased from 10000 to 14000 but two already have 15046 & 16355

BIBLIOGRAPHY

Primary Sources

Devon Heritage Centre

DHC: 1262M/o/E/5/16, Correspondence with J. M. Lester, Bennerley Furnances, Exmoor Mining Syndicate and others with catalogue of sale 1913, concerning Exmoor Minerals, 2 files: 1917 (45) 1917–1919 (92), 1917–1919

DHC: 1262M/o/FD/46, Personal Diary of the 3rd Lord Ebrington, 1914–1916

DHC: 1262M/o/FD/47, Personal Diary of the 3rd Lord Ebrington, 1916–1918

DHC: 1262M/o/FD/48, Personal Diary of the 3rd Lord Ebrington, 1918–1921

DHC: 1262M/o/FH/42, Typescript of Work of Lord Fortescue during First World War, Post 1919

DHC: 1262M/o/O/LD/112/97, Typed sheet – Distribution of Agricultural Labour in Devonshire, 11 December 1918

DHC: 1262M/o/O/LD/112/154, Typed sheet detailing Acreage of Grassland ploughed since the Outbreak of War, c. 1918

DHC: 1262M/o/O/LD/113/127, Typed letter from Fortescue headed Devonshire Patriotic Fund, 28 April 1915

DHC: 1262M/o/O/LD/113/135, Letter written by Emily Fortescue, 14 August 1914

DHC: 1262M/o/O/LD/114/2, Typed letter from Fortescue to unnamed general about recruitment scheme, 26 June 1915

DHC: 1262M/o/O/LD/114/4, Typed letter to Fortescue from Pitcairn-Campbell, 12 July 1915

DHC: 1262M/o/O/LD/114/8, Typed letter Ref to Pitcairn-Campbell from Fortescue, 21 July 1915

DHC: 1262M/o/O/LD/114/12, Typed letter to Fortescue about Farmers' Battalion, 22 July 1915

DHC: 1262M/o/O/LD/114/20, Typed letter to Fortescue from Colonel Gretton, 8 August 1915

DHC: 1262M/o/O/LD/114/22, Typed letter from Fortescue to Colonel Gretton, 10 August 1915

DHC: 1262M/o/O/LD/116/42, Newspaper Cutting – The Great Canvass, 20 November 1915

DHC: 1262M/o/O/LD/120/30, The War an Appeal to Devon Men and Women issued by the Devon Parliamentary Recruiting Committee, 1 February 1915

DHC: 1262M/o/O/LD/129/7, Letter from Fortescue to the Mr Asquith and Lloyd George referring to the separation allowance and recruitment, 14 September 1914

DHC: 1262M/o/O/LD/136/3, Newspaper Cutting of an article comparing recruitment in Devonshire for the First World War with that of a recruitment drive in 1794, c. 1914

DHC: 1262M/o/O/LD/136/4, Booklet titled 'Red Cross and Voluntary Aid in Devonshire during the War', 30 May 1920

DHC: 1262M/o/O/LD/139/1, Pamphlet on the history of the Devon and Cornwall War Refugees Committee, c. 1919

DHC: 1262M/o/O/LD/143/37, Draft letter from Chairman of Devon Agricultural Executive Committee discussing threat by disgruntled farmers to put cattle in fields laid up for hay. Table of police numbers and stations on back of sheet, 30 May 1918

DHC: 1262M/o/O/LD/153/3, Memoranda on recruiting, 1914

DHC: 1262M/o/O/LD/153/5, speech (incomplete), 1914

DHC: 1262M/o/O/LD/155/9, Typed return of Tractor Ploughing from the Devon Agriculture Executive Committee, 18 January 1918

DHC: 1262M/o/O/LD/155/39, Typed letter to The Rt. Hon Earl Fortescue from H. J. Butler, Tractor Representative, statistics, circular and balance sheet, 1 May 1918

DHC: 1262M/o/O/LD/155/45, Typed notes, entitled – as to the Clean Cut in Devonshire and additional hand written notes, June 1918

Parliamentary Papers

Board of Agriculture and Fisheries, *Agricultural Statistics for Great Britain, with summaries for the United Kingdom, 1917. Vol. LII., Parts I. to III (Agriculture: Statistics)*, (London: HMSO, 1918)

Board of Agriculture and Fisheries, *Agricultural Statistics for Great Britain, with summaries for the United Kingdom, 1918. Vol. LIII., Parts I. to III (Agriculture: Statistics)*, (London: HMSO, 1919)

The National Archives

TNA: CAB-23-2, War Cabinet minutes, 100, p. 109, http://filestore.nationalarchives.gov.uk/pdfs/large/cab-23-2.pdf (accessed 5 February 2018)

TNA: CHAR 4/4, WAR CHARITIES ACT 1916: List of Registers, Cheshire (Maple)-Devon (Exeter), Devon and Cornwall War Refugees Committee, 1916

TNA: MAF 80/4998, Devon War Agricultural Committee, 1915–1918

TNA: RAIL 446/1, Lynton and Barnstaple Railway Company, Proprietors' minutes, 1895–1923

TNA: RAIL 446/2, Lynton and Barnstaple Railway Company, Board of Director's minutes, 1895–1922

Newspapers
Baily's Monthly Magazine or Sports and Pastimes
The Daily Mail
The Devon and Exeter Gazette
The New York Times
The North Devon Journal
The Telegraph
The Times
The Western Morning News and Daily Gazette
The Western Times

Secondary Sources

Articles and Books

Barnett, L. Margaret, *British Food Policy during the First World War* (Boston, MA: George Allen & Unwin, 1985)

Batten, Richard, 'Book Review: *A Kingdom United: Popular Responses to the Outbreak of the First World War in Britain and Ireland* by Catriona Pennell', *War in History*, Vol. 22, 2 (April 2015), pp. 252–253

Beadon, Colonel R. H., *The Royal Army Corps: A History of Transport and Supply in the British Army*, Vol. II (Cambridge: Cambridge University Press, 1931)

Bilton, David, *The Home Front in the Great War: Aspects of the Conflict, 1914–1918* (Barnsley: Leo Cooper, 2003)

Black, Jeremy, *The Great War and the Making of the Modern World* (London: Continuum, 2011)

Brock, Michael and Eleanor Brock, eds, *Margot Asquith's Great War Diary, 1914–1916: The View from Downing Street* (Oxford: Oxford University Press, 2014)

Bowser, Thekla, *The Story of V.A.D. Work in the Great War* (London: Imperial War Museum, 2003)

Butler, David and Gareth Butler, *British Political Facts*, 10th ed. (Basingstoke: Palgrave Macmillan, 2011)

Cahalan, Peter, *Belgian Refugee Relief in England during the Great War* (London: Garland Publishing Inc., 1982)

Cannadine, David, *The Decline & Fall of the British Aristocracy* (London: Picador, 1992)

Cawood, Ian, *The Liberal Unionist Party: A History* (London: I. B. Tauris, 2012)

Chope, R. Pearse, ed., *Devonian Year Book 1914* (London: The London Devonian Association, 1914)

_____, *Devonian Year Book 1915* (London: The London Devonian Association, 1915)

_____, *Devonian Year Book 1916* (London: The London Devonian Association, 1916)

_____, *Devonian Year Book 1917* (London: The London Devonian Association, 1917)

_____, *Devonian Year Book 1918* (London: The London Devonian Association, 1918)

Collins, William, *Herefordshire and the Great War, with the City and County's Roll of Honour* (Hereford: Jakeman & Carver, 1919)

Collyns, Charles Palk, *Notes on the Chase of the Wild Red Deer in the Counties of Devon and Somerset: with an appendix descriptive of remarkable runs and incidents connected with the chase from the year 1780 to the year 1860* (London: Lawrence and Bullen Ltd, 1902)

Connelly, Mark, *Steady the Buffs! A Regiment, a Region, and the Great War* (Oxford: Oxford University Press, 2006)

Craig, F. W. S., ed., *British Parliamentary Results: 1885–1918* (London: The Macmillan Press, 1974)

_____, *British Parliamentary Results: 1832–1885* (London: The Macmillan Press, 1977)

Dalley, Stuart, 'The Response in Cornwall to the Outbreak of the First World War', *Cornish Studies*, Vol. 11 (2003), pp. 85–109

David, Edward, *Inside Asquith's Cabinet: From the Diaries of CHARLES HOBHOUSE* (London: John Murray, 1977)

'Devonshire and the War', in R. Pearse Chope, ed., *Devonian Year Book 1915* (London: The London Devonian Association, 1915), p. 40

Dewey, Peter, 'Food Production and Policy in the United Kingdom, 1914–1918: The Alexander Prize Essay', *Transactions of the Royal Historical Society*, Vol. 30 (1980), pp. 71–89

_____, 'Nutrition and Living Standards in Wartime Britain', in R. Wall and J. Winter, eds, *The Upheaval of War: Family, Work and Welfare in Europe, 1914–1918* (Cambridge: Cambridge University Press, 1988), pp. 197–220

_____, P. E., *British Agriculture in the First World War* (Routledge: London, 1989)

Dod's Peerage, Baronetage and Knightage, etc of Great Britain and Ireland for 1915 (London: Dod's Peerage Limited, 1915)

Ebrington, Viscount, 'Stag Hunting', in A. E. T. Watson, ed., *Fur and Feather Series: The Red Deer* (London: Longmans, Green, and Co., 1896), pp. 197–284

Evered, Philip, *Staghunting with the "Devon and Somerset", 1887–1901: An Account of the Chase of the Wild Red Deer on Exmoor* (London: Chatto & Windus, 1902)

Fletcher, Walter Morley, *The University Pitt Club: 1835–1935* (Cambridge: Cambridge University Press, 1935)

Fortescue, Hugh, *A Chronicle of Castle Hill: 1454–1919* (London: W. H. Smith & Son, 1929)

Fortescue, John, *Records of Stag-Hunting on Exmoor* (London: Chapman and Hall Limited, 1887)

_____, *The County Lieutenancies and the Army, 1803–1814* (London: Macmillan and Co., Limited, 1909)

_____W., *My Native Devon* (London: Macmillan and Co., 1922)

_____, *A Short Account of Canteens in the British Army* (Cambridge: Cambridge University Press, 1928)

French, David, 'Spy Fever in Britain, 1900–1915', *The Historical Journal*, Vol. 12, 2 (Jun 1978), pp. 355–370

Gatrell, Peter, *Russia's First World War: A Social and Economic History* (Harlow: Pearson Education Ltd, 2005)

Gliddon, Gerald, *The Aristocracy and the Great War* (Norwich: Gliddon Books, 2002)

Goss, Fred, *Memories of a Stag Harbourer: A Record of Twenty-Eight Years with the Devon and Somerset Stag Hounds, 1894–1921* (London: H. F. & G. Witherby, 1931)

Gray, Todd, *Lest Devon Forgets: Service, Sacrifice and the Creation of Great War Memorials* (Exeter: Mint Press, 2010)

Grayzel, Susan R., *Women's Identities at War: Gender, Motherhood, and Politics in Britain and France during the First World War* (Chapel Hill, NC: University of North Carolina Press, 1999)

Gregory, Adrian, *The Last Great War: British Society and the First World War* (Cambridge: Cambridge University Press, 2008)

Grieves, Keith, '"Lowther's Lambs": Rural Paternalism and Voluntary Recruitment in the First World War', *Rural History*, Vol. 4, 1 (1993), pp. 55–75

_____ ed., *Sussex in the First World War* (Lewes: Sussex Record Office, 2004)

_____, 'Introduction', in K. Grieves, ed., *Sussex in the First World War* (Lewes: Sussex Record Office, 2004), pp. ix–xli

_____, 'The Quiet of the Country and the Restless Excitement of the Towns: Rural Perspectives on the Home Front, 1914–1918', in M. Tebbutt, ed., *Rural and Urban Encounters in the Nineteenth and Twentieth Centuries: Regional Perspectives* (Manchester: Conference of Regional and Local Historians, 2004), pp. 79–97

_____, 'War Comes to the Fields: Sacrifice, Localism and Ploughing Up the English Countryside in 1917', in I. F. W. Beckett, ed., *1917: Beyond the Western Front* (Leiden: Brill, 2009), pp. 159–176

Gullace, Nicoletta F., *"The Blood of Our Sons": Men, Women and the Renegotiation of British Citizenship during the Great War* (New York: Palgrave Macmillan, 2002)

Hammerle, Christa, 'Diaries', trans. by Andrew Evans, in M. Dobson and B. Ziemann, eds, *Reading Primary Sources: The Interpretation of Texts from Nineteenth- and Twentieth-Century History* (Abingdon: Routledge, 2009), pp. 141–158

Healy, Maureen, *Vienna and the Fall of the Habsburg Empire: Total War and Everyday Life in World War I* (Cambridge: Cambridge University Press, 2004)

Heathcoat-Amory, Roderick, *Reminiscences* (n.p: privately published, 1989)

Horn, Pamela, *Rural Life in England in the First World War* (Dublin: Gil and Macmillan Ltd, 1984)

Horne, John, 'Introduction: Mobilizing for "Total War", 1914–1918', in J. Horne, ed., *State, Society and Mobilization in Europe during the First World War* (Cambridge: Cambridge University Press, 1997), pp. 1–17

_____, 'Remobilizing for "Total War": France and Britain, 1917–1918', in J. Horne, ed., *State, Society and Mobilization in Europe during the First World War* (Cambridge: Cambridge University Press, 1997), pp. 195–211

Jebb, Miles, *The Lord-Lieutenants and their Deputies* (Chichester: Phillimore, 2007)

Jenkins, T. A., *Gladstone, Whiggery and the Liberal Party, 1874–1886* (Oxford: Clarendon Press, 1988)

Jones, Clyve and David Lewis Jones, eds, *Peers, Politics and Power: The House of Lords, 1603–1911* (London: The Hambledon Press, 1986)

Keating, Jenny, *A Child for Keeps: The History of Adoption in England, 1918–45* (Basingstoke: Palgrave Macmillan, 2009)

Kelly's Handbook to the Titled, Landed and Official Classes for 1915 (London: Kelly's Directories Ltd, 1915)

Kennedy, Rosie, *The Children's War: Britain, 1914–1918* (Basingstoke: Palgrave Macmillan, 2014)

King, Alex, *Memorials of the Great War in Britain: The Symbolism and Politics of Remembrance* (London: Berg, 1998)

Kirkby, Andrew, *In the Cause of Liberty: Exeter Trades Council, 1890–1990* (Exeter: Sparkler Books, 1990)

Kowner, Rotem, *Historical Dictionary of the Russo-Japanese War*, 2nd ed. (London: Rowman & Littlefield, 2017)

Mair, Robert Henry, ed., *Debrett's House of Commons and the Judicial Bench* (London: Dean & Son, 1886)

Martin, Peter, '*Dulce et Decorum*: Irish Nobles and the Great War, 1914–19', in A. Gregory and S. Pašeta, eds, *Ireland and the Great War: 'A War To Unite Us All'?* (Manchester: Manchester University Press, 2002), pp. 28–48

McDermott, James, *British Military Service Tribunals, 1916–1918: 'A Very Much Abused Body of Men'* (Manchester: Manchester University Press, 2011)

Middlebrook, Martin, *The Kaiser's Battle* (Barnsley: Pen & Sword Military, 2007)

Neville, Julia, 'Devon County Council and First World War Food Production Policy: A Challenge to Landlordism and Squirearchy?', *The Devon Historian*, Vol. 86 (2017), pp. 63–75

Noakes, Aubrey, *The County Fire Office, 1807–1957: A Commemorative History* (London: H. F. & G. Witherby Ltd, 1957)

Offer, Avner, *The First World War: An Agrarian Interpretation* (Oxford: Clarendon Press, 1989)

Osborne, John Morton, *The Voluntary Recruiting Movement in Britain, 1914–1916* (New York: Garland Publishing, 1982)

Page, John Lloyd Warden, *An Exploration of Exmoor and the Hill Country of West Somerset with Notes on its Archaeology* (London: Seely and Co Ltd, 1890)

Parker, David, *The People of Devon in the First World War* (Stroud: The History Press, 2013)

_____, *Exeter: Remembering, 1914–18* (Stroud: The History Press, 2014)

_____, *Edwardian Devon, 1900–1914: Before the Lights Went Out* (Stroud: The History Press, 2016)

Pelling, Henry, *Social Geography of British Elections, 1885–1910* (London: Macmillan, 1967)

Pennell, Catriona, *A Kingdom United: Popular Responses to the Outbreak of the First World War in Britain and Ireland* (Oxford: Oxford University Press, 2012)

Pershing, John J., *My Life before the World War, 1867–1917: A Memoir: General of the Armies John J. Pershing*, ed. John T. Greenwood (Lexington, KY: University of Kentucky Press, 2013)

Philpott, William, *Bloody Victory: The Sacrifice on the Somme* (London: Abacus, 2010)

Prior, Robin and Trevor Wilson, *The Somme* (New Haven, CT: Yale University Press, 2005)

Proctor, Tammy M., *Civilians in a World at War, 1914–1918* (New York: New York University Press, 2010)

Purseigle, Pierre, 'Beyond and Below the Nations: Towards a Comparative History of Local Communities at War', in J. Macleod and P. Purseigle, eds, *Uncovered Fields: Perspectives in First World War Studies* (Leiden: Brill, 2004), pp. 95–123

_____, 'Introduction, Warfare and Belligerence: Approaches to the First World War', in P. Purseigle, ed., *Warfare and Belligerence: Perspectives in First World War Studies* (Leiden: Brill, 2005), pp. 1–37

_____, '"A Wave on to Our Shores": The Exile and Resettlement of Refugees from the Western Front, 1914–1918', *Contemporary European History*, Vol. 16, 4 (2007), pp. 427–444

_____, '"Wither the Local?" Nationalization, Modernization, and the Mobilization of Urban Communities in England and France, c. 1900–18', in W. Whyte and O. Zimmer, eds, *Nationalism and the Reshaping of Urban Communities in Europe, 1848–1914* (Basingstoke: Palgrave Macmillan, 2011), pp. 182–203

_____, 'Home Fronts: The Mobilization of Resources for Total War', in R. Chickering, D. Showalter and H. V. D. Ven, eds, *The Cambridge History of War: Volume IV: War and the Modern World* (Cambridge: Cambridge University Press, 2012), pp. 257–284

Readman, Kristina Spohr, 'Memoranda', in M. Dobson and B. Ziemann, eds, *Reading Primary Sources: The Interpretation of Texts from Nineteenth- and Twentieth-Century History* (Abingdon: Routledge, 2009), pp. 123–140

Richardson, Ralph, *Through War to Peace, 1914–1918: Being a Short Account of the Part Played by Tavistock and Neighbourhood in the Great War* (Tavistock: Jolliffe & Son, 1919)

Robb, George, *British Culture and the First World War* (Basingstoke: Palgrave, 2002)

Simkins, Peter, *Kitchener's Army: The Raising of the New Armies, 1914–1916* (Barnsley: Pen & Sword Military, 2007)

Sondhaus, Lawrence, *The Great War at Sea: A Naval History of the First World War* (Cambridge: Cambridge University Press, 2014)

Stanyer, Jeffrey, *A History of Devon County Council, 1889–1989* (Exeter: Devon Books, 1989)

Stevenson, David, *1914–1918: The History of the First World War* (London: Penguin, 2004)

_____, *With Our Backs to the Wall: Victory and Defeat in 1918* (London: Penguin Books, 2012)

Strachan, Hew, *The First World War, Volume I: To Arms* (Oxford: Oxford University Press, 2001)

Tennant, A. J., *British Merchant Ships Sunk by U-Boats in World War One* (Penzance: Periscope Publishing Ltd, 2006)

'The Family of Fortescue', in R. Pearse Chope, ed., *The London Devonian Year Book 1910* (London: The London Devonian Association, 1910), p. 36

'The Office of Lord Lieutenant', in W. M. Ormrod, ed., *The Lord Lieutenant and High Sheriffs of Yorkshire, 1066–2000* (Barnsley: Wharncliffe Books, 2000), p. 3

'The Winter Conference', *Charity Organisation Review*, New Series, Vol. 39, 230 (February 1916), pp. 62–93

Thorpe, Andrew, *A History of the British Labour Party*, 4th ed. (London: Palgrave, 2015)

_____ and Richard Toye, eds, *Parliament and Politics in the Age of Asquith and Lloyd George: The Diaries of Cecil Harmsworth, MP, 1909–1922* (Cambridge: Cambridge University Press, 2016)

Toye, Richard, *Lloyd George & Churchill: Rivals for Greatness* (London: Macmillan, 2007)

Tregidga, Garry, ed., *Killerton, Camborne and Westminster: The Political Correspondence of Sir Francis and Lady Acland, 1910–29*, Vol. 48 (Exeter: Devon and Cornwall Record Society, 2006)

Vincent, John, ed., *The Crawford Papers: The Journals of David Lindsay Twenty-seventh Earl of Crawford and Tenth Earl of Balcarres 1871–1940 during the Years 1892 to 1940* (Manchester: Manchester University Press, 1984)

Waites, Bernard, *A Class Society at War: England, 1914–18* (Leamington Spa: Berg Publishers Ltd, 1987)

Ward, Paul, '"Women of Britain Say Go": Women's Patriotism in the First World War', *Twentieth Century British History*, Vol. 13, 1 (2001), pp. 23–45

Wasley, Gerald, *Devon in the Great War* (Tiverton: Devon Books, 2000)

Weston, Corinne Comstock and Patricia Kelvin, 'The "Judas Group" and the Parliament Bill of 1911', in C. Jones and D. L. Jones, eds, *Peers, Politics and Power: The House of Lords, 1603–1911* (London: Hambledon Continuum), pp. 527–539

White, Bonnie J., 'Volunteerism and Early Recruitment Efforts in Devonshire, August 1914–December 1915', *The Historical Journal*, Vol. 52, No. 3 (2009), pp. 641–666

_____, 'Feeding the War Effort: Agricultural Experiences in First World War Devon, 1914–1917', *Agricultural History Review*, Vol. 58, Part I (2010), pp. 95–112

_____, 'Sowing the Seeds of Patriotism? The Women's Land Army in Devon, 1916–1918', *The Local Historian*, Vol. 41, 1 (February 2011), pp. 13–27

_____, 'Wigwams and Resort Towns: The Housing Crisis in First World War Devon', in N. Mansfield and C. Horner, eds, *The Great War: Localities and Regional Identities* (Newcastle upon Tyne: Cambridge Scholars Publishing, 2014), pp. 97–118

_____, *The Women's Land Army in First World War Britain* (Basingstoke: Palgrave Macmillan, 2014)

Who's Who, 1914 (London: Adam & Charles Black, 1914)

Williams, John, *The Home Fronts: Britain, France and Germany, 1914–1918* (London: Constable, 1972)

Winter, Jay, 'Recent Trends in the Historiography of Britain and the First World War: Cultural History, Comparative History, Public History', in H. Berghoff and R von Friedeburg, eds, *Change and Inertia: Britain under the Impact of the Great War* (Bodenheim: Philo, 1998), pp. 87–97

_____, and Jean-Louis Robert, eds, *Capital Cities at War: Paris, London, Berlin, 1914–1919* (Cambridge: Cambridge University Press, 1999)

_____, 'Paris, London, Berlin, 1914–1919: Capital Cities at War', in J. Winter and J-L. Robert, eds, *Capital Cities at War: Paris, London, Berlin, 1914–1919* (Cambridge: Cambridge University Press, 1999), pp. 3–24

_____, and Antoine Prost, *The Great War in History: Debates and Controversies, 1914 to the Present* (Cambridge: Cambridge University Press, 2007)

Winter, J. M., 'Propaganda and the Mobilization of Consent', in H. Strachan, ed., *The Oxford Illustrated History of the First World War* (Oxford: Oxford University Press, 1998), pp. 216–226

Winton, Graham, *'Theirs Not To Reason Why': Horsing the British Army, 1875–1925* (Solihull: Helion & Company Limited, 2013)

Websites

'1914–1918 International Encyclopaedia of the First World War', https://encyclopedia.1914-1918-online.net/home, (accessed 20 November 2017)

'Australians at Exeter', 1914–1918, British Pathé, https://www.britishpathe.com/video/australians-at-exeter/query/Devon (accessed 14 December 2017)

'Captain Ludovic Heathcoat-Amory', Christ Church Oxford, http://www.chch.ox.ac.uk/fallen-alumni/captain-ludovic-heathcoat-amory (accessed 4 October 2017)

Chudley, Ron, 'A Brief History of Freemasonry in Devon', ed. D. Purnell, Provincial Grand Lodge of Devonshire, https://www.pgldevonshire.org.uk/information/provincial-history (accessed 10 September 2017)

'Ebrington, Hugh, Viscount (EBRN872H)', Cambridge Alumni Database, University of Cambridge, http://venn.lib.cam.ac.uk/cgi-bin/search-2016.pl?sur=&suro=w&fir=&firo=c&cit=&cito=c&c=all&z=all&tex=EBRN872H&sye=&eye=&col=all&maxcount=50 (accessed 20 November 2017)

'Exmoor Historic Environment Record', Exmoor National Park Authority, http://www.exmoorrher.co.uk/home (accessed 12 December 2017)

Fortescue, Denzil, 'Denzil Fortescue b.1893 Recollections 1974', http://fortescue.org/site/wp-content/uploads/2012/11/DGFRecollections2.pdf (accessed 12 December 2017)

'Lady Margaret Fortescue summary1', Exmoor Oral History Archive, 2001, http://www1.
    somerset.gov.uk/archives/Exmoor/fortescuesummary1.htm (accessed 20 March 2018)
'Lord French', 1917, British Pathé, https://www.britishpathe.com/video/lord-french/
    query/Devon (accessed 14 December 2017).
Madigan, Edward, 'Morality in Wartime Britain', http://podcasts.ox.ac.uk/morality-
    wartime-britain-video (accessed 14 January 2013).
'On This Day in Trinity House History – 28 March | Trinity House History', Official
    history blog of the Corporation of Trinity House of Deptford Strond and its lighthouse
    service, incorporated 1514, https://trinityhousehistory.wordpress.com/2014/03/28/
    on-this-day-in-trinity-house-history-28-march (accessed 9 February 2018).
'Oxford Dictionary of National Biography', https://www.oxforddnb.com (accessed
    8 December 2017)
Purseigle, Pierre, 'Violence and solidarity. Urban experiences of the First World War',
    27 September 2012, http://www.pierrepurseigle.info/violence-and-solidarity-urban-
    experiences-of-the-first-world-war (accessed 20 February 2013)

Unpublished Theses

Batten, Richard, 'Devon and the First World War', PhD thesis, University of Exeter,
    2013
Dawson, Anthony Michael, 'Politics in Devon and Cornwall, 1900–1931', PhD thesis,
    London School of Economics, 1991
McDermott, James, 'The Work of the Military Service Tribunals in Northamptonshire,
    1916–1918', PhD thesis, University of Northampton, 2009
Monger, David, 'The National War Aims Committee and British patriotism during the
    First World War', PhD thesis, Kings College London, 2009
White, Bonnie, 'War and the Home Front: Devon in the First World War', PhD thesis,
    McMaster University, 2008
Young, Derek Rutherford, 'Voluntary Recruitment in Scotland, 1914–1916', PhD thesis,
    University of Glasgow, 2001

INDEX

DEVON AND CORNWALL
RECORD SOCIETY

(Founded 1904)

Officers 2017–18

President: Dr S. Roberts BA, MA, PhD, FSA, FRHistS

Chairman of Council: Dr T. Gray BA, PhD, FRHistS

Hon. Secretary: E. Babbedge BA Hons, Dip AA, PGCE

Membership Secretary: K. Osborne BA, MA, PhD, AMA

Hon. Treasurer: M. Billings MSc, BA, PGCLT, FCA

Hon. Editor: Professor A. J. Thorpe BA, PhD, FRHistS

The Devon and Cornwall Record Society promotes the study of
history in the South West of England through publishing and
transcribing original records. In return for the annual subscription
members receive the volumes as published (normally annually).
For further details see
http://www.devonandcornwallrecordsociety.co.uk/

Applications to join the Society should be sent to
The Membership Secretary, Devon and Cornwall Record Society,
Devon Heritage Centre, Great Moor House, Bittern Road, Exeter EX2 7NL,
or emailed to
membershipDCRS@btinternet.com

DEVON AND CORNWALL
RECORD SOCIETY PUBLICATIONS

Previous volumes are available from Boydell & Brewer Ltd.

A Shelf List of the Society's Collections, ed. S Stride, revised 1986